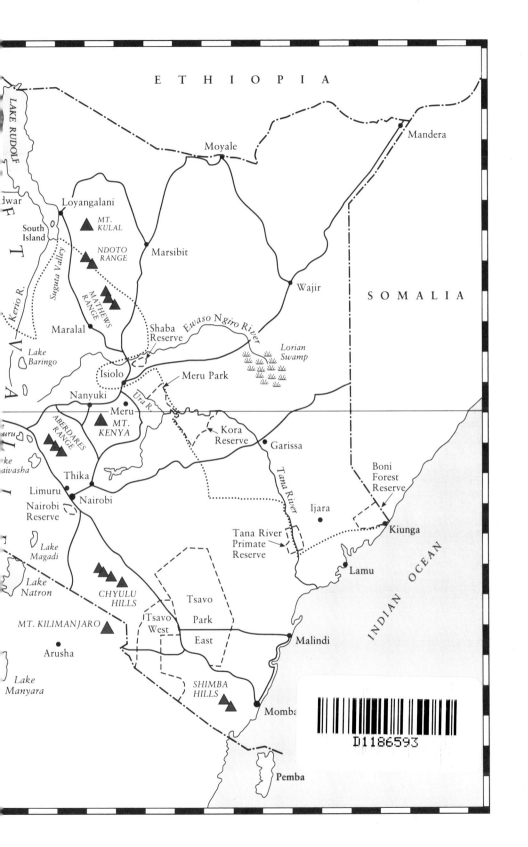

ETHIOPIA

Moyale

Mandera

LAKE RUDOLF

Loyangalani

MT. KULAL

NDOTO RANGE

Marsibit

Wajir

SOMALIA

South Island

dwar

Suguta Valley

MATHEWS RANGE

Kerio R.

Maralal

Shaba Reserve

Ewaso Ngiro River

Lorian Swamp

Lake Baringo

Isiolo

Meru Park

Nanyuki

Ura R.

Meru *MT. KENYA*

Kora Reserve

Garissa

ABERDARES RANGE

uru

ke aivasha

Thika

Tana River

Boni Forest Reserve

Limuru

Nairobi

Nairobi Reserve

Ijara

Kiunga

Lake Magadi

Tana River Primate Reserve

Lake Natron

CHYULU HILLS

Tsavo Park

Lamu

INDIAN OCEAN

MT. KILIMANJARO

Tsavo West

East

Malindi

Arusha

Lake Manyara

SHIMBA HILLS

Momba

D1186593

Pemba

The Great Safari

ADRIAN HOUSE

The Great Safari

The Lives of
George and Joy Adamson

HARVILL
An Imprint of HarperCollins*Publishers*

First published in Great Britain in 1993
by Harvill
an imprint of HarperCollins*Publishers*
77–85 Fulham Palace Road,
Hammersmith, London W6 8JB

2 4 6 8 9 7 5 3 1

© Adrian House 1993

A CIP record for this title is
available from the British Library

The author asserts the moral right to be
identified as the author of this work

ISBN 0 00 272082 5

Photoset in Linotron Ehrhardt by
Rowland Phototypesetting Ltd, Bury St Edmunds, Suffolk

Manufactured in the United States of America

This book is dedicated with love

TO PERELLA

for many reasons,
not least of them her calm acceptance
of so many lions and lionesses
in our life for so long

ACKNOWLEDGMENTS

I would like to thank first the Trustees of the Elsa Conservation Trust, who have kindly given me access to all the Adamsons' papers, photographs and paintings needed for this book. Jean Aucutt, Secretary of the trust, and the successive wardens of Elsamere, Joy's house on Lake Naivasha, now a conservation center, have been unfailingly helpful.

In England I have received special help from Joy Adamson's sister, Dorothy (Dorle) Cooper; Joy's cousin Mary Pike; George's lifelong friend the late Dr. Angela Ofenheim; Dr. Jan Gillett at the Royal Botanic Gardens, Kew; Sir John Johnson, lately British High Commissioner in Kenya, who read through the typescript and saved me from many errors; and Bill Travers and his wife, Virginia McKenna, whom I have consulted on all aspects of the book. I also warmly thank, for help and information, John Aspinall, Sir David Attenborough, Harry Birkbeck, Brigadier Percy Blake, Mark Boulton, Pamela Carson (Newton), Jill Duncan (Librarian of the Institute of Psycho-Analysis, London), Georgina Edmonds, Stephen Ellis, Nick Gray, William and Morna Hale, Richard Hennings, Susan Holmes, David Hopkinson (Assistant Registrar, University College London), Elspeth Huxley, the late Lady Jeans, Elizabeth Mackenzie, Alex Maitland, Anthony Marrian, Chris Matchett, the late Robert Nimmo, Hans Oppersdorff, Humphrey Osmond (archivist of Dean Close School, Cheltenham), F. W. Robins, Ronald Ryves, Keith Shaw, David Shirreff, Sir Richard Turnbull, Dr. Bernard Verdcourt, Connie Whitfield and Nigel Winser (Expeditions Director of the Royal Geographical Society, London).

In Kenya I have received the most generous hospitality and help from Peter and Mary Johnson; Monty and Hilary Ruben; Kuki Gallmann, who kindly allowed me to quote from her journal; Ken Smith; Anthony and Rose Dyer; and Jens and Tutti Hessel. I also warmly thank, for help and information, Jack Barrah, Jonny Baxendale, Osman Bitacha, Esmond and Chryssee Bradley Martin, Omari Bwana (Deputy Director of the National Museums of Kenya), Constance Cohen, Douglas Tatham Collins, Shaura Dirkicha, Iain and Oria Douglas Hamilton, Rodney Elliott, Ted Goss, the late Ian Grimwood, Nigel Guild, Patrick Hamilton, Brian Heath, Abdi Ibrahim, Mark Jenkins, John and Joan Karmali, Dr. Mary Leakey, Dr. Richard Leakey, Makedde, Mahomed Maru, Richard Matthews, Gideon Matwale, Dr. Andrew Meyerhold, Millicent Morson, Samuel Mwaura, Dr. Perez Olindo, Tom and Yvonne Pedersen, Gilfrid Powys, Peter and Sue Robertson, Dr. Paul Sayer, Wernher Schillinger, Phil Snyder and Jason Witney. I thank also Mohamed Amin and Duncan Willetts.

In other parts of the world I have also received the kindest hospitality or help from Dr. Sue Hart at her Eco Link Centre in South Africa, Betty Leslie Melville (Steele), Bob and Nora McRae, Dr. Wolfgang and Ingrid Koos, Betty

Henderson, Helen Wolff (who generously spared the time to read the typescript of the book), Tony Fitzjohn, Dr. Jane Goodall, Dr. George Schaller and Alan Davidson. I warmly thank, for information, Heidi Bally, David Bateman, Harry Benson, Professor R. L. Brahmachary, Merrell Dalton, Dr. Toni Harthoorn, Margot Henke, Ros Hillyar, the Hunt Institute for Botanical Documentation (Pittsburgh), Inge Ledertheil, Leo Lobsenz, Neil Lindsay, David Mackie, Sister Mary of Lourdes, Gareth Patterson, Carol Perkins, the late Susanne Peschke-Schmutzer and David Prestland-Tack.

For help in research I depended throughout on the wise advice and translation from the German of Ernestine Nowak in Vienna. In England Lisa Matthews and James Burleigh kindly helped me with research. I cannot thank Pat West sufficiently for typing the entire script immaculately and then revising it with equal precision through innumerable drafts.

Finally I would like to thank Richard Johnson of Grafton for suggesting the book to me and Christopher MacLehose of Harvill who commissioned it. Harvey Ginsberg, who accepted it for William Morrow in New York, and Bill Swainson of Harvill have been editors such as all authors pray for but seldom find. Toby Eady has been my ally from the beginning.

ADRIAN HOUSE
Easter, 1993

CONTENTS

ILLUSTRATIONS

All the illustrations are printed courtesy of the Elsa Conservation Trust except where otherwise acknowledged.

MAPS

PROLOGUE

It has always been impossible to make a safari—originally a day's journey—in Africa without encountering the unexpected. The arrival of the white man merely increased the permutations of chance.

On patrol as a game warden in the Boni Forest, George Adamson and his brother, Terence, came across an old African lying unconscious beside the track: an empty beer gourd lay nearby. A very large python was attempting to swallow him but since it had managed to get its mouth around only one of his feet it had finally reached an impasse at his groin.

George and Terence killed the snake with a revolver, pulled it off the old man's leg, wrapped it round him as a caution against the perils of drink, and continued their pursuit of some poachers.

When the Harvill Press, who jointly with Collins published all the Adamsons' books, asked me to write the story of their lives, I had no doubt I would encounter some surprises along the way, however well I had known both George and Joy.

I first met Joy in 1959 when she brought into Collins, where I worked as an editor, her embryonic script of *Born Free*, the story of the lioness Elsa she and George had adopted, raised and returned to the wild: with it were several massive photograph albums, some bound in lion skin. Over the next twenty years I was continuously embroiled in the detailed business of her books, lectures and films and last saw her only three weeks before she was stabbed.

I did not meet George until I started to go to Kenya regularly in 1977. In 1985 I helped him write his book *My Pride and Joy*, and I planned to stay with him—as I did once a year—in September 1989. At the end of August he was shot.

Danger, like the unpredictable, is an inevitable element of any prolonged safari in East Africa. To some it is a desirable spice; George and Joy became addicted to it and in the end, as with many addictions, it proved fatal.

The essence of a successful safari is a sensitive response to one fundamental principle: the interdependence of every part of the whole, beautiful, pulsing world through which we travel.

George in his work as a game warden and Joy as an artist who painted remarkable records of the flora and tribal traditions of Kenya had to understand the evolution of the landscape, the rhythms of the climate, the growth of plants and trees, the natural movement of the birds and the animals and the adaptations of the indigenous tribes to all of these. The longer I followed their safari the more convinced I became that physics, biology, and the activities of the mind, imagination and spirit belong to a single continuum.

George, especially, learned to live in exceptional harmony with this timeless pattern. It was therefore a jolt to discover that during the temporary but murderous Mau Mau upheaval, precipitated by the white man's presence in a black continent, he was obliged to turn his rifle on men.

The written sources on which this book is based are primarily those left by George and Joy themselves. The most remarkable of these are George's diaries, kept night after night for more than sixty years; the most intimate are Joy's pocket diaries preserved from 1945 to 1975; the most moving is a sequence of letters George wrote Joy a few years after they were married. For access to them, I am deeply in debt to the trustees of the Elsa Conservation Trust, the charity to which they both left their estates. Many other people, thanked in the acknowledgments, have lent me letters and documents, or given me information.

When I first read the most intimate passages in the diaries and letters I felt uneasy about using them. However, I then realized George and Joy had deliberately preserved them in the full knowledge that their activities aroused curiosity throughout the world and that they might die at any moment. I have therefore quoted them because they throw critical light on a number of mysteries.

I have tried to talk to all the most significant witnesses, but many are dead and I have not been able to see others, though not, I think, to the detriment of the book's authenticity. I have also been to the most important settings in Kenya but while George and Joy travelled on foot, rode mules or sailed in a makeshift canvas boat, I cheated and went in a small plane or Land-Rover—sometimes with the help of George's godson, Jonny Baxendale.

Neither George nor Joy was a scholar; nor am I. I have therefore not loaded this story with dates, references and scientific names.

Acknowledgments, the source of each indented quotation and a select bibliography are given at the end of the book.

I would make two points about the quotations from Joy's and George's writing. The first is that because Joy, an Austrian by birth, never fully mastered English, all her books required a degree of "translation" and editing. I have therefore treated her letters similarly, except in a few cases where I have left them verbatim in order to give the flavor of her written—and spoken—use of the language. George expressed himself formidably on paper, though I have sometimes paragraphed his prose.

Second, it has often been necessary to abridge passages from letters, diaries, reports and books, but to avoid distraction I have not indicated omissions with the customary elipses ... I do, however, assure the reader that I have never used translations, editing or abridgment to alter the sense or mood of the writer. In Joy's case this has sometimes been difficult because her mental and emotional processes were so mercurial that occasionally two adjacent diary entries, two consecutive letters or even two passages in the same letter are at odds with each other. I have therefore found it wisest only to accept her opinions of people or controversial events if they are corroborated by a second source.

Perhaps the greatest surprise for most readers will be the difference between the impression of Joy they received from her books or the film of *Born Free*, and the character who emerges from these pages. Once or twice George's behavior, too, seems out of character. Because I do not believe biographies should attempt to protect the image of public heroes by omitting or camouflaging uncomfortable facts I have tried to tell nothing but the truth, although this is not always easy as anyone will know who has listened to two honest accounts of the same accident.

If any reader is tempted to rush to judgment, may I just say this. Although he survived Joy by nearly ten years, George never once spoke ill of her; and although she was married to him for thirty-five, and twice initiated divorce proceedings, she never longed for his companionship more than at the very end of her life.

The influence the Adamsons exerted on the attitudes of a whole generation, of which there is concrete evidence, was due to at least three factors. First, they loved and were loved by a lion—the most potent archetype to have emerged directly from the animal world. Second, they recognized and vividly described the extraordinary and hitherto unsuspected potential of a wild animal's character and behavior. Third, their impact derived further strength from their concern for each animal as an individual. By the time I came to finish this book Joy's convictions and George's whole way of life persuaded me to accept the truth that was central to their later years: an animal's rights should be as inviolable as our own.

If it is wrong to thrash a human being, draw his nails, subject her to involuntary medical experiment, to lock him up or kill her without trial, it is morally wrong to treat an animal in this way. The more evolved the animal the greater its potential to suffer, and since it is handicapped by the double disadvantage of not speaking our language or possessing a vote, we have a double duty to protect it. Its unnecessary injury, captivity or death diminishes each one of us.

On the other hand, through their vision, courage and generosity, the Adamsons enlarged us by advancing our knowledge of animals, and by extending our concern for both them and the planet on which we all live.

Part I

THE GAME WARDEN
& THE ARTIST

1906–1955

The Lion is the King of Beasts, but he is scarcely suitable for a domestic pet. In the same way, I suspect love is rather too violent a passion to make, in all cases, a good domestic sentiment. Like all other violent excitements it throws up not only what is best, but what is worst, in men's characters . . .

Marriage is like life in this—that it is a field of battle, and not a bed of roses.

ROBERT LOUIS STEVENSON
Virginibus Puerisque

ONE

A Merry Christmas

1942–1943

1

Just before Christmas 1942 George Adamson rode into the life of his future wife, Joy, at the head of a train of camels. They had both been invited to a party by the District Commissioner at Garissa, on the Tana River in Kenya.

The precise date of George's arrival is lost because that December is one of the very few months in the entire sixty years covered by his diaries that is illegible. The discolored wartime pages are pitted with termite tunnels.

The improbable repercussions of that little rooftop gathering can still be felt today. For the penniless game warden from the remote Northern Frontier Province and the unknown Austrian artist it led not only to fame and unexpected fortune but to a succession of adventures, culminating in their murders nine years apart.

The District Commissioner was stationed at Garissa because of the strategic position of its bridge, halfway down the river. The Tana links most of the important themes and events in the Adamsons' lives, as it connects so many in the story of Kenya and its wildlife—for it is the longest and most important river in a country where existence, survival, and daily behavior are dictated by landscape and climate.

The Tana is born on Mount Kenya, which straddles the equator. Once a volcano far taller than its present height but worn down by the forces of nature, the mountain is usually covered in cloud and permanently frosted with snow and ice. The river therefore never runs dry, unlike most of the others in the country.

Both the Kikuyu, an agricultural tribe, and the northern Maasai, who are pastoralists, each understandably locate their God on this awe-inspiring mountain from which He dispenses rain for their fields and their cattle.

When the clouds do clear from the three icy peaks of the mountain, the moorlands just below them become an Elysian field. The sun lights up golden everlastings and piercing blue delphiniums, while the melting snows gather in runnels and rush down through the forest and ravines to the thirsty plain below.

The Tana makes its way to the sea through scenes of aridity and lushness, beauty, peace and brute savagery, all typical of East Africa whose landscape is as varied and complex as any in the world. Here the earth's surface has been ridged and cracked by the immense pressures and faults beneath and pocked by volcanoes that have pushed up through it and erupted with dramatic effect.

Once the inexorable process of erosion had clothed it with soil, this unique mosaic of habitats—high- and low-lying, freezing and torrid, rain-drenched and parched, fertile and desert, all of them spinning in a privileged position close to the sun—was able to accommodate any form of life that chose to evolve. As a showcase of creation, East Africa is still matchless in the miraculous variety and profusion it offers.

The Tana winds through this world like a lifeline. Villagers draw off its water for their simple crops of maize and bananas. Furrows scratched too close to the banks cause the precious soil to wash into the river when it rains, but the pastoral tribes still drive their herds of hundreds of thousands of sheep, goats and camels to drink in what looks like flowing red cocoa.

In 1958, George and Joy released their orphaned lioness Elsa on a tributary of the Tana, in what is now the Meru National Park. Sitting under a fig tree beside the stream, Joy started to type *Born Free*, the book that caught people's imaginations all over the world and earned what at today's values was more than two million dollars.

A lifeline for some, the Tana is a death trap for others. Once she was free, Elsa learned to pounce on a kudu or waterbuck when it came down to drink in the evening. Crocodiles, like rotten logs, lie in wait for a goat or a child splashing past in the shallows. Fish eagles drop from their trees to grab a barbel or tilapia.

As warden, George had to keep a protective eye on the game along the river. Some of the finest elephants in Kenya, with tusks weighing more than a hundred pounds each, sought sanctuary in the thickest riverine bush near a steep, rocky hill named Kora.

The Tana is one of the natural frontiers in Kenya. There is constant tension between the cattle tribes on one bank and the Somali camel herders on the other. Except in towns, the pastoralist has always carried his bow and arrows, his spear, and a knife—like the slim *simi* that was used to kill Joy in 1980. A lightning stock raid, a grazing dispute, a hijacked load of poached ivory, or a personal vendetta can quickly lead to bloodshed.

The Tana is a frontier in another sense too. Since the end of the last century the Somalis have progressively pushed southward into Kenya, extending their grazing toward the heart of the country. The "Somali Line" along the river was drawn, although challenged every year, as the absolute limit of their range. George set up his last camp three miles south of the Tana at Kora Rock. In 1989 he was shot in the bush there by three Somalis armed with automatic weapons.

About one hundred and fifty miles downstream from Kora the Tana River Primate Reserve protects seven species of monkeys, including two—the Tana mangabey and red colobus—that are endangered. However remote East Africa may seem to you, or if the loss of a species of monkey seems little more than regrettable, remember this (if your religious beliefs allow you to): whoever you are and wherever you come from you are inseparably connected with East Africa and you are descended from a primate.

The formation of the Rift Valley eighty miles to the west of Mount Kenya, and the volcanic activity that followed, shrank the vast East African rain forests in which the primates lived and also created the savanna surrounding them with new sources of food, easy access to water and different types of refuge. Responding to these threats and opportunities, some of the primates dropped out of the trees, stood up and started to investigate this new world. The ash from a volcano that erupted three and a half million years ago made a perfect cast of their footprints at Laetoli; the fossil bones of some of their descendants were preserved in Olduvai Gorge.

Just over a million years ago, still later descendants of these primates, immediate forerunners of our own species *homo sapiens sapiens* were ready to leave their East African cradle and cross the land bridge into Europe and Asia. Their curiosity led them on to the sea and thence to the rest of the planet.

2

Malindi is one of the ports that has served successive, but unsuccessful, waves of seafarers who hoped to exploit the hinterland of what is now Kenya.

From the years before Christ to the nineteenth century, Greeks and Romans, Chinese and Indians, Arabs and Portuguese, managed to establish trading posts, mosques and the occasional fortress along the coast of East Africa. Fort Jesus, founded by the Portuguese in 1593, dominates the old harbor at Mombasa.

Sea-lanes from India and the head of the Red Sea converged farther north and ran down the littoral of Africa to the island of Zanzibar. Dhows brought woodwork, brass, silk, cottons and dates and carried back cargoes of mangrove poles, frankincense, ivory, gold, monkeys and slaves.

Whatever the ravages of slavery farther south, man and nature combined in Kenya to repel the stranger. It was a formidable alliance: roving bands of fearless and bloodthirsty tribal warriors, especially the Maasai; a deep and hostile belt of thornbush; the often lethal attention of malarial mosquitoes; tsetse flies that dealt death by sleeping sickness to man and his companion in conquest, the horse; and lions and elephants that threatened violence by day and by night.

Despite these hazards, by 1900 the European scramble for Africa was well under way and a commercial company had begun to build a railway from the port of Mombasa to the fertile shores of Lake Victoria. When the project ran into predictable problems the British government assembled some plausible reasons for bailing it out. For instance, the scheme would forestall occupation by the French or the Germans and also check any spread of the Arab slave trade. In 1901 the railway was completed and by 1905 Kenya became a fully-fledged British protectorate.

The first exodus, begun a million years before, was reversed and the newcomers found that the land in what is now Kenya was only very sparsely populated. Its inhabitants had plenty of room in which to hunt, work the soil or follow the rains with their flocks and herds. The distribution of land was informal. For instance, some areas were traditionally lived in or grazed by particular tribes; clans or families adopted and cultivated others until they were exhausted, then they moved on.

Man lived in an alliance with nature and survived on its dividends;

in no case did he plunder its capital by eroding the land and devastating the forests. It was a pattern of life that intruders from Europe could too easily disturb.

Kenya Colony, as it became in 1920, was ruled by a governor representing King George V in Great Britain and serving the elected government in Westminster under the eye of the Colonial Office. On special occasions he wore a gold-braided uniform, a dress hat cockaded with plumes, and a sword. He ran the colony through a service of administrative officers or commissioners who were responsible for each of the seven provinces and the districts into which each was divided.

District commissioners came in all shapes and sizes with minds, hobbies and passions to match. They might well become obsessed by a favorite tribe but it was frowned on to take a bedmate of one of these peoples. Doing so might not mean automatic dismissal but would almost certainly entail transfer to one of the remoter areas of the Northern Frontier. To a desk wallah in Nairobi or a careerist in the south, this was the equivalent of Siberia, but for a real man a northern posting was the ultimate accolade, enjoying the same cachet as the North West Frontier in India. Isiolo, the gateway to the province, was in reality a frontier town, complete with police post and barrier: "Kenya" began south of the border.

These backbones of law and order were supported by pink-necked European officers of the Kenya Police, who dealt with the more serious crimes. The routine work in the African areas was carried out by tribal police, resplendent in a compromise of red fezzes, tunics, loincloths and bare feet.

Like the police and the game wardens, the livestock and veterinary officers, who told the Africans what they might or might not do with their animals, were socially accepted in the District Headquarters, or *boma*—which means "stockade" in Swahili. They could more than hold their own with a hand of cards, a shotgun or a bottle of gin.

The salt of the earth in the Public Works Department, and the Asian—often Goan—revenue officers and clerks upon whom the whole administration depended, were invited to tennis but not to sit down to dinner.

Although it may seem that the apparatus of colonial control was designed largely for the benefit of the European settlers, such was not the case.

One of the earliest, richest and most influential of the settlers was

Hugh Cholmondeley, the third Lord Delamere, who first reached Kenya overland from the north in 1897. Three years earlier, while he had been on an expedition into Somaliland, his ankle had been seized and chewed by a lion. His Somali gun bearer courageously grabbed hold of the animal's tongue and was horribly mauled for his pains, but surprisingly only the lion succumbed in the fracas.

Delamere's energy and determination were prodigious. He sunk fortune after fortune in pioneering new strains of cattle, sheep and wheat to overcome problems of climate and disease. Since his fellow farmers could find no one to process their grain and their milk, he invested in a mill and a dairy. Finally, when the economics of transport became a nightmare he challenged the railway management, the shippers, the governor and the mandarins in Westminster.

Delamere's battles were fought precisely because the Kenyan government was not concerned primarily about the settler. As early as 1911 the Governor's secretariat had devised a policy of "Paramountcy," but the paramount interests were those of the native Kenyans. Their traditional lands were to be protected and on no account were they to be coerced into working against their wishes.

Furthermore, scarcely any white man left the country richer than when he arrived. Many lost or gave away whatever they brought in and many forfeited even their lives.

Although most of the immigrants were conscientious and hardworking, an all too visible minority of lightweights floated on the surface of Kenyan society. They made a serious business of hunting big game, shooting sandgrouse, playing polo and racing—an irritated rhino interrupted one of the earlier race meetings. They ate, drank, dined and sometimes danced at Torr's Hotel in Nairobi, or at the fashionable country club in Muthaiga on the outskirts. Both there and in their airy and comfortable houses in the "white highlands" they made an almost equally serious business of fornication. According to Byron, who knew about such things:

> What men call gallantry, and gods adultery,
> Is much more common where the climate's sultry.

Second, third and fourth marriages were commonplace and alcohol was the least noxious of the artificial aids to their pleasures. Nevertheless it was said that one venomous snake which had bitten a settler died of alcohol poisoning within a few minutes.

Nairobi and the highlands are well over 5,000 feet and although a medical authority identified two of the effects of long periods at high altitudes as instability and erratic judgment, lack of moral, rather than atmospheric, pressure lay at the root of these problems.

The trouble with the white froth in Kenya was that, like spoiled children, they ignored the fundamental precept "Do as you would be done by." This was a formula for disaster when they mingled with the decent, or indeed when they set off each other's more basic emotional reflexes.

Raymond de Trafford, whose elegant decadence charmed the satirist Evelyn Waugh when he visited Kenya in 1931, was shot in Paris, though not fatally, when putting an end to an affair that had blossomed in Kenya. An even more ruthless adulterer, Lord Erroll, received commensurate retribution: he was shot behind the ear.

Despite a murder trial it was never proved who pulled the trigger — a mystery that obsessed another sophisticated observer of social perversity, Cyril Connolly.

One potential suspect was Major Cyril Ramsay-Hill whose wife Erroll had seduced and eloped with. Ramsay-Hill had followed them to Nairobi station, where he saw the well-known cab man, Ali Khan, dressed in his picturesque breeches, tunic and Stetson, standing by his horse and cart.

According to George Adamson, Ramsay-Hill shouted, "Lend me your whip, I've got to beat a dog!"—which he did when he found Erroll on the platform.

In the end Erroll married Mollie Ramsay-Hill, ran through her money and plied her with the drink and drugs that killed her. Years later Cyril Ramsay-Hill told Joy he had refrained from murdering Erroll himself: "Better lose one's wife than one's life."

Mingled with this whole human brew, giving character to both the broth and the froth, were men and women with genuine gifts as writers, scholars and artists. One was a Dane named Karen Blixen, who was married to Baron Bror Blixen, a Swedish white hunter and roué, whom she accused—contrary to the evidence—of infecting her with syphilis. She struggled to grow coffee on the Ngong hills, while her friend, the beautiful and thrice-married Beryl Markham, trained racehorses and became the first pilot to fly the Atlantic solo from east to west.

Both women took as their lover the English aristocrat and white hunter, Denys Finch Hatton, who was as fond of literature and modern music as he was of killing big game. When two of King George V's sons, the Prince of Wales and his brother Prince Henry, came out to Kenya, both women entertained them with intimate dinners and dances; the royal safaris were organized by Blixen and Finch Hatton. Beryl Markham succeeded in having affairs with both princes simultaneously without the other knowing.

Both women also wrote books, Karen Blixen *Out of Africa* under the pen name Isak Dinesen, and Beryl Markham (with the help of her third husband) *West with the Night*—classic accounts of farming, hunting and flying in their exotic world.

A rather different cluster of scholars and specialists gathered around the Coryndon Museum in Nairobi. Its leading figure, a trustee, and from 1940 to 1945 its acting curator, was Louis Leakey. He was fired with a passion for ideas and knowledge, and his excavations to uncover the secrets of man's emergence as man were often inspired.

He also had a flair for finding the right women to realize his dreams. His divorce and second marriage in 1936 to Mary Nicol disturbed his father, a missionary to the Kikuyu, and shocked his university colleagues but it was a perfect example of his instinct. From the day she set foot in Kenya, Mary Leakey began her own excavations and years later made her sensational finds at Olduvai and identified the hominid footsteps at Laetoli for what they are.

Louis Leakey also spotted early the unusual talent of another very gifted young woman, who had recently married Peter Bally, a Swiss botanist at the Coryndon Museum. Bally, a meticulous botanical artist himself, was teaching her to paint the plants he collected in his work. For some reason he objected to the name Fifi always used by her family and friends, so she began to call herself Joy.

While the Ballys built themselves a home, they rented the guest house in Louis and Mary Leakey's garden. It was there, sitting on the floor and helping to sort a tray of fossil bones in 1939, that Joy heard on the radio that war had been declared. Almost immediately Kenya was mobilized as a base to take on the Italian forces threatening the country from the borders of Ethiopia and Somaliland.

Despite the campaign against the Italians and wartime restrictions, Peter and Joy were able to move freely about Kenya and East Africa in search of new plants, especially those that might be used for medicinal, edible or other practical purposes. Thus it was that they set off for Garissa at the end of 1942 to look for a group from which dyes could be extracted and to examine some chromium deposits that might also yield pigments.

3

By December 1942 British victories in Ethiopia and Somaliland had liberated an unaccustomed flow of Italian wines and cosmopolitan spirits, encouraging the District Commissioner (DC) at Garissa, William Hale, to give a small Christmas party. His wife, Morna, who was an enthusiastic botanist, knew Peter and Joy Bally were on the Tana and pressed them to stay for it.

The other guests were three old friends—George Low, the livestock officer, his wife, Lois, and George Adamson, the game warden responsible for the desolate wilderness of the Northern Frontier and, more recently, for the Garissa district as well. George had a reputation as both a recluse and a survivor of hair-raising adventures.

After fifty years, neglect has left its marks on the old DC's Arab-style house near the Tana River. It is abandoned; a grove of tall palms has grown up and dwarfs it; and the outside staircase has been pulled down, leaving a scar in the plaster, no longer white. The flat top on which the Hales entertained, and where they slept under mosquito nets, has been built up in wood and roofed over with rusting corrugated iron.

When they had been greeted by the DC and his wife, the Ballys set up a tent for themselves and their little dog in the shade of the trees by the Tana and ringed it with a couple of strands of barbed wire to keep out the hippos—an optimistic measure. George Adamson, naked after bathing in the river, had once been chased off a sandbank by an angry male, and one of his game scouts, who had tried to discourage another from chewing his grass hut during the night, had been bitten in two.

All her life Joy loved a party at Christmas: the tinsel, the presents, the music and a chance to dress up. She threw herself into the preparations while Morna Hale amused her with stories of George's adventures.

The most celebrated occurred at the end of an exhausting safari in search of the Queen of Sheba's gold mines. Defying the winds which can gust across Lake Rudolf (now Lake Turkana) at 80 miles per hour, he took a shortcut back across the water in a boat that he and his companion had cobbled together by stretching their groundsheets over some branches.

George had been even luckier to survive a more recent ordeal. After being savagely mauled by a lion in the morning, he was charged the same evening by a demented elephant. His sudden appearance now, with a camel train and in a wide-brimmed hat, further stimulated Joy's romantic imagination. His hair was reddish-gold, his beard neatly trimmed in a goatee and his eyes a piercing blue.

Joy took Morna's warning that his conversational repertoire was limited to only three responses—"Oh," "Really?" and "How extraordinary!"—as a challenge to extract a great deal more from him.

While George dismounted and soaked in a hip-bath, Joy withdrew to her tent and put on a fashionable and wonderfully inappropriate silver evening dress. As the serious drinking began on the roof, the local Somalis and Orma from across the river gathered around the house for an *ngoma,* or dance.

Night falls fast on the equator at about seven o'clock every evening. The Gioffi's gin and the whiskey effectively primed the spirit of Christmas while chanting broke out among the Africans below.

Joy maintained that George quickly put back several glasses of whiskey and asserted that it never made him drunk. She and Morna took it as another challenge and introduced brandy into his soup, his gravy and his pudding. Before long he and the other men discarded their black ties and exchanged their dress trousers for their regular evening apparel—a *kikoi,* or length of cotton wrapped around the waist. When some of the party went down to join in the dancing, George and Joy remained on the parapet and sang their heads off.

Next morning he woke up with his boots on the pillow and a very hazy memory of the evening before. Joy looked out of her tent to see shreds of her silver dress hanging from the barbed wire.

When George had stopped at Garissa he was on his way to patrol a particularly harsh stretch of country, the Boni Forest, near the coast. No one had been there for a long time and he suspected it was a hotbed of poachers. He was therefore dismayed when the Ballys told him they would be delighted to accept his invitation to join him. He had no recollection of having made the offer and feared that a talkative and overdressed artist with a dog would be a serious liability on this difficult assignment. Nevertheless, out of courtesy, or for some more personal reason, he agreed they should come.

George discovered that both the Ballys had been married before and that Peter was considerably older than Joy. He was pleasant-looking and highly intelligent. He also spoke very good English.

Joy, on the other hand, poured out her words in a torrent very difficult to understand until George's ear became attuned to her strong Austrian accent. But her sparkling blue eyes caught and held his attention as she cross-examined him or delivered a discourse on one of her enthusiasms—botany, painting and music. Slim and vivacious, she was only too easy to look at, even if it was difficult to hear what she said.

She was obviously passionate about animals, especially her cairn terrier, Pippin, and when offered a mongoose near the bridge at Garissa, she bought it and took it down to the river where the Hales and their guests went swimming. The mongoose quickly disappeared into the bush and eluded the overqualified search party composed of the DC, game warden and livestock officer sent after it by Joy.

Africans strolling on the bridge watched with amusement as the Europeans bobbed about in the water near the pontoons. Later Joy discovered they were having bets as to which of the *wazungu* (white people) would be eaten by a crocodile first.

Thus far the various accounts of George and Joy's first meeting agree but there are several versions of what followed. Joy's, in books published twenty or thirty years later, are understandably reticent, although a few additional details survive in unpublished paragraphs drafted for her autobiography. George was also circumspect in his books but the opening and uneaten pages of his diary for early 1943 are revealing.

He set off on foot with the Ballys at the end of December. The tents and other baggage were loaded onto the camels which followed them along the unmade dirt road that more or less kept to the river. There were plenty of diversions: Peter Bally darted off into the under-growth to take a specimen of a rare or unknown plant and George stopped to point out the spoor of an elephant or question herdsmen about trouble from lions.

George enjoyed the companionship of both the Ballys, and Joy in turn was fascinated that George could interpret so much about the life going on all around them in the bush. She was particularly impressed when he showed her a trick he had learned from the Njemps on Lake Baringo: by calling "imm, imm, imm" he could arouse the curiosity of the crocodiles which immediately glided over to investigate the source of the sound.

It was a normal enough start to a safari, but then came George's diary entries, only a week after he and Joy had first met.

January 1 While we were walking along Bally was some way behind, Joy suddenly caught me by the hand and said she loved me. I was flabbergasted and felt very embarrassed.

January 2 Went along the river bank with Joy and called a croc. She radiated sex and I only just managed to keep a hold on myself.

Each evening they left the track to camp in the bush or near the river. George would catch fish or shoot a bird for their supper. There were lions nearby to add a frisson to the tension. Joy says they roared in the night, and George shot an antelope as a "kill," hoping to lure one close to the camp.

January 6 In the evening we had drinks, while I went into the bush Joy filled up my glass with neat brandy. I pretended not to notice and drank it down. When we were going to bed our eyes met. If Bally had not been there we would have slept together.

Although George makes it quite clear that he was not in love, he was increasingly impressed by Joy's qualities on safari. His original apprehensions were groundless: she was sensibly dressed in leather gaiters, khaki shorts and a halter top and wore, as she did on safari to the end of her life, a small pith helmet known as a "Bombay bowler."

Occasionally the going made it necessary to mount the camels. Joy had never ridden one before and she was soon bleeding and chafed to the bone. It was extremely painful but she never complained.

A week later the situation was almost out of hand.

January 12 Joy asked me whether, if we got married, she would spoil my life—I said she could make it and I believe she could.

January 13 Yesterday at our midday halt, Joy and myself were sitting on the ground next each other skinning a Vulturine guinea fowl. Presently we touched and it was like an electric current through me. It would be a very dirty trick to take advantage of the situation.

January 14 Went out for walk with Joy and she told me that Bally is impotent, pretty tragic. During the night I heard Joy crying. I'd like to help her—Bally seems a very decent fellow, but at the same time he is a bit of an "old woman" and I can quite understand a woman like Joy wanting a man with red blood in his veins.

George knew that there was only one thing he could decently do and he told Peter and Joy that he would have to leave them at Ijara. The Hales would pick them up in their truck and take them to the picturesque port of Lamu.

Privately George resolved that he would never see either of the Ballys again. With the whole of the vast and remote Northern Frontier demanding his attention, it would not be difficult to achieve.

January 15 The Ballys and Hales started back for Garissa by lorry. Sorry the Bs have gone, they were good company on the safari. She is an exceptionally good walker and does not mind hardship and would make a wonderful companion for a man like myself. As they drove off her eyes literally looked into my soul.

TWO

Out of India

1906–1924

1

George may have been a man of few words in conversation but he could use them very effectively on paper. He was also truthful. For reasons that will emerge later, the account of his meeting with Joy given in his diary is more reliable than the versions in his or her autobiography. Occasionally a change of pen, ink or emphasis in the handwriting suggests an entry has been added later and some significant events are entirely omitted. But there is no evidence of falsification: who else would faithfully record his shots that missed?

Joy undoubtedly made the first moves, although George's heart had been touched once or twice before, and there was no doubt that "red blood" ran healthily in his veins. The best insights into his early life and relationships come from the written word—his letters, diaries, reports and two books.

The Adamson family were Irish and could trace their ancestry back to the seventeenth century. The signet ring George was wearing when he was killed bore the family crest—a lion.

George's father, Harry, served in the Royal Navy before starting an indigo plantation in Etawah, in northern India, on the Jumna River, about a hundred miles downstream from Agra and the Taj Mahal.

George's mother, Katherine, belonged to a Scottish family, the Lauries, and her mother had lived through the Indian Mutiny as a child. Her parents owned Laurie's Hotel in Agra. Katherine married Harry Adamson at Etawah in 1905, George was born on February 3, 1906, and christened George Alexander Graham Adamson, and his younger brother, christened Terence Graham, was born in 1907.

At about this time the indigo industry was badly hit by the development of chemical dyes in Germany, and Harry Adamson, a versatile

man and self-taught engineer, went to work for the Maharaja of Dholpur, about forty miles from Agra on the opposite side of the Jumna. Even-tempered and good with men, he was engaged to reorganize the Dholpur army and build its railway.

Dholpur had a reputation for producing fine soldiers, horsemen and wrestlers. It was a state of about a quarter of a million people and a thousand square miles. Very dry and hot in summer, much of it was agricultural land; the rest comprised rocky hills and desert, not unlike Kenya.

Tigers, leopards and bears inhabited the forest in the southwest of the state, and elsewhere wolves, hyenas and antelope were commonly seen. As a young boy, George had bloodthirsty dreams of shooting a bear and was taught to use a rifle by one of his father's sergeant majors.

The Maharaja, once a crack small-game shot, tired of killing and would wander out into the forest and mimic the birds which, like the shy Sambar stags, came and fed from his hand.

When writing his first book, *Bwana Game*, George began jotting down his earliest memories. He must have mislaid the writing pad, for the memoir suddenly breaks off and was never included in the book. He starts in 1910 when he was four years old.

I saw Halley's comet one night, stretched in fiery splendour across the sky. From where we stood on the roof of a half-ruined palace of Akbar's day it was reflected in the waters of a small lake called Tal Shai. Within the next day or two we heard of the death of King Edward VII.

My father being in charge of the Dholpur State railway we often had a special train to ourselves to visit outlying stations. The train stopped whenever my father felt like taking a shot at a black buck near the line with his black-powder Schneider, loaded with rolled brass cartridge cases.

Soon after we arrived in Dholpur a punitive expedition was organized with the State army against a fortified village called Jhiri, which was in rebellion. I remember the troops in bright blue uniforms, with yellow facings, boarding a train with muzzle-loading artillery pieces and armed with Martini-Henry rifles. My father was in command of the State troops, who were aided by a more up-to-date contingent from the neighbouring state of Bharatpur, under the command of Captain Cole.

In the ensuing action against Jhiri the only casualty was the gallant Captain. While riding his horse and calling on the insurgents to surrender, his big toe was shot off.

About a mile from our house, across a sandy plain, there was a Hindu temple. One night the priest in charge was murdered. My mother gave strict instructions to Balgit and Bebari, the two menservants whose job it was to look after us when we went out for our daily walks, not to take us anywhere near the scene.

Our sense of morbid curiosity was strong and somehow we persuaded, or perhaps blackmailed, our escorts to take us to the forbidden temple. The first evidence to meet our gaze was a long white pugaree dangling from the stone gutter overhanging the temple wall. Presumably this was the murderer's escape route.

With rousing excitement, mingled with fear, we entered the courtyard to be assailed by loud wailing from the womenfolk. They were not in the least averse from taking us to the chamber where the corpse was lying, pointing out the numerous sword cuts on it. My most vivid memory is of gore all over the room and hundreds of termite wings sticking to the drying blood.

We had a charming young governess called Miss Blünn, with whom I was great friends, but to whom my brother Terence must sometimes have been a sore trial. He had an incredibly obstinate streak.

On one occasion Miss Blünn asked him to spell "cat." Whether he thought it was beneath his dignity, or did not like her tone of voice, he simply went dumb. As a punishment he was locked in the lavatory. But he created such a rumpus by beating the door with an enamel jug that he was let out.

At length Miss Blünn got married, which was inevitable with her looks and charm. It was therefore decided that our further education should be accomplished in England, far away from the infection of an Indian accent. Up till then Terence and I still spoke Hindustani far better than English. In fact we usually conversed with each other in the language.

Before they left for England George and Terence received a gentle inoculation against this impending separation from their parents and home. Each year during the hot season they were sent up to the narrow terraces of the hills at Simla, together with most of the British wives and children from Delhi, and stayed at the Longwood Hotel. It was a world of blue skies, tennis, cricket and riding; of picnics, bands and concert parties; of ice cream, cake and lemonade.

At first Katherine Adamson went too; later she sent the boys with Miss Blünn, who saw that they wrote to their parents. Katherine kept their letters, with many later ones from their school in England.

From the ages of seven and eight the boys' different personalities— George's sanguine view of the world and Terence's love of plants— are already discernible.

George writes:

1914

Dear Mummie

... Terence and I are having a dreadful time, Miss Blünn beats us twice a day and gives us only one milk dish and only half a toast.

We went in the buggy and an enormous flash of lightening frightened Stuffybags [our horse] last night ... I must do some lessons now, so good-bye.

With much love from George.

JUNE 28, 1915

We went to the dentist on Thursday and we did not funk it a bit and even Terence did not make a fuss.

Last night I took Miss Blünn khud climing. It was frightfully slippery and she was very unhappy. I got a long root like a rope and pulled her up and I lent her my khud stick. Next time I will take my lassoo ...

JULY 12, 1915

I feed myself on sausages and hunter's beef so I am never hungry.

I am very sorry to hear you have got boils and that it is so hot.

We are going for very long walks if the rains do not come.

We want a dog badly.

The germs of Terence's lifelong botanical interests are beginning to stir:

Dear Mummie,

I want my two watering cans bringing up by Auntie Rose because I shall want them in the rains.

George and I have built a hiding place and as I was digging when Miss Blünn and George were out shopping I killed a little snake and a senterpead with my shoe.

I have picked many pretty flowers. We have ate many wild strobries.

Lots of love from Terence.

We went to the Lieutenant Governor's house on Wednesday because there was a show. I liked the countries best.

Britannia came in and then Scotland, Ireland and Australia, Canada and Africa, all dressed up. Scotland *was* funny, she could not get real thistles so she had to use artichokes instead. India was dressed in gold and Australia had a cowboys hat and a stock whip. Africa had a big spear and some feathers.

Another of Terence's characteristics is also emerging: he was his own man to the end of his life.

I have read your letter and I will be good the first day, the next day I will be naughty and so on.

I have got a lot of wire to trail creepers on when we get back.

We frighten Miss Blünn every day at tiffin by getting behind the door and jumping at her.

George remembered Miss Blünn with great fondness. Like all the women who later most attracted him, her family came from continental Europe.

2

During the First World War, in September 1916—when George was ten and Terence nine—Katherine set off with them to England. George recalls the voyage, and then his memoir breaks off.

At Bombay we boarded the good ship *Elysia* of the Anchor Line. The first excitement was gunnery practice with the lone 4.7 inch mounted on the stern. Most merchantmen were armed at this time of the submarine menace and indiscriminate sinking of ships.

The Suez Canal was lined by British and Australian troops. Port Said had been bombed on the morning of our arrival. The explosion was said to have decapitated a Greek woman but this time we were unable to view the victim.

The trip through the Mediterranean was exciting because of the ever present danger of encountering a German submarine and the ship followed a zig-zag course.

We arrived in Liverpool on a foggy morning and reached London just in time for a Zeppelin raid. All I can . . .

George and Terence never set foot in India again. Instead they embarked on one of those curious upbringings inflicted on children of the Raj that were calculated to stiffen their upper lips. In this it was extraordinarily successful with the Adamson boys, although it must have wrung their mother's heart for she was sensitive and loved them very much.

As soon as they reached England, Katherine took the boys down to Cheltenham, a Regency spa at the foot of the Cotswold hills. Their school, Dean Close, frequently confused with its larger neighbor, Cheltenham College, numbered about two hundred boys. Its headmaster was Dr. W. H. Flecker.

The tall redbrick buildings rose out of an almost treeless expanse of football, cricket and hockey fields; there was no privacy for junior boys in its high, echoing classrooms and dormitories. The regime of Low Church puritan services, compulsory games, monotonous food and one bath a week reflected the values of its founders.

For news of home George and Terence were entirely dependent on letters and cuttings from the Indian papers. George read them with avidity: when riots broke out he thought it would be best to shoot Gandhi, and he asked if Lord Reading was any good as Viceroy.

From his own letters he seems much the same as any other schoolboy, though few, spotting an Indian on the other side of the hedge, could yell out in Hindustani and ask him what on earth he was doing in Cheltenham. He has some nice turns of phrase and flashes of humor, occasionally writing in pencil by torchlight and "in deathly fear of being caught by a prefect."

I saw Aunt Mia. She has got a specimen of a companion, I never saw such a face in my life . . .

I had to get a new pair of football shorts. They were not short, they were long, and I could stow away a pig in them . . .

I am afraid I am an awful chap at writing letters. Scripture prep is the only time I feel inspired . . .

Good heavens that mango pickle is d—— hot. No one here dare steal it. I offered it to some people and it nearly lifted their scalps off . . .

There are several references to Terence's idiosyncrasies. "Terence has got quite a collection of caterpillars. Remember those fish worms that got loose in the cabin at Marseilles?" In 1922, when Terence was fifteen, George writes, "Terence is exactly the same as before, he loads up his pockets with stones, nails and bits of iron." He was still doing it sixty years later.

There is no hint of unhappiness in the letters and if the boys got bored at school they devised new forms of mischief for which they were occasionally beaten. George illicitly boiled eggs over a Bunsen burner, crawled over the roofs, played hooky in a teashop and baited the local gamekeeper. Oddly, Katherine did not discourage George from smoking; when he was sixteen he wrote home for, and received, a box of 555 cigarettes and a four-inch cigarette holder.

Nevertheless as the years go by, a note of nostalgia creeps into his letters. In 1921 he writes: "When will you be coming to England? It seems a long time since you were here. I always think of you and Dad at night and often dream of Dholpur. The other night I dreamt I was chased by a boar."

Virtually every year Katherine made the hot and smelly voyage back to England, arriving in June. She would come down to Cheltenham and spend most of the summer holidays with her sons. Harry also came over a couple of times. They must have stopped at Mombasa and Cape Town on the way, for in a letter George asks his mother to take a photograph of an aunt in Nairobi. It was a signpost to the future.

By the time George left Dean Close both independence and integrity were deeply engrained in his character, qualities that must have owed something to the place where he spent eight formative years so far from home. One of his contemporaries, F. W. Robins, said this about him seventy years later.

I remember George particularly sitting next to me at meals. I got the feeling of a great strength of character—the ability to accommodate other people but at the same time to stand up to bullies, as I remember gratefully myself a number of times.

The aspiration of a school like Dean Close was to impart to its boys the character of a gentleman, self-reliance and esprit de corps. In all these aims it perfectly succeeded with George. In three others it signally failed: the infusion of social conformity, the competitive spirit and its own brand of religion—"one of the dullest in the world" according to a contemporary of George's, who became successively a priest, a lay missionary in India and an anthropologist specializing in sexual mores.

It seems unlikely that the school did much to excite the imaginations of its pupils, despite the achievements of two of its old boys— the poet James Elroy Flecker (son of the headmaster) whose *Hassan* was set to music by Delius, and Francis Bacon, one of the most highly regarded British artists of the twentieth century. George's mind was not closed to the arts, but his eyes and ears were simply never opened to them.

He won no distinctions at school. He simply took a few form prizes and played in the second football and hockey elevens: lance corporal was the highest rank he reached in the school cadet corps. Even so, in the first century of the school's existence no Old Decanian has become better known throughout the world.

THREE

Dreams of Gold

1924–1934

1

When Harry Adamson retired from Dholpur in 1924 he decided to settle in South Africa. He therefore sent George a ticket to Cape Town. But Harry and Katherine liked Kenya so much when their boat put in at Mombasa that they decided to stay and George joined them there.

By the time he arrived Harry had already bought a coffee farm at Limuru, about twenty miles north of Nairobi toward Lake Naivasha. The green and fertile country had been cleared for farming, so there was very little game, but the birds were lovely. Crowned cranes, tall and golden-crested, stalked around the pools. Colobus monkeys with capes of silky white hair flowing over their black fur swung through the trees.

The Adamsons' house, like many others at that time, was picturesque but primitive—a so-called banda thatched with grass. European settlers had first arrived only about twenty years earlier and had much to learn. Harry Adamson fared no better as a coffee farmer than Karen Blixen had at Ngong. Today tea flourishes all around Limuru but the altitude is too high for coffee.

At first George helped his father but was quickly depressed by the monotony, "one coffee bean looked exactly like another." He felt no more fulfilled as a plowman, a bailiff on a hundred-thousand-acre farm, a trucker or cutting sisal for sacking with his friend David Hobden.

On the other hand, goat-trading with two friends, Hugh Grant and Roger Courtney, was too lively; the goats were constantly breaking out of the lorry and died when transferred to a different climate.

George outlived both his partners. Roger Courtney had a brother who never touched a drop and was known as "Sacred" Courtney;

Roger, who very much enjoyed his sundowner, was nicknamed "Profane." "Profane" died up-country of Blackwater fever and was buried with a funnel in his grave to receive libations from whoever was passing. The Somali herdsmen, who had admired him but were Muslim, would drip in some milk.

A cluster of legends surrounded Hugh Grant. He had won a Military Cross in the First World War for his part in hand-to-hand fighting: a silver stud on his knife handle signified the life of an officer, the brass studs were for those of other ranks. When the Provincial Commissioner once missed a duck with a sighted shot from his .22 rifle, Grant picked it off from the saddle with his pistol. After he joined the Moral Rearmament movement—it found a crop ripe for harvesting in Kenya—he confined himself to killing with a bow and arrow until the Second World War, when he recruited George to his private army of cutthroats.

In April 1927, Harry Adamson died. He had been aware that the altitude at Limuru could be dangerous for his heart but liked the place so much that he would not move. Terence, who was teaching himself to become an engineer, had rebuilt the house in stone. He now took over the farm and looked after his mother. People warmed to her, although her poor hearing gave her an air of aloofness. George thought Terence took after her: she was sensitive, observant, methodical and an expert gardener. She planted plums and peaches around the house, from which she could see Mount Kenya in one direction and Kilimanjaro in another.

George in the meantime embarked on a few further enterprises with David Hobden. They sold milk in whiskey bottles, making their rounds through the rutted and puddled streets of Nairobi in a disintegrating truck; they worked behind a bar in Limuru; and they ran a bus-cum-mail-and-carrier service to Arusha. This was bankrupted by the cost of replacing axles and springs and by the loss of a consignment of matches that ignited itself on the way.

George was later lured into one last enterprise with Hobden, selling insurance in Kenya and Uganda. George's competitor in the field, a defrocked priest with delirium tremens, usually got the better of him but before George gave up he had his first brush with marriage. He was twenty-four.

We arrived late in the evening at an attractive little hotel. The sole occupant of the lounge appeared to be a young man of pleasing appearance. Some time later I realised that our companion was a lady; she was a geologist.

We became very friendly and while Hobden went on his insurance errands, I went sight-seeing with Miss Ledeboer, in her car. We had several pleasant days together and at the end of our stay decided to have a farewell party. I retired early as I felt a bout of fever coming on. Miss L. and Hobden continued the party until the early hours.

In the morning I was informed that it had been decided that Miss L. and myself should get married. We were all to go forthwith to the local magistrate's office for the civil ceremony. Never having considered matrimony at such an early stage of my life I was staggered at all the implications. While Miss L. was a very charming girl she was unusually powerful and determined. Had I not seen her clout an African who had been insolent and send him reeling?

I suggested that Miss L. and Hobden should go ahead in their car and that I would meet them at the magistrate's office. As soon as they were out of sight I headed south at full speed; when later we met the atmosphere was distinctly chilly.

It was another five years before he really fell in love, and another seven before he lost his virginity.

Although during these early years in Kenya George was undoubtedly a rolling stone, he was propelled by two principles that guided him all his life: he was determined never to be bored and equally set on not compromising his freedom.

In between jobs he would do maintenance and repairs on the house, the farm and any transport. He became an expert handyman and mechanic. His favorite recreation, which also helped keep him financially afloat, was to go on a hunting safari with Terence.

They would set off after antelope with their shared .405 Winchester rifle and a few precious rounds of ammunition. If they were successful they loaded their kill onto the sidecar of their motorbike. Occasionally they would take out a license for rhinos or elephants. Rhino horn sold quite well and the feet were bought for tobacco jars. An elephant license cost £25, but the tusks might fetch £50 or £100. On any serious safari they took the man who laid the foundations of George's skill as one of the outstanding trackers in Africa.

We would never have got anywhere without Mosandu, our Dorobo tracker. The Dorobo are past masters of the ancient traditions of the hunt. Mosandu taught me to understand wind, scent, sound and spoor. He could interpret the age and sex of an animal from its tracks, and knew how fast it was moving, if it was lightly or badly wounded, and if it was dying. He could tell from the clarity of the trail, from rain drops or dew on the spoor, or perhaps from the trace of an insect, how old the prints were. If the spoor petered out he would pick it up again from dislodged pebbles, broken twigs, bent blades of grass, or torn cobwebs. If an animal had lain up, under a rock or bush, he would identify it by licking his palm and pressing it to the ground, so that any hairs there would cling to it.

The lessons George learned from Mosandu reinforced the self-reliance he had developed during his eight years in England without a real home. The next eight in Kenya provided his further education and practical training.

2

In 1929 George took on two formidable tasks.

By January large swarms of locusts were already sweeping south into Kenya. The government mobilized a team of control officers to combat them, including George, who was posted to Karpedo in the Baringo district. His workforce consisted of fifty men, half Pokot and half Turkana. He had no difficulty in telling which tribes the men belonged to since they wore no clothes and the Pokot were circumcised while the Turkana were not.

Apart from his pipe, his whiskey, his diary and his rifle, his closest companions were his dog, a pointer named Hindoo, and the team of donkeys he assembled. For the next thirty years, although he sometimes had the use of a truck, donkeys became his Land-Rover. Whatever he needed for his work or for himself was loaded onto their backs in rawhide panniers. George walked or rode on a mule.

He traveled faster than the donkeys and often pushed ahead so that one day when they and their drovers took a wrong fork, George was left to spend the night alone in the bush, mercilessly bitten by mosquitoes. It was not just the mosquitoes that bothered him.

He had seen lion spoor that day, so he settled down with his back against a tree and his rifle across his knees. Since it had been too dark to collect fuel for a fire, sleep was out of the question. As time went by the lion began to call and gradually drew nearer—at one time it was only fifty yards away.

Hungry, bitten and cramped, George was off at first light and found hordes of "hoppers." Soon after leaving the egg, locusts look like small black grasshoppers. It is difficult to convey to anyone living in a country free of locusts the horror of a plague. A swarm can travel up to forty miles in a day and darken the sky in living clouds, brown, pink or yellow, according to the phases of the insects, numbering millions. They may cover an area fifty miles long by fifty miles wide and continue to fly over for three days, adding to the sense of doom with the "muffled roar" of their wings. At night the swarms settle down on bushes and shrubs; by morning every leaf has been stripped.

When they are laying, each female digs a little hole and drops into it fifty or a hundred eggs that will hatch out as hoppers that cannot take to the air for another five weeks. Some people find this phase the most frightening as an army of billions, rustling their wings and crunching their jaws, eat their way across lawns, fields and plantations, devouring every morsel of green. Once after a plague of Egyptian proportions, the Maasai lost every blade of their grazing and in consequence every cow they possessed.

At that time the hopper stage was the only one during which the locust was vulnerable. Control officers were therefore issued with stirrup pumps, sacks of bran and five-pound tins of arsenide of sodium. A solution of arsenic was then sprayed on the crops in the locusts' path, or mixed with the bran and laid out for them as "bait." This latter method of control was extremely effective, but also held dangers. Some villages, with only a few goats to their name, refused to put down bran, in which the proportion of arsenic was minimal. They said that the birds that had fed on the locusts had all disappeared and their stock was dying from bait not starvation.

To drive home his confidence that his bran was safe George fed some to Hindoo, his pointer. Terence, who was engaged in similar work, used to go a step further. He munched a handful himself in front of the mesmerized elders.

When the plague was finally exhausted George was recruited to explore routes for new tracks to improve the mobility of locust control in the future.

George relished his lonely and itinerant life and was given a gang of Turkana and a lorry so that he could build a control road linking Karpedo, at the source of the Suguta River, with the valley of the Kerio.

The Suguta emerges from springs in the ground and flows north along the bed of the Rift until it is prevented from joining Lake Rudolf by a barrier of volcanoes. The valley, without much water for months on end, is intolerably hot, reaching 140°F in the shade, if shade can be found. The glare off the sand, white as snow, and the shimmering rocks is blinding. For Wilfred Thesiger, the last great explorer on earth and the ultimate arbiter, the Suguta is the most interesting desert in Africa.

Seen from the air, it is exquisitely beautiful, its sand and lava swirling and undulating in psychedelic patterns. The waters of the river gush hot from their springs and converge in a channel of sand whose colors shift from gold to salty white, tinged with squirls of coral and veins of viridian. Thereafter it is joined by delicate little water courses leading up into the dunes like tendrils or roots. Here and there patches resembling lichen turn out to be scrub, fighting for survival.

Not until the valley widens is its full grandeur revealed. A single rust-colored cathedral of rock rises out of the sand, and the sides of the Rift shelve back in terraces as if the Grand Canyon had been forced open by invisible hands. Toward the north lava spills over the sand, black ink on white paper, and seems still to be moving. Beyond it the volcanic hills are twenty shades of gray, brown and pale mauve. One cone, almost entirely surrounded by the lake, floats in the water like a giant jellyfish.

Three lakes in the craters of volcanoes at the end of the valley, alive with different algae, glow like a ruby, a sapphire and an emerald.

The view from the highest crag above the Suguta challenges any in the world. Even through binoculars men and donkeys below are as ants. In fact the animals and birds that inhabit the valley do not attempt to move in the heat of the day but come alive at night.

George and his Turkana followed their example. They worked by night and did not touch food or drink till the sun left the sky. When, at last, they reached the Kerio the DC came out to greet them, the first white man George had seen for fifty-two days. His qualifications as a pioneer were now complete.

3

Like any other qualified man, George wanted to make a living, and there were only two ambitions to which he ever admitted. One was to strike gold or precious stones. The other, harbored since childhood, was to become a game warden.

In December 1932, after alluvial gold had been found at Kakamega in western Kenya, George joined the rush to stake out and register a claim. He was supported by two friends at Limuru: Jack Dyer, who owned a farm, and Nevil Baxendale, who worked on it. Because there was a farming depression in Kenya at the time, Dyer encouraged the young men to seek their fortunes by prospecting.

Baxendale, who towered over George, was the ideal friend and companion. Strong as an ox, self-confident and amusing, he was a brilliant shot, fisherman, boat builder and sailor. They set out on their quest with their faithful companions, Hindoo and Yusuf, their emaciated cook.

In *Bwana Game* George gives a brief and practical account of how they worked at Kakamega. They staked out a claim along a stream they believed to be gold-bearing and assiduously panned their stretch of water. Sometimes they were rewarded and could extract from the rubble a few ounces of gold that they hid in a sack guarded by a rhinoceros horn viper. They called the snake Cuthbert Gandhi because, like the Indian leader, he would periodically fast nigh unto death.

At the end of the year the last of the gold was handed over to the bank and Cuthbert Gandhi to the Coryndon Museum. The price they received for the gold exactly covered their costs without a penny over.

They returned to Limuru, where Jack Dyer had persuaded them to take up another of his enthusiasms. His business may have been farming but his heart lay with boats. He built a number at Limuru, naming several of them *Osprey*, and took them by trailer either to the coast or the thirty-odd miles to Naivasha, one of the loveliest lakes in the country. For several years George and Nevil spent much of their spare time on the lake, sailing, racing or fishing from *Osprey*. The boats were tied up at The Anglers Rest, now a Masonic lodge.

At the end of 1933 they planned another prospecting safari down the Kerio River to the west coast of Lake Rudolf. Failing any luck there, they would look for the Queen of Sheba's mines, which legend located between the eastern shores of the lake and Ethiopia. It would be a long walk.

They set out in February, taking Hindoo, who was so keen he would even point at a tortoise, but he was bitten by a tsetse fly, fell sick, and George had to shoot him. Another of his dogs had died of dropsy and a third was killed by a porcupine whose quills pierced his heart.

When Yusuf heard George and Nevil were on safari again he walked a hundred miles to join them. He had a way with the donkeys and was a master chef in the bush. Wild spinach soup, smoked catfish and guinea fowl roasted with mushrooms and *posho* (maize flour) were all in his repertoire. It was just as well since George was always running out of conventional supplies, including tea and tobacco.

Like those of the Tana, the banks of the Kerio are shaded with palms, figs and acacias. George also found bushes of cordia gharaf whose orange berries he ate as protection against scurvy. Despite the shade, the air along the river is exceedingly hot and to get sufficient ventilation termites must build their towers of red earth twenty feet high. It is hotter still when the river leaves the hills and trickles into the lake through a delta of sand on which sacred ibis cluster and crocodiles doze in the blazing sun.

Just before reaching the lake, George and Nevil bumped into a young man who turned out to be the assistant DC from the Turkana District headquarters at Lodwar. It was their first meeting with William Hale.

Since they had so far found only a few specks of gold, they could not resist the lure of Mount Kulal, looming out of the haze on the other side of the lake. There was a chance that one of its ravines would lead to the mines. The eastern shore was out of bounds, and they had no permit to go there, but their minds were made up.

They recruited a new set of donkeys and, to help Yusuf, employed two naked Turkana, a man named Tobosh and his friend.

Before they all set off they shot a hippo "as lean as a greyhound," and presented it with their compliments to the Turkana chief. They stocked up their own larder with a 15-pound catfish caught from a canoe they made with their tarpaulin and some doum palm stems.

There can be no lakeshore on earth that is barer, bleaker, hotter and windier than the southern circuit of Lake Rudolf. A moderate wind blows at 40 miles per hour, taking your food from your plate and flinging stinging sand in your face. The grit, stones and rocks slide from under your feet, slash your shoes and raise impassable walls.

For mile after mile George, Nevil and the donkey party slithered along the lava that sloped down to the pebble beaches and was cut across by dry riverbeds. Then lacerating knife-edge outcrops forced them up the slippery scree into the unforgiving pink rocks of the Loriu hills. George wore a loincloth so that his sweaty trousers did not rub his scrotum raw. A donkey died of exhaustion.

Hungry as they were, the small flocks of flamingos, pelicans and cormorants dotted along the shore did not tempt them, for their flesh was fishy and rank; the tasty Egyptian geese nesting on a cliff were out of reach. Nevil caught several Nile perch of 30 to 40 pounds which made excellent eating, and when the occasional gazelle appeared, he proved the better shot. It was only when George got home he realized that the rifling of his barrel had worn smooth.

It took three weeks to reach the south end of the lake and there the lava marshaled itself to repel them. Gray, writhing and networked with crevasses, it was almost impossible to cross, yet George and Nevil persisted and made their way up Teleki's volcano, which was still smoking when the Austrian explorer had found it fifty years before.

In another week they were among the palm trees of the lovely and still untouched oasis at Loyangalani. They did not laze by the warm waters of its pools as visitors to the modern lodge there do, but went straight inland across the twelve miles of sand to the mountain.

There is no gold in Mount Kulal, as they quickly realized from its volcanic formation, so they made their way back to the shore and trekked north for another ten days. Soon they passed the little settlement of the El Molo, a tribe of a hundred living in tiny reed huts on the lakeshore. They were the only people George saw during the entire 150-mile journey around the lake.

The absence of human beings, despite the prevalence of game along the foot of the mountain and permanent water in its ravines, was one of two enigmas that puzzled George on this march. The other was the mystery of South Island which rises like the back of a dinosaur out of the southern end of the lake. The El Molo endowed it with legends, but no European had set foot on it.

North of the El Molo, the sand dunes seemed to rise and fall to eternity and the outcrops of rock among which the two men occasionally stopped to prospect were some distance from the water. At Moite Hill George and Nevil turned back, exactly six weeks after reaching the lake. Their time and their food had run out.

In the light of all they had endured it is not surprising that they conceived a plan to take a shortcut home in another improvised boat. In the first week of June they started to build it in a wide flat *lugga*, or dry riverbed, called Serr el Tommia, just north of Porr Hill, that looks like a pyramid of rock.

The design of our boat was based on a wooden frame, made from the branches of the acacias growing above the riverbed. None of the branches were straight, so they had to be broken and rejoined with thongs from an antelope we had skinned a few days before. My job was to sew our groundsheets together for the hull and to tailor a sail from our bedding. Donkey boxes were adapted for the rudder, a leeboard and oars.

In high spirits we sent Tobosh off with his companion, the donkeys, the remains of our food and all our possessions except for a gun, and a cooking pot we kept as a bailer.

That evening we weighted the boat with stones, so it would not be blown away, and retired to sleep in the riverbed. When we woke in the morning the boat was in pieces. Jackals had come in the night and devoured all the thongs.

They had to replace the thongs with acacia bark, and they supplemented their last food with salvadora berries and a goose George shot.

At 3.00 pm, three days after Tobosh and the donkeys had left us, we pushed out onto the lake. While Yusuf bailed, and the little boat concertinaed with the waves, Nevil and I rowed for six hours until well after dark and our hands were raw. As we paused to check our position against the silhouette of the Loriu hills, which had appeared dimly ahead of us, I heard a sound in the distance like waves under a gathering wind.

Nevil and I strained our ears; we suddenly realised it was the croaking of a thousand frogs and we must be close to shore. Half an hour after we landed the wind really did get up and a gale blustered over the lake until well into the following day.

While George and Nevil were sailing north toward Lodwar, Tobosh and his companion cheerfully caught them up only a week after their departure with the donkeys. Reunited, the party set off across the sandy plain to Lodwar, where they were given an exuberant welcome by the DC, and Willie Hale. Hale pressed them to a basin of succulent goat stew. He also explained why the opposite shore was deserted. Gelubba raiders from Ethiopia had recently robbed, raped and dispatched or dispersed the tribes people who normally roamed it.

The two men reached home at the end of July and a month later George picked up on the wireless a tragic piece of news that provided a rider to his crossing of the lake. Just after it, a scientific expedition to Rudolf, led by Vivian Fuchs, had left two men on South Island. They had vanished, and despite intensive searches by air, only an oar from their boat and a helmet had been found. George determined that one day he would cross to the island and search for clues to their fate.

Was it the challenge that had driven him and Baxendale to walk so many miles in such terrible conditions? Dr.eams of gold can hardly have been enough, even though one of George's closest friends said that to the end of his days he never walked anywhere without scanning the ground for a glitter or gleam.

When asked what he would have done if he had really struck gold George replied, "Probably retired to the coast and drunk myself to death." He wouldn't have; he could not have stood the boredom of dying that way.

FOUR

Changes of Heart

1935–1942

1

As with most other diaries, the disclosures in George's are not confined simply to the words of its entries. The writing varies from tight to flowing and sometimes loose, perhaps depending on his mood or how long after sundown it is. There are a few cryptic symbols and odd abbreviations. Periodically there are gaps for weeks on end. These occur between jobs or safaris, or when there was someone to talk to in the evenings. The diary often filled the place of a companion at the end of the day.

He used the pages in the front and the back, considerately provided by the publishers with useless information and irrelevant pro formas, for practical or sentimental notes. He recorded the formulas for mixing arsenite and curing leopard skins and lists his guns. In 1934 he already had quite an arsenal: two heavy rifles for stopping elephants, buffalo and rhinos; two medium Winchesters; a .22; two 12-bore shotguns; a .55 Colt revolver and a .32 Walther automatic.

Despite the record in his diaries George was a good, not a bad, shot. About the only notes of satisfaction are when he kills an oryx and, later, an impala at 250 yards and shoots six ducks with his last six cartridges. Willie Hale, who was often on safari with him, says that quite apart from his skill, which was great though not exceptional, his outstanding bushcraft enabled him to reduce the length of his shots and increase the chances of a kill.

At the beginning of 1935 George jotted down various addresses, including Gethin & Hewlitt's, a firm that employed him to take out hunting safaris on and off for the next three years. Another address belongs to Angela Ofenheim. She and her brother Ernest were the first clients he took hunting.

Angela, known as Tony in the family, was no older than George, then twenty-nine. She was the daughter of an Austrian doctor who had become a naturalized Englishman when he was young, and she was a fully qualified doctor herself. Tall, slim, dark and attractive, she handled a rifle with confidence and enthusiasm. Nevertheless, the fact that she was a woman, and perhaps her upper-class English manner, decided George to assay her real worth.

He quite deliberately took her and her brother over the roughest ground and the steepest slopes of the Ciana hills in search of quarry. Tony, who had spotted what George was up to and was determined not to lag behind, shot a fine roan antelope and on the same afternoon wounded an eland that George finished off.

Four days later Tony hit one of three fine lions after George whispered at her, "Shoot girl, shoot!" It was too late to follow it up that night. Next morning they lost the tracks of their lion but came across a freshly killed wildebeest, its blood still flowing, and the spoor of the other two lions they had disturbed on their victim. George thought that the first lion must have got away, but the next morning he found it, dead. It was one of the largest he had ever encountered. More than fifty years later its head still hung on the wall of Tony's farmhouse in England.

With a buffalo and rhino added to their score, the Ofenheims took George back to Limuru, dined with his mother and went on to Nairobi. Tony found Katherine Adamson eccentric but welcoming; Terence was also there but he was overshadowed by George.

Tony had certainly passed George's stringent appraisal, for he wrote in his diary that night: "The end of the most enjoyable safari I have ever been on, with two of the most charming people one could wish to meet."

The liking was reciprocated and a week later all three set out again on impulse to hunt bongo, shy and very beautiful chestnut antelope with lustrous eyes and delicate markings, which live in the depth of the forest on the Aberdare Mountains, where the going is extremely tricky and tough.

The party was short of almost everything, shared a small tent and in the evenings knocked back rum *bilis* together. Ernest ricked his knee and George sprained his Achilles tendon; Tony alone, to George's amusement, was unscathed. To restore their pride the two men polished off her flask of brandy—she was beginning to make her mark.

February 18   T. is really a splendid girl, full of fun and always cheerful, even after a hard day. I'm beginning to get very fond of her.

Toward the end of their stay in Kenya the Ofenheims were very shaken to hear that their father had died, and Katherine Adamson insisted that they should spend the night with her at Limuru: Ernest was only twenty-one.

The next day George waved good-bye to the Ofenheims at the airfield and then collected the shotgun they had given him.

March 1   Tony has gone away with my heart. If I was in a position to, I would marry her any day. I must write to tell her of my sentiments. I have her image continually before my eyes.

George you idiot, you're getting sentimental and its not in your line, so chuck it! Don't think about things of that sort until you have made a fortune.

George tried to tell Tony some of his feelings when he wrote to her. Her answer was charming and kind "but not the sort I wanted." It was only ten years later that he discovered she felt much as he did. In the meantime the friendship rooted in their safari, and regularly refreshed by their letters, grew into one of the most valuable of his life. Strengthened by the affection and laughter of their very rare meetings, it flourished until he died.

2

By then George had a very clear idea of the life he wanted to live— active, independent, adventurous and preferably in the wild and desolate landscape of northern Kenya. If not there, he was always happy to take his clients down to the Mara in the south, a great plain divided from the Serengeti in Tanganyika (now Tanzania) only by the invisible frontier between the two countries.

In the hard years between the two world wars, safari clients did not swarm into Kenya during the dry seasons as they do today, so for the next three years George interspersed professional safaris with trips in search of beeswax, leopard skins, hides and frankincense resin.

He took out Belgian, German, American and British clients, including two who were soon to return to his life from an unexpected direction, Dr. Jex-Blake and his wife, Lady Muriel. The doctor was a Nairobi heart specialist; his wife was tall and beautiful and, like him, an expert botanist and gardener. During the First World War she had cut off her hair and gone with two friends to nurse the Serbians among the extremely primitive conditions of the Balkan front.

The Jex-Blakes were much more interested in watching animals and looking for rare plants than in hunting, and increasingly George himself saw the point of shooting animals with a camera rather than a gun; he took as much pride in getting his clients a good picture as he did a fine trophy.

On the photographic safaris in the Serengeti it was the lions that most impressed George, apart from the sheer numbers of other game, and a passage in *Bwana Game* expresses a change of heart that occurred at this time.

One evening we came on a magnificent lioness on a rock, gazing out across the plains. She was sculptured by the setting sun, as though she were part of the granite on which she lay. I wondered how many lions had lain on the self-same rock during countless centuries while the human race was still in its cradle. It was a thought which made me reflect that though civilised man has spent untold treasure on preserving ancient buildings and works of art fashioned by the hand of man, yet he destroys these creatures which typify the perfection of ageless beauty and grace. And he does so for no better reason than to boast of a prowess achieved by means of a weapon designed by man to destroy man, or to use their skins to grace some graceless abode.

There is something prophetic about this description of his feelings twenty years before he and Joy adopted the lioness Elsa. Elspeth Huxley includes it in her anthology *Nine Faces of Kenya*, and Bill Travers, who played George in the film of *Born Free*, read it at George's memorial service in London in 1990.

The recent bruise on George's heart must have ached a little when his old friend Nevil Baxendale announced his engagement in June 1935 and married in November. George could not go to the wedding because he was racked with malaria, an affliction common to almost anyone who frequently sleeps out in the tropics.

The best defenses against the mosquito-borne disease are to wear clothing that covers as much of the body as possible and use the protection of gauze windows or mosquito nets. Leading the life he had chosen, George had little chance of avoiding malaria. He therefore suffered the consequences: ague in which the body shivers and the teeth chatter with cold, followed by a slow dry heat with burning skin, and finally an outbreak of drenching sweat. This cycle may be repeated over anything from six hours to three days.

Taken in advance, quinine can reduce the impact of malaria and it is also the specific for the disease itself. Medical science therefore constantly sought to improve its prophylactics and antidotes. Unfortunately over the years mosquitoes grew increasingly immune to them, while an excessive dose could produce a condition at least as frightening as the disease itself.

Malaria is recurrent. Periodically throughout his life George would "feel awful" and have to take to his bed every six or twelve months. A bout can be brought on by any accident or shock to the body. Once, when he was celebrating his return home, the capsule of a soda machine exploded in his face; the next day he had a temperature of 104°F.

In the future his personal safaris in search of skins and wax were made alone with his donkeys and a handful of Africans, chief among them a man named Rotich who acted as an interpreter among the tribes not speaking Swahili and opened his bargaining.

Wild honey was prized by any tribe that had no easy access to sugar—it was an essential ingredient of home-brewed beer—and George calculated that wherever there was honey there must also be wax. He therefore planned to scour the country.

Some of the tribes hollowed out logs and hung them in trees to attract the nesting bees. Others followed honeyguides, inconspicuous brown birds about the size of a thrush, that set up a chatter and flutter their wings whenever they sense a chance of leading a man to a bees' nest. Having taken part in the ritual a number of times, George knew that while the Africans took the honey and rewarded the birds with the grubs, they normally threw away the wax; he would persuade them to save it.

Although George returned from one safari with a hundred pounds of beeswax, he constantly found that in the excitement of laying hands on the honey, his suppliers had either forgotten to save the wax or had better things to do than collect it. His trading in skins and hides did little better.

He saw virtually no other Europeans when he was out in the bush, although one evening he was accosted by an American who asked him point-blank, "Do you know Jesus?"

George realized his reply was unconvincing and after accepting the man's invitation to have supper at the mission station—he was very hungry—quickly took a couple of tots of rum "which made me feel ready to meet dozens of missionaries."

Not long after this, the voice of a tempter, which had kept silent for remarkably long, began to whisper to him.

On my safaris I seldom met anyone of my own kind to talk to and there were times when I was assailed by temptations of the flesh.

There was one little river on which I used to camp where the women would come down to wash and bathe. Two girls made a habit of progressively revealing their charms with the object of securing my attentions. In other places the girls seemed to have a collection of skirts which grew shorter and shorter as our acquaintance grew closer.

Sometimes I left it a little late but rather than succumb to such overtures I would seize my rifle and stay out in the hills or until I or the girls had grown weary. My men could not understand and asked if I suffered from some physical impediment.

In the end I allowed nature to take its course in the company of a beautiful girl from the Nandi tribe.

He wrote this in his diary.

January 3, 1937   In the morning Rotich came to me and told me that a girl was waiting for me in the bush by the river below camp. I found her rather bashful, good looking, and about twenty years old. She was absolutely clean and no smell.

His first sexual experience gave him intense pleasure and there were several more of these meetings. By the end of the week the girl spent a whole night in his tent.

The Nandi women, like those of the Somalis, can be extremely beautiful to Western eyes. George told one of his old friends that he recorded these favors so discreetly in his diary—with only the small sum of money with which he gave her and two initials—that years later he could not at first remember what they signified!

3

While this initiation was being completed, another one was just beginning. In September 1936, George met someone who changed his life forever. He stumbled on the man's camp near the Kerio River, a bower of freshly cut green branches surrounded by a carpet of leaves. He was a keen British Israelite, a sect that believes the past and the future of the world can be read by interpreting the detailed measurements of the Egyptian pyramids.

For three or four nights George listened attentively to his new friend, Captain J. T. Oulton—a man in his sixties—who explained why he always slept with his head to the north, whether in the bush, some house or a city, and why he would not touch immature food such as lamb or an egg.

George took all this with a pinch of salt. His letters from school deplore the prospect of a Sunday with two sermons, and once he reached Africa he seems to have relinquished any vestige of formal religion or belief in God.

On the other hand, Oulton's stories about his early life in Kenya— he had arrived in 1898—engrossed George, as did his account of his job. He was a game warden, at present scotching a plague of hyenas with poison. It was a grisly business, unlike the excitement of the rest of his work—outwitting and arresting poachers, protecting villagers and herdsmen from harassment by rogue elephants and man-eating lions, and making sure that hunting parties respected the terms of the licenses he had issued to them.

At this time the Game Department consisted of only five men and a sixth who was responsible for fish. Their chief, Captain Archie Ritchie, might have stepped out of a novel by John Buchan or Dornford Yates. He was tall and upright and his hair and mustache were gray, almost white. He had acquired an excellent degree in zoology, served in the French Foreign Legion at the beginning of the First World War, transferred to the Grenadier Guards and had been awarded several medals for gallantry by the British and the French.

He did not endear himself to the more puritanical members of the administration by traveling about in a yellow Rolls-Royce fitted with a box body—to carry safari equipment—and a large hippo tusk mounted on the radiator. He was also perfectly happy to allow one of his wardens to patrol narrow game trails on a Harley-Davidson motorcycle, with a giant Kamba game scout clutching his rifle on the pillion. They cut quite a dash when they turned up in Nairobi.

Since Kenya is a little larger than France, Ritchie's men were spread very thinly over the ground. This was especially true of the Northern Frontier, and its warden, Captain Whittet, was quite unable to protect it adequately.

Oulton, impressed by George, advised him to apply to the Game Department for a job and promised to recommend him to the office in Nairobi. But George had several more safaris contracted with Gethin & Hewlitt.

He also wanted to make a few more of his own with Terence, and with a young man as different from the reserved and ascetic Terence as can be imagined. Alick Kirkpatrick, whose family lived in Limuru, belonged to the jeunesse dorée of Kenya. Good-looking, hard-drinking and fond of women, he had inherited a baronetcy and reflected a certain amount of glory from his half-sister, Beryl Markham, who had just made her celebrated solo flight across the Atlantic from England to Nova Scotia.

However content George was to be alone for weeks on end in the bush and however silent he might be in new or mixed company, he had a natural courtesy and humor that enabled him to get on with his clients or anyone else. His broad-brimmed hat and neat red-gold beard grown to protect his skin from the sun, gave him an unself-conscious but distinctive style and there were always friends delighted to see him in Nairobi, Limuru and Naivasha.

It was perhaps fortunate that George did not immediately follow up Captain Oulton's suggestion that he approach the Game Department because Archie Ritchie was away in Malaya for most of 1937, giving advice on game management. As it was, George's application coincided not only with Ritchie's return but with the climax of a correspondence initiated by Elspeth Huxley, who had been shocked by the scarcity of game she had seen on a recent safari in the Northern Frontier District (NFD).

Over the years Elspeth Huxley's pen has often been effective. For instance, millions of people discovered Kenya for the first time when her book *The Flame Trees of Thika* was adapted for television. But as early as 1938 she commanded great respect there for her recently published biography of Lord Delamere and was able to sting the authorities into action with a scathing letter that she sent to her cousin by marriage, the eminent biologist Julian Huxley. He was a member of the Fauna Preservation Society and ensured it reached its target. The Northern Game Reserve was in the NFD.

FEBRUARY 9, 1938

I went up from Isiolo and was travelling about for three weeks entirely in the Game Reserve . . .

In the whole time we saw exactly one rhino in the Reserve. The DC, who has known that country well for some time, said that five years ago we should have seen rhinos every day in whatever direction we had chosen to go—it was famous, or notorious, for being crawling with rhino . . .

The trouble is that the Game Department is hopelessly understaffed. The nearest European officer to the Northern Game Reserve is at Meru, which is not even in the Reserve itself, but south of the southern boundary . . .

I understand that before he left, Ritchie was continually trying to get additional funds to provide for one or two young and completely mobile European wardens who would be continually on safari in the Reserve, but that he wasn't able to extract the money from Government. The position is farcical, in that everyone for hundreds of miles around hears when the Game Warden at Meru is about to make one of his periodic forays into the Game Reserve, and of course all the poachers evaporate like the dew until the Warden has returned to Meru, when they emerge again and slaughter more rhinos.

This indictment was forwarded to the Colonial Office in London, which in turn passed it on to Government House in Nairobi, where it finally produced action.

In June, George walked two hundred miles with his donkeys and three companions to help manage a hunting lodge at Isiolo. No sooner had he got there than a telegram arrived from the Game Department offering him a job as a "Temporary Assistant Game Warden" of the Northern Frontier District.

George borrowed a car and drove straight to Nairobi. On July 14 his appointment was confirmed. Tom Oulton had been as good as his word; his recommendation, coinciding with the pressure from London, meant that from now on George would use his four rifles for managing rather than hunting the colony's game.

Fortuitously he was to be based in Isiolo and could stay on at the hunting lodge—then known as the Rest Camp. It consisted of a group of round thatched huts attached to a central thatched cottage. Before long George was able to buy it as the Game Department headquarters.

From the outset George knew that in Archie Ritchie and Gerald Reece, the Commissioner in charge of law and order in the NFD, he had two of the ablest men in Kenya to support him. Wasting no time, he enrolled and equipped a handful of game scouts, mastered the legalities of arresting and prosecuting poachers and prepared his donkeys for a four-month safari to the boundaries of the Northern Game Reserve.

The trip took him up through the Mathews and Ndoto Mountains, over much the same ground that Elspeth Huxley had traveled. There were areas where the Turkana had wiped out all the game—they killed the giraffes for their meat and hides, and rhinos for the horns they needed to pound the giraffe skin into buckets and pliable sandals.

George made twenty-five arrests. A quiver of surprise ran through the reserve, including the European farmers who were not entirely blameless of shooting game without licenses as meat for their employees. By December, George was able to go down to Nairobi to present his first report to Archie Ritchie.

The picture was far from black. George had seen many herds of elephants, some two or three hundred strong; on one day he found the spoor of forty different rhinos; there were plenty of rare greater kudu; and near the Ewaso Ngiro River the giraffes were untroubled. He and Ritchie began to work out a plan to protect this precious yet vulnerable domain as large as the British Isles.

4

George soon became very good friends with the Brown family who owned the Rest Camp. He also quickly conceived a passion for a French girl he met there named Juliette Fremder. She worked as the secretary of a hotel in Nanyuki, which later became famous as the Mount Kenya Safari Club.

July 24 Juliette has made a deep impression on me, am thinking about her the whole time. In the evening we went out for a walk, managed to pluck up enough courage to get Juliette away from the others and, after great hesitation, was bold enough to ask her to let me kiss her.

With the help of letters, George kept the tenuous flame of his romance flickering during his frequent safaris.

As soon as he returned to Isiolo, the Browns lent him a car and he raced to Nanyuki to fetch Juliette.

November 22 Spent a wonderful day with Juliette, went out for a long walk in the morning. Really she is the most wonderful girl and I feel I couldn't do without her for long. I suggested we might get married later on and she agreed, that is if I get a permanent job and somewhere to live.

Good thing that this has happened to me as I was rather going to seed and would probably have ended up by keeping a native woman. There is no doubt the girl is capable and clever and would look after me and civilise me a bit. The only doubts I have are on my ability ever to settle down into a family man.

By this time George is irrevocably in love and facing up to the serious implications.

November 26 Devil of a business this being in love. I wander about like an idiot with unseeing eyes, but its a marvellous state to be in. J. is a girl in a million and I'm the luckiest man in the world.

In the last ten days before Christmas George had a very busy time. He had to go to Limuru to see his mother and on to Nairobi in order to present his report to Archie Ritchie. His exiguous salary of £360 per year and Ritchie's intimation that there was a good chance that he would be taken on permanently gave his confidence a boost.

His mother lent him £250 to buy a car, "a new half ton model," and came with him to choose a handbag for Juliette for Christmas.

Christmas was a considerable success and the next weekend he went down to meet Juliette at the Norfolk Hotel in Nairobi.

December 30 Sent a note in to Juliette who was in her room, came out and joined us in drinks. J. has already got everything tied up for this evening, going out with that fellow Henderson. God knows what she sees in him, a really nasty piece of work. In fact J. seems to have some very peculiar friends. Really I don't think it is much good me trying to compete. I do not possess the necessary social accomplishments.

George spent New Year's Eve alone.

At the beginning of George's diary for 1939 there is a barely legible note requesting that "if anything happens to me" Miss Juliette Fremder be informed. It is sadly ironical, for she failed to keep a rendezvous or to answer his letters. When he finally heard from her, he was out on patrol.

March 22   Mathews Range. Got a hell of a letter from Juliette, fairly wiping the floor with me! Made me feel a pretty poor sort of worm at first, afterwards I'm afraid I saw the funny side of it and gave way to unseemly mirth.

Time is often the best healer of the heart but George's ability to detach his point of view from his feelings also helped. His work, too, distracted him from his private frustrations.

There is no doubt that George positively enjoyed the dangers as well as the independence of his life. Within a few months he was charged by a rhino that had recently killed a woman: fortunately his shot went home. Twice he came face-to-face with lions in very thick bush and the second time he was really shaken. A third experience brought him into still closer contact with a lion.

He had gone to Arsim in the Ndoto Mountains where a Samburu manyatta—a group of mud huts housing people and their cattle at night—was being attacked by a pride. One lion had entered the manyatta, dragged a Samburu outside and started to eat him. When his brother attempted to rescue him, he was bitten in the shoulder by a second lion but managed to get away. The lions were said to be killing daily and George arranged to stay at Arsim for a week so that as soon as information came in he could go after them. There was also an additional threat from a deranged elephant that was persecuting the village.

George soon caught several poachers but had to wait for reports of the lions. After two or three days the peace of the morning was shattered when a huge, trumpeting elephant charged past his tent in pursuit of a donkey. A few minutes later George noticed a Samburu wandering off in the same direction. Before he could call out a warning there was another great bellow from the elephant and the Samburu shot by with the beast at his heels.

Fortunately the elephant vanished into the forest, and George, bored with waiting for news of the lions, strolled down a valley alone, in search of their spoor.

I saw a lioness crossing my path about a hundred yards ahead. I had a shot at her and she rolled over, but was up again in an instant, and made off into a patch of long grass before I could get in another shot. I had seen blood on her shoulder, but rather low down: cautiously I walked around the cover. There were no tracks leading out. Then I climbed a tree, but could see nothing, so I went up close to the grass and hurled stones in; still there was neither sound nor movement.

I had just turned my back to set off when there was a low growl behind me; spinning round I saw the lioness starting to charge. I took a quick shot but still she came on. I was not unduly worried because I felt confident of stopping her with my next shot at close quarters. I worked the bolt of my heavy magazine rifle. It jammed! I realized that I was helpless.

As the lioness reached me I tried to ram the muzzle of the rifle down her throat. She bit it savagely and tore it out of my grasp. Then she reared up and seized me by the right forearm which I had put up to protect my throat. She hurled me backwards to the ground. I can remember getting to my feet and seeing the lioness standing a few feet away and myself trying to draw the hunting knife which I wore on my right side, but my arm was numb and powerless. The lioness came at me again and caught me by the left thigh, again bowling me over.

When George had recovered himself there was no sign of the lioness. He later told friends that his chief recollections of the attack were the appalling stench of the lion's breath and the numbness, not pain, in his arm.

As I waited and waited for the lioness to show herself my head began to throb and I felt the sun burning my skin.

47

When I could not stand the suspense any longer I began to crawl very slowly toward the rifle, expecting the final charge at any second. It seemed to take an age before I got my fingers to it yet I found I had just enough strength to drag it and myself to the shade of a tree. Propped against the trunk I managed to unjam the spent case and work a new bullet into the breach. I fired two or three rounds in the air, hoping they would bring help.

Several Samburu arrived, bringing my camp-bed as a stretcher. By now I was beginning to suffer from the symptoms of malaria, as so often happens after a shock, and they can be so severe that I felt I was quite likely to die from a combination of these and septicaemia. However, I luckily had with me a bottle of sulfanilamide pills I was taking for a poisoned finger; a lion wound may look clean on the outside, and can be treated with disinfectant on the surface, but the bacteria on the teeth and claws will quickly cause gangrene under the skin. While I was still conscious I scribbled an SOS to the District Commissioner at Marsabit.

During the night, as George floundered between sleep and delirium, he was jolted awake by the snort of his mule which was chained to a tree outside his tent.

Simultaneously her chain snapped, an elephant screamed and a dark shape loomed in front of my tent. My cook lying beside me thrust a light rifle into my hands and propped me upright against the tentpole. Oblivious to the searing pain I raised the gun and fired.

The elephant swerved and next morning was found dead, about eighty yards away. I hovered on the edges of consciousness in excruciating pain and cried aloud when my dressings were changed. In the meantime the Samburu elders shook their heads and prescribed doses of mutton fat, which I knew to be their version of extreme unction.

Four days after George had been mauled, the DC turned up about 11:00 P.M. He had sent a wire for a plane and then set off on the 150-mile journey to George.

After a very painful drive back to Maralal they found two RAF bombers waiting for them. Although Europe was a long way off, large contingents of Italian troops were occupying Ethiopia and Somaliland,

48

and would pose a formidable threat to Kenya should Italy declare war on Britain. An air force presence seemed the best response to it.

Early the next morning George was strapped into a kind of straitjacket and pushed through the bomb hatch for the flight to Nairobi, where he was met by Archie Ritchie. He quickly recovered in hospital.

While George was lying semidelirious at Arsim he thought of writing to Juliette, ". . . but haven't got the energy. What's the good anyway?" This is the last reference to Juliette in the diary. War was only three months away and she must have left Kenya for he never saw or heard of her again. Nevertheless his brief encounter with her brought home to him a fundamental longing.

This is a wonderful life I lead, only one thing missing and that is someone to share it with. Someone, a woman, to express one's hopes and fears to and talk over the day's happenings and someone to give one encouragement and someone to work and strive for. Wonder if I shall ever meet the girl of my dreams?

FIVE

Cold Feet on Mount Kenya

1943–1944

1

Between his escape from the jaws of the lioness in 1939 and his encounter with Joy in 1942, George had been too busy in remote places, as a game warden and attached to Military Intelligence during the Italian campaign, to look for a wife.

Joy's manifest attraction to him may have revived thoughts of marriage, but he was determined to suppress them in her case. Although he was indifferent to religion, he respected another man's marriage.

News of Joy's feelings for him had traveled fast among his friends in Isiolo and Garissa. When he bumped into Alys, the wife of the Provincial Commissioner, Gerald Reece, who liked Joy but thought her unbalanced, she strongly advised him to avoid becoming involved with her.

A little later Archie Ritchie sent for George to discuss the NFD. When he arrived in Nairobi he went straight to the Norfolk Hotel to book himself a room, leaving his car in the courtyard. To his amazement, he was shortly given a message to say that a Mrs. Bally would like to speak to him. Joy had recognized his car and invited him to dinner the following evening at their house on Riverside Drive. George mumbled an excuse and hurried to his meeting with Ritchie.

That night he wrote in his diary: "I *must* try to avoid her. I am *not* in love with her, but she attracts me greatly—sex I suppose." On this evidence it is difficult to accept Joy's assertion in her memoirs that it was George who first fell in love.

George's good intentions were undermined the next morning when he bumped into Peter Bally who urged him to change his mind. Thinking he must be on safe ground, George acquiesced, but at dinner Joy constantly pressed his hand under the table and he felt his desire for her rising again.

Perhaps naïvely George was still unsuspecting two days later when Bally asked him to come around next afternoon. However, he sensed something was amiss when Joy herself answered the door—all the servants were off and Peter was at the museum. Apart from Pippin, he and Joy were entirely alone.

Many years later George mentioned that there was a book of erotic drawings lying open on the table—Bally had a taste for such things. After a little, Joy asked George what he felt about the book and plied him with several drinks. She then embarked on a long and intense account of her marriage and it became crystal clear she was after something more lasting than a brief liaison.

March 18 She wants to get a divorce and to marry me; she has discussed it with Peter and he wants it. I do not know whether I want to marry her; I do not want to behave like a cad, least of all hurt her. I am single, past my youth and I want to have a wife some day—why not risk it? It will be something positive if I make her happy.

Well I "burnt my boats" and now I am in honour bound to marry her. I think it will not be difficult to fall in love with her.

Presumably the reference to burnt boats means that George made love with Joy, as he did several times over the next week or two, taking her out to the Mbgathi Gorge on the edge of what is now the Nairobi Game Park, and up into the forest on the Ngong Hills.

According to George he quickly told Bally everything that had occurred between him and Joy, and Bally raised no objections to a divorce and Joy's remarriage.

Joy left her version of the men's conversation in a passage drafted for her autobiography, *The Searching Spirit*, but omitted it, along with a number of other passages, since both men were still alive. This source will be referred to again as her draft memoir.

Peter hinted to me that it might be a good idea if I married George, who was much younger and more fit to offer me a life which I seemed to love. I was torn between my love for Peter and watching him getting more and more depressed by being unable to keep up with my activities.

He talked the situation over with George and they arranged that

I should marry George. I only agreed as I could not bear watching Peter becoming more and more unhappy.

Neither of the men can possibly have realized the labyrinth of problems into which this apparently civilized accommodation would lead them all. First, George had to report it to Ritchie. He was putting his job at risk by appearing to break up a marriage and then marrying the divorcée, but Ritchie knew from Bally himself, and from Dr. and Lady Muriel Jex-Blake, who had taken Joy under their wing, that the marriage was already doomed. When he realized he could not turn George from his decision he promised to speak to the Chief Secretary.

At eleven o'clock precisely Ritchie reached down into the bongo skin bag that always hung from his desk and pulled out a bottle of gin: they needed the restorative badly. George found the habit of an eleven o'clock vodka or gin infectious and never threw it off.

At the end of a week George was told he was officially in disgrace. Nevertheless, provided the divorce and remarriage were discreet, he would be able to continue to serve in the department. In the meantime he was to take two weeks' leave with Joy in order to provide the necessary evidence of adultery. George immediately reported this to Peter Bally and agreed with him on the course they would all follow.

Exactly a month after their meeting outside the Norfolk Hotel he took Joy to The Pig and Whistle in Meru to provide the evidence for the divorce proceedings. There he found an irrepressible character from Isiolo, Colonel Bryan Abbay—ex-Indian army, inveterate sportsman, tireless raconteur and assiduous drinker—sitting in the bar with a friend. George quickly explained the object of his mission and the friend offered himself as a witness.

When George and Joy closed the door of their room and set the process of law in motion they were caught like two leopards in a cage. George's chief memory of that night was the discomfort of the bedbugs, while Joy preserved a copy of the affidavit Peter Bally was obliged to sign, swearing that he had not in any manner "connived at or condoned the adultery."

The deed done, George took Joy back to Isiolo, where they went out on safari and he gave her some shooting lessons. "She doesn't need much teaching: damned good shot!" He was no longer in any doubt about his feelings.

April 24   I do love Joy, in fact I am frantically in love with her. This has been the most wonderful experience of my life. Joy means everything in the world to me and I now long for the time when we are married.

His idea was that Joy should camp near Isiolo until the divorce came through nine months later. But Gerald and Alys Reece would not countenance it. As officer in charge of the Northern Frontier, Reece was a despot but a benevolent and amusing one, much loved by his subordinates, who all referred to him as "Uncle." He was determined to respect the Chief Secretary's injunction, while Alys must have prayed that Providence would intervene before the divorce went through.

Providence had a good try.

April 26   I realised today that Joy has doubts about our marriage being a success. My God—is she another Juliette? No, it can't be, she is in a very nervous state over the divorce and it is understandable.

April 29   She still loves Peter and I am terribly afraid that she may go back to him before the divorce is through.

For the next two months Joy stayed with friends and tried to sort out her feelings. In May she sent George a letter that allayed all his worries and made him very happy. In June she put in a dramatic appearance at Isiolo.

June 24   In the course of the afternoon Joy turned up in a hired lorry. Very upset and wanted to dash off to Nairobi, appearing at the divorce case in court and telling the judge that the whole thing was "collusion" with the idea of getting the proceedings stopped and saving me! She said she had decided she did not want to marry me or anyone again.

George took her camping the next day and calmly explained the disagreeable consequences for all three if she went to the court at this stage. He also warned her of the bleak future she would face if she didn't marry him after the divorce went through.

Joy's draft memoir has a slightly different slant.

This short time was enough for me to realise that George and I had little in common other than our love for wild life and the irresistible NFD. I begged him to let me return to Peter but he was as adamantly determined to marry me as Peter was to get a divorce. In the end I had to give in, especially as George threatened to commit suicide if I didn't marry him.

A few years later George set down an account of these months that refers to this last allegation.

One day she would show passionate love towards me, the next day she did not want to meet me again. During this period I know she wrote several letters to Bally. I wrote her a good many and some of them were pretty foolish. In one of them, when I thought she was going to leave me in the lurch, I believe I told her that if she rejected me, life for me would be finished and that I would go out of my way to try and get myself killed by some wild animal in the course of my work.

By now Joy and George recognized she was happiest when she was on safari, preferably with flowers to paint. In August she therefore decided to seek relief from the pressures closing in on her and to camp on the moorlands of Mount Kenya until her divorce came through in January.

2

Joy's decision to spend several months on the moorlands, which rise from about 10,500 feet to 14,500 feet, was astonishing but typically courageous, especially since her seclusion was planned to coincide with one of the two rainy seasons when the flowers are at their best. It meant nights of snow and bitter cold, with clouds, mist and rain closing in during the middle of the day.

While Joy's willingness to face her lonely ordeal was further proof to George that she was the perfect companion for his life in the wilderness, she saw Mount Kenya simply as a sanctuary in which to resolve her dilemma.

Although Mount Kenya bestrides the equator, the axis of the earth wobbles so that before and after the June solstice, when the sun passes over the Tropic of Cancer, the snow on the north face melts. By the December solstice the axis has tilted the other way, and with the sun over the Tropic of Capricorn, the south face melts. At any time of the year it is therefore possible, by making an eight-hour circuit of the mountain, to experience all four conventional seasons in one day.

Mount Kenya has always exercised a powerful spell on men's minds. It is the home of Lengai, the Kikuyu god; in 1899 Sir Halford Mackinder engaged a Swiss guide to help him make sure he was the first European to reach its top; three Italian prisoners of war, tantalized by the sight of the mountain, escaped from their camp and gave themselves up as soon as they had scaled it; and even while Joy was making her camp on one flank, her first husband, Ziebel von Klarwill, by an odd coincidence, was prospecting a route to the summit up another. Men have risked, and lost, their lives on the mountain in response to its challenge—congestion of the lungs on its heights has often proved fatal.

Joy's access to it was made possible through the help of an eccentric scholar-gypsy, Raymond Hook, who was obsessed by the mountain and befriended many people attempting to tackle it. Hook was about sixty years old and had farmed at the foot of Mount Kenya for twenty-five years.

He surrounded himself, indoors and out, with a menagerie of animals, domestic, tamed and wild. Chickens nested under the beds, a cobra lived in the laundry basket and antelope grazed with his cattle. He was the first man to trap a bongo and ship it to Europe; his favorite hobby was to lasso cheetahs on the plains and train them for hunting or racing.

His half-brother, Hilary Hook, whose outrageous personality and wit are pickled in an unforgettable television profile and his memoirs *Home from the Hill*, swears Raymond caught his cheetahs by the tail. He helped his brother train them to race greyhounds in England, using the stadium at Staines, but as they averaged 20 miles an hour faster the bookies refused to take any bets.

Joy had been warned Hook would charge her "through the nose" for his help, but it was essential. In any case she loved his stimulating company. He read ancient Greek and even hieroglyphics with the same ease as newsprint, discoursed on the Egyptians and Assyrians as if they were old friends and was plotting every combe and tarn on the mountain that had never been properly mapped.

An expert naturalist, he was familiar with the subspecies of mole shrews and mole rats and the green ibis that were unique to the mountain.

He offered Joy horses and mules to carry up her equipment and advised her on the tents she needed: one for Pippin and herself; one for her Samburu gun bearer Lembirdan, on loan to her from George, and her cook; and a "studio" of bamboo poles in which to paint. He promised two of his men would bring her weekly supplies and her mail.

The track up the mountain first led through a rain forest of giant junipers and podocarpus—primitive conifers related to the yew. Their branches were festooned with lianas and dripping with Spanish moss. Elephants and buffalo moved through the half-light that was also haunted by leopards, bongo, bushbuck, giant forest hogs and colobus monkeys. But apart from the occasional cry of a redheaded parrot or a monkey, the silence was almost unbroken, the loudest noise perhaps the buzz of a carpenter bee or the click of a flycatcher's beak as it snatched at an insect.

Above this, the trail ran through a wide belt of dense and soaring bamboos, forty feet tall. Their dead leaves crackled underfoot while the living rustled overhead. The huge tubular stems creaked and rattled in the breeze and when the wind blew across a broken stem it gave out an eerie moan. The only paths through this dense mass had been forged by buffalo and elephants whose prints were fresh on the ground.

Now and again the trees opened out into a glade, carpeted with grass and delicate green ferns. Butterflies floated in shafts of sunlight or settled on the moisture at the edge of a stream trickling under the trees and cascading into a steep and rocky ravine.

Toward 11,000 feet the bamboos began to thin and shrubs filled their place, while on the edge of the moorland the last of the trees appeared, hagenia—rosewood—and hypericum, whose yellow flowers attracted the sunbirds.

At Raymond Hook's suggestion Joy pitched her camp here, in a lovely little glade and next to the trunk of a tree up which she could escape if bothered by elephants.

The views from the moorlands were sensational. Two hundred miles to the south the dome of Kilimanjaro sparkled in the sunshine: as Evelyn Waugh observed, Africa's is a diamond light, not the amber sunlight of Europe. In the other direction earth and sky met on the horizon a hundred miles away, the shadows of drifting clouds mottling the golden plains below like the skin of a giant giraffe.

Looking up, the eye traveled over the tufted grass, lichen-covered rocks, flowers and weirdly shaped shrubs on the moors to the snow-fields and glaciers surrounding the pinnacles—Batian the summit at 17,058 feet, Nelion about 40 feet lower and Lenana, the highest attainable by amateur walkers and scramblers.

During August and September Joy concentrated on her paintings. It was thrilling to find blood red gladioli, dark blue or turquoise delphiniums and flaming red-hot pokers, their pigments richer than those she had seen in the Alps, emerging from a protective layer of snow at least a foot deep. Out on the moorland giant heathers, lobelias and groundsel—senecios—grew up to a good twelve feet tall, the groundsel taking perhaps two centuries to reach their full stature and putting out their flowers only after the first thirty years. Joy would sketch with a hot water bottle on her lap and Pippin on her feet to keep them warm. By the time she left she had finished more than seventy pictures.

Just as the plants adapted to the altitude, so did the fauna. Eland and buffalo developed larger bodies and thicker coats but spent less energy on the growth of their horns; jackals and hyraxes produced warmer fur; the mole rats, naked elsewhere, grew strong chestnut hair. Birds, too, responded to the conditions. The striking scarlet-tufted malachite sun-bird sipped the lobelia nectar, and other species of sunbird, which normally never mingled, congregated on the giant lobelias and senecios. It was bad luck for the hyraxes and mole rats, which had especially adapted to this habitat, that the superb-looking Mackinders eagle owls had also adapted and hunted them by moonlight.

In the first two months there were few intruders apart from a buffalo that squeezed between the tents at night: Joy hugged Pippin close to her and he held his breath so as not to give himself away. She christened the interloper "Uncle Joseph."

Her sole contact with the world below were the weekly deliveries by Raymond Hook's men. However, in October her isolation was interrupted by a succession of visitors. There was a flow of young servicemen eager to get to the top of the mountain, and George came for a week and then for weekends. He would drive 60 miles from Isiolo, leave his car on the slopes and walk up through the forest for two hours, sometimes arriving after dark. On his first long visit he and Joy planned an assault on Lenana.

It needed a tough reconnaissance but although Joy was slower, she was absolutely tireless and ready to attack the peak early the next morning. The climb meant braving steep scree, loose rocks and frequent danger at the slippery edges of precipitous drops. Just what Joy faced that day was played down by both of them—as indeed they made light of their whole experience on the mountain.

Fortunately letters written by a Canadian pilot and a British sailor bring alive with remarkable freshness the extreme rigor of their exploits on the roof of East Africa.

Alan Davidson, on attachment from the Canadian Air Force, was one of the personal pilots to General Platt, the Allied Commander in Chief, and was on leave with Ripley Bogle, a graduate of both Edinburgh and Oxford, who was immediately on excellent terms with Raymond Hook. Davidson's letter home is condensed with his blessing.

The weather was glorious and we awoke to find the peaks towering above us—the sun throwing off rainbows from the glaciers.

Raymond Hook is fanatically devoted to animals. First of all there is George the cheetah which he uses for chasing buck on the plains. George has dinner in the dining room—it's quite an experience to have him sniffing around your legs while you try to concentrate on your meal.

Then there is Lucy, a full grown chimpanzee—truly a loveable creature. She is very well trained and obeys orders implicitly. When told, she will undo your shoes and take them off, shake hands with you and ask to be kissed—a favour I passed up. She really is amusing, but the day following our introduction she threw Hook to the ground and took a nasty bite out of his leg. Hook explains it as temperament.

He also keeps puff adders which he sells to the local clinic to extract the venom used to stop "bleeders." Then there is a lynx, a full grown eagle, a buffalo, an eland and a kudu.

He let us have a guide, two boys, three horses and three mules to pack our equipment to the base camp. He then explained he wanted us to look into a new valley which had never been explored by a white man and find the source of a large stream.

Eventually we arrived at the "Dame's Camp," owned by a lady botanist who is drawing the flora of the mountain. A lonely life for a woman of 35-odd years. She made us very welcome and soon we were drinking cups of tea and eating peanut scones.

Davidson and Bogle were delighted by Joy's informed, inquisitive and humorous conversation over supper in the glow of the campfire.

His account of his ascent of Lenana with Bogle reveals how tough the conditions were.

When night falls at 14,500 feet it is really cold, so we had a small primus stove burning in the tent and arranged to do all our cooking in with us. I don't know how the boys keep warm, for we have sleeping bags and four blankets apiece and its still none too hot—they have only have one blanket.

The following morning we were awakened early by snow drifting in through two holes in the roof of the tent. We thought this was going to keep us under ground for the day, but by six-thirty things had cleared.

I found a very steep face covered in snow that was frozen like a sheet of ice and started cutting footsteps across it with an ice axe. Then without warning I was heading down the mountain at terrific speed. My ice axe was lost at the first bump but I managed to get right side up, saw the rocks rushing towards me, and hit feet first.

We finally reached the summit after much hard work. The day was perfect and the view—well it has to be seen to be appreciated. We put our names on a scroll on top.

Finally back to the "Dame's Camp." We found she had another visitor named Adamson who is the game ranger of the NFD. His job is to shoot animals that make a nuisance of themselves.

That evening was spent in telling stories around a lovely big fire. Finally, when sleep could no longer be denied, we rolled into bed to die.

Davidson had done a little hunting in Canada and was as excited by George's stories of the bush as Bogle was by Joy's knowledge of Egyptian sculpture. If anything, the last evening in her camp was more animated than the first. It was twenty-five years before Davidson came back to Kenya and saw George again. After that they never lost touch.

The letters from the British sailor are signed only "Leslie"; he wrote in 1963 after reading *Born Free*. Enclosed with one was a six-page reminiscence in which he recalled an angry rhino butting a tree in the rain forest, the bottle-green gloom of the bamboos and the sudden quiet in the night as frost silenced the rushing waters of the stream beside his tent.

What follows is extracted from his two letters.

In the late months of '43 you, Joy, were camped at about 11,000 feet on Mount Kenya, not far from the head of the Mackinder Valley.

I was completely enchanted by your tales of Europe and Vienna and George—apparently a modern Chevalier Bayard, the knight *sans peur et sans reproche*.

The stay on the mountain was so lovely I hated returning to reality, but during the descent just below the bamboo forest I met George and found him very much as you described.

So often I have thought of you two . . . and no matter where I have been in this strange and fascinating world, the vision of Joy, George and the mountain has haunted me.

George's romantic appearance on the mountain, Joy's profound admiration for his courage and their instinctive trust in each other when confronted with danger did not stifle Joy's growing misgivings.

She was aware that both her friends and his believed that they were fundamentally incompatible, and she only now faced the fact that, although George enjoyed reading, he was almost entirely ignorant of Europe and the arts, which meant so much to her.

Joy was wise to be worried by the cultural chasm between them but less so in her choice of a helping hand to haul her back from the brink. When George discovered she and Peter Bally were exchanging letters, and that she even planned to go down to Nairobi to see him, he was both infuriated and alarmed. He extracted a promise that their correspondence would cease and stepped up his visits.

At first he seemed successful. Joy was moved by his devotion when he appeared late one night after narrowly avoiding two elephants, exhausted and soaked by the pouring rain. Next day she came out with him to look for "Uncle Joseph" whom she had twice stumbled into near the camp and who was terrifying her cook, a cheerful and normally staunch Kikuyu named Kifosha. After a stalk they found him. Joy fired first; she hit the buffalo but it came straight for them.

George fired second; the buffalo still came on until it suddenly crumpled and toppled into a gully, George's bullet in its heart.

There was an atmosphere of Gothic melodrama about Joy's last month on the mountain. The monsoon broke and gales swept down from the snowfields and into the forest with accelerating force, knocking over trees and snapping their branches. Joy, already tense, lay awake expecting disaster and became "a sleepless wreck."

Meanwhile George was seen at Isiolo by Archie Ritchie and Gerald Reece, who told him to take a week's leave in Nairobi over the New Year so that he could marry Joy quickly.

He was in for a shock when he reached Joy's camp on Christmas Eve.

December 24   Got up to Joy's camp about 2.15. She stared at me in a startled way and asked me if I had got a letter (which I hadn't). It was breaking off and a farewell. Peter had written in a condescending way, suggesting the possibility of her going back to him in a vague future. Joy more upset than ever before. I was firm and put it to her that she *must* decide now one way or the other.

Went out for a walk to talk over things. On the opposite slope saw a buffalo. I went straight off and shot it.

The marriage was on and off every few hours over Christmas, and it cannot have helped that a strange young couple had turned up in the camp. This is from Joy's draft memoir.

During these months I had become aware that Peter meant more to me than my own life. I knew that he had gone through a vital crisis, both psychological and medical, and that he had wanted to be legally free in order to get the right perspective on himself and our marriage. But he had often reassured me that we should regard this period as a testing time of our feelings for each other and I therefore set all my hopes on a genuine and happy reunion when it was over. Naturally I had explained all this to George but realised my efforts only made him more determined to marry me.

Joy was right about George.

December 27   Left Joy, omens favourable! Arranged to go to her on Saturday and help her pack up. Received her letter but as I had promised to burn it without reading it I did so, although it was a great temptation. If Joy goes out of my life, I do not know what I shall do. It will be the second time in my life and too much.

On January 2, when Joy called in to say good-bye to Raymond Hook, he asked her to stay the night and waived any payment, saying that since he could no longer get up on to the mountain to see the flowers he would very much value two of her paintings, which she willingly gave him.

At dusk a boy came into her room, placed a brazier under an aquarium of tropical fish on a stand and closed the windows tight. That night she was nearly asphyxiated but dared not open the window for fear of killing the fish.

3

When Joy reached Nairobi on January 3, 1944, she went to stay with a family named May. Her divorce was expected to come through at any moment and George found her very difficult.

She was, in fact, distraught. Although she had given George repeated undertakings to marry him and not to see Peter Bally, she later maintained that these were blackmailed out of her by his threat to get himself killed.

Aware of her anguish, Bally must have equivocated in a mistaken response to her pleas for a reunion. What he had intended as assurance of his continuing friendship she interpreted as an offer of remarriage.

She therefore made straight for the museum—only to find that in anticipation of an embarrassing confrontation he had left for a three-month safari in Ethiopia.

Joy could only find one last card to play.

January 7 This morning after the Mays had all gone off to work I noticed Joy seemed to be in a very emotional state. She started to play the piano and to sing. After a few moments she broke down and told me that she was going to die, she had taken poison, swallowed a whole bottle of [M&B] 693.

I wouldn't believe her, she took me up to her room and showed me the empty bottle. I was frantic with grief. She refused to be taken to a doctor but eventually I forced her to come with me to Dr. Jex-Blake.

Only by looking at Joy's earlier life is it possible to discover what drove her to reach for that bottle.

SIX

Out of Austria

1906–1944

1

In Joy's house at Lake Naivasha a birthday book lies open at the date on which she was born—January 20. She has added the year, 1910.

The quotation for the day is so apt that it almost prompts the suspicion that she allowed it to influence her behavior.

> Like Dian's kiss, unasked, unsought,
> Love gives itself, but is not bought;
> No voice, nor sound betrays
> Its deep, impassioned gaze.

One early admirer always thought of her as Diana, goddess of the hunt. At almost every stage of her life, even before Elsa came into it, people tended to notice something leonine in her appearance and behavior.

After their first parting, George had recorded the powerful impact of the gaze from her blue eyes—they were equally capable of expressing love, inquiry or anger.

She was volatile, romantic and troubled, like the society in which she grew up. Passion—in every sense of the word—constantly simmered inside her and frequently boiled over. It is difficult, in fact, to understand her without briefly glancing at the disintegrating world of the Austro-Hungarian Empire, ruled by the House of Hapsburg, into which she was born.

It stood at the crossroads of eastern Europe. The Balkans lay to the south; Germany and France to the west; Poland and Prussia to the north; and to the east stretched Asia, the cradle of the Slavs, Magyars, Huns, Tatars and Mongols. In 1918 the Hapsburg Empire was defeated at the end of the First World War and quickly dismembered. Joy was eight years old.

Silesia, in which her family had large estates and where she spent the happiest days of her childhood, became part of the new Czechoslovakia. Vienna, where her grandmother—the most influential figure in her life—lived, had been the proud capital of the Hapsburg Empire for more than six hundred years: now it was a head without a body, in a state of economic and psychological trauma.

Joy always described herself as Austrian. She was born into the country, lived for some time in its capital, and when she was twenty-five married an Austrian. Her blood was not so easily labeled.

Her mother's family, like half the population of Austrian Silesia, were German by origin, while one of her great-grandmothers was Polish. And two astute women—one a lifelong friend and sculptress, the other Joy's American publisher whose mother was Austrian— saw hints of Asia in her face. Quite independently they were convinced that a trace of Mongol or Hun in her blood must account for the set of her eyes and her cheekbones. In her teens her friends called her "Cheetah" because of the slant of her eyes.

2

Joy's father, Viktor Gessner, was an Ober Baurat—a civil servant with qualifications as an architect or engineer. During the First World War, as a captain, he commanded a motorized unit on the frontiers of Poland.

Her mother, Traute (neé Greipel), was twenty-two when Joy was born. Charming and intelligent, she was musical and also painted in watercolors, and sometimes oils, and had a special gift for flowers.

They lived in Troppau in Silesia, on the border with Poland; today the town is in the new Czech Republic and known as Opava. Reasonably off, they could afford Milli, the cook, and girls to look after their children. Their eldest daughter, also called Traute, and Joy were born there in 1908 and 1910.

Joy's arrival was a disappointment to her father, who wanted a son. They gave her the family names Friederike Viktoria, but her father insisted on calling her Fritz, treated her as a boy and encouraged her to dress as one. The rest of the family called her Fifi.

The best picture of what Joy was like as a child comes from a birthday letter her mother wrote to her in about 1970.

> As you were very high spirited and quick in your movements you were not allowed into the salon alone because it contained much glass and china. But when you were three the door was left open, you rushed in and broke several valuable porcelain figures. As a punishment you were made to sit on a dining-room chair, next to the sideboard, until you apologised. This you refused to do and after several hours we had to think of an excuse to let you go. You were afraid of nobody except a bogey called Bubutz, invented by Milli to keep you in order.

On one occasion Joy was put to rest after lunch on the sofa in her father's study, but she found a box of crayons. Thinking the plain green wallpaper could do with some flowers, she added them happily until Milli came to get her up.

Her mother goes on.

> You had a passion for flowers. Once Milli gave you a pot of violets for your birthday and you wouldn't leave them to go to school.
>
> You also loved music and could read it before you knew the alphabet. When you had earache all you wanted me to do to ease the pain was to play Chopin. When you hurt yourself you never complained, even if you bled . . .

Joy maintained she never had any difficulty with music because everyone in the family sang and played instruments; she herself loved dressing up and giving solo cabaret performances. Together the family performed chamber music and sang snatches of opera the way others did nursery rhymes. But it was not only music Joy was good at.

> In school you learned very quickly, almost too quickly, and although you got a "1" in each of your exams, your teacher had to give you "2" for Application so you did not feel superior to the rest of the class.

Every nuance of these stories remained true of Joy for the rest of her life.

By far the most exciting times of her childhood were spent in

Silesia, on the family estates of her maternal grandmother, whom she called Oma. Oma, born Friederike Weisshuhn, was married to Joy's grandfather for only two years before she was widowed. She had then married Wilhelm Pretz.

The Weisshuhns' estates and forests had been in the family for many years; they also owned paper factories near Freiheit (now Svoboda) in Bohemia. It was Joy's great-grandfather, a young German who married into the family in the 1870s, who first persuaded them to make paper from their trees and their sympathies were German rather than Czech.

The family's country house was called Seifenmühle. Large and built of wood, it stood on the side of a little wooded valley. A stream ran below, feeding a swimming pool.

Joy and Traute would find up to a dozen other children at Seifenmühle, cousins and friends from Austria, Germany, Yugoslavia, Italy, England and America. There was an inscription over the door:

> Ten were invited, twenty came,
> Water the soup and make them welcome.

The head of the family was Joy's great-grandfather, a large, jovial and enterprising figure, who presided over the annual harvest festival. He was the first man in Silesia to own a car and to introduce hydro-electric power to his factories. His wife bore him fourteen children but toward the end of his life his heart is said to have strayed. At eighty-two he died and was succeeded by Uncle Karl, his eldest son.

Seifenmühle was a paradise for the young, with its swimming pool and a slide, tennis, boating, riding, make-believe lion hunts in the woods—Joy was often the lion—target practice and serious hunting for partridge, hares, foxes and roebuck. Joy enjoyed the keepers' company but hated seeing fox cubs bred or trapped and then used to train terriers; and she was filled with remorse when she stalked and shot a buck.

But for all the happiness she found at Seifenmühle, two uncomfortable truths came home to her. The first was that one or two of the Weisshuhns pitied the Gessners for being less well-off. They lived in villas, she in an apartment; they had leather-soled shoes, Joy had nails in hers to stop them from wearing out; they had whipped cream on their cakes, hers and Traute's had whipped white of egg. She always remained sensitive to social distinctions.

The second was far more serious: her parents were growing apart. A young woman of immense charm, animated and loving a party, Traute Gessner was bored with her husband. Perhaps the birth of their youngest daughter, Dorle, in 1918 was designed to bring them together again. To make matters worse Traute had fallen in love with another man.

Although Joy loved and respected her father, who told the children stories, encouraged them to observe the habits of insects and birds and was often affectionate, he also frightened her. She felt he sometimes ignored, teased, or punished her excessively. On one occasion he was scolding her when visitors arrived. She was obliged to shake hands with a smile while he painfully squeezed her other hand in his own.

Joy worshipped her mother but quoted an early experience to illustrate the coldness she later attributed to her. During the First World War Joy lavished devotion on Hasi, her favorite rabbit, an albino. At lunch, after a rare stew, her mother lightheartedly informed them that they had just eaten Hasi.

In 1922 Joy's parents decided to divorce. Her father was too serious minded, her mother rather too gay and romantic, and the love she felt for the other man was too powerful. She went to Vienna and married Hans Hofmann, her nephew's tutor at Seifenmühle. From all accounts he was intelligent, amusing and excellent company. The main flaw in his character, rigid anti-Semitism, emerged only later.

Joy never recovered from the sense that her parents had betrayed her. Above all she could not tolerate the idea of her mother giving precedence to anyone else in her life. The bitterness went on burning inside her, flaring up and subsiding but never dying out, until her mother's death fifty years later.

For a time the three sisters lived with their father at Troppau until it was decided that Traute and Joy should move to Vienna with Oma.

Dorle remained with Viktor Gessner: then he too remarried and Joy's resentment was compounded. She seldom saw Dorle or her father again and completely lost touch with the Gessners.

3

For the next four years Joy went to a boarding school.

Always restless, she left it early and continued her studies while living with Oma and her husband, Wilhelm Pretz. Oma was alive, warmhearted, large-bosomed and romantic—tears sprang to her eyes when she sang Schubert at the piano. She was dark and tall, unlike her second husband who was older, much shorter and red-haired—"a little red slug" to one irreverent niece. Life was not always easy because Pretz had a son named Heinz who resented sharing the family apartment with Traute and Joy.

After two years Joy received her Staatsprüfung in Klavier, an excellent piano-teaching diploma, in 1927. She then took a course in dressmaking for which she received a Gremium diploma in 1928. At the same time she went to evening classes in typing and several of the applied arts.

By then she was between eighteen and twenty, and despite two unpleasant encounters in Troppau—one when a man had flashed her in the park and the other when she had been stopped after dark and asked if she had hairs between her legs—her mother had never answered her questions about the fundamentals of sex. She and Traute were still ill-informed when they went to live with Oma in Vienna.

This was a pity, if not hazardous, since both sisters were extremely, if differently, attractive. Joy once remarked wistfully that if she had a face as pretty as Traute's, and Traute had a figure like hers, they would both be irresistible. A young doctor at Seifenmühle said the same thing another way: he observed it was strange how he always thought of Traute with her clothes on and Joy with hers off.

Their cousin and contemporary Mary, coming from England to stay with them for the first time, saw exactly what he meant. She remembers walking down the street in Vienna behind Joy and Traute when a car went past and stopped ahead of them. The young driver walked back and said with a smile that each man who had passed them had turned for a second glance; he therefore had to see for himself what they looked like from the front.

Joy's close friend, Susi Hock, remembers how Joy, always beautifully dressed in clothes she had made for herself, caused men's heads to swivel in the street. "Even my brother, who was training to be a clergyman, was not immune to her charms."

Perceptive and generous, Oma did everything she could to distract Joy from her misery since her parents' divorce, to develop her confidence and ease her into the world of men. She sent her off skiing in the mountains on weekends and arranged for her to have lessons in dancing. When the highlight of the season came around, the ball in the Hofburg Palace, she gave Joy tickets and helped her plan an elaborate dress.

Unfortunately Joy found her partners dull, regarded their dueling scars with contempt and said they trod on her toes. On the other hand, she was a great success among the art students, many of them Jews—their parents were still the cultural yeast in Austrian society— with whom she worked and went skiing. Two of them proposed to her and a third, a Hungarian of whom she was very fond, was prevented from doing so only by serious illness. Still comparatively ignorant of the world, Joy was shrewd enough to decline these first offers.

Traute was different—pretty and clever but unwise. Anxious to get away from her jealous step-uncle, Heinz, she was the first of her contemporaries to marry. A young Austrian, who was working in Argentina, returned briefly to Vienna and was befriended by Oma and the girls. On the voyage back to Buenos Aires he proposed to Traute by letter—and was accepted. They married by proxy, Herr Pretz vouching for Traute, but the marriage was not a success and before long she returned to Vienna—with a baby boy. Her husband, named Erdmann, followed later and when their son was sixteen they divorced.

Traute's marriage and departure produced an almost immediate, and no doubt subconscious, reaction in Joy.

She called the second chapter of her autobiography "First Love," although it also describes her first marriage. The lover, the first of many in her life, receives only one paragraph; her husband, the first of three, no more than a dozen. Yet the former was far more significant, both because of his impact on Joy and the effects of the subterfuge that surrounded their love.

One evening in 1930, she was given a ticket for the Gschnas, the Arts ball that came at the climax of the Vienna carnival. She persuaded Oma to let her go, slashed one side off her Hofburg dress and decorated her body—and what remained of the dress—with grease paint.

She was both fascinated and scared to find the stately Künstlerhaus transformed into an underworld by the suggestive murals and Bacchanalian throng. But before she could escape she was grabbed by the shoulders with the words: "You are mine." In her draft memoir it was "Don Giovanni" who seized her, in the published book it was "a masked Apache." Joy goes on:

Thus I was swept into my first love affair. It aroused emotions sometimes almost beyond what I could bear. When, after two years, it ended I was left with a little dachshund called Plinkus and a deep wound in my heart, which took a long time to heal.

That is all she ever said and sixty years later it has been difficult to discover more. However, with clues from Susi Hock, a reference in one of George's letters, Joy's photograph albums, a further hunt through Joy's autobiography, *The Searching Spirit*, and the memory of her cousin Mary, it is possible to reconstruct one of the most bizarre and formative experiences of Joy's life.

A remark by Susi Hock about her early friendship with Joy produced the first hint that there was a significant experience to be investigated. "My parents really did not like me seeing her: they thought she might be a bad influence as she had eloped with a young man to Italy. That sort of thing was not done in Vienna in those days, you see."

Since she could remember no more about the episode I asked another early friend, Susanne Schmutzer, a sculptress living in Vienna. She thought the story unlikely because Oma would never approve. Joy had indeed written in her draft memoir, "I never did anything behind her back and always talked over my problems with her."

Almost at a dead end, I decided to turn to the correspondence and photographs for help. Two of George's letters suggested that her first lover was a Jew with a name like Scheier (he spelt it Shire)— and there, in the 1930 album, her lover poses for the camera as an Apache, with Joy in her half-and-half dress, gazing into his eyes.

Joy does not mention his name but her photographs show the places they visited during the next two years. The Apache leaning on the roof of a little coupé parked by a fountain in a Swiss village tumbling with geraniums; both of them together in Viareggio, the piazza in Venice and the Lido; and Joy's lover in front of the Signoria in Florence. Susi Hock was right.

Not only that. The following year Joy and the young man spent the spring, summer and autumn traveling together all over Europe— Austria, Italy, Monte Carlo, France and Switzerland, though carefully avoiding Germany. They explored the most famous beauty spots, the greatest cathedrals and palaces, the finest museums and galleries. Joy kept a plan of their route over the Alps and a note of the restaurants they went to in Paris.

The year after, in the summer of 1932, they cruised up the west coast of Italy from Sicily to Genoa and a much older couple appear in the photographs with them. Who are they, and what did Oma think about it all?

The answer is deliberately concealed in Joy's memoirs. There she describes another set of travels, making no connection between them and her elopement.

Just before she and her lover went off to Italy for the first time, Uncle Karl, head of the family in Silesia, asked Oma, his sister, if he might borrow Joy as a chaperone. Like his father's, his heart had a way of straying and his marriage was less than satisfactory. His consolation was an actress and singer with whom he wanted to share some of the more romantic corners of Europe.

Oma, victim of an arranged marriage herself and kindhearted, had come to adopt a "long leash" view of such attachments, provided they were managed with tact and no one got hurt. Her brother's proposition seemed providentially timed. Obviously Joy and men could no longer be kept apart; she and Uncle Karl had better protect each other's reputations with a smoke screen of so-called propriety.

Joy's reference to her travels with her uncle in *The Searching Spirit*, which never once mentions the existence of her own companion, is brilliantly ingenious.

> It proved a very happy time for all of us. This was my first visit to Switzerland, Uncle Karl generously lent me his car so I was able to go exploring in all directions . . .
>
> To make it all the more pleasant, behind all this sightseeing was the knowledge that by my presence, or rather my tactful absence, I was enabling two people to be very happy.

The coupé in 1930 must have been Karl's; the dachshund Plinkus makes his appearance in 1931; and by 1932 the quartet has grown sufficiently confident with one another to travel and be photographed together.

The confidence was possibly ill advised. Joy had received several suggestions that she should model. She had rejected an invitation to ride a white stallion in Reinhardt's *The Miracle*, but then Karl's mistress offered her an introduction to a theatrical agent and she accepted it.

When the meeting took place in a private room of the fashionable

Café Sacher, the little hunchback agent dimmed the lights and asked Joy to play the role of a young wife trying to win back the favors of her erring husband, as played by himself. She simply burst out laughing and torpedoed her career as an actress.

Almost the last pieces in the jigsaw of this whole masquerade were supplied by Joy's cousin Mary. She remembered very well one uncle's speechless fury at the effrontery of Joy's elopement and the mutual camouflage she and Karl afforded each other. In the eyes of most of the family his taste was deplorable and his actress a fifth-rate singer.

The curtain fell on Joy's romance when the young man decided to go to America. Joy wanted to go too, and no doubt argued her case very strongly, but for once the family adamantly opposed her. When the Apache stuck to his guns that was the end of the affair.

Recently Joy's sister Dorle added a postscript to this love affair, which could explain many of the events in Joy's life that are otherwise difficult to account for. She says that the lover was the son of a rich banker; that Joy became pregnant; and that when the young man refused to marry Joy and insisted on going to America, she was obliged to have an illegal abortion. After it she was dangerously ill.

There is no question that the consequences of the entire experience were far graver than a wounded heart and far longer-lived than her dachshund.

4

When not traveling with her lover Joy had studied fine metalwork for two years at the Kunstgewerbe Schule. Then she apprenticed herself to a painter of miniatures. She did not stay long but her time with him taught her to observe her subjects in the minutest detail.

Heartbroken and abandoned, she found the black clouds of guilt and depression that often follow an abortion had gathered over her head. It is difficult to penetrate the gloom of this period. The chronology in her memoirs is obscure, her photograph albums for 1933 and 1934 reveal nothing and she managed to conceal her worst melancholy from her closest contemporaries. In her disturbed state she submitted to the fashionable panacea of Vienna—its own brainchild—psychoanalysis, spending an hour each day on an analyst's couch.

She had come to detest her mother, especially after her stepfather had begun to show signs of anti-Semitism. This hatred was aggravated when her mother telephoned one day and told Joy "in a detached and insensitive voice" that her father had just died of a disease of his spleen, which was to be preserved at the Medical Museum in Prague.

While the analyst was probing into her past, Joy had started going to lectures on psychiatry and noticed how morbidly introspective she and some of her friends were becoming as they explored this new science. She refers to this danger in her draft memoir.

> How fatal such self-tormenting analyses can be became clear when I was told that Austria was second only to Sweden in its record of suicides. This might be explained by the tendency in both countries to dissect the mind to such a degree that sensitive people are driven to despair.
>
> I narrowly escaped such a fate but luckily, or perhaps unconsciously, left a chance of being rescued before it was too late.

Impatient with her analysts, she turned to sculpture as a student of Wilhelm Frass, who had done a fine bust of her in 1931.

The professor welcomed her with open arms and initiated her into all the techniques needed to master the mysteries of marble, stone, clay, bronze and wood—her favorite medium, which slowly released her forms from its grain. Frass also took her home to play chamber music with his wife and two sons. For Joy, this was the finest kind of healing that Vienna could offer, and when she was suddenly faced with a moment of horror—a drunk ran under a car in which she was traveling and was killed—she needed it.

She had always been terrified of death, but now she was able to exorcise her fear by transmuting the dead man's figure into images of clay and finally of wood.

Oma must have found it very difficult to decide when Joy was genuinely suffering or indulging in dramatics. Her affectionate nature usually seems to have given Joy the benefit of the doubt and in 1933 she let Joy prepare for an examination that would enable her to study medicine at the university. Despite difficulties with her new subjects she went to a number of parties and incessantly skied in the winter.

Herbert Tichy, who remained a close friend for thirty years and became one of Austria's leading photographers and travel writers, said she was an excellent skier. Walking down Regent Street in

London one day, her cousin Mary Pike did a double take when she saw a life-size Joy on skis, smiling at her from a travel agent's window, the epitome of a Tyrolean snow maiden. Someone had pirated a photograph of her and used it for a poster.

Susi Hock and Susanne Schmutzer remember her as a center of attraction at parties, and Herbert Tichy recalls his sister standing on the stairs looking down at Joy when a cousin, Viktor von Klarwill, tugged her sleeve.

"Who is that girl?" he asked. "I am going to marry her!"

Von Klarwill, who was known to his friends as Ziebel, saw Joy every day for the next three weeks and then proposed. He made a very good living as a car dealer; he had inherited the title of Ritter from his father; his mother was a Jew.

Ziebel von Klarwill's friends thought him eccentric for preferring the natural world—especially birds, the mountains and skiing—to the sophistications of city life. In an attempt to escape he had written to the lone inhabitant of one of the Marquesas Islands in the Pacific, asking if he might join him. It was a curious choice, for the archipelago lies in the tropics, never sees snow and is singularly short of flora and fauna. However, the hermit turned down his proposal.

On the other hand he was accepted by Joy, and they were married at Ramsau on July 28, 1935. Shortly before, Susi Hock had married a world-famous mathematician and astronomer, Sir James Jeans, and had gone to live in England.

Joy and Ziebel made an enviable couple—good-looking, intelligent, gifted and charming. They were well enough off to indulge their passions for travel, music and skiing. They also had the foresight to see which way the wind was blowing from across the German frontier. They investigated plans for migrating to Tahiti, Tasmania or California, and were also in touch with a Swiss farmer in Kenya.

Meanwhile, in the summers of 1935 and 1936 they stayed in northern Italy, traveled through the South of France to Avignon and Carcassonne, drove north to Chartres and Paris and then turned into Belgium and Holland. Wherever they went they derived pleasure from the buildings, the history, the paintings and the scenery.

From November to April they skied, sometimes sleeping in primitive huts with neither windows nor doors—or occasionally in a small tent. One weekend, in the spring of 1937, when the lights of Central Europe were dimming again, they drove to the snowy slopes on the Weisshuhns' estates near Svoboda. There, against the advice of a doctor, Joy, who was pregnant, went out on her skis once too often and suffered a miscarriage. She had been warned that if this happened she might not be able to bear children later.

Joy had wanted a child, and her miscarriage brought on a renewed bout of depression and guilt. To add to her sorrow, Plinkus had died. It was therefore decided she should take a boat from Genoa to Mombasa and stay with the Swiss friend in Kenya, both to restore her health and to look for a farm. She concealed the second purpose of her journey to protect Ziebel's business. As a half-Jew, he thought it imperative that no one should know he was planning to leave Austria for good.

On the way to catch her boat at Genoa they stayed with some friends who were all agog at the uncanny predictions of a local fortune-teller. With two thoughts dominating her mind Joy could not resist trying him out.

I scribbled down two questions. One—was I going to continue living where I was at present? Two—would I have children?

I did not sign the paper, or give my address, but placed it in a sealed envelope and asked my friends to keep the reply until I called for it.

Joy sailed for Africa on May 12, 1937. She was anxious at the prospect of traveling alone to an entirely new world but as they parted Ziebel embraced her and told her all would turn out for the best.

The best for whom? There is a troubled look in her eye as she stares into the camera from her deck chair on the boat, and Ziebel detected trouble from the letters she wrote him from Kenya. But he had no idea of the extent of the problem until she confessed it on her return some weeks later.

She said that on the voyage out a Swiss botanist, Peter Bally, had joined the ship at Egypt; baldly, he and she had fallen in love, embarked on an affair and now wanted to marry. According to Joy, Ziebel was crushed by the news, which is hardly surprising.

Long afterward Joy wrote that she had been aware, before she went to Africa, that her values in life were quite different from Ziebel's, but it is hard to discern the evidence of this. She makes a further charge that, in all fairness, should not have been leveled at him—he spoiled her too often. It is difficult to reconcile this with another of Joy's allegations—that Ziebel was far too intent on pursuing his bachelor interests of climbing, skiing and parties, to adapt himself to her artistic tastes.

Ever since Joy had left her parents her grandmother had sought to console her or disarm her temper with acts of generosity or by meeting her wishes. Perhaps it was she who had spoiled Joy too often, from the goodness of her heart.

5

Joy first set eyes on Peter Bally when he joined her ship after it passed through the Suez Canal. She had just spent a few hectic days trying to see as much as possible of the Tutankhamen treasures in Cairo and then snatching a dazzling glimpse of the coral fish on the coast of the Red Sea.

This is from her draft memoir.

> I noticed especially one man of about forty who aroused a sensation in me I could not understand and tried to suppress. I rejoined the group of passengers I knew but this man drew my interest again and again, and I felt I had known him all my life. Next morning I was more than glad when he asked me to be his partner at deck tennis.
>
> Was this real LOVE? I thought I knew love, but this was so different, so natural, so simple. I just belonged to him and it was good. Peter and I spent most of our time together, although we were both bewildered as neither of us was free to marry.
>
> I had just left a most kind and loving husband who had entrusted me with a great decision in our lives, and here I was in love with Peter—which I had no moral right to be.

Peter Bally was then aged forty-three. He belonged to a family well known for its shoe business, but his father had broken away to become the successful director of a chemical company in Germany. Peter had therefore studied chemistry at Zurich University, joined a pharmaceutical company in India and later taken a job as an industrial chemist with an oil company in Tanganyika, where he turned to botany and was just completing a book on medicinal plants, *Die Heil und Gift Pflanzen Tanganyikas.*

He was tall, vigorous and good-looking. Cultivated, courteous and gentle, he spoke excellent English, with only a faint trace of an accent, and fluent Swahili. He was, and continued to be, attracted by younger women and had a penchant for risqué books and pictures. He was in the process of dissolving his recent first marriage because his wife refused to accompany him to Africa.

Bally was on his way to Cape Town but had business to do in Nairobi, while Joy went on to stay with Ziebel's Swiss farmer friend up-country at Kitale. There she suffered not only from emotional turmoil but also from dysentery and malaria. She was able to paint a few flowers but for obvious reasons was in no state to look seriously for a farm.

> I battled during the next week to suppress my feelings and live up to all Ziebel had entrusted in me but it was a hopeless struggle. When Peter finally arrived and was in a similar state we decided I should return to Austria and give my husband a fair chance to arrange what should be done.
>
> With a heavy heart, an even heavier feeling of guilt, and with a new consciousness of real love, I left the sunny highlands of Kenya though I knew it would not be for long.
>
> I had not seen the real Africa, but its vast expanse, its strong unbroken wilderness and its very grandeur had impressed themselves on me.

It is doubtful whether Ziebel ever had a chance of altering the course of events. He was shattered by the news of Joy's betrayal. Although they drove through Europe in an attempt at reconciliation, Joy spent several months without him in Switzerland, on an archaeological dig in Zurich and also saw Bally's brother, a psychiatrist, there. In the end the dispirited Ziebel allowed their divorce to go through in six months.

Joy left Vienna for Africa the second time in March 1938, on the eve of the Nazis' arrival in the capital. The only person who came to see her off at the station was Susanne Schmutzer. Hans Hofmann was openly a Nazi, which would account for the absence of her family.

Before she left Joy collected the fortune-teller's answers to her questions: she would live in the tropics, have to learn English and would bear no children. Determined not to be discouraged, she took a short course in how to manage childbirth in remote places, beyond the reach of a doctor or midwife, and designed her new wardrobe so that it could be let out if she became pregnant.

Her return to Africa was a colossal gamble. She could not speak English fluently, she had little or no money and she had known Peter Bally for only a few weeks. Luckily for Joy he was not only attracted by her physically and mentally, but he was also chivalrous. He told one of his closest friends that she had thrown herself at him on the boat and although he had enjoyed their brief affair, he was amazed when she returned to Kenya, having burned all her boats in Europe and expecting to marry him.

Peter Bally possessed modest private means and had just been appointed botanist at the Coryndon Museum in Nairobi. There was neither any financial nor, according to his brother, any medical reason why he should not marry Joy. The wedding took place on April 4, 1938, and they moved into the Ainsworth Hotel close to the museum.

Almost immediately Joy was catapulted into the life she loved so well for the next forty years. For three months she and Peter lived under canvas with the museum expedition on the Chyulu Hills in southeastern Kenya. A recent volcanic formation, the chain offers a spectrum of habitats from the totally arid to lush rain forest.

Peter, an expert and meticulous botanical artist, instantly recognized Joy's gift and encouraged her to paint some of the specimens he collected. Disgusted by her attempt at the delicate gloriosa lily, she tore it up: Peter stuck it together again. It was the beginning of her serious career as an artist.

Disliking both her nickname, Fifi, and Friederike, he suggested she now name herself after the joy she had brought into his life. Henceforward she called herself, and signed all her paintings, Joy.

The expedition, comprising many specialists from the museum, was supported by 150 porters with whom Peter was on particularly good terms. Accurate as Joy was as an artist, she was less so as an author. Her autobiography attributes Peter's authority with the men to his left-handedness and his monocle, both of special significance to their tribe. Peter later protested that he was right-handed and had only once worn a monocle, as a joke.

Life in the Chyulu Hills was extremely rigorous; quite apart from the stiff climbs over very rough ground, there were occasional encounters with buffalo and other big game. Joy claims that after a time she suffered increasing discomfort and suspected she had once more miscarried.

Only after their return to Nairobi was she properly introduced to life in the capital. Peter Bally had already made an excellent impression on the senior people he met through his work: Louis and Mary Leakey, Dr. van Someren, curator of the museum, Archie and Queenie Ritchie and the Jex-Blakes.

Lady Muriel was particularly kind to Joy, recognizing in her the same ardor, enterprise and disregard for danger and hardship that had taken her to nurse the Serbs during the First World War. She had a comfortable house, a famous garden, a coffee farm and a string of horses which she invited Joy to ride with her.

It was both a great challenge and a compliment when Lady Muriel asked Joy to illustrate the second edition of the book on which she was working with her husband, *Gardening in East Africa,* for it meant painting specimens from every climate and altitude in Kenya, Uganda and Tanganyika.

Very soon Lady Muriel began to fill Oma's place in Joy's life and she badly needed the support. She found the formality of this professional society—so different from the temperamental license of Vienna—an increasing strain. It was a relief to relax in the evenings and speak German with some of Peter's Swiss friends.

The Leakeys were also very friendly, leasing the Ballys their garden cottage while they built their own house, which would not be ready until October 1939, and inviting them to see their excavations in the Rift Valley. Peter and Joy also joined one of Mary's expeditions to the Ngorongoro Crater in Tanganyika. Nevertheless, in prolonged proximity both the Leakeys found Joy's restless conversation exhausting.

Just before the outbreak of war, in September 1939, Ziebel von Klarwill and his mother, Elsa, managed to escape from Austria and arrived in Kenya. It enabled Joy to go some way toward making reparation for her desertion. According to her friend Susanne Schmutzer, Joy worked hard at painting flowers and sold the pictures to support the von Klarwills.

Ziebel must have lost everything he possessed in Austria, and he immediately set about making a living in the business he knew—cars. Joy never once mentioned publicly her early help, and Ziebel displayed exquisite tact in conveying to her his lasting affection only through the rarest and most sensitive gestures.

After her possible miscarriage Peter had given Joy a puppy, her cairn terrier Pippin, who was her constant companion when she was alone and even joined her when she went to paint at the museum. The dog had a weird musical sense and would perform a duet with her when she struck up an aria from Mozart or Verdi, always finding perfect pitch. On safari he slept under a mosquito net for protection from tsetse flies.

Although Peter and Joy still collected plants together she had, soon after their original safari in the Chyulu Hills, started to go off without him. The first occasion was when she climbed Kilimanjaro—19,340 feet—with A. S. Thomas, an ecological botanist from the Entebbe gardens, near Kampala, in Uganda. She regarded getting to the top of a mountain as a moral exercise in defeating the temptation to give up.

A far longer and even more ambitious expedition was a safari in the Belgian Congo—now Zaire—with Dr. Sally Atsatt, a Dutch zoologist from the University of California at Los Angeles.

In a fit of the compulsive suspicion to which he was sometimes prone, Louis Leakey, who had been working for the Security Services since the declaration of war—and who may have been aware that Joy's stepfather was a Nazi—telephoned a border post through which the women were passing and had them painstakingly searched on the grounds that Joy was an Austrian and her journey questionable. Fortunately for her future as an artist, Joy had simmered down by the time she returned to Nairobi and passed the incident off as a joke.

The Ballys' new house in Nairobi was simple but convenient. Peter painted sliding screens in it with a dry-country landscape to which Joy added some wydah birds. Peter also created a garden, planting only indigenous species.

One morning while Joy was painting a rare white delphinium she found a policewoman at the door with a warrant for her internment as an enemy alien. She tried to brush the intrusion aside but an escort was waiting and she was taken to a convent at Loreto on the outskirts of Nairobi. Being Joy, she insisted on bringing Pippin, her paint box and the white delphinium, much to the astonishment of the disgruntled and polyglot detainees already waiting at the convent.

Joy always kept the letters Peter wrote to her in English during the next few days. In his efforts to get her released he immediately went to his well-placed friends who alerted the authorities to the injustice.

JUNE 28, 1940

My poor darling,

... Ritchie is doubtful whether your leaving for Mau Summit can be prevented. You cannot make exceptions of this kind under military orders.

But do not let that discourage you for a moment. We shall all do our best to get you out as soon as ever possible and you can be assured that I shall keep things going all the time. Do not take things too tragically ...

JULY 1, 1940

On Saturday morning the Private Secretary to His Excellency rang me up unofficially, telling me that the Governor had instructed the Chief Secretary to get on with the case with the utmost dispatch.

It's fortunate too that we have influential friends like the Jex-Blakes and the Ritchies who have all done their best to help you.

Their interest and regard for you is also obvious. Mrs. Ritchie, for instance, remembered at once that you loved Vermouth and it was she who suggested to put the flask into your provision basket ...

How is Pippin taking it all? I am so very glad that you were allowed to have him with you; he will occupy you and he too is a true friend! He is just a furry bundle of love, isn't he? Give him my love too!

Joy's detention, on the lofty escarpment above the Rift Valley, did indeed last only a few days longer before the Governor signed her release.

It emerged that the cause of Joy's arrest was that the Jex-Blakes, when quizzed, had told the police they had heard German spoken in her house. The conversation was, of course, purely innocent. To show the Jex-Blakes that she bore them no ill-feeling, Joy gave Lady Muriel the finished painting of the white delphinium, but the episode must have brought home to her how precarious her position in Kenya was, even with friends who had the ear of authority.

On the surface, at least, everything seems to have gone well between Peter and Joy up to this point, but in July 1940 he became seriously ill with kidney problems. Joy says that after he had been treated his doctors advised him to take a three-month break in South Africa.

George and Joy on the Tana River in January 1943, when she fell in love with him at their first meeting. Her cairn terrier, Pippin, is beside her.

Above: George's parents, Harry and Katherine Adamson. *Left:* George (*left*) with his brother, Terence, at Dean Close School, Cheltenham, in 1923.

Above: Seifenmühle, Joy's great grandfather's large house in Austria-Hungary (now in the Czech Republic). *Left:* her Weisshuhn great grandparents. *Below left:* Joy's grandmother, Oma, with her second husband, Herr Pretz. *Below right:* Joy (*right*) with her parents, Viktor and Traute Gessner, and her sister Traute in 1918.

1930s. *Left:* George (*right*), Terence and a friend watch wild honey being taken from a tree. *Below:* George beside the boat made from sticks and groundsheets, bound with strips of bark, in which he crossed Lake Rudolf in 1934.

Left: Tony Ofenheim, with whom George fell in love in 1935 and who remained an affectionate confidante until his death. *Right:* Joy, while cruising with her first lover in 1931.

Joy at the Vienna Arts Ball in 1930. "My shoulders were grabbed by a masked Apache. I was swept away into my first love affair. After two years I was left with a little dachshund and a deep wound in my heart." *Below left:* The car in which the lovers eloped.

Joy and her first husband, an Austrian, Ritter Viktor von Klarwill, who had a passion for mountains and skiing.

Joy and her second hus-
band, the Swiss botanist
Peter Bally, who taught
her to paint flowers and
persuaded her to adopt
the name Joy.

Right: George on safari with Joy in 1943.
Below: Joy with Pippin, during her four months on Mount Kenya, where she waited for a divorce from Peter Bally. The ladder provided an escape route from elephants and buffalo.

George and Joy on Mount Kenya in 1943. She painted more than seventy flowers but both she and George were tormented by her growing doubts about her promise to marry him.

Joy was fascinated by elephants. *Right:* Her copy of a prehistoric rock engraving, 1944. *Centre:* She stands proudly beside an elephant she shot in 1945. *Below:* She photographed this perfectly formed embryo in 1947.

Above: Joy's lovers in 1948.
Left: A. B. Simpson,
a DC. *Right:* Assistant
Superintendent A. L. Griffith,
with Joy's cairn terrier,
Pippin, and his dachshund.
Left: Joy prepares for a dip,
fully clothed, in Lake Rudolf.

Joy's photograph of this turbaned Korokoro elder (*left*) demonstrates both the likeness and authenticity of her portrait (*right*).
Below: An Isukha in circumcision: "awe-struck boys stand plastered with ashes and ochre."

Left: As they moved into the Sahara in 1953 Joy changed into her floating toga and straw hat.
Below: Heading through the Hoggar Mountains for the hermitage of Assekrem.

1955. *Far right:* Joy shows off her colobus cape against the rock engravings she copied onto sliding doors at Isiolo. *Right:* Her wooden carving of a Rendille woman. *Below:* Joy on South Island, Lake Rudolf.

Above: George at the end of a bird shoot, 1954, with (*left to right*) an officer attached to the Inniskillings, Robert Nimmo and Joy.
Left: George receives his MBE from the Governor, Sir Evelyn Baring.

It is very likely that something more than a convalescence was responsible for this separation. Later Peter said that he felt as if Joy's erratic behavior was driving him to a breakdown. According to him she was compulsively unfaithful and appeared to do everything she could to avoid having a child by him.

While Peter was in South Africa, Joy remained in Kenya and helped look after the children of the officer in charge of the Northern Frontier, Gerald Reece, who lived in Isiolo. Fortunately for Joy, the family was about to spend two months in the log cabin they had built on Mount Marsabit, with a view across the everlasting expanse of the NFD. Joy was enraptured by the scenery and determined one day to explore it.

There was no glass in the windows of the cabin, but wire netting kept out a leopard that was keen to make a meal of the dogs. The night watchman was allowed to sleep in the kitchen after he had twice been nuzzled by a lion on the veranda.

Joy took the children for walks through the misty forest, painted flowers and listened to the gramophone under the trees with Alys Reece or went riding with her. Joy unburdened herself of the difficulties besetting her marriage.

On a lighter note, she and Alys entertained the officers of a battalion returning from Ethiopia—with a steeplechase. There were not enough horses to go around and the missing mounts were made up with mules, donkeys and camels.

When the family party returned to Isiolo, Joy was exceedingly upset by a letter reporting that one of the steeplechasers had broadcast his surprise that she, as an Austrian, had been allowed to entertain the army. Gerald Reece quietly took her into the garden with a torch and showed her a tree whose branches were laden with small birds roosting overnight on their long migration to Europe. He took one down and, stroking it, placed it in her hands.

"Isn't this of far greater importance than anything in your letter?" he asked quietly, and took her in to listen to her favorite music.

When human beings seemed to fail her, Joy often sought the solace of music; it was perhaps the key to her soul. Only one piece of sustained writing survives in her early, handsome, free-flowing script. It describes—in German—her response to the opera she loved best.

APRIL 1940

This morning my husband gave me a recording of *Der Rosenkavalier*. This music is for me an essential part of a world that does not exist any more. The mixture of races and cultures in Austria formed a unique combination from which the works of its famous composers and writers emerged.

After the 1914–18 war Austria changed and only a few of them remained, but I was lucky enough to share their experience and all my life I will be homesick for them. *Der Rosenkavalier* belongs to those times.

The only luxury I brought with me to Africa was a porcelain figure of Richard Mayr as Baron Ochs in the opera. As I play the record I can hear his voice that I heard so often in Vienna and Salzburg. In my mind's eye I can see his cheerful face and shivers run down my spine—he is dead now.

How often I walked home after a performance, too full of the music to bear anyone's company. I love every note, the rich harmonies, more and more each time I hear them.

Peter Bally, like Ziebel von Klarwill, understood this side of her nature but neither man was able to fathom or manage the whole.

Peter felt far fitter when he returned from South Africa, but Joy wrote this in her draft memoir about their search for a very rare plant near Lake Rukwa in Tanzania:

> I was in good form after Marsabit and never felt tired at the end of a day's walk. This seemed to depress Peter who could not keep up and felt that perhaps he had overestimated his recovery.
>
> It did not help when I told him I was sure that it was the sixteen year difference in our ages that was responsible—not his illness.
>
> After our return to Nairobi he became even more depressed and retired into his shell which made it difficult to help him.

Joy's version of these growing troubles has to be looked at with caution. Peter later proved he was neither impotent nor lacking in stamina: he survived a fractured skull in a plane crash, and at the age of eighty-six drove himself to Mombasa and back—600 hundred miles—in a day.

Joy's account of Peter's reaction to her remarkable success as a flower artist is also at variance with other evidence. In 1941 Lady Muriel arranged an exhibition of her work in Nairobi; Lady Moore, the Governor's wife, commissioned her to paint twenty flowers for presentation to General Smuts, the Prime Minister of South Africa and a botanist; and finally she was asked to provide eight flower paintings for table mats in the Royal Lodge, Kenya, and twelve native trees for Christmas cards to be distributed by the *East African Standard*.

Joy wrote: "However much I tried to keep Peter to the forefront, my paintings were always preferred, which hurt me more than it hurt Peter." Her remark is received with disbelief by Peter's friends, who say that he never showed anything but satisfaction in her success, both for the pleasure it gave her as an artist and him as her tutor.

Whatever mistake Joy may have made in bringing her second marriage to an end, Peter was undoubtedly relieved to see her go. Prudently he withdrew to Ethiopia when his divorce was due to come through and while—he presumed—her marriage to George Adamson went ahead.

SEVEN

For Better for Worse

1944–1946

1

George was afraid that Joy might be dying when they arrived at the Jex-Blakes' house. But the doctor took one look at the empty bottle of tablets and gently told her she was a sham.

The pill known as M&B 693 was widely prescribed for pneumonia and other conditions now treated by antibiotics. They would do no lasting harm, merely make her feel sick for a few days. Talking to George alone, Jex-Blake advised him not to insist on immediate marriage but to give Joy a few months in which to calm down. George agreed and in his diary that night wrote: "Oh darling, why did you? If it is so terrible I will not insist on marriage."

His compassion might have induced him to delay the wedding and conceivably give up Joy altogether, but he was irretrievably in love. If he waited too long Peter Bally's return would upset the applecart again, and his job would be at risk if the whole process of divorce were to end in a public fiasco.

He therefore felt cornered by forces too powerful to fight against, and the next day he insisted that Joy make up her mind to marry him immediately; if she did not he would leave Nairobi, never to see her again.

Joy was also snared. She saw with absolute clarity that, for all her affinity with George on safari, and her admiration for him, their temperaments were unsuited and he was incapable of sharing her passions for painting and music. Apart from that she was no longer in love with him and was tortured by her renewed obsession with Peter. The prospect of isolation with the one man and separation from the other was intolerable, yet she could see no alternative means of survival. She lacked money; her family were seven thousand miles away in Vienna; and although her two cast-off husbands were living in Kenya, the first was penniless and the second had made his present attitude plain by leaving for Ethiopia.

Furthermore, the stepdaughter of a Nazi, she was living in a colony governed by the British who were at war with her own country. Some of its most consequential figures—the Ritchies, Jex-Blakes and Reeces—had twice rallied to her and George's support but would not help her again if she reneged on the marriage. Joy recognized there was no escape, and her rage at being trapped, though sometimes dormant, never worked itself out.

Her divorce came through within a week and at 3:30 P.M. on Monday, January 17, 1944, she and George were married by the District Commissioner in Nairobi. There were only two witnesses, their host, Mr. May, and a lawyer named Kaplan. Apart from his commitment to Joy in the words officially prescribed, George made a private vow that however much their feelings toward each other might change he would always do his best to be a good husband. He never forgot it.

He briefly noted in his diary that the Mays gave a party after the ceremony, but the wedding night was a serious disappointment to him.

George's house at Isiolo stood a few miles outside the town. It consisted of a large rectangle with a rondavel at each end; the whole was thatched with grass. The wooden walls were daubed inside with whitewashed mud or lined with bamboo. The glass in the windows and wooden boards on the floor were luxuries.

The kitchen, a few yards away, formed part of a circle of other rondavels containing two guest rooms and George's workshop, office and Game Department stores.

Joy introduced color into the house; her pictures shared the walls with a huge buffalo skull and other trophies. The indestructible sofa and chairs made by Italian prisoners of war were covered with zebra and lion skin, and a man came twice a year from Nairobi to tune her upright piano.

George and Joy were generous hosts but their staff was often adequate in numbers only. She was an exacting employer who did not suffer fools gladly and never listened properly when addressed in Swahili, the lingua franca of East Africa. She spoke it atrociously herself and unfortunately was apt to mistake incomprehension for insolence.

Apart from Pippin, she and George shared the house with a variety of orphans—from tiny weaverbird chicks to a baby giraffe, they were always welcome. In the early days Joy confined herself to mongooses, and over the years she had twenty. When they were angry their noses bled.

Joy's favorite, Metternich, once strayed from the house and her searches were fruitless. A few days later George was shooting guinea fowl four miles away in the bush when Metternich, who must have heard Pippin barking, pranced up in delight. The mongooses were sufficiently house-trained to sleep in Joy's bed but savage enough to attack and kill snakes.

In Nairobi Joy had been close to the hub of things—the station and airfields; hotels and clubs, offices and shops; the cathedral, hospital, theatre, cinemas and library, also, of course, the Coryndon Museum. Isiolo was different. It was where the rough road north to Ethiopia passed through two lines of ramshackle huts. Off its main street were a few bungalow offices, a mosque, a church and a prison; its main life revolved around the market near the police barrier, where every car heading north from the town had to stop and register the names of its passengers.

In addition to the Superintendent of Police the other Europeans stationed in Isiolo were the Provincial and District Commissioners, with their wives, and the livestock officer, George Low. Apart from his veterinary work, he had to act as middleman or whole-saler on behalf of the government, buying all the livestock for sale in the NFD. His wife, Lois, a cheerful and immaculate hostess, was equally impeccable as his bookkeeper in the dustiest villages and manyattas.

By far the greater part of George's work was done in the field and Isiolo was simply his base. But wild animals are no respecters of places or people. A lion killed an impala on the Reeces' lawn and an elephant grew partial to the DC's tomatoes. George bitterly resented having to shoot innocent intruders when they followed the dry riverbed into the town in search of a meal. His colleague Jack Bonham felt much the same: in protest at a DC's intolerance, he shot a trespassing elephant on his vegetable shamba but refused to remove it.

For Joy, Isiolo was almost bearable in short spells, thanks to the company of Alys Reece and Lois Low, the consolation of her piano and the hopes raised by the arrival of the Royal Mail Service—delivered three times a week by a portly Sikh in a scarlet shirt and spotless white turban. But if the days were usually lackluster, the nights were frequently hideous.

Until they married Joy made no criticisms of George as a lover; afterward she regularly, if not invariably, rejected him in bed, as she had so often refused Peter Bally. It was unlucky that before George could take her out on safari, where she usually recovered her good humor, he was summoned to Nairobi. Joy went with him.

2

Archie Ritchie had sent for George to help deal with a pride of lions that were causing embarrassment in what is now the Nairobi game park.

To ensure they remained on view they were often fed near a lone tree that provided a landmark. Perhaps as a result the lions grew a little lazy about hunting game, for after some soldiers had escaped from detention in the barracks nearby only their boots and feet could be found. This of course enhanced the glamor of the Lone Tree pride and on fine weekends up to two hundred cars would turn up to watch it, and families brought out their picnics. Archie Ritchie had to act quickly before a more gruesome picnic occurred.

Reluctantly he asked George and a colleague, Eric Rundgren, to eliminate them. To shoot a pride of eight lions, more or less simultaneously, was an almost impossible task, especially in the fading light at the end of the day when the crowds had dispersed. Joy described the scene.

The pride had to be located when they were hungry. The next step was to chain a wildebeest carcase to a tree, close to a stream where there was enough undergrowth to conceal two cars. All this had to be done with the wind in the right direction so the lions were not suspicious.

Then we waited. It seemed an endless time until the vultures started circling and guided the first lions to the bait. Finally all eight were tearing at the kill and cuffing each other. I had never been so close to even one lion before.

Suddenly there was a deafening volley of shots, followed by lions leaping across each other, stumbling, rolling over, tearing blindly to get away in different directions, but only to collapse after a few steps.

More shots, more growls, and then the almost human cries and whimpering of the dying lions.

Joy was profoundly unsettled by this visit to Nairobi, not because of the lions but because of the proximity of Peter Bally. Back in Isiolo the tail of the trapped leopardess started to twitch.

Late one night she began taunting George about the native women in his past and his "lunatic" mother, who was now suffering from the onset of senile debility. He retorted that she had nothing to be proud of either. It caused an outburst.

June 11 She got in a fury and walked off to find someone to take her to Nanyuki. I ran after her and forced her to come back. She went off to our guest house—this was too much for me, had a struggle and forced her into our room. She half mad, kicked and bit and insulted me again. I lost my temper and got her by the throat and half choked her.

This was one of the rare occasions when George was unable to restrain his physical response to Joy's provocations. She lost few opportunities of resurrecting the memory: he confided her provocations to his diary and thereafter held his peace.

It is impossible to know exactly what occurred when Joy and George, or Joy and Peter Bally, were entirely alone. Making love is like playing duets on two pianos: the strength and timing of the impulse to play may be entirely different, while the range, tuning and temperament of the instruments may vary like the skill and experience of the players. If they regularly stumble, grow discordant or utterly come to grief, much more than pleading or coercion is needed to put things right.

The only way George knew of countering Joy's hostile moods was to take her out on safari. So they went briefly up into the Mathews Mountains, her first real glimpse of the NFD since their marriage. Their bizarre rapprochement is best recounted in George's words.

July 12 This has been our first real safari together. Joy has shown herself to be ideally fitted for the life and has been a wonderful companion—but nothing more than that, not once has she slept with me.

On the way from Wamba stopped at the pool near Archers Post in order to bathe. Joy would not go in because she did not want to be seen naked by her husband. Every night on this safari she has never failed to say "don't look" when she was having a bath. It sounds absurd but repeated daily it nearly drove me crazy.

During the next fortnight letters shot backward and forward between Joy and Bally, whom she went down to see in Nairobi. He obviously realized her state was abnormal, for he offered to pay for her to be treated by a psychoanalyst in South Africa, and to George's anger she accepted.

George found there was little he could do with Joy until August, when he swept her off from this emotional battlefield to give her an extended experience of the beauty and exhilarating freedom of the Northern Frontier.

3

The two-month safari startled and gave a sharp lesson to the poachers hunting in the heart of the Mathews range and along the shimmering shores of Lake Rudolf. George steadily captured a string of prisoners, including Adukan, the most notorious of the Turkana who had twice tried to kill his pursuers, once rolling a boulder down on to a patrol. George and Adukan quickly became excellent friends.

The expedition was a tour de force in another sense. Despite her previous expeditions in Kenya, Tanganyika and the Congo, Joy discovered through George an extra dimension to Africa.

They traveled rough, riding on mules ahead of the donkeys and game scouts. Sometimes they were nine hours in the saddle, with the temperature rising to over a hundred. They lost five donkeys from exhaustion or hunger and two to lions.

A close friend of Joy's said she was frightened by only two things in Africa: punctures and elephants. Now she was put to the test. One night she had to hold George's torch high while he shot a marauding elephant sixteen paces away in the maize.

The next day they were taken to see the furrowed earth, littered with a few rags and bones, where an elephant had killed a man the week before and come back each afternoon to plow up the ground with his tusks. George was convinced from several incidents like this that elephants have a sense of death, both human and their own.

Joy's first view of Lake Rudolf took her breath away. The impact of this vast expanse of water lying in a rocky inferno almost as barren as the moon is astonishing. For more than a hundred miles its waters stretch northward into the haze. That day they were neither jade nor the sulky slate-gray they become under clouds, but bright blue and choppy with white horses.

The shore looked as if it were lined with cotton wool. When they approached it the white mass suddenly disintegrated as hundreds of gulls, terns and plovers, ducks, geese and herons, storks, ibis and spoonbills, rose into the air with pelicans, flamingos and fish eagles.

Joy derived great pleasure from collecting curiosities for the Coryndon Museum. Louis Leakey had given her a killing bottle for insects and traps for small reptiles and rodents, along with tracing equipment. Twice she spotted rock faces engraved with remarkable bestiaries— a mammoth, a rhino, a long-horned antelope, giraffes and camels— which she copied.

By the lake she caught a chameleon with white feet and white markings; she gathered chalcedony, fossil fish and an unfamiliar yellow-flowered portulaca. She found a turtle that could flatten its carapace, and seeing that the El Molo were using the shells of another rare species as plates, she bartered for one.

The crocodiles in the lake were ubiquitous and nearly capsized their boat in the dark. George had to kill eleven near their camp and from her bed Joy shot one approaching the mouth of her tent. She therefore only swam in a safe offshoot of the lake with her goggles, where she caught two brightly colored fish that seemed completely alien to these waters.

Taking their last look at the lake, George and Joy noted a cove on South Island where a small boat might land if the wind were to drop. She became as eager as he to solve the mystery of the missing scientists. Then she plunged into the lake fully dressed, as she had done several times each day, to cool herself for the baking trek to Mount Kulal.

At the foot of the mountain they watched a statuesque Rendille woman, her hair fashioned with fat and red ocher into a tall and elegant cockscomb, lead a train of a hundred camels, their wooden bells clonking, to the water in one of the deep and narrow gorges that almost sever the mountain into segments.

It was impossible to take the donkeys to the summit of Kulal, and

Joy had to work her way along the last knife-edge crest with her legs dangling on either side of it. At the top, she sat on the very edge of an abyss several thousand feet deep to paint the view across a fissure to the limitless desert beyond. "To convey its awe-inspiring grandeur I had to take three sheets of paper and sketch it in sections."

A fire of blazing cedar logs kept them warm at night but did not deter an attack on the donkeys by three lions which had been prowling the forest and preying on the Samburu cattle. Firing three shots, George drove off one, wounded another and killed the third. The Turkana will happily eat *posho*, fish, goat or rank hippo meat; and the next day Adukan and his confederates—the least cooperative of whom had been roped for security—polished off the lion, to the disgust of the other tribesmen.

To feed them, George shot a buffalo and, too late, found her calf hidden in a thicket. Joy took it to her heart and was obliged to buy a milk cow to feed it. Refusing to abandon her orphan, she decided to travel a hundred miles with it to the one man she knew would adopt it, Raymond Hook. Several days later a remarkable procession set off.

George and Joy were in the lead with Pippin and a dwarf mongoose on the front of her saddle; next came a camel on which the baby buffalo lay in a palanquin padded with grass, the milk cow with her calf and the donkeys; George's scouts with their prisoners brought up the rear on foot. By now George had persuaded Adukan to join his staff.

Joy's first eight weeks at large in George's domain were packed with more adventures than most of us experience in a lifetime. She tried to translate them into words but the article was never accepted. She felt her sketches of the landscape also failed to capture its magic, although the bars of music she scribbled on the backs of them may have been nearer the mark.

Much more important, the safari proved to her that the Northern Frontier, which she had always looked on as a promised land, was something far better than a conflation of her dreams: it was real, and she never escaped from its spell.

On the way back to Isiolo she stopped and sent a wire to Thomas Cook postponing the passage she had booked to South Africa.

4

Joy was thrilled by her reception when she went to Peter Bally and Louis Leakey at the museum.

The chameleon, portulaca flower and collapsible turtle were new to science. The other turtle shell was wanted by the British Museum. The nearest relatives of the two colored fish lived in West Africa. The animals she had traced—which she and George never found again despite several searches—turned out to be the first prehistoric engravings recorded in East Africa.

Her elation at the response of the scientists and scholars, and renewed contact with the cultural traditions of Europe personified by Peter Bally, now produced an inverse reaction to the unharnessed natural forces represented by George. She was incapable of controlling the pendulum's swing. As a result she began to compile a case against the man she had enticed into a marriage he would otherwise never have contemplated seriously.

It is difficult for anyone who knew George well to believe he would remain dirty longer than could be helped; Joy now claimed he did. It was also her perennial cry that he smelled of tobacco and whiskey, that they could not afford his smoking and drinking and that he often drank to excess. Joy further charged that he was stupid, uncultured and silent.

This was the man that she herself had gone out of the way to choose as her third husband. He had always smoked but was seldom if ever seen to drink immoderately. He had great common sense and showed considerable intelligence when he turned his mind to a subject. It is fair to ask what difference a degree in the humanities would have made: "culture" had not saved her two previous husbands from dismissal. Perhaps it was as well for her that George did keep control of his tongue.

Joy's indictment of George at this time ends with two final counts: that he was mean and a liar. Anyone looking impartially at a game warden's salary of about £700 per year in 1944 would know that he had not a penny to spare on luxuries or whims. George drank his whiskey, Joy had her vermouth, they both liked to entertain friends. By the time he had paid for these, their food, staff and petrol, nothing was left over. As for his lies, it is impossible to pin one down.

Before the end of the year in which she was married to George, Joy was literally beyond reason and announced in December she was going to spend Christmas with Peter. This is what George wrote on the final page of his diary that year.

My feelings now are an utter longing for Joy and that life for me without her is an empty wilderness.

Then again I am assailed by a red fury that I should have been so contemptible as to have put up with words and insults—insults to my deepest feelings from a woman who has proved herself to be unworthy of a decent man's love—a woman who has failed to make a success with four men! 1st, Jew, 2nd, Klarwill, 3rd, Peter Bally, and 4th, myself! Surely all four of us couldn't be "outsiders," it is just possible that Joy is a little to blame.

There is no logic or sense of obligation or duty in the woman. Her private convictions, in her own mind, justify all her actions, regardless of morality.

Joy was away from December 18 until February 2. One of the greater and odder inaccuracies in her autobiography is that she places here, at the end of 1944, a six-week safari she and George made to the Belgian Congo—that expedition occurred five years later.

Since her entries for the Congo are among the fullest in her diaries for the years 1945–1975, it is unlikely she forgot they existed. It is more probable she dared not risk consulting the early diaries for fear of stirring up the pain, and perhaps the shame, that lay buried in them.

In fact Bally refused to spend Christmas with Joy and for six weeks she stayed with friends on their farm in the White Highlands.

In February 1945 she and George went down to Nairobi for the weekend. They camped out at Lone Tree and for three days were both painfully locked with Bally in what Joy calls a "post mortem," during which she aired her most wounding grievance against George—that he was not a suitable father for any child of hers because his mother was mad. It cut no ice that George had already consulted a doctor about the implications of his mother's illness and had been assured that it involved no risk of this kind.

George had to put up with both Joy's taunts and Bally's offer to provide him with grounds for divorce but only on the understanding that he would not afterward marry Joy.

George's diary on the Monday after this distressing weekend, dur-

ing which she had thrown the early-morning tea tray at him, went to
the heart of the matter.

February 19   Joy accused B. of encouraging her to believe that he
still hoped that they might come together, had actually told her
before the divorce went through that they might have an artificial
child together. He tried to deny it but I really believe that Joy was
speaking the truth. The man is an absolute moral coward! I don't
for a minute believe that he wants Joy back—but he hasn't got the
guts to tell her so plainly.

George was right: Bally had told Archie Ritchie that he had no desire
whatever to take Joy back, but had been alarmed by another threat
of suicide.

Having made little impact in Nairobi, Joy repeated her attacks
on George's mother and Terence. No doubt Katherine Adamson,
feebleminded as she had become, was trying to Joy. No doubt, too,
Terence expressed in looks if not words what he thought of her
intolerable behavior. But while the brothers settled their mother into
the Silverbeck Hotel in Nanyuki, Joy rampaged against the lunatic
and the idiot, as she called them.

This time she went too far and was shocked by the ferocity of
George's anger. At the climax of a row she threw a chunk of limestone
at him.

In May, Joy went down to Nairobi again to see Bally and to consult
doctors, both about her psychological problems and physical—probably gynecological—health; she had regularly been running a temperature.

To describe her condition as hysterical would be glib, but there is
no doubt that a sudden longing for a child, or fear of not having one,
increasingly preyed on her mind, and she drew a meticulous ovulation
chart at the end of her diary that year.

While the Nairobi doctors struggled to help her, Joy burned her
fingers painfully going through Bally's desk in the Museum when he
was away. George later described what happened.

She read through his private diary and discovered that he was
having an affair with another woman. This led to the most awful
scene, she went to his house, refused to leave until he was obliged
to call on friends for assistance to get her out. The friends had to

call in a doctor who had to give her morphia to calm her, before she would leave.

There were several immediate sequels to this drama. For a month Joy continued to importune Bally, possibly to provide her with a baby by artificial insemination. Weak as he seems to have been with her, it is impossible to believe that a man so respected by his friends for his decency would have contemplated it without George's wholehearted consent. At the end of June Joy records: "Talk with Peter—final parting—very alone."

It was not a final parting, but her obsession seemed to subside, possibly because of the work of the doctors and George's insistence, by letter, that she entirely alter her attitude to their marriage and cease to sign her paintings Joy F. Bally.

> *June 13* She has applied for a visa for Switzerland and seems determined to go. Well, we'll see what happens. I've had enough and if she goes for good, so be it, it will not break me. Asked her for letter of "desertion" which I will use at the end of the necessary three years to get a divorce.

Apart from George's firmness and her medical treatment, one other factor may have helped restore Joy's balance. In the first week of July the museum paid her £925 for 185 of her flower paintings. Although this was only £5 each, it was a colossal windfall, almost one and a half times George's annual salary, and the equivalent of at least £20,000 today. For the first time since she had left Bally she was confident that if the worst came to worst she would not starve. What is more, the war in the West was over and she might even be able to get back to Austria.

On August 25, George was camping at Garissa, where they had first met. Suddenly Joy arrived looking very thin and ill but pleased to see him. That night they made love for the first time in a year.

5

Joy and George spent most of the remaining months of 1945 together. During six weeks' patrol along the Tana, George captured a number of poachers and one night Joy shot an elephant that was raiding a shamba near the river.

The rest of the time she spent mostly at the coast, where their adventures stimulated Joy to break ground as an artist in two important new fields.

She embarked on the first enterprise while staying in Malindi with a notorious couple called John and June Carberry while George was flown to Nairobi for treatment for dysentery.

The Coastal Province is a world of its own, a green strip lying between the harsh hinterland and the white sands fringing the Indian Ocean. At sea level it is both hot and humid, with a constant monsoon, strong or gentle, blowing southward from October to March, and northward for the other half of the year. The two rainy seasons coincide with these changes. The soil is wonderfully fertile for root crops, coconuts and dates, mangoes, papaws and limes. The air is scented with spices, jasmine, woodsmoke and drains.

The coastal people are mostly descended from maritime invaders; many are Arab, the majority Muslim. Mombasa, in the south, is the largest port in East Africa. Malindi, now a seaside resort but in the 1940s a sleepy fishing village, lies about halfway up the coast. The old Arab trading town of Lamu, the northernmost port in the country, is still used by dhows. Its Arab architecture—intricately carved doorways and shutters, shaded Moorish arcades, verandas and balconies, thick whitewashed walls and minarets—remains unspoiled.

George's recovery, and return to meet Joy at Malindi, coincided with the festival of Id-el-Fitr, celebrating the end of Ramadan. Its climax was a ceremony in the white coral rag hall on the seafront when the population, tricked out in their finery—the women in billowing gowns, beads, bangles and turbans, the men in cloaks, caftans and headcloths—gathered like a scene from the *Arabian Nights*. The DC arrived in a starched white uniform and the Liwali, the distinguished and much loved leader of the local Muslim community, in his most imposing robes.

Joy was so overwhelmed by the unexpected profusion of color and the distinctive character in so many of the faces that she conceived an instant ambition to paint them. She was prepared to start with a portrait of almost any one from the crowd. The next day, while she was adapting the DC's veranda as a studio, softening the glare and preparing a background with blankets and mats, she found to her consternation that the Liwali himself had decided to sit.

Above her diary entry for September 10, 1945, she later added in red ink, with a large exclamation mark, that this was her first portrait.

It opened the way for her most significant work as an artist, a government commission which took her another eight years to complete.

When George went back to work Joy stayed on in Malindi at the Carberrys', with whom she had little in common. At the heart of the fast set in Nairobi, June Carberry had spent the night of Lord Erroll's murder staying with his mistress, Diana Broughton, and her husband, Jock, who was accused of the murder. June Carberry smoked and drank brandy and soda through most of the day. Joy's diary is suddenly sprinkled with drinks, dinners, parties and even roulette.

June, like Joy, was utterly dauntless, and if she fancied a man would go after him. Like Joy, also, her feelings about men were ambivalent. She was once heard to bark in her brassy voice a remark of which Joy would have approved. "My God, I hate men. I'd trust my dog more than any man. I'd tell it things I'd never tell a man."

Joy was flattered by the Carberrys' friendship, perhaps because John had inherited a peerage which he then abandoned. After that he had gone to prison for eighteen months and grown increasingly sadistic—inserting gramophone needles into his horses' bits to see if they induced them to race faster. He caused his fifteen-year-old stepdaughter Juanita to be thrashed so cruelly while he watched that she at once rode, in agony, to the nearest police station and had herself removed from his "care." Forty years later she became a friend and warm supporter of George.

Monster as he was, Carberry lent Joy a harpoon and some goggles and introduced her to yet another, perhaps the most exquisite, dimension of Africa. Nine years before he had lent Beryl Markham the plane in which she flew the Atlantic.

To swim through the myriads of tropical fish on a coral reef is an experience part aesthetic, part sensual, that has no equal on earth. The colors of the fish are as many and varied, as striking and subtle, as any devised by the artists of the Renaissance; their gold has not been dug from the darkness of the earth but streams fresh from the sun. Because the coral is alive, its formations take on shapes, colors and textures that human architecture can never hope to emulate.

Awareness of the dazzling variety of color, of unimagined shapes in continuous and unfrightened movement all around you, of a quality of light unique to the element of water, is heightened by a further phenomenon. You are free, silent and weightless and you feel you are actually flying through this miraculous world.

At the beginning of November, George took Joy on a patrol through the Boni Forest, north of Lamu, to a derelict fishing village called Kiunga, close to the border with Somalia.

At Kiunga Joy explored a second new sphere of endeavor as an artist. She began to record the scintillating tropical life she had discovered just below the surface of the sea. She and George were taken out to the reefs by an entertaining old Bajun called Dilimua in his dhow. Whereas Joy wanted to paint fish, Dilimua was only concerned to eat them.

He sent George and Joy down into the chilly sea, again and again, for the succulent crayfish which they had to shoot between the eyes— not an easy feat since Carberry's harpoon was handmade and erratic. The crayfish in the deep, and very cold, water tasted far better than those from the reef.

Joy found all the fish she needed to paint. As she had at Lake Rudolf, she wrote down her impressions at the time; later she wove them into *Born Free*.

Some of the corals were pagoda-shaped, others looked like the brains of giants, while some fanned out like mushrooms patterned with purple rosettes or were furrowed by emerald creases.

There were the buried clams, their mouths a deadly trap, just showing above ground; the poisonous stone fish which kept perfectly still against a coral rock except for its amber-coloured eyes that followed every move and gave it away; and the crayfish with their sharp hooked armour.

Joy found that she had to sketch the colors of the fish in the dhow before the scales faded. In the evenings she hung the fish on threads to make accurate drawings of their shapes which altered when they dried. Finally she packed the fish in salt and sent them to the museum where plaster casts were made that she later colored herself.

Joy worked furiously, often long into the night, sometimes painting eight or ten fish a day. In the end she completed about eighty finished portraits of the fish which glow with a wonderful brightness. Her collection was bought by Sir Ali Bin Salem, head of the whole Arab community on the coast, and presented to the Mombasa Museum in Fort Jesus.

When the sea was rough, there was no point in trying to goggle, so Joy walked inland through the long grass with a gun bearer and Pippin on a lead.

She was fascinated by the ruins at Ras Chiamboni, just across the border in Somalia, whose origins were unknown but suspected to be Arab. They boasted two phallic towers or obelisks, as did similar ruins close by and at Gedi, near Malindi. The phallus always excited her interest and she went to great trouble to obtain phallic symbols from the Turkana and Boran.

On another day she lost all sense of time trying to prize some giant fossil clams from a bed of coral stranded far back in the bush. On the way home in the dark she suddenly felt a blast of warm breath from in front of her and simultaneously heard a low growl. Her gun bearer fired: a dark mass withdrew and charged again before disappearing after a second shot. The next day George said the spoor was a lion's.

Kiunga and Lake Rudolf became the two places most treasured by George and Joy, to which they returned again and again, and where they took Elsa as soon as they felt she was ready to go on safari.

Today, threatened by armed refugees from Somalia and linked to the outside world only by a tenuous sand track, Kiunga is still unmolested by tourists or developers.

6

On her return to Isiolo after Christmas Joy began to make a number of tribal sketches, often joining George on his game control safaris, and sitting up at night for leopards and lions. He describes a night on which she waited with him for a pride of cattle raiders.

February 24   About 1.00 am a single lion appeared which I shot in the shoulder. It went and stopped about two hundred yards off, could only see its eyes and hear growls. Had a shot and again hit it, eyes disappeared.

About 5.00 am heard lions at kill and switched on the light and saw four lionesses, gave Joy first shot. She killed it with a bullet in the chest and it fell a few yards from kill. I shot a second which dropped about fifteen yards off. A few minutes later one of the remaining lionesses returned but we let it go.

Joy had no inhibitions about killing at this time: she frequently shot zebras, oryx, steinbok and gazelles to feed George's staff. In May, writing to Louis Leakey about the possibility of the museum buying another hundred of her flower paintings, she added she had just shot her "first" elephant—presumably she meant her first under license. It had decent tusks of 82 lbs and 79 lbs. In a photograph she stands proudly beside it, but she noted in her diary that "now all the excitement and shine" of hunting an elephant had gone.

It was quite understandable that, once it became clear African wildlife was heading for extinction and she had launched her crusade to protect it, she drew a veil over her shooting.

Similarly George was never squeamish if he felt it was absolutely necessary to shoot an animal—or a man—however much he hated killing. When he had to cull up to fifty antelope and zebras a day for a month on end, to clear land for cattle at the beginning of the war, he detected with disgust the blood lust it released. On certain occasions, and in changing circumstances, he too kept silent about some of his killing.

Both Joy and George showed the greatest concern for anyone mauled by a lion, since the wounds would almost certainly turn septic. George mentions, though Joy does not, that at this time a five-year-old girl was taken by a lion and rescued by her family only after she had been badly bitten. Joy carefully dressed her wounds with M&B 693 and took her to hospital. A DC recalled watching George treat a similar case with extraordinary tenderness.

During the middle of the year Joy's disturbed obsession with Bally erupted yet again. She insisted on sleeping alone in the guesthouse and once in a rage against George tugged at the hairs on his chest; yet there were times when she doodled affectionate cartoons in his diary. Her feelings for Bally were just as unstable.

George, Bally, Joy herself and her friends grew increasingly worried about these violent and conflicting moods which pulled her in opposite directions almost simultaneously. Her condition perfectly fits some lines of Coventry Patmore's about love.

> He that but once too nearly hears
> The music . . .
> Is thenceforth lonely, and for all
> His days as one who treads the wall
> Of China and, on this hand, sees
> Cities and their civilities
> And, on the other, lions.

Joy suffered because she was as equally drawn to both men as she was to both sides of the wall. Paradoxical, sexual, alternating between elation and despair, her condition clearly called for diagnosis and treatment.

The chance came in June 1946 when Joy heard that her grandmother, Oma, had died and decided to go to Europe in order to see her family. She would look for a doctor who could help her, and an artist to teach her the basics of portraiture. Lady Muriel also encouraged her to show some of her flower paintings to the Royal Horticultural Society in London.

She and George were on safari at the beginning of August when she did a quick and striking portrait of him—blue-eyed, fair-haired, firm-featured and romantic. It is not accomplished, but she did it to prove to herself that she could catch a likeness in her portraits, and she succeeded.

The next day she received confirmation of her passage for August 29. Both of them were sad. Yet even on her last night in Kenya she made it clear she wanted to turn the clock back. George wrote, "She is still obsessed by P.B. My God, I pray for him to die."

George and Joy said a hurried good-bye on the deck of the *Winchester Castle* at Mombasa. These are his reflections that night, after three years of marriage.

August 29   Feel very sad as the future is so doubtful and God knows whether she will come back to me. It is a definite end of the first stage of our married life. Mixture of a little happiness and much unhappiness.

This time only she can decide whether there is to be a future or not. She was terribly upset when we parted.

EIGHT

A Gold Medal

1946–1947

1

When the *Winchester Castle* had made the open sea and was heading north up the coast of Africa, Joy watched a whale and then began to write. She was sharing a cabin with eleven other women.

She also started to sketch some figures for a chess set she planned to carve in ivory—the pawns were to portray different tribes. An old colonial hand with an erudite interest in the peoples of Africa offered her an introduction to the editor of the *Geographical Magazine* when they reached London.

The prospect of confronting the furies that had gathered around her early life and three marriages was daunting, and for reassurance she had made assignations with two men, one on the boat and another in London.

On the fifth night out, in the heat of the Red Sea, there was a party on board. Joy notes in her diary: "No Dorian!" She does not mention his surname. Dorian had been with her and George on the Tana and during her month alone at Malindi they had dined and been to various parties together.

To Joy's relief he boarded the ship the next morning when it put in at Port Sudan. His company added a tingle of excitement to the voyage. She painted his portrait and they discussed the various permutations of friendship between men and women.

September 9 Rather outspoken. Dorian: "I am clever enough to keep in love but not to marry."
Well the journey was much more pleasant like that.

When the ship docked Joy felt very lonely, but her spirits lifted as soon as she reached James and Susi Jeans who had invited her to stay.

Apart from his eminence as an astronomer, physicist, mathematician and author, Sir James was also an excellent organist. By this time Susi was internationally famous, giving organ recitals in London, Paris and Vienna. There were three Baroque organs in the house, one an exact replica of Bach's in Leipzig.

Joy's first full day in England was warm and sunny. Susi's friends arrived in the afternoon with their instruments, and music went on well into the evening. When the guests had all left and Susi had gone upstairs to put the children to bed, Joy and Jeans stood talking by an organ. Suddenly he went pale, began to gasp and collapsed. He died at two o'clock in the morning, and Joy suggested a death mask should immediately be cast.

Forty-five years later Lady Jeans still played the organ, the death mask lay on a table in her music room and she recalled with a glint of affection and humor Joy's first visit to England. "She was wearing a matching fur hat, coat, gloves, boots and handbag—all made of lion skin . . . She had brought with her some bits and pieces of ivory which she wanted to carve into chessmen. She was especially keen to start work on a giraffe for a knight and a phallic tower she planned for one of the castles, but found the ivory too hard for her knife. I suggested she should try a dentist's drill."

Following the line of the conversation, I asked Lady Jeans if Joy had seen an analyst in London. She smiled. "I introduced her to a doctor—Paul Kane—who agreed she ought to get help from someone. Having listened to her carefully he strongly recommended that it be a *woman*!"

The doctor he found for her in Hampstead was Barbara Lantos. Older than Joy, she was from a German-speaking family and had studied in Berlin and Paris before the war. Professionally Dr. Lantos saw analysis as a prelude to therapy rather than as a cure in itself and was more concerned about getting at the behavior of the ego or conscious mind than at "the unconscious." She published papers on relations between parent and infant, on connections between the body and the mind, and on aggression. There was another on sublimation—the direction of drives, such as the sexual, out of abnormal and into more acceptable channels; in other words, self-control. Her closest colleague had especially studied those attempted suicides whose real intent was to put an end to the objects of their early fixations rather than to their own lives.

Joy moved into a room nearby and saw Dr. Lantos each day. Badly in need of a dentist she persuaded one to deal with her teeth and also to lend her a drill for her chessmen. She then set about getting as much as she could out of the rest of London.

She meticulously followed up her various introductions. She took her tribal sketches to the *Geographical Magazine,* delivered her flower paintings to the Royal Horticultural Society and canvassed every suitable publisher to commission a set of flower illustrations. She was able to shortcut the waiting list for the Slade, then probably the finest art school of its kind in England.

There were women—and men—to dine with: Dorian appears, and in November there is a brief note in her diary: "Dorian. Love!" She also made friends with a socialist Member of Parliament who had a post in the new Labour Government, Julian Snow. For the time being the second of her assignations was delayed.

Apart from her analyst, Joy's course at the Slade was her principal preoccupation. According to their records she attended classes five or six times a week, from October 7 to December 19, and in 1947 from January 14 to March 24. The terms cost her £17 and £12 respectively.

The famous professor, Henry Tonks, had retired, and Joy found the first-year tuition too academic and formal; so she gate-crashed the life classes and no one objected. Her drawings show a good sense of line and her portraits in watercolor may have caught a likeness but are crude and over-colored. Nevertheless the course boosted her confidence and provided her with a valuable qualification.

At one stage Joy wrote eleven begging letters in the hope that a foundation or benefactor would finance a series of tribal studies when she returned to Kenya, but she was as unlucky in this as she was in finding a publisher for her flower paintings. Her chess set also ground to a standstill because the ivory proved too hard even for her drill, and when she tried to soften the chips in vinegar they simply flaked.

Her spirits rose when the editor of the *Geographical Magazine,* Michael Huxley, so much liked her tribal sketches that he said he would publish them with an article: Alys Reece agreed to write the text.

Joy's next success was even more heartening.

2

On February 18, 1947, the Royal Horticultural Society in London awarded Joy their highest honor for a painter—their Grenfell Gold Medal. Because there was no official citation we do not know which particular qualities most impressed her judges but the impact of her paintings was clearly remarkable because the gold medal had not been awarded during the previous twelve years.

A proper appreciation of Joy's work, her methods and an informative listing of her paintings could not have been attempted without the help of Mr. Jan Gillett, who first met her in 1952 when he went out to Kenya from the Royal Botanic Gardens at Kew, near London, while preparing his *Flora of Tropical East Africa*. Their paths crossed again when he returned to Kenya in 1965 as botanist in charge of the East African herbarium, attached to the museum in Nairobi.

Joy had begun to paint flowers seriously in order to give herself a raison d'être on museum safaris with Peter Bally and to help support the von Klarwills. She continued to paint during her marriage to George, partly because it provided her with an absorbing occupation wherever she found herself and partly to keep in touch with Bally.

Botanical painting has a long history, particularly distinguished in Austria, as in England, Germany, France and Holland. Although Joy never mentions him there was an outstanding sixteenth-century flower artist, born in Zurich, whose family name was the same as Joy's—Konrad Gesner (or Gessner).

Flower paintings fall into two classes the scientific or useful on the one hand, and the beautiful or decorative on the other. The former originated in drawings and woodcuts for identification in early herbals and medicinal works. Peter Bally belonged to this tradition.

Without being an exceptional botanist he was conscientious, an excellent field naturalist and a good diagnostician. His research on medical plants made him especially interested in the narcotic or antibiotic properties of thorn resins chewed by the Maasai for sore throats and latex from euphorbias applied to open wounds to burn out septic flesh. He specialized in succulents, such as aloes, long used as purges.

His plants, meticulously drawn and colored, were accompanied as needed by buds, fruit, seedpods, sections, roots and a scale; he gave details of each plant's identification, location and dating. Joy frequently failed to provide such details.

He was an ideal tutor for Joy. Although she was an amateur—

serious and dedicated but usually unpaid—her work was, in the opinion of experts at Kew, as accurate as his. She "had an eye for a plant," a sense of where to look for it, or to identify it by its habitat. As in all her work, botanical, anthropological and later ethological, she was intelligent and inquisitive, but she acquired her knowledge impulsively and eclectically. Nevertheless her paintings were naturalistic and authentic. The quality of Joy's work is uneven. Her better paintings are not simply accurate, they have a freshness, vitality and grace that lift them off the page. They also enjoy a boldness and vigor lacking in the work of many contemporary botanical artists, which may have something to do with the nature of Africa's flora and its light.

When her work was exhibited by the Royal Horticultural Society at the time of her award it was said that "she combined artistic layout with scientific accuracy not seen since the days of the great Dutch herbalists," who reached the high ranges of flower painting during the seventeenth and eighteenth centuries.

Most of Joy's flowers were painted between 1937, when she met Peter Bally, and 1947, after which she concentrated on her tribal portraits. During those years she completed about five hundred, not to mention several hundred line drawings. Few of the flowers had been photographed in color or accurately painted before, and her collection is therefore a pioneer achievement.

Many flower artists of the past received full justice when their work was reproduced from metal plates through the processes of engraving, etching or aquatint—often with a finish of hand coloring—and later by lithography, printing from treated stone or zinc.

Joy has been less well served. Altogether forty-seven of her paintings were reproduced as plates in the second, third and fourth editions (1939, 1949, 1957) of *Gardening in East Africa* edited by Dr. Jex-Blake, and another thirty-one appeared in *The Indigenous Trees of Uganda Protectorate* by W. J. Eggeling (1951) and *Kenya Trees and Shrubs* by P. G. Greenway and I. R. Dale (1961). She provided black and white line drawings only for Muriel Jex-Blake's *Some Wild Flowers of Kenya*.

Sadly the quality of Joy's color work simply does not survive in the double distortion of reduction to octavo format and the process of commercial letter-press printing prevalent in those decades. The closest any reproductions come to revealing the true character of her paintings are the nine quarto flower plates in *Joy Adamson's Africa* (1972), which was photolithographically reproduced and printed by

Brüder Rosenbaum, the family of her friend Susanne Schmutzer in Vienna.

It is a tragedy that such fine work has been seen by so few people, for only a minute proportion of the millions familiar with Joy Adamson's books and films are aware of her gifts as an artist.

Louis Leakey lobbied tirelessly for money to buy her paintings for the museum. Here is an extract from a letter Joy wrote to him on January 8, 1955.

> I have in front of me a letter which you wrote on March 13, 1953. If you have a copy, please read through it—otherwise I will send you the letter. You mentioned that you have 204 flower paintings which belong to the [museum] and 132 which belong to me and which are on exhibition. About the 132 which are still my property: if the Trustees want them, please try to raise the money—even if it is in instalments. I had these pictures now for 7–8 years at the Museum and I think it is not unfair to ask for a decision.

After very considerable effort, Leakey raised the necessary money and on September 7, 1957, Joy, who was on safari to Lake Rudolf with George and Elsa, sent the museum a receipt for £1,000 for 120 of these paintings.

Joy's pictures require careful preservation and full cataloging. They also deserve rotating display in the museum gallery and regular exhibition elsewhere, both in Kenya and abroad.

The loveliest books of botanical illustration have often brought their publishers to ruin, as did the classic portfolios of Redouté and Thornton, but it should be possible with a suitable subvention to produce a handsomely illustrated catalogue raisonné of her work. It would both be a fitting memorial to her and open the eyes of future generations to the botanical treasures of East Africa.

3

As soon as George heard of Joy's gold medal he sent her a cable of congratulation. It was just one in a series of letters and telegrams they each noted in their diaries. Joy was erratic as ever: she alternated between telling George she was homesick, sending him a pastel portrait of herself for Christmas and summoning him to London—and postponing her return to Kenya and warning him that she saw no future in their marriage.

At the time her second and long-awaited assignation was about to take place. Peter Bally, who had sailed up the west coast of Africa, arrived in London at the end of February. For a week they went to see Dr. Lantos each day, singly or together. Joy tried to fill their evenings with concerts or the opera. At the end of the week there is an enigmatic note in her diary: "Peter at Dr. Lantos. Miracle."

On the strength of whatever had happened she wrote to tell George that she wanted to end their marriage—though making no mention of Bally.

In March she left for Austria, going by way of Zurich, where she planned to meet Bally whose family lived there. However their reunion proved a grave disappointment because he clearly had no intention of resurrecting either their marriage or, it appears from the evidence, their intimacy.

Traveling through a defeated and occupied Austria in 1947 was like playing an elaborate board game. In 1945 America, Britain, France and Russia had divided the country into four areas of occupation. Progress depended on your nationality, the zones you wished to enter and which authority would stamp your permit. Where you stayed, where you ate and in which class or compartment you traveled were officially regulated. Joy was fortunate: although she had not obtained permission to go to Vienna, her British passport allowed her to enter the French-occupied zone of Vorarlberg, near Innsbruck, to ski with her family.

At first she felt endowed with a halo, being British; it was only after a few days when members of her family, and friend after friend, turned up to ski with her that she realized how tragically the country was racked by suspicion. Ex-Nazis—like her stepfather—and resistants, progressives and conservatives, Germans and Czechs, partisans and opponents of Russia, France, Britain and America wrestled with their hatreds, tragedies, secrets, ambitions and the battle to survive.

This was the dark legacy of the Hapsburg Empire and two world wars, so often concealed by images of chalets and edelweiss, and by echoes of Johann Strauss. Joy personified both sides of the coin. Like the field marshal's wife in *Der Rosenkavalier*, one of her cheeks smiled while a tear ran down the other. As she talked, laughed and drank wine, she learned the details of her stepfather's imprisonment for working in one of the Nazi-controlled ministries, and the expropriation by the Russian-controlled authorities of the entire Weisshuhn estates.

Despite a number of applications Joy failed to get permission to go to Vienna, so she returned to London. She spent two days in Paris with Julian Snow. He becomes Ju or St Julian in her diary and must have been an excellent guide, for he had studied at the Sorbonne before taking his first job in Africa in 1930.

Once they were back in London she needed only ten days, with Snow's advice, to obtain a permit for Vienna, particularly since she could claim that she was not only visiting her mother but had to consult an eminent psychoanalyst, Dr. August Aichorn, recommended by Barbara Lantos.

Joy seemed to move through the half-lit world of postwar Europe like a flickering candle with a retinue of moths. She had a farewell lunch with Dorian, who sent her a telegram with his love on the morning she left for Vienna. As her train crossed the border into Austria, she was worried by the crush of elderly people in the corridor outside her empty compartment and invited some of them in.

To her absolute astonishment there, behind them, stood not just one of the two men who had proposed to her more than fifteen years before, but both!

A few days later Julian Snow arrived, and although he received some rough treatment from her, he joined in all the reunions with her family and old friends, among them Herbert Tichy, whose sister had introduced her to Ziebel von Klarwill, and who talked of coming to Africa one day.

Nevertheless, it was a grim month for Joy. Her mother and two sisters were hungry and depressed, and her mother still wore the same dresses that Joy remembered from ten years before. It was hardly surprising that all three were caught in a time warp of that period. Her mother openly stood by her husband and counted the days until his release. In her heart she must have wished Germany had won the war.

Twenty thousand houses in Vienna had been damaged or destroyed by bombing and fighting. The streets were the dark and sinister thoroughfares immortalized in Graham Greene's *The Third Man*— like the sewers they were rat runs for black market traders in almost anything from bread to diamonds or, more precious still, penicillin. There had been more than 150,000 Jews, including many of Joy's best friends, before the war; only a fraction now remained.

In every sense Joy felt an outsider. Estranged from her mother, she was bored by her elder sister, Traute, and Dorle had grown up almost a stranger. She was so worried about her younger sister that she suggested she too should see Dr. Aichorn.

August Aichorn was a leading Freudian psychoanalyst who had made his name for his treatment of male juvenile delinquents. He believed that their antisocial behavior stemmed from inadequate child–parent relationships or the death of a parent. In such a case the ego might not achieve proper sublimation of its desires in keeping with acceptable behavior. The superego or conscience, which should override these desires and moderate gratification, failed to do so. As a result anyone who stood in the way of such indulgence was hated. Unfortunately his approach to Joy, both older and a woman, totally failed. The one word "Betrayal" is scribbled in her diary. Aichorn fared no better with Dorle.

It is probable that the roots of Joy's disturbance or psychoneurosis were embedded in the recurring conflicts between her wishes and their fulfillment—her thwarted feelings for her parents, her first lover and her husbands, and her failure to do justice, in her own eyes, to her gifts. Sir George Pickering, a Regius Professor of Medicine at Oxford University, believed that the achievements of many artists, scientists and religious leaders derived from frustrations of this kind.

His book *Creative Malady* argues that Florence Nightingale and Mary Baker Eddy, both extremely uncomfortable associates, harnessed their neuroses to advance their lifelong and enduring achievements. He adds that analysis, or any other such alleviation of their conditions, would have robbed them of the passion that secured their success.

When Joy's permit expired at the end of a month she raced back to England. She was genuinely grieved to see her mother reduced to such straits. She respected Traute's efforts as a journalist and writer to earn enough for herself and her son; she had written a standard "Lives of the Saints" for Austrian schools and a miracle play performed in the state theater. Joy had also tried to help Dorle overcome her problems. Nonetheless, the visit to Vienna left her empty and drained the residual drops of her family affection. From then on she felt alone in the world, and no more than a sense of duty toward her mother and sisters remained.

It took Joy only a week in London to tie up all the loose ends there, write to George telling him not to meet her at Mombasa and catch the boat at Tilbury.

Despite the treatment she had come so far to find, neither of her doctors had been able to exorcise her furies. But although she had not been able to shed her emotional dependency on Bally, in another and very important respect she had changed. She now felt qualified to assert her economic independence as an artist.

Essentially European and sophisticated in her background, talents and tastes, she was about to fling herself once more into the life of the beautiful, but dangerous and untamed, continent she had adopted, as if aware that although it could not give her peace of mind it might still offer her the chance of fulfillment.

NINE

Frontiersman

1938–1947

1

While Joy was enduring the roar of traffic in London, Paris and Vienna, George went about his business among the lions of Africa. During the ten years that she had spent painting wildflowers, he had been covering the Northern Frontier and the Tana down to the coast for the Game Department. A brief spell with the army during the war accounted for his only absence.

When war was declared against Germany in 1939 he had wanted to join up like Terence, who served with the Royal Army Service Corps in transport and then as a garrison engineer. George, however, was told to patrol the Samburu country in case the Italians in Ethiopia decided to show where their sympathies lay and strike across the border. If this happened, he was expected to deter the Samburu from stampeding down into the European farmlands. His front was about two hundred miles long; his force was six game scouts and eight tribal policemen.

In June 1940 the Italians finally declared war on the Allies and George was released from the Game Department to join the army. His military career vacillated between frustration and farce, although the occasional jab of activity set his adrenaline flowing.

At first he was attached to Military Intelligence. Sleeping out under the stars, he recruited scouts from Somaliland—where they fiercely resented the Italian occupation—to report on the movement of troops. Their observations sometimes caused headaches because the scouts could not differentiate between a lorry and an armored car, or a caterpillar tractor and a tank.

George and his men were involved in only one skirmish, and that opened with a five-hour march in the heat of the day and culminated in an elaborate encircling movement. The scratch force included some West Africans who kept pointing their loaded rifles at George's feet, a British NCO who fainted and a platoon commander whom George recognized from his school days and who lobbed grenades into the wrong depression, allowing the enemy to escape and retaliate.

During the first major advance into Somaliland in February 1941, George joined a new force of irregular cutthroats led by his old friend Hugh Grant, who had set aside his bow and arrow for the duration.

"All who take the sword will perish by the sword," according to St. Matthew—and it was true of Grant. After the war he became a DC among the Maasai and was involved in a dispute with one of them over his favorite cow. The warrior threw a greased spear at Grant with such force that it ran right through him. The Maasai was able to pick it up and run off, but he was caught and hanged for murder because the greasing was evidence of his intent.

The advance moved so fast that George was left, fuming, to help police the occupied territory. By the use of cunning and brute force, he broke up a mob that had come to lynch an Italian on his farm. He also restored another farmer to his banana plantation, had the man's house rid of the excrement dumped in it and recovered his tractors by threatening to have the Somali ringleaders hanged from a tree if they did not comply with his orders.

According to Joy, George used to say it was necessary to instill fear in order to exercise authority. It was so uncharacteristic of him that perhaps he made the remark when telling these war stories. Nevertheless, it is also true he once beat an old Dorobo poacher until he revealed where he was hiding his spear, his bows, his traps and his larder of meat. Joy also said that she was convinced George would have arrested and strung up his grandmother had he found her poaching.

For the next few months George was posted to Afmadu, a small station in the desert. He lived alone except for an attractive Somali companion of whom no more is known than her name, Fatima, and the twinkle in George's eyes when he mentioned her.

In the evenings he would sit on the veranda with his sundowner and before the light faded blaze away at rats and salmon-pink cobras with a heavy machine gun mounted on a tripod that had been left behind by the Italians. In the mornings he fed another Italian legacy, a lame ostrich wounded in the fighting. He also took a nightjar chick into his infirmary until the mother returned and adopted it.

In August 1942, to his immense relief, he was released from his duties and could return to his job. But just because the two European powers had called a halt to their fighting on African soil it did not mean that George's experience of killing in Africa had come to an end.

2

By the time Joy went to Europe, change was in the air and not long afterward Gerald Reece was appointed Governor of Somaliland. He was replaced as Provincial Commissioner by an equally remarkable man, Richard Turnbull, who once said of George, with a touch of irony: "He was a very brave man. A year never went by without his being nearly killed by some wild animal or other."

It was true, although no one was ever less given to heroics. During his first decade with the Game Department he must have been charged or threatened by more than a dozen animals—twice by hippos, twice by rhinos, once by a buffalo, several times by elephants and five times by lions.

On the face of it this sounds reckless, if not like sheer stupidity, but it wasn't. William Hale, who succeeded Archie Ritchie as Chief Game Warden in 1949, said that when it came to dealing with a dangerous animal George was unsurpassed.

Although the department was slowly expanding, with fourteen wardens instead of the original six, each commanding an average of more than twenty scouts, it was still a brotherhood. Hale's assistant was George's old hunting companion Sir Alick Kirkpatrick, whose enjoyment of women and parties had not been diminished by his wartime service in the Air Force. At least half the wardens had fought with the army, and one was a brigadier.

There were, in addition, about two hundred honorary game wardens who included men from every walk of life—the police, vets, white hunters, farmers and scientists. Terence was one.

Always a loner, Terence developed an intuitive skill in countering crop raids by elephants and buffalo. He knew the buffalo so well, and their reluctance to return to the same place twice, that he could anticipate their moves. On moonless nights, with the lightest of rifles, he waited until they were almost on top of him before he fired; he shot more than forty this way. In a hurry one night he went out in only his pajama trousers and the cord came undone as he fired.

The Game Department's authority was of course derived from the Government, whereas the first National Park, set up outside Nairobi under Mervyn Cowie in 1946, was responsible to a board of independent trustees.

Other members of the cast enforcing the game laws were the district commissioners, who acted as magistrates before whom George prosecuted poachers and illicit traders, and the police officers, who were called in to help with the more serious cases of villainy. Very occasionally George was asked to support the DC or the police, as in the case of this incident he described in a letter to Joy.

At Banya a police patrol of eleven men had run into a band of over forty raiders and in the ensuing battle had killed five Gelubba at a cost of nearly four hundred rounds of ammunition and one askari hit in the finger! As a result the natives were not in a friendly mood.

A few days later the DC arrived and had to conduct an enquiry into the fight. I went along with him, together with a strong escort of Police. It was a most gruesome sight, bits of bodies lying about torn to pieces by hyenas and vultures.

The Veterinary Department and the game wardens supported each other very closely in the field. One of their officers, Harry Benson, who was based in Isiolo and shared many adventures with George from 1938 to 1954, is a forthright Australian. Over ninety, with a mind as sharp as a *simi*, he wrote this from South Africa about George.

He was as tough as goats' knees, could walk incredible distances and go hungry for long periods.

He was a very good tracker, far in advance of the average black or white man—I would say on a par with the Australian aboriginals whom I knew very well, being raised amongst them in Queensland.

He had an uncanny sense of knowing that he was in the close vicinity of his quarry, whether an animal or poacher, and was utterly without fear of man or beast, but cautious with it. He was an excellent shot.

A simple man, his whole life was bound up with nature and all it meant. His love of wild life was incredible, yet he could control it fairly.

Control it he had to, in different ways and with the extraordinarily limited means at his disposal. It was a challenge he loved, except for the paperwork: his reports, his accounts and preparations for appearing in court.

Once a month he assembled and paid all his game scouts and mustered his tribal police known as *dubas*. Only thumbnail sketches of some of these characters can convey the gulf that divided their way of life from those of their contemporaries throughout most of the world.

Olo was a brave but impetuous Somali. George describes how he and two Boran guides, one named Godana Dima, ignored his warning and chased a lion he had wounded.

Next thing I knew, there were several shots, a loud roar, and growls and yells. I raced up to see the lion on top of Olo, it left him and came towards me and I killed it. Olo had fired one shot as it got to him. It seized him by the thigh and shook him like a rat before dropping him. Olo got up and caught the lion by the chin and fought it.

Godana Dima dashed in and tried to spear it, but the weapon was a very poor one and merely cut the skin. Nothing daunted, he recovered the spear and using both hands stabbed it into the lion's flank. This time the spear just bent but it caused the beast to leave Olo and that was when I shot it.

George was so impressed by Godana Dima's spirit that he immediately engaged him as a scout and they were still together when George shot Elsa's mother eight years later.

Munda belonged to the Kamba tribe, famous as carvers and hunters. He asked George for leave so that he could have himself cleansed from an evil spell placed on him and his family. George refused and sent him to hospital, and although Munda was cured of his malaria he died. After that George allowed his men to go home to see their own witch doctor in similar cases—and they always recovered.

Lodogia, a Dorobo, was one of George's earliest and most reliable trackers. A witch doctor successfully cast off a fatal spell on him for which his fee was two goats, five pounds of tobacco and a bottle of brandy.

Lowakoop was another Dorobo, a notorious poacher whom George and his scouts tracked along a heavily trapped trail to his mountain cave. They failed to find him there but captured instead his Samburu mistress, abducted from the plain below. The cave was packed with his snares, spears, bows, arrows, poison-brewing apparatus and magic powders for casting spells on his prey. Only by using the Samburu girl as a lure was Lowakoop finally trapped. As soon as he was let out of prison George gave him a job.

Gobus, a Turkana poacher, became an especially loyal game scout and later gave George a talisman to protect his life during the Mau Mau rising. Gobus had an extraordinary experience with elephants one time when he was returning to camp with his aged mother. On the way he had to answer a call of nature and told his mother he would catch up with her shortly.

The old woman was half blind and in the gathering darkness took the wrong path. After going some way, she realised that she was lost. In the manner of her kind, she made herself comfortable at the foot of a tree and decided to spend the night as best she might.

Gobus hurried on to the scouts' lines expecting to find his mother. A search was made but, owing to the darkness, it was unavailing. The old woman under the tree fell asleep.

Late at night she was aroused to find herself surrounded by elephants. A young bull stood over her and felt her with his trunk; she told him in Turkana to "get out." He backed away, and again approached and felt her over: again she told him to "be gone." He then tore off thorny branches and carefully covered the old woman under a great pile until she was completely imprisoned. To add insult to injury, he urinated over her.

Next morning a Turkana herding goats saw the pile of thorns and, hearing cries for help, released the old woman who was little the worse for her frightening experience. It is well known among natives that elephants will cover over the body of a human they have killed.

Lembirdan, George's most intelligent and trustworthy scout, was the Samburu he had lent to Joy when she was on Mount Kenya. Well set-up with cattle, he could not resist the adventure of a game scout's life. When an elephant that had already killed several men chased him to the edge of a precipice, he turned and shot it at such close range that he was splashed with its blood. While he and George were after another elephant, George had to retreat and tripped in its path. He was saved by Lembirdan, who stood firm, fired and deflected the elephant's pursuit. George resolved never to turn his back on a charging animal again.

3

During the year that Joy was away in Europe George could once more throw himself single-mindedly into his work. News of stock and crop raids by lions, leopards, buffalo and elephants, or of plagues of hyenas and baboons, reached him all too fast. On the other hand, he had to organize his network of headmen, ex-scouts, traders, informers and gossips to send him tips of flagrant or covert poaching activity.

From the beginning of time the tribespeople had lived off the animals who shared the land with them, taking no more than was needed for themselves and their families. Suddenly the white man laid down laws about what might be hunted, where, when and how. It was breathtaking arrogance and George used his authority with great understanding, especially in times of severe drought or other hardship.

Wrongdoers never knew where he and his scouts were going to turn up next. By tireless tracking, assiduous searches in hollow baobab trees or under prostitutes' beds, raids, ambushes and the occasional use of a roadblock, he usually got to the heart of the matter.

He loathed all forms of cruelty as he did wanton killing. The worst suffering was inflicted by traps and snares: concealed pits lined with sharpened stakes, weighted drop spears hanging from branches and triggered when their ropes were nudged, head-height snares along game paths and—most brutal of all—snares fashioned from wire hawsers and attached to heavy logs so that when an elephant or giraffe stepped into them the wire bit into their flesh. The animal could get no purchase to snap the wire and the log might drag behind it for days before it died or was found by the hunter and killed.

The most lethal weapon—far more effective than an obsolete rifle—was the poisoned arrow. In George's territory there were two sources of poison, Ethiopia and the Giriama tribe on the coast.

As a botanist, Peter Bally was fascinated by the way in which the Giriama prepared their poison. This is from an account he wrote for the Chief Game Warden:

> The ingredients vary with the tribe and the district but always contain *Acokanthera;* where this tree does not occur *Strophanthus* or *Adenium* may be used to substitute it. All three belong to one family of plants containing very strong heart poisons.
>
> So far as is known the poison consists of four ingredients.
>
> 1. An extract from *Acokanthera*. The individual trees vary in toxicity and the best poison is obtained from the twigs of those under which dead birds or rats are found.
>
> 2. Juice from the leaves of *Aloe rabaiensis* which dries into a black, splintering lacquer, extremely bitter, used in small doses as a powerful purge.
>
> 3. The root bark from a tree of the family *Rutaceae* which has a pungently foul smell.
>
> 4. The body of a shrew which is said to make the wounded quarry escape in a straight line (apparently the habit of shrews).
>
> It is said that when fresh the poison will kill an elephant so fast that he will fall before he has covered 500 yards.

The Boni, who were neighbors of the Giriama and had an ancient, even aboriginal, hunting tradition, acquired the poison to tip their four-foot arrows, fired from six-foot bows with a pull of a hundred pounds. The poisoned arrowheads were wrapped in leaves to preserve their potency and avoid accidents.

Although elephants and rhinos were prime targets they were not the only victims of commercial poaching. If I had to choose one animal that epitomizes all that is beautiful, savage and mysterious in Africa it would be the leopard. So prized was its skin that it was relentlessly hunted throughout Ethiopia, Somalia and northern Kenya.

Sadly it has not been just Renaissance princes and artists like Titian and Rubens, Turkana and other tribal coxcombs, or a cosmopolitan plutocracy and Hollywood stars, who have found leopard skin irresistibly lovely. The proliferation of central heating not only modified indoor clothing but fueled a demand for fur coats when people left the new warmth of their homes. Fashion quickly responded and nothing was more alluring than leopard skin. The finest for depth and softness came from Somalia.

In Kenya there were few white households that could resist having one or two leopard skins stretched out on a chair or the floor, or pinned as a trophy to the wall. Joy particularly loved the skins.

Lower down the scale of merchandise were spiral horns, elephant and wildebeest tails for fly whisks, elephant-hair bracelets and trinkets worked from hoof, bone, tooth and claw.

With unremitting vigor, George managed to keep poaching in his sprawling domain at tolerable levels. Offenders were arrested, roped and marched for trial to the nearest DC. The guilty were fined or possibly committed to a spell in what they good-humoredly called "Hoteli King Georgei." There they were sheltered, clothed and fed in congenial company until they emerged from prison and returned to their hunting. George gave this account of one year's work.

There were over eighty convictions for game offences, including twelve at the coast. These involved the deaths of about ten elephants, twelve rhino, fifteen giraffe, two lions, two leopards and a few lesser animals.

Compared with the massacre that devastated the elephant herds and virtually wiped out the rhinos forty years later, modern poaching had not yet come of age.

If poaching control smacked of playing cowboys and Indians, the supervision of licensed hunting occasionally descended to the level of cops and robbers.

It was George's task to issue licenses in his area: a licence listed the type and number of game each gun might shoot and the "block" of territory that might be hunted. Certain of the larger animals were subject to a fee and could be shot only in the company of a professional "white hunter" under the strictest conditions. For instance, no animal might be shot close to a car, and any game wounded must be immediately followed up and accounted for.

Once or twice offenders who were caught red-handed by George and who tried to defy him by driving off had to think again when he shot out their tires or put a bullet into the radiator. Small game and bird shooting was less stringently controlled, but George set the limits of each season according to whether nesting was early or late.

Usually the white hunters who saw themselves as a corps d'élite, numbering fewer than twenty in Kenya, were on the side of the angels. They were highly skilled and efficient, tough, brave and excellent shots. If found breaking the law they lost their licenses and their livelihoods.

Beyond that, their reputations depended on obtaining for their clients the maximum number of outstanding trophies. If they found poachers disturbing their favorite hunting blocks they immediately reported them to George or the police.

A white hunter had to match his prowess as a sportsman with the skill of a diplomat. On safari his shower water in camp had to be piping hot and his cocktails ice-cold. He could never be short of a blanket, a steak or a suitable anecdote. Above all he could never run out of patience. Nevertheless, he sometimes did, as George recounts in a letter to Joy.

I met again the Mexican multi-millionaire Pasquel. He has been out with five other Mexicans and a Russian strong-man as personal bodyguard; his job I think is to deal with irate husbands whose wives Pasquel has seduced. They had as hunters, Eric Rundgren, Myles Turner, Roberts and young Blacklens (the son of our ex-grocer, a very nice lad).

First of all Turner had a big row and left them, then Rundgren had a serious quarrel which nearly ended in a fight and he also left them—all over their peculiar methods of hunting.

After a pleasant chat I went and had a look at their huge pile of trophies, among them I saw the heads of two "baby" greater kudu. He said, "Oh, we have such a short time left and even a little kudu is better than none!"

I went back to the Game Department, told William that I wanted to run Pasquel in for the two baby kudu. William stuttered and stammered and finally put me on to Alick Kirkpatrick who promptly said confiscate the heads and get all the evidence.

Eric Rundgren had indeed left the safari as the result of a scrap, but not with one of the Mexicans. George passed the story on to Joy.

Eric Rundgren turned up and he told me all about his adventure with the leopard and he was very lucky to get away with it. When it charged it got on top of him, then he managed to get on top of it and pin it to the ground, all the time receiving terrible bites.

Eventually, in desperation, in order to avoid his face being bitten, he stuffed one hand down its throat. In the meantime the two brave Mexicans stood by and did nothing until a boy dragged one of them by force up to the leopard and made him shoot it.

Today commercial hunting is highly controversial. Nevertheless in the 1940s and 1950s, probably no more than an average of 150 elephants and 125 rhinos were shot under hunting license each year, while altogether the licenses brought in more than £20,000, or approximately half the annual cost of running the Game Department.

At the end of the 1970s, after legal hunting was abolished, poachers were killing more than 5,000 elephants a year in Kenya, with not a penny of the proceeds going to the state. The game had lost the eagle-eyed and jealous protection of the professional hunters, and as George had predicted, the finest elephants were the first to go, leaving a population "little bigger than hippos with tusks like toothpicks."

It is an equation worth pondering in a continent where governments need to earn every penny they can from their natural resources, and where amenities like wildlife, more prized by the outside world than by the electorate, must be shown to earn their keep if they are to survive.

4

It was when the animals in the NFD were at their most troublesome that George had the best chance of getting to know them well. In a crisis he might have to study them, or wait up for them, for days and nights on end before he could decide how to handle them.

Arguments still rage about which is the most dangerous animal in Africa after man and the mosquito. A solitary buffalo, cunning and, if wounded, implacable in its determination to defend itself and destroy its enemy? A startled and shortsighted rhino, long and wrongly assumed to be insensitive and antisocial, but in any case fearless because it has nothing to fear but a bullet? A strident cow elephant, relentless in the use of her flailing trunk, stabbing tusks and pounding feet to defend her calf? Or a lion that is hungry, old, wounded, antagonized, or that for some other reason has acquired a taste for human flesh?

George tried to work out the best way to take on all these hazards yet keep his killing to a minimum. In some ways a determined buffalo was the most difficult to cope with, but he avoided disaster throughout his professional career, although one cracked a few of his ribs and broke a bone in his foot. In a tight corner, rather than turn his back, George applied a simple technique. His godson once watched him, relaxed and standing sideways on a narrow track, while an angry rhino thundered toward him. At the very last second he gave a neat little jump backward into the bush and the creature hurtled harmlessly past.

Almost the only occasion on which he admitted to being scared was when he tried out a new stratagem to protect the fields around a mission that were being raided by elephants. His tactic was to wait in the elephants' path, hoping his scent would disperse them: if one turned aggressive he would shoot it, believing it would deter the rest from returning.

February 25   Put my plan into execution and getting to within thirty yards of some cows, shouted. Out came a cow, screaming. My right barrel turned her and the second got her through the heart. The rest of the herd made off.

February 26   Came on the tail of a vast herd, feeding in very dense cover. I was really frightened. Sat down and thought over the situation for twenty minutes or so. Having come deliberately with the intention of being charged, I could scarcely back out! Found a small open space with a mound at one end which gave me a clear view. Started talking loudly to my men. The elephants just turned away and went off in a stampede with shrill trumpeting.

It is impossible to approach an elephant on foot in the bush without a feeling of awe at its sheer size and power; of respect for the intelligence in its eye and its sensitivity to scent; of admiration for the beauty of its tusks and the cleverness of its trunk; and of fear at the havoc it could inflict if it abandoned its restraint for only a few seconds.

To watch a family, a clan or a large herd of elephants at close quarters intensifies and broadens these feelings because it is obvious that their social life is subtle, complex and in many ways like our own. A herd is not a random group of elephants but a gathering of families around a matriarch whose female relations keep in touch for the comfort and safety of numbers. An elephant's life span is about the same as ours. To some extent a cow must rely on her own strength, initiative and extraordinary memory, but she enjoys company and needs a degree of security and family support while she educates her offspring.

It is for these reasons that both the solitary confinement of a female in a zoo, and the systematic slaughter of matriarchs because they carry sizable tusks, are criminally cruel.

Each time a mature female comes into season, males who have been living singly or loosely together, shadowing the herd of cows and calves, pick up her far-reaching, low-frequency rumblings, well below the range of our own ears, and follow them to her. After mating a male will stand beside her but will probably be displaced by a larger or more assertive one. He in turn may be ousted by a superior rival. Since the female ovulates at the end of her cycle the seed of the most powerful will prevail.

The older the elephant the more ivory it makes each year, and the old males carry the heaviest of all. Often the oldest are found with one or two younger bulls acting as askaris or sentinels. Elephants are not normally aggressive except in defense of their young: if they are, it is almost invariably because they are suffering from festering bullet wounds or wire snares biting into their feet or their trunks.

Patiently and enthralled—usually at dawn or at dusk but sometimes in the magical light of a full moon—George watched the private lives of these great animals. He witnessed a pair mating not alone, as he had been told, but in the middle of a restless and inquisitive herd. He was entertained by the games of the young and their lessons in feeding, bathing, safety procedures and social decorum. On two occasions he watched elephants support a wounded companion on either side and bear it off into the safety of the forest. The Somalis in the Lorian Swamp told him how a herd had sent out scouts to search for an alternative water supply when their own ran dry. Together he and Joy once kept utterly silent while a group of bulls quietly carried off and hid the bones and tusks of their dead leader.

Elephants succeeded in terrifying George as nothing else had. Several times they tried to kill him, but his respect for them continued to grow.

The certainty of conflict with elephants occurred only where they could not resist plantations, especially in the south of George's territory. Temptation for lions, in the form of cattle and goats, was rife all over the NFD. Running warfare sometimes filled every hospital bed in the missions with cases of mauling. The boldest and hungriest lions were quite unafraid.

Years later, wiseacres who criticized George for "destroying the lion's natural fear of man" in those he released were speaking from prejudice or ignorance. Here is an episode from *My Pride and Joy*.

Up at Lalalei the Samburu reported that nine of their men had been eaten by lions in the previous twelve months. The day before I could get there a youth was killed while herding his cattle. I went to the scene and found that three lions had gone through the herd and chased the boy around a bush before killing and eating him. It was extraordinary that they should choose him in the middle of so many cattle. That night we made a particularly strong thorn boma around the cattle, the donkeys and ourselves, but a lioness tried to break in and I shot her. Two hours later I was woken by the donkeys and going to investigate with a torch and revolver saw another lioness trying to break through. I emptied my revolver at her but she vanished.

In the morning when a ranger brought me tea, he pointed to the sand around my sleeping bag. About eighteen inches from my head was the spoor of yet another of these man-eating lions— which I found extremely unnerving.

George and his patrol followed the lions into some scrub which they drove in line.

Just as we emerged from it there were loud yells and then a growl from the left of the line. I saw the end ranger go down under a lioness; seconds later the man next to him ran up and fired his rifle into her ear. We expected the first man to be badly mauled but he was unscathed and was mercilessly ribbed by his colleagues for having cried out. This second lioness, like the one in the night, appeared to have no physical cause for her man-eating though I found a fresh graze across her chest from one of my revolver shots.

We had a ten-hour chase after the third lion, a male, which finally lost patience and turned on us with a furious charge. He too showed no physical defects to account for his grisly behavior. This experience combined with a number of others convinced me that following up a lioness, especially if she is wounded, is much more dangerous than going after a male. He will growl and give away his position: she will stay hidden in silence and is launched on her final, lightning charge before she lets out her snarl.

It was a charge like this that caused George to shoot Elsa's mother and obliged him to begin his study of lions in earnest.

Far more often he saw prides when they had fed, and were resting together, perhaps sprawling on their backs. Then he could appreciate the atmosphere of the family circle. He was touched when a magnificent male tolerated impertinent youngsters stalking and killing the tuft of his tail, if a lioness suckled the cubs of another who had gone off to hunt and by the displays of liking and loyalty that hold young males together when they are cast out, as adolescent bull elephants are, from the family.

He grew sensitive to their every movement and noise, and to the telltale sounds—or absence of them—uttered or suppressed by other creatures alarmed at their presence. Several times he was alerted to the unexpected maneuver of a lion by the sudden silence of cicadas by day or crickets after dark.

He frequently observed the rituals of the lions' courtship and mating. Alerted by the scent of a female in estrus, a male would approach her, usually to be rebuffed at his first attempt. If he persisted she might accept him after a few token cuffs. At the climax he would nip her on the side or nape of the neck, then she would roll over on her back and purr.

The final performance might last no longer than a minute but it was usually repeated three times an hour throughout the day and night. On one occasion George broke camp five days after the nuptials had begun nearby, and they were still continuing.

If elephants won his respect, lions compelled his admiration, and increasingly he stood up for their right to the minimum of interference from man. Nevertheless, there were some circumstances that leveled the odds between them.

5

However generous nature can be in East Africa, it can also be mercilessly mean. Drought is a recurring affliction even more devastating than war, killing hundreds and thousands of people and millions of animals, domestic and wild.

In 1951, the eight-mile-long lagoon of the Lorian Swamp, the destination of the Ewaso Ngiro River and sole source of water for a large population of Somalis, entirely dried up. The young, the sick and the old were failing. Every leaf and blade of grass disappeared and the swamp's muddy bed became as hard as concrete, networked with cracks. Hyenas and jackals scavenged for the last of the fish; emaciated antelope and elephants and forty thousand livestock lay dying or dead all around; vultures were too bloated to take to the air.

When George and Joy approached, in response to a call from the Somali chief, Abdi Ogli, they were overwhelmed by the stench of putrefaction. A camel had been cemented in mud to its neck for thirty-six days but when George touched its head it opened an eye. He shot it as he did many other animals in extremis.

His main task was to drive off or kill elephants competing so desperately for the last of the water that they were attacking people and their stock. They tried to seize *debes* or gourds from the water carriers, and even damp loin cloths off men who had been scooping water from holes dug twenty feet down. When George shot one elephant standing defiantly over an improvised well it crumpled on to a sheep too feeble to move out of its way.

Total disaster was finally averted, when far away in the mountains where the Ewaso Ngiro rises, the rains broke. The river began very slowly to seep down its course like melted milk chocolate, first filling the cracks and the waterholes dug in the bed and then slaking the parched earth before it could make real headway. Joy wrote: "herds of camels, sheep and goats appeared as if by magic, and stood knee-deep in the water, bleating and gurgling."

Caught in the spirit of general elation, she and George jumped in the car and hurried upstream to watch the reborn river flow over Chanler's Falls in a spectacular cascade. Normally prudent, they stood in the gorge overhung by rock, just below the falls, staring as the debris and two huge tree trunks tipped over the edge. When the sluggish stream suddenly flash-flooded and raged through the narrow canyon they were nearly drowned.

6

These were the days before ecology had come of age and before two Nobel Prize winners, Konrad Lorenz and Niko Tinbergen, opened our eyes to the wealth of knowledge and self-knowledge to be gathered from a sensitive and systematic look at the way mammals and birds behave in the wild.

George Schaller had not yet produced his famous scientific study *The Serengeti Lion*, Iain Douglas-Hamilton his findings about the family behavior of elephants at Manyara or Jane Goodall her revelations about the tool use, loyalties and internecine warfare among the chimpanzees of Gombe. Nor had Dian Fossey embarked on her obsessively dedicated surveillance of the gorillas in the Virunga Mountains which proved fatal to her but brought hope for the great apes. Compared with all these scientific accumulations of fact, George Adamson's were the random observations of a wandering naturalist.

On the other hand, he enjoyed one inestimable privilege that these zoologists lacked, and that will probably never be available to anyone again. For years he had been able to walk for weeks on end across vast tracts of an Africa quite undisturbed by man's building, planting or other perceptible interference. For days his senses and mind were continuously focused on the landscape and its inhabitants as they had naturally evolved since the beginning of time.

The groan of an approaching lorry had no chance of impinging on the silence often disturbed only by the sigh of the wind or the whisper of insects; there were no jet planes to rip through the peace; he never carried a radio.

The integrity of these safaris was further preserved by his acceptance of the dimension of time inherent in unspoiled space. The sun became his clock, the moon his calendar, and his pace was the stride of a camel or his own two feet. This tempo was dictated by the earth over which he was moving and which pulsed like an organism as it absorbed air and moisture, circulating them through soil and underground tubes and cavities for nourishment.

In fact an extremely persuasive thesis was advanced by James Lovelock in 1971 that Earth, or Gaia as he calls it, *is* a living organism contained within the finite membrane of its atmosphere and sustained in a state of balance by bacterial life on the surface and in the depths of our landmass and oceans.

In the same way that we are familiar with our domestic timetables or office routines George knew by heart the annual, monthly and circadian rhythms of the earth and its creatures.

Like the innocent, most take their sleep when the sun has left the sky. Elephants drop off after midnight and have been known to snore. The giraffe will doze for an hour or two at a time but never rest its neck on the ground for more than five minutes. The vultures, sun-birds and cicadas sleep in the trees or creepers, butterflies close their wings and the aloes their petals.

When the light begins to thicken, the lion stretches after its long siesta and the hyena emerges from its burrow, both in need of flesh and blood. The bat, the wide-eyed bush baby and the hooting owl begin to hunt through the acacias for moths, eggs or scurrying mice. The crickets start to chirr and the hanging flowers of the baobab open and scent the darkness.

Up above, the spinning of the Earth seems to turn the compass of stars. The twinkling constellations guide nomads through the cool of the night to their seasonal grazing; falcons, swifts and other migrants steer north by them to the long summer days of rich feeding, vital while they raise their young.

As the Earth rocks back and forth on its axis, every six months, another, slower, rhythm determines the length of the days, the flow of the winds and the timing of the rains, while our annual orbit of the sun alters again our exposure to the stars.

Each of these phenomena, creating alterations in light, magnetic fields, temperature and moisture, stimulates other changes—leaf growth, fruiting, the secretion of hormones and release of irresistible urges. These in turn activate the dynamics of existence, feeding, hunting, migration, the adoption of territory, battle, mating, nesting, birth, aestivation—seclusion during the desiccation of the dry seasons—and death.

Once he became part of this pattern George acquired an astonishing understanding of its animal life and its tribes—whether hunters, nomads or tillers of the soil—whom he was there to protect and restrain. He was therefore able to sense in which way they would act or respond in any situation.

Animated by the same forces that governed the lives of the elephants, the lions and the tribesmen, he shared with them the genetic imperative to mate and sire offspring. He therefore found Joy's behavior baffling and painful. But unlike her he seemed imbued with the sanity that derives from the protean wholeness of the organic world. He remained at one with himself, firmly grounded in the land he had adopted as his home and that he hoped to go on exploring with her.

As a way of life it was, of course, still prey to violence, cruelty and pain, but not at the degraded level or on the titanic scale developed and introduced by the West. This is the impact Africa made on Carl Jung in 1926.

> I had the good fortune to taste the world of Africa, with its incredible beauty and its equally incredible suffering, before the end came. Our camp life proved to be one of the loveliest interludes in my life. I enjoyed the "divine peace" of a still primeval country. Never had I seen so clearly "man and the other animals" (Herodotus). Thousands of miles lay between me and Europe, mother of all demons. The demons could not reach me here—there were no telegrams, no telephone calls, no letters, no visitors.

George was so devoted to this world that he once risked forfeiting promotion and ten years of pension rights in order not to leave it.

> When I look at Wargess and Kulal in the distance I realise what I am losing. I have a passionate love for the mountains and valleys and all the country I know so well.

George, in his generation, was not alone in crossing the bridge between the ancient and the modern. Laurens van der Post forged an almost mystical union with the Bushmen and the Kalahari desert. Wilfred Thesiger's identification with the Bedouin and sands of Arabia was more earthly but just as intense. All three knew with sadness that these immemorial ways of life, embodying precious human values, were likely to vanish before they were dead.

George's long spells in the Northern Frontier gave him a remarkable sense of perspective. "Mr. Adamson has eyes which can see a long way ahead," a boy of five once told his mother.

It was an observation many people made, meaning it both literally and metaphorically. His marathon safaris also developed atavistic virtues vital to the survival of a nomad. The daily calls on his self-reliance and courage steadily strengthened his resolution and confidence. His remote independence secured his freedom from conventional values, including ambition for power, riches, possessions or fame.

This lack of concern for himself went hand in hand with respect for other people and sympathy for their troubles. Altruism, or some degree of self-sacrifice, is an adaptation advantageous to human and some other societies, in which it is not practiced equally by all individuals; indeed, if it were, that society would be in danger, for a healthy community thrives only if it also possesses a balancing element of aggression to secure and maintain its position in the rough-and-tumble of the world.

To some extent the complement of these opposites, the yin and yang of Joy's and George's characters, may have accounted for the inexplicable survival of their marriage. Beneath Joy's increasingly emphatic warnings from Europe that she wanted a divorce and George's exasperation with her behavior, each must have recognized in the other some vital element missing in themselves, for he was still eager to see her again.

As time went by, George's friends noticed that his deepest compassion was reserved for those least able to look after themselves—the animals. It was a latent trait, owing nothing to the tribal traditions of East Africa, for the tribes had no need for it. Never before had man killed there to excess. The practice had been brought in by the Arab and the white man.

George's effortless ability to commute between two cultures, the one of arrows, camels and mud huts, the other of rifles, lorries and corrugated iron, fitted him perfectly for life on a frontier, including the one between the past and the present.

TEN

Cries from the Heart

1947–1953

1

George had a problem. Joy had written a curt letter telling him not to meet her on her return from Europe and that she would be staying with friends at Karen. His instinct told him that she might not really mean this and that if he was not there to greet her she would always hold it against him. Since he longed to see her he decided to compromise and meet the boat train at Nairobi.

July 14   Waited for nearly an hour before train came in. The most anxious wait I have ever had. Was standing near the end of station, saw Joy, she seemed to look directly at me and then deliberately away as her carriage flashed past. Heart went down! Must meet whatever the reception, raced down platform, Joy saw me and waved. Seemed really glad to see me and asked why I hadn't met her at Mombasa! Why I hadn't brought Pippin?

Joy was in fact so pleased to see George that she canceled her arrangements at Karen and came back to his mother's house in Limuru, where he had left Pippin so Joy would not feel her dog was being used as a pretext for his meeting her. They celebrated with champagne.

Although her letters had grown ominous her present warmth was typical of her mood swings. During the next few months she was outwardly relaxed toward George while covertly badgering Peter Bally to take her back.

According to an account in George's files, Joy's mood changed when he followed her down to Nairobi during the week before Christmas. He found her painting in the museum again. She had switched away from flowers—to moths, a chameleon, a sunbird, a hornbill and a crowned crane—but was nevertheless sharing a room in the Coryndon with Peter Bally.

> The old associations, and I suppose his near physical presence had a disastrous effect, and all the infatuation for Bally had returned in increased measure.
>
> I thought it scandalous under the circumstances for her to be in the same room as Bally. Bally assured me in front of her that he did not want to have anything to do with her, that she was pestering the life out of him and that he was at his wits' end.
>
> Joy was very hysterical and started in front of Bally accusing me of endless brutalities, blackmail, etc. She said if I did not grant her a divorce she would use every means at her disposal in achieving her object.

Two days before Christmas, George went to the Game Department office and received a message from Joy saying she wished to see him.

> Bally came over and asked me to postpone my meeting with Joy for half an hour as he was in the process of writing her a letter, which he would show me, to make it absolutely clear that he had not the remotest intention of ever taking her back.
>
> In due course I went over to the Museum and found Bally and Joy together. She was in a really dreadful state, I was afraid she was going insane, she was raving, threatening to commit suicide, making all kinds of accusations against him.

During the week after Christmas Joy went to a lawyer and told George he thought she had a case for divorce on the grounds of cruelty. He prepared the record that is quoted above and below for his own lawyer.

> Joy ignored my efforts at a reconciliation, and packed up her things. When she was ready she demanded that I should put all her luggage in the car and take her down to Nairobi.
>
> I refused and told her that it was scarcely reasonable to expect me "to help my own wife in running away from me" and that if she wanted her things she must make her own arrangements. I then instructed my boys to put them in a room which I locked up. We went to Nairobi and I as usual deposited her at the Museum.

Just before lunch there was a phone message from the Resident Magistrate, Roberts, to say that Joy had lodged a complaint with the police, who had referred her to him. She had told him that I refused to hand over her things and that she was afraid of personal violence if she went up alone to get them.

Roberts was very decent and it was agreed that I should hand over Joy's things to her in the presence of the acting Chief Game Warden.

Joy's principal allegation against George was of the violence he had used to restrain her on the night—soon after they were married—when she had first flung herself at him in a fury and then flounced off through the darkness in search of a lift to Nairobi. She swore she could call a European policeman who had witnessed George striking her, although there was not one within miles of their house that night.

Within a week George's lawyer told him that Joy simply had no case against him. It is possible that George had the beginnings of a case against her since for two years she had refused to sleep with him.

Sometimes it is difficult not to see the proceedings as a drama conceived, presented and starred in by Joy. On one occasion she bumped into all three husbands talking together at a street corner in Nairobi. Von Klarwill had settled down in the country and now made his living from a climbing club he had started at Nanyuki, near Mount Kenya. Before long, however, she found her cast deserting the stage.

George returned to Isiolo. He would neither give her the grounds to divorce him nor divorce her himself, although she confessed to having met Bally in Europe. The lawyers could not build bricks without straw; and finally Bally promised decisive action to end Joy's suspense and took it. He disappeared on safari.

Joy's behavior aroused in those who knew her well anger or despair; in those who did not it provoked gossip and laughter. After her death flippant stories began to circulate about what her husbands were feeling, although nobody dared attribute one to George.

Peter Bally is supposed to have said, "All the world is mourning Joy today except her three husbands."

Ziebel von Klarwill is alleged to have observed, rather more lightly, "If I were still married to Joy I think I would be pushing up the daisies by now."

None of these stories reflects her husbands' true and fundamental feelings about her when she died.

Ziebel von Klarwill wrote a letter to two of her closest remaining friends, Peter and Mary Johnson, in which he tried to express the emotions he still felt for the woman he had married forty-five years before.

> May I seek refuge in another language, as one is wont to do when expressing a deep feeling? *Je l'ai aimé de tout mon coeur* ... I see her young, radiant, beautiful, strong, untiring, and searching, searching ...

Peter Bally also mourned her but, out of deference to George, refrained from attending her funeral. Instead, at the age of eighty-five, he went to the mortuary to pay her his final respects. Afterward he told the Johnsons that "she looked as beautiful as if she was still eighteen."

George seldom, if ever, spoke about his deepest feelings for Joy, but there is evidence of them. In the film of her funeral his emotion is manifest and he flicks a tear from his eye with the back of his hand. A few years later he spent a whole evening at Kora talking about Joy to Alan Davidson—the Canadian who found them on Mount Kenya in 1943—and his wife; the three of them were alone. When their little plane had left the airstrip next morning Davidson's wife, who had not met George before, said, "From the way he spoke about Joy last night I felt George was still in love with her."

2

Joy's behavior after the collapse of her divorce proceedings was deceptively mild. Instead of turning her into a thwarted fury again, her mercurial personality devised a new and perhaps more dangerous role for her.

Distinguished visitors of all kinds were constantly cast up at Isiolo, as if on Circe's isle, in search of the legendary enchantment of the Northern Frontier. Because of his growing reputation, George was invariably asked to organize their safaris, and some of the travellers quickly succumbed to Joy's spell.

At about this time the American Attorney General arrived, followed by a trio of European aristocrats—Baron Buxhaeveden, Count Seilern and Prince Windischgraetz—who sought George's advice on where to find the best trophies and largest bags of birds. The prince, inevitably known to George and his colleagues as "Windyscratch," was said by some to be the epitome of a noble sportsman and by others to possess the blood lust of a pathological killer mingled with religious scruples: he was once found beside a burning mound of "5,002 olive pigeons," weeping tears of contrition.

Biologists were another species drawn to George's domain, among them a Dr. Bengt and his colleague. George wrote to Joy:

> Your dear friend was here for a few days. He disgusted me by shooting six bush babies along the river, and then five Grevy's zebra. He had certainly made a fine collection of rats and probably decided after our trip it was safer to concentrate on lesser fauna!

Joy's spell over one scientist was so potent that, according to a DC, George had to take precautionary measures.

> I remember hearing that George booby-trapped her tent with rope and tin cans so that her suitor aroused the whole camp trying to get into it at night.

In February 1948 Dr. Olaf Hedberg, a Swedish botanist, and Dr. Ake Holm, a world authority on spiders, arrived with a party from Uppsala University intent on studying the flora and fauna on the higher mountains of Kenya, Uganda and Ruanda-Urundi. One of these naturalists, alarmed to find himself face-to-face with nature, sat up all night, fully dressed and armed. When a family of elephants ambled to within thirty feet of the tents he leapt into his lorry.

The Swedes were so bewitched by Joy that they let her join their expedition and she spent the next three months with them in the Ruwenzori Mountains and Mount Elgon. It is impossible to tell from her laconic diary entries how intimate she became with Ake Holm, but their relationship was obviously intense and tempestuous.

Just after Joy, Holm and Hedburg left the Ruwenzoris to collect plants on Mount Elgon, back in Kenya, she recorded an extraordinary coincidence:

We had a blow out and had to spend the night at a small inn. There were only a few people in the dining room, but two of these were Peter Bally and a woman.

Meeting him so unexpectedly at such a remote place was more than I was prepared for. Because my wounds were painfully ripped open again, I tried to control my emotions by concentrating on sorting out plants.

However, during a tormenting night I vowed that this forthcoming trip up Elgon would be my last botanical effort; I only continued with it so as to include this important mountain in my collection of the Alpine flora of East Africa. From then onwards I intended to concentrate on painting Africans in their traditional costumes.

When the Swedes left Joy showed no inclination to go back to Isiolo. She went briefly to Nairobi and then returned to western Kenya to start work on her tribal record, although she had still not found anyone to commission it.

Having spent so much time away from George since their marriage, she scarcely seemed to miss him, yet she quickly protested if there was a gap in the flow of his long, vivid and often humorous letters.

This one opens with a quotation from a dispatch he had just sent to the Chief Game Warden.

After being away for two months, I find that the house is just about a ruin, large gaping holes in the roof, many of the beams eaten through by ants and in imminent danger of collapsing altogether. I guarantee that if you were to see the place now, you would agree that it is not fit for any civilised man to live in, let alone a woman . . .

JUNE 20, 1948

My dear Joy,

The note [above] is in the nature of an "Official complaint." Really the house is quite impossible, owing to the very high wind there is a shower of earth falling the whole time. I am not going to ask you to come back under the present conditions, it would drive you crazy.

The two remaining ostriches are doing fine, the cock has just started to get his black feathers. The two dogs are also growing fast and have great games with the ostriches; today Bully appeared with half a hare, frightfully proud; soon after Fifi brought in the other half! Then they were sick all over the place.

If you are still in Nairobi when you get this, will you please try and get me some medicines for my hounds—mange, ticks and fleas, worms, and anything else you can think of—and have it all put down to my account. Also please, needles (not too small) and cotton, white, khaki and black. I must mend some of my clothes!

Poor mother is back in Mathari Hospital. I did so much hope that at last we had got her fixed up for good with the couple at Limuru, but she became impossible.

Why did you cry on your birthday? Wish I could help you. Tell me everything, is it still Peter? Perhaps if we got divorced he might take you back. There is no sense in us both being unhappy; if either of us can do anything to help each other, let us do it.

By October the stress of prolonged separation, with Joy so near— only a few hours away—and yet so far, was telling.

Isiolo
OCTOBER 18, 1948

Dear Joy,

Do you remember this letter you wrote to me? You must have been genuinely in love with me then—you could never have written like that if it was just sexual attraction.

I started by looking upon it as just another affair, like I had had with other women. I would go back to the NFD and perhaps next time I came to Nairobi on leave would carry on where we had left off and be good friends.

Then all my defences were broken and I was touched to the bottom of my heart by your evident sincerity and passionate love and the fact that you gave the whole of yourself to me, and did not hesitate to give up everything of your old life for me.

Then as you know the whole situation changed. Your feelings and love for me lasted a bare fortnight, mine have lasted five long years.

As she moved from tribe to tribe, with only Pippin and her cook Kifosha for permanent company, Joy looked to the local DCs and officers in other departments for help. Like the wanderers Circe had turned into wolves to protect her, they gave her a sense of security; they also produced models for her. In her draft memoir she wrote this.

> Some took advantage of this situation but as we were dependent on each other's company for several weeks I tried to divert their flirtation into friendship. On the whole I survived unscathed.

I had heard many stories that Joy was repeatedly unfaithful on these safaris, but since the alleged lovers were never named I decided to discount them unless I found concrete evidence for their existence.

There are innumerable reasons why men and women commit adultery. They are blown into it by the breezes of waning self-confidence, boredom, irritation or mischief; swirled into it by the dangerous currents of vanity, curiosity, romanticism or loneliness; get caught in a riptide of sexuality; or, headed for the rocks of divorce, clutch at the groping hand of a possible new partner.

When I began to research this period of Joy's life she seemed to be running through the gamut of these experiences, and clues to them began to surface without probing.

For instance it was alleged that when a DC named A. B. Simpson was sued for divorce, his wife cited Joy. A little later a botanist volunteered that in 1952 the Provincial Commissioner at Isiolo had forbidden him to take Joy to Mount Marsabit in search of plants as she had just been having an affair with the police officer there. He could not remember the man's name, but the PC could: it was A. L. Griffith.

On reading through George's letters to Joy, I discovered that in September 1948 Joy stayed with Sandy Simpson and his wife at Kabarnet in western Kenya. In November George mentions to Joy that he has got wind that "Griff" Griffith had to rescue her from the wrath of his wife at Lodwar, farther north. He twits her about it, but the rest of his letter is not amused.

> Got back today from safari and received your letter from Lokitaung. Still the same! Blame me for everything. Alright my dear, I am a brute and you are an innocent woman who has been put upon by a bounder.
>   Life is too short to go on quarrelling, besides it is pretty futile and childish to do it through the post. If you want a nice row,

much better to come here, there would be plenty of Doum palm nuts and elephant balls to throw at me!!

I was hoping there might be a slight chance of you coming along for Christmas, very foolish of me—now of course I see that you would rather spend it alone.

For a very different reason, I intend to spend the time alone, because I cannot bear the thought of being among people who are making merry because they are happy, and I am not. You know the ordeal it is to try and pretend you are enjoying yourself when in reality your heart is breaking.

My intention is to set off on a donkey safari. I expect to land up at Laisamis about New Year. Oh, Christ, Joy, why not come along? If you want to, send me a wire, I can always wait a week or so. Never have I seen the country looking so lovely.

George's cri de coeur went unheeded and Joy remained at Lokitaung for Christmas. Something or someone was keeping her there.

Among her more personal photographs and keepsakes were snapshots of two tall, good-looking, unnamed men who appear curiously alike. One holds a dachshund on his lap, and in another photograph appears to be nude. With them was a Christmas card for that year that Joy had drawn, but not sent, of a naked figure with a paintbrush in his hand and a dachshund at his feet. It took a hunt through the main albums to identify the two as Simpson and Griffith, who had a dachshund and with whom she swam in a rock pool. I also discovered through police contacts that Griffith was not only a well-known ladies' man but also an amateur artist.

This letter from George elicited the truth of what Joy had been up to.

FEBRUARY 4, 1949

Got your very welcome letter yesterday on my birthday. I had a good few quiet laughs over it. What on earth does it matter to you whether I snore like a monster or breathe like an asthmatic rhino if you have no intention of coming back to your loving husband? I would gladly have bits cut off my nose and even my ears, of which I am so proud, if I knew it would bring you back . . .

My dear old Joy, I have been thinking a great deal about the question of divorce. I told you that in the end I would do what was right. For all the five years we have been married, I always hoped that, if you could throw off the influence of Peter, things might come right between us. Now I am convinced it is no good going on.

I intend to find out what Government's attitude would be supposing I let you divorce me. If it won't completely jeopardize my career, I think I will go through with it.

I trust you, that if I let you divorce me, you will not try to claim alimony. Naturally, I would always want to help you if you were in need. After it is all over I want to try and save up some money in case I do get married again.

George's diary describes the effect of this overdue firmness.

February 11 ... Joy had come in answer to my last letter. Naturally I was overjoyed to see her after all these months. We celebrated with champagne.

February 12 We had a very pleasant day together and returned in the evening. She told me about everything which had occurred since we parted last July and it was a revelation!

While at Kabarnet she fell in love with the DC, A. B. Simpson, a married man with two children, and six years younger than herself! Apparently the S.'s marriage was unsuccessful and "on the rocks." Joy and S. had come to an understanding that she would keep away from him for six months while he gave his marriage another trial, then if still a failure (presumably), Joy and he would get married. S.'s wife knew of the situation and agreed to the arrangement.

Then Joy left Kabarnet and a few weeks later went to Lodwar and met A. L. Griffith of the police. He took her with him to Lokitaung and then began a sordid love affair lasting the best part of a month, which came to an abrupt end on the arrival of Griffith's wife. Joy, as always, was in deadly earnest and believed and trusted that Griffith would leave his wife and marry her. Too blind to realise that all Griffith wanted was to have an affair, it gave her a great shock emotionally.

However, after getting over Griffith, she still felt in love with Simpson but also began to realise I might still be the best man for her. The situation to-day is that Joy does not want to lose me, yet she is not willing to give up Simpson—altogether intolerable!

It is impossible to give Joy's side of the story; her letters do not survive. All that exists is her diary.

> *February 12* Off to Neumann's camp. Lovely day! Feeling very fresh. Something so utterly different; George, thank God (?), more independent of me. I respect him more. Same filth, same smell, but home!

> *February 13* If I don't give him a divorce he will call Griff into camp. Threat?

George was indeed utterly outraged and wrote immediately to both Simpson and Griffith.

> Posted registered letter to Griffith, one that he will not like and which I hope frightens him. The swine.

Circe, having made her confession, withdrew to continue her painting.

This is George's last entry on the subject.

> *March 8* Mail from Joy and also a wire from Fort Hall saying that she had received letter from Simpson and that everything was to be alright between us, ending with congratulations and love!

Two days after Joy had told him about Simpson and Griffith, George had gone out and experimented with his new tactics for dispersing elephants that he knew might result in being trampled to death. Now his mood was rather different. He threw a party for the entire European population at Isiolo.

3

From 1948 to 1953, while Joy concentrated on her tribal paintings, the full story of which is told in Chapter 12, she was away from George for an average of eight months each year. Given the stresses of the marriage, these separations probably kept them together.

On the occasions that Joy, in search of models, did join George on safari, she was often—but not always—the ideal companion of their earliest journeys. With a temperature of 104°F she rode on in the heat of the day wrapped in wet sheets; she made no complaint when George used her rubber shoes as fire lighters at the end of a night of torrential rain they had spent without a tent; and she was interested rather than perturbed when a lion, and later a leopard, wandered into their camp at night.

On the other hand, there were occasions when George must have wished her elsewhere. David Shirreff, a DC in the Samburu country, described one of them in a letter.

The Government decided to move several thousand Turkana tribesmen who had settled in Isiolo back to their home district of Turkana. The job of supervising the move was given to Don Stone, DO at Isiolo, an ex-fighter pilot with one eye, and George Adamson, who was accompanied by Joy. By the time they reached my district, Stone, George and Joy were travelling in three separate camps and hardly speaking to each other.

Joy had the rather disconcerting habit of walking about naked except for a very brief pair of pants, not the sort of behaviour which the elders at Baragoi expected of a white woman.

I remember I told her to put a shirt on when attending a stock sale and she thought I was rather stuffy.

Shirreff may have been the first officer to ask Joy to cover her breasts, but others did too, including one who told her he had seen better among the Giriama at the coast.

The Adamsons were not the only couple in the NFD to have their marital differences. George described to Joy the predicament of one of the DCs who had rebuked her immodesty.

His wife has turned out to be a nymphomaniac and has been whoring around with any and every man who cared to have her, her husband apparently looking on and not minding. One day he did take a kiboko [rawhide whip] to her, but afterwards she boasted that he had spoilt the effect by apologising to her. Such is life in the NFD. In comparison, we must be quite an ordinary happily married couple!

There is a sequel to the story of the relocation of the tribesmen. George was asked to help with another Turkana move a few years later. Their witch doctor prophesied it would never take place, and on the morning the trek was due to start George Low told George to cancel it: he had discovered foot-and-mouth disease among the cattle.

While Joy was away George persevered with the strenuous task of extracting government funds for his new house—and finally succeeded. It was only possible to make the allocation stretch to their needs by persuading Terence to build it.

After the war Terence had emerged from the army with a demobilization suit and a small gratuity. To protect the suit from the climate and ravening insects he sealed it in a *debe*, or oil drum, and buried it. Ten years later he dug it up, went around the world, wore it out and burned it. It was the only time he left Africa.

He invested the money in a half share of The Pig and Whistle at Meru, which he bought with George's old drinking companion Colonel Abbay. Being a teetotaler he used to glower at any customers who ordered a second tot of spirits and mutter, "*Another!* Don't you know what it will do to your stomach?"

Since the colonel, who had an insatiable affection for the bottle, swallowed what the customers would otherwise have paid for, the inn had to be sold after two years. Terence's next venture, working for mica, was no more profitable and he was therefore delighted to help George with his house.

Constructed of local stone, it was set in a horseshoe of hills a few miles outside Isiolo, commanded magnificent views and possessed a room large enough for Joy's easels and the new piano she bought with her income from painting flowers. On the sliding doors that closed off the veranda she painted a copy of the rock engravings she had found near Lake Rudolf.

In June 1950, George realized his mother did not have long to live and arranged to meet Joy in Nairobi, where she agreed to visit Katherine Adamson, but stayed separately from George.

June 10 Went to see Mother in the morning, decidedly weaker but still able to talk and hear us. In the afternoon Mother much worse, I do not think she can last the night.

Got back to the hotel about 11.00 pm Terence told me that Mummy had died.

So ends the life of my mother at the age of 75. She was the most wonderful mother to us, always unselfish and understanding in our troubles until her mental breakdown in 1942, after which her life was miserable.

Just before she died, Katherine begged George always to see that Terence came to no harm. He made her a promise and faithfully kept it.

A week after the funeral, when Joy had returned to her painting, George ended a letter to her with these thoughts.

I hope and try to believe that Mother has gone to a better life and is with my father now—but who knows?

I will always be grateful to you for seeing my mother this last time. You were very sweet to her and I know by the way her eyes lighted up when she saw you that you made her happy.

Well Fifi Darling, it is getting late and I must go to bed. Take care of yourself.

A few days later still George wrote to her that a producer called Jack Swain who was making a film for MGM had, like so many other wanderers in need of help, pitched up on his doorstep.

Pity you are not here to help and bring in the romantic touch— "love interest"! Swain was all prepared to meet you and brought an enormous bunch of flowers for you, most crestfallen when I told him you wouldn't be here until Monday. You are missing the chance of a lifetime! You might have been the heroine in a thrilling drama of the NFD.

I love you . . .

Your potential film star, George.

In fact George did feature in the film *Stronghold of the Wild*, released by MGM in 1952. Joy also had a part in Swain's African adventure but not in the film. George noted:

July 1 Spent the morning finishing off the last scenes. Then came the parting with Swain. An incredible situation suddenly developed.

Joy was away down the far end of the manyatta ostensibly taking photographs. Swain walked down to see her; a long and intimate conversation took place which was obvious even at a distance. Joy and Swain returned, she very obviously under strong emotion and in tears, Swain looking a bit sheepish. I was very angry, quite justified I think! Every letter from her before she came said she was longing to be with me. Now, after five days of my company, she falls for the first man she meets! Incredible, she has absolutely no control over her emotions.

A strange postscript to the episode is the cartoon of the parting doodled by Joy in George's diary!

4

George did his best to persuade Joy to focus her mind constructively on their future, together or apart. At times he was worried that Bally's effect on her was still as potent as ever.

Intending to do both men a favor, George put his brother, a knowledgeable botanist, in touch with Bally. Joy intercepted Bally's reply.

Letter from Peter regarding the plants, which Joy insisted on seeing, furious that I had helped him by suggesting Terence as suitable collector.

Her violent hatred toward P. makes me uneasy as in my opinion it merely goes to show that she is still very much bound up in him and it is only one step from hate to equally violent love. I will never feel safe until Joy can display indifference toward P.

Even her love of Simpson had not exorcised her fixation on Bally, nor had her affair with Griffith satisfied her craving for physical proof of men's admiration. Her diary suggests that she was unfaithful with at least half a dozen other men.

By this time her younger sister, Dorle, had moved to England, and although he had never met her George began to exchange letters with her. Her relationships with men seemed almost as unhappy as Joy's, and George offered her advice, sent her a little money and poured out his heart to her. He told her he thought Joy must have suffered from some "unbearable hurt" in her past: today Dorle believes it was her abortion. He said that Joy had offered him a degree of license with other women but he had no desire to take advantage of it.

Given his appreciation of attractive women, his physical vigor, and Joy's relentless refusals and infidelities, it would be surprising if he had not; but I have not come across a scrap of convincing evidence in the diaries and letters, or through the grapevine, that he did so. Whenever anyone who knew him well talks about him, the word "gentleman" sooner or later crops up. It is possible that he did occasionally seek or accept consolation from other women, but he left no trace behind to implicate them.

He did, however, constantly tease Joy in his letters about his flirtations with a variety of sirens including "a most charming woman with whom I almost fell in love—good looking, plenty of money, very interested in animals and keen to come out on safari."

One letter took a much tougher line.

I simply am not prepared to remain content with seeing my wife for a couple of fortnights in the year. The mere fact of my being married and yet having to live alone is *driving* me to drink. Apparently it does not matter to you and you do not feel the need for sex. Therefore live your life alone and let me go free to find another wife.

I tell you that there is someone else of whom I am fond and if I was free I believe she would marry me tomorrow, and be willing to give me a child in spite of my lunatic mother. I do not believe that I could have the same passionate love for her as I used to have for you, but I think that mutual fondness and companionship are in the long run more worthy and lasting, particularly if there is the bond of a child.

In our marriage there was a definite break when I learned of your "affairs" with Simpson and Griffith. Try as I would I could not retain the same trust and respect for you.

Nevertheless my dear, I am still very fond of you and want to give our marriage every possible chance if you will also try to do your part.

In spite of being forty, you have retained your looks and it would not be difficult to find another husband but time will not wait for anyone and you have not so very many years left in which to start a new marriage. I am convinced that your most difficult period of your life is going to be at "the change of life". You will then be in desperate need of love and understanding and of a husband who will stand by you. If you feel that I am not the right man (which by now you ought to know) then don't lose any more time. You have often spoken of a man (Fitzpatrick I think) who wants to marry you. Perhaps he could give you more than I can.

We have *got* to come to a decision, before both our lives and chances of happiness are wrecked for ever.

Three comments should be made on this letter. First, there is no clue to the identity of the woman George refers to as a possible wife—if she ever actually existed. Second, although George applies the word lunatic to his mother it seems she suffered from premature senility rather than madness. Third, Joy did meet a man named Fitzpatrick on the social circuit of Nairobi from time to time, but there is no evidence he asked her to marry him.

There was, however, one woman whose friendship meant more to George than any other. When Joy went to England he gave her the address of the woman who had captured his heart in 1935, Angela Ofenheim, the doctor always known as Tony. It is noticeable that from then on when he sent off one of his more impassioned letters to Joy he was apt also to write to Tony. He clearly poured out his heart to her as well as to Dorle. One day he wrote this to Joy.

Together with yours, I received a wonderful letter from Tony Ofenheim after a very long time. I will quote some of it and you will realise what a fine woman she is.

"No George I have never married . . . I was not fortunate enough in being able to find a man whose life I could share and carry on my work at the same time. Sometimes it is possible, but I was not lucky. Although I do what used to be a man's job and am capable of earning my own living, I am not a feminist and have very strong views about marriage. Sacrifices have to be made by both parties but the woman's job is to follow her husband and fit in with his way of life, and if she is not prepared to do that the marriage can never be a happy one.

"At the time I knew how you felt about me, a woman knows that by instinct, and I could have so easily felt the same way about you. In fact I did, and it took a lot of willpower not to let it come to anything as in my saner moments I realised that in the long run I wouldn't be happy giving up all I had worked and striven for, for so many years, and I knew eventually the call of medicine would be too strong and I would make you unhappy.

"Perhaps being recalled to England so suddenly (when my father died) saved us both from a lot of heartache."

George seems to have been saved from heartache with Tony, only to run into it with Joy, and yet there is one letter to Joy in which he expresses alarm at the prospect of an unhappiness even more daunting than the present one.

Well, you certainly are an idealist and one day, perhaps, Kenya will give you your due and you will become "Dame" Joy Adamson. After all many women have been "Damed" for much less. By the time you have finished, I think I also will be entitled to a knighthood, for being such a long-suffering and patient husband!

I realise Joy that you are doing a fine and great work with complete unselfishness, but do not let it become your master, because there is another side to life, which although less spectacular, is just as important. That is to build up a home and family and a happy married life.

I can go on for the rest of my days, living in the country I love, among my wild animals, and doing my job. But there is always the aching void of loneliness, having no one to share my daily life with me, and no future to look forward to, except being alone always. I am terrified of the time when I have to retire because I am too old to do my job and pray God that I do not live to see that day.

At the heart of this letter lies the idea of raising a child or children and it was this shared ambition, however simplistic on George's side, and however convoluted and ill-starred on Joy's, that now held them together against all the odds.

ELEVEN

A Child?

1947–1953

1

However late they had left it both George and Joy were approaching a point when they realized at the same time how empty life might become without a family. George wrote:

NOVEMBER 29, 1948

You say you want desperately to have a child, I also want one before I am too old. Isn't it possible that a child might bring us together? The love which you are incapable of giving me might find its fulfillment in a child of ours.

Since this letter to Joy was written during her simultaneous infatuation with Simpson and Griffith, it received short shrift. A few months later George tried again.

FEBRUARY 3, 1949

Funny! I have just remembered it is my birthday. Nearly 9 pm! Well, I am four years ahead of you, soon be an old man! Really Joy you must think seriously about the question of a child, that is if you want one. I know your arguments by heart about having a house, etc., but "time" will wait for no one. One day you will find that it is too late. It would be tragic, particularly for you. We are almost past it, to see our child grow up before us and reach maturity.

Again Joy's response was so negative that George was convinced she was determined not to have a baby.

In reality Joy had not made up her mind; it was in a state of contradiction and chaos as it had been from the beginning. However often she refused him, there were one or two occasions each year when they consummated their marriage and George expressed optimism about the future.

At first the question of a child may have been connected with the issue of divorce. His friend Harry Benson put it to me like this.

> Some of his closest friends persuaded George to contact a firm of lawyers in Nairobi with a view to divorce. She at that time was living with a man at Nanyuki only fifty miles from Isiolo. She got to hear of the move to divorce her and shot off to Isiolo and had George in bed right away. End of the divorce.

If an action were to be started Joy wanted the initiative and timing to be hers, not George's. The belief that George might be able to sue her either for divorce or restitution of conjugal rights if she denied him continuously may well have accounted for her occasional, if grudging, acquiesence.

After they had both stayed in Nairobi—though in different places—at the time of his mother's death, George wrote a letter attempting to find a way out of the maze.

> JUNE 16, 1950
>
> Why did you not live with me in Nairobi? Twice I suggested it and you made every excuse possible to avoid it on both occasions.
>
> If the prospect appals you, then please do not come, as I do not want a wife who gives herself as a sacrifice to an unpleasant duty. Also, continuing in the vein of frankness, and that you should not arrive here under false pretences, I have burnt all my "rubber things" and absolutely refuse to use them because they are things one uses for a prostitute and not for one's wife.
>
> Naturally if you are not feeling well when you come here I will not force myself on you. Joy, I want this time together to be really happy for both of us and we must try to give each other as much as we can in a positive way. If you want a child, and I long for one sometimes, the prospect is not too bad. Between us we are better off than most people.

This letter seems conclusive evidence that Joy was not pregnant in June 1950. On the other hand there is a passage in her autobiography that can be attributed only to the first half of 1950, in which she wrote this.

However varied and interesting our life often was, it was also very restless and insecure and I had another miscarriage, the third now by three husbands. I badly wanted a child, but evidently had not the mentality of a brooding hen, and I felt very distressed.

This raises several questions. If she so much wanted a baby, and had become pregnant in the first half of the year, how is it that there is no reference to it in any of George's fifteen letters to her surviving from those six months, no reference to it in her diary entries and no irregularity in the cycles she ticked off on the calendar each month? Did conception and miscarriage really occur? It is a doubt that arises again later.

The reference in George's letter to contraceptives—together with others in their diaries and letters—strongly suggests that he alone used them. Given Joy's frequently expressed phobia of having a baby by him, why didn't she use a contraceptive of her own? In view of the life she led, and the number of doctors she saw, it is astonishing if she did not actually possess a diaphragm. Nevertheless, it is possible, for at the end of her 1948 diary, when she was having affairs with Simpson and Griffith, there is a formula for taking ergot, a substance sometimes used for inducing abortion.

There is further evidence of Joy's complex attitude to a child in George's diary toward the end of 1950.

> *October 24* Long three page letter from Joy, most disturbing, will not agree to ever having a child by me. Suggests artificial insemination through some friend of hers, C—— M—— I should think. Under no circumstances will I agree to such a course unless Joy is prepared to go with me to a specialist, Carothers for preference. If he says it is unwise for me to be a father, then I shall be prepared to consider artificial insemination. But not simply because of Joy's neurotic and probably quite groundless fears.

The next morning George wrote to her very sharply indeed and threatened a lawyer's letter to follow. But, as he told Joy's sister, Dorle, he had a reputation for being "foolishly good-natured."

> In the afternoon I relented and packed up a parcel for Fifi containing two boxes of chocolates and 300 shillings in cash and a loving letter. She does not deserve it but I love the woman and I can never be angry with her for very long.

A CHILD?

This soul-destroying pattern of unsynchronized or conflicting moods and desires might have gone on indefinitely but for one event. In 1951 Peter Bally married again.

2

The new Mrs. Bally was Swiss, like Peter, but much younger than he and even Joy.

The fact that very soon she was expecting a baby must have wounded Joy's pride. It was bound to appear that far from Bally being impotent, she herself was either unable to arouse his attentions or was infertile.

Bally warned his wife how strongly Joy might react and he even fitted a grille to the porch in case Joy tried to force an entry to their house. In fact Joy never referred to Bally's marriage in her diary and simply withdrew to the coast to continue her painting. If the wound festered it did so unseen.

During the next few months Joy appears to have engaged in one or two liaisons that began optimistically but quickly fizzled out. She saw Dorian—the admirer who sailed to England with her—but he probably realized she had been offering her favors elsewhere and was very cool toward her.

Just before Christmas George had a stroke of luck—he was posted to take over the coastal district of the Game Department for three months and conceived the quixotic plan of canoeing down the Tana in a Fol boat to surprise Joy for Christmas. Delayed by unforeseen hazards, he reached her on Boxing Day, camped in a grove of mango trees, where she was astonished but delighted to see him.

Just as her sister Traute's unexpected marriage precipitated Joy's elopement to Italy with her first lover, so Bally's baby seems to have activated a genuine resolve to start a family of her own. In April, when she and George returned to Isiolo together, there is a cryptic note: "First time without horror."

By the time Joy went back to the coast in August to continue her tribal record they had been reassured by Dr. Carothers, the government psychiatrist, that there would be no danger in bearing a child by George. Her gynecologist must also have believed it was possible for her to have a baby for he advised her to have her fallopian tubes blown out. Chronic inflammation or infection of the fallopian tubes can be one of the consequences of a clumsy or unhygienic abortion, inhibiting conception.

In September Joy went into hospital at Mombasa. She described the episode in her draft memoir.

> I badly wanted a child and George took leave to spend time with me immediately after this small operation. We camped in the nearby Shimba Hills, hoping to get a glimpse of the rare Sable antelope which only occur in this lovely range overlooking the Indian Ocean. It was an ideal place for a second honeymoon.
>
> I felt really happy when George promised to be more loyal to me from now on and I soon became pregnant. But when I discovered George had betrayed me again soon after he left me I had another miscarriage.

There is no doubt that Joy really hoped for a child during the next few years. Several parents noticed that Joy was moved to tears when she looked at their small children or babies. She confided her longing not only to her doctors but to her closest women friends in Isiolo. But she seems to have been as ignorant about conception as she was of contraception.

At least twice, after spending a night with a man on earlier occasions, she jotted down "baby," or "child!" as if conception would inevitably occur. She seems to have been under the same misapprehension at Shimba Hills.

The memoir is baffling, because her diary records a monthly period occurring two weeks before the operation and again two weeks after it. In other words, there was no interruption of her menstrual cycle that continued regularly throughout the year. The "pregnancy," like the one she refers to two years before, must have been illusory: perhaps pride or some other emotion caused her to dissemble.

There is another curiosity in Joy's claim that she miscarried because George "betrayed" her: she implies—though no more—that he was unfaithful to her, whereas all he did was to stay with two of his oldest friends, Denzil and Denzilla Pedley, whom he had consulted about marrying Joy during the heady weeks of their first meetings in Nairobi. For some reason Joy not only disliked Denzilla, but suspected George of once having an affair with her. If he did there is no trace of it.

For George to avoid the company of everyone Joy disliked would have entailed becoming a hermit; she would have proscribed his mother, his brother and his closest friends, along with his pipe and tobacco. Recently she had seized his whiskey bottle on safari and stuffed it out of reach down the tunnel of a termite mound.

She was also notoriously intolerant of George's servants and was said to have thrown stew over one *toto* (kitchen boy) because it was not hot enough. A DC told me she had asked him to have another boy beaten when he burned her soup: he refused.

George put his finger on it.

Yes Joy I still have the toto with me and he is turning into an excellent servant. Other people remark how good my servants are and I am not going to sack him until you have settled down with me. After a time, if you still can't get on with him, I will get rid of him, but not just on a whim because every thing and person connected with me is abhorrent to you, like my dog Kim.

Although she was unkind about Terence to George her real feelings about him were mixed. Friends thought she was embarrassed by his nervous mannerisms—hesitations in his speech, uninhibited scratching and a noticeable habit of twitching his shirt collar, which probably devloped as a result of his often solitary life.

From 1950 to 1955 he carried out locust and game control near Isiolo, Garissa, and then Voi—where she saw him after her latest "miscarriage." She was always aware that he resented her treatment of George. On the other hand, their idiosyncratic paths in that remote country had a curious way of crossing and when this happened she was delighted to walk through the bush with him, learning from his encyclopedic knowledge of the trees and plants.

3

In case I have failed to set aside any male prejudice, conscious or unconscious, in examining Joy's relationship with George I think the following should be said.

The inescapable whiff of his tobacco and his monstrous snoring may sometimes have been unbearable from her point of view. Careless of his own comfort and safety, he was probably cavalier with Joy's.

His prolonged silences, sometimes lasting several days, can have

been no fun for anyone who loved talking as much as Joy did, especially since he had no ear for her great alternative delight, music. And
although he was an avid reader, enjoying most of the same books
that she did, they had no common ground in the field of painting.

Often finding George uncongenial as a companion and lover she
was driven by irresistible urges—physical, psychological or hor-
monal—to seek satisfaction elsewhere, but her infidelities would
scarcely have raised an eyebrow among her contemporaries had she
been a man.

It is also true that until Terence finished building the new house
in 1950 Joy was entirely justified in not wishing to start a family
which, by his own calculation, George could not have supported at
the time.

On the other hand, Joy's storms shocked by their violence and
George was occasionally obliged to defend himself physically: Peter
Bally had similar experiences with her. Sometimes George slapped
her face in an attempt to restrain her; sometimes he wrestled with
her; occasionally she was hurt and would have to see a doctor.
Although painful, and recorded by both of them, these occasions
were very rare. Nevertheless, Joy tended to exaggerate and embel-
lish—even invent—them, maintaining that several times George
tried to throttle her.

On a lighter note, George was never sure whether Joy really
intended to hit his private parts when she threw a knife at him—he
supposed not because her aim was always so erratic.

Just as shocking were her verbal assaults on George. It was only when
I began to help him collect material for *My Pride and Joy*, after she was
dead, that I realized how much emotional pain she must have inflicted
on him during the early years of their marriage. It is difficult to understand why he put up with so much from her for so long.

I finally came to the conclusion that once his romantic illusions
had been shattered there were still three powerful forces that held
him to her. She remained a wonderful and probably irreplaceable
companion on safari. He did his utmost to honor his original vow to
prove a good husband, even if their feelings toward each other altered.
And, above all, she elicited the profound compassion he felt for
anyone, or any animal, that was in trouble or suffering. Only he, and
perhaps Bally, recognized that her compulsion to hurt others must
have derived from pain in her own mind and heart.

When researching this book I became so puzzled by Joy's behavior that I asked Dr. Matthew Cullen, a psychiatrist, if he could help me understand her better. He knew the bare facts about Joy from *Born Free*, but little else. I therefore sketched in the basic complexities of her family background and marriages, and tried to answer some extremely pertinent questions he raised about them. A week later he offered a diagnosis.

He believed that her childhood relations with her father, her parents' divorce, her later reactions to her mother, and also her first love affair, had led to a distinct personality disturbance. Technically there are several types of these disorders, and they may overlap, but one, in particular, describes Joy's behavior with great precision. This is extracted from its definition in *The Oxford Textbook of Psychiatry*.

Histrionic Personality Disorder.

In a normal personality, minor histrionic traits can be socially advantageous.

When these qualities are exaggerated in histrionic personality disorder they become less acceptable. The person dramatises himself as a larger than life character; he seems to be playing a part, incapable of being himself.

He appears vain, inconsiderate, and demanding and may go to extreme lengths to force other people to fall in with his wishes. Emotional "blackmail," angry scenes, and demonstrative suicide attempts are all part of the stock-in-trade of such a person. He displays emotions readily, exhausting others with tantrums of rage or dramatic expressions of despair. He seems to feel little of the emotions he expresses, he recovers quickly and often seems surprised that other people are not prepared to forget the scenes as quickly as he is himself.

With these qualities is combined a capacity for self-deception that can at times reach astounding proportions. The person goes on believing himself to be in the right when all the facts show that he is not. He is able to maintain elaborate lies long after other people have seen through them.

In histrionic personality disorder, the sexual life is also affected. Especially in women there is often sexual provocation combined with frigidity. They engage in displays of affection and are flirtatious, but they are often incapable of deep feelings and may fail to reach orgasm.

However different this profile is—especially in its indications of megalomania and dishonesty—from the popular image of the Joy Adamson who wrote a series of best-selling books, who featured in some remarkable films and television documentaries and who lectured all over the world, in the opinion of people who knew her very well it is tragically accurate, although it deals with only one side of her personality. So carried away could she become by the version of events that best suited her mood, case or view of the world, that hostile testimony from her, particularly toward George, but also toward anyone else who crossed her, needs the closest examination before it is accepted.

There is further pathos in Dr. Cullen's opinion that at the time Joy was desperately seeking psychological help the only treatment was a long course of analysis in Europe. She could neither have afforded it nor stood the claustrophobia of spending months or years in a city. In any case, analysis has never been able to guarantee a cure.

As a sick animal may instinctively select the right diet, choose seclusion or rely on a companion for food and protection while it cannot fend for itself, Joy's intuition seems to have led her to the mountains and Kenya, and to three extraordinarily magnanimous husbands.

The bargain was not entirely one-sided, for everyone who knew Joy intimately derived great pleasure from her vitality, talents, courage and joie de vivre. She helped to ease Ziebel von Klarwill's first year in exile from the Nazis; to Peter Bally she brought both credit and lasting delight in her success as a botanical artist; while with George she raised Elsa and together they created a legend.

4

Joy seems to have received almost greater reassurance and consolation from her small cairn terrier than she did from the combined resources of the Alps, the great East African peaks and her three husbands. Pippin's company and devotion had never once failed her during the most turbulent period of her life. Unlike the mountains, he was accessible wherever she went; unlike other available love his was entirely uncritical.

Peter Bally had given her the dog to console her after she supposedly lost a baby in 1938. Since then Pippin had braved every imaginable climate and landscape, from the glaciers of Mount Kenya, through the forests of Kulal and the plains of Meru, to the parched sands of the Suguta Valley. By 1949 his constitution was exhausted: he began to stiffen up and his nose bled.

Knowing he was ill, George turned up at Joy's camp when Pippin was finally dying. They sat up all night with the little dog and George buried him in the dark at four in the morning—"with part of myself," Joy wrote. George understood very well what she must be suffering.

His own two dogs, Bully and Fifi, had recently died after eating poisoned hyena bait. Their replacement Kim—whom Joy so disliked—was a handsome cross between a Ridgeback and a mastiff, but he suffered repeatedly from the diseases and parasites of the bush and was finally killed by a pack of village curs. Neither George nor Joy ever kept a dog again.

On the other hand, a succession of orphans found refuge in their camps or in the enclosure at Isiolo, even though this frequently led to heartbreak. Attempts to save the lives of a young impala doe, a small Grevy's zebra and a baby elephant were in vain. One of the two surviving ostriches was killed by a snake and Oscar, the other, also came to a sticky end.

A cock ostrich can be aggressive and viciously dangerous. Turn and face it with a stick, or a handful of stones, and it may keep its distance. To run is fatal: it will chase a man and kill him, slashing through the muscles of his back with its powerful claws.

When Oscar first grew obstreperous he was given a dose of his own medicine by a wild cock which chased him ignominiously into the kitchen. After that he went berserk. It might have been amusing when he tore the clothes off the *toto*, but when he jumped up and down on the groom and broke two of his ribs he signed his own death warrant. Other adoptions, the mongooses for instance, were happier. Success largely depended on how much was known about a species and how young an orphan was when Joy took it in.

A rock hyrax she adopted and christened Pati Pati became as important to her as Pippin and took the place of a child in her life until she adopted Elsa.

The dark-furred rock hyrax, or dassie, looks like a large guinea pig. It is diurnal and experts say that it is related to the rhino. Because Pati was brought to her when she was only a day or two old, she imprinted on Joy—in other words accepted her as her mother since she was the first animate presence that she saw. She was therefore never tempted to stray in search of her own kind.

She spent much of the day on Joy's shoulder and slept near her at night. Her personal tastes and habits were curious. Wild hyraxes use a regular rock from which to excrete and Pati immediately adopted the lavatory at Isiolo—she even tried to push visitors like Elspeth Huxley's mother and the DC's wife off it. In fact it became so important to her that George had to make a miniature one for her use on safaris, during which she rode a mule with Joy.

A vegetarian, Pati developed a liking for alcohol—knocking bottles over, drawing their corks with her teeth and enjoying a good binge. If obliged to drink water she preferred the chill taken off it. Each evening she joined Joy in her bath, crept down her naked stomach and sipped the warm water, grinding her teeth to convey her satisfaction. This is how Joy came to feel about her.

> Thanks to her I had found an outlet for my frustrated need to care and love. I knew that George needed both but in a way he seemed to be unable to show his feelings and thus made it impossible to respond. How often did I try to tell him that I loved him only to get his grunt, "What did you say?" before falling back into his characteristic introverted silence.

Joy's formal record of the tribes began on her own initiative in 1948, became a government commission in 1949 and was nearing completion in 1952. By then there were rumblings of discontent, both great and small, that were to have an immediate effect on her and George's short-term plans and in the long run to transform entirely the face of Kenya.

For the first time in his life, George began to face serious criticisms from his superiors and colleagues. They felt he was no longer in effective control of his game scouts or tribal police. It would be hardly surprising, given the inordinate stress and demands Joy imposed on him, if his energy was not sometimes sapped and his mind distracted from his work.

Quite apart from that, he had not been on leave outside Africa since he had arrived there in 1924, and his only spells away from his district had been during his time with the army in 1941 and two months in the Belgian Congo with Joy over Christmas 1949. Willie Hale therefore put down his foot and told him to take overseas leave. By then he had accumulated an entitlement to more than 700 days of absence, so there was no alternative but to accept with good grace!

• Dissatisfaction of an infinitely greater order began to find violent expression among members of the Kikuyu tribe at just this time. On February 5, 1952, Princess Elizabeth, visiting Kenya with her husband the Duke of Edinburgh, went to Treetops Hotel to watch the game at the water hole. Her father died that night and on the following day she returned to England as Queen Elizabeth II.

As her plane left the airstrip at Nanyuki, on the slopes of Mount Kenya, smoke was seen rising from five grass fires started as protests. During the previous two weeks there had been far more serious acts of arson committed by devotees of a movement known as Mau Mau that was sworn to the overthrow of the British colonial regime.

For the past four years activists among the Kikuyu, the cleverest and most ambitious of the tribes, had been secretly, and not so secretly, recruiting under oath men and women who would stop at nothing to get rid of both the white man and any African who remained "loyal" to him.

In October, the new Governor-General, Sir Evelyn Baring, announced a State of Emergency, the arrival of a British battalion from the Suez Canal Zone and the arrest of the man widely believed to be masterminding the disturbances, Jomo Kenyatta.

At the end of the year, and in the beginning of 1953, the Mau Mau began their bloodthirsty work in earnest. Four isolated European farmers, the six-year old son of one of them, Councillor Tom Mbotela in Nairobi, and Chief Hinga in hospital at Kiambu, were all brutally murdered and mutilated. Equally ruthless, and on a far wider scale, were the atrocities committed against any Kikuyu, living on farms or in villages, who resisted or even showed themselves half-hearted toward the movement.

It was reckoned that only one sixteenth of Kenya was seriously affected by the Mau Mau revolt, but its epicenter—round Mount Kenya and the Aberdare Highlands—lay at the heart of the country. Both the principal roads between Isiolo and Nairobi, which ran either side of the mountain, were therefore at risk.

It was just as well that Joy's tribal pursuits were nearly at an end and that she planned to accompany George on his reluctantly taken overseas leave.

TWELVE

Twilight of the Tribes

1947–1953

1

Joy's adventures as an artist during the five years she concentrated on painting the tribes led her into some curious scrapes.

One day, after completing the picture of an elder wearing a large headdress of ostrich plumes, a monkey coat and a spear, I took a stroll up a lonely valley.

I must have come close to his home for suddenly he appeared at the top of the hill dressed in the clothes in which he had posed for me. As soon as he spotted me he came tearing down the slope, shouting and waving his spear. I thought he was doing it for fun.

When he came closer I realised he was going to charge me and I had to run as fast as I could to escape.

His chief was furious with the sitter for going back to his hut and restoring himself with too much home-brewed beer.

On Lake Baringo she was less afraid of the Njemps warriors in their lion-mane helmets and armed to the teeth than of the hippos that emerged from the water and approached her tent in the night with deep, reverberating grunts.

At Lokitaung, in Turkana country, she took great care not to tread on the nocturnal carpet vipers in the dark: although they are only a foot long, their bite can cause a fatal internal hemorrhage. While she was at Kakamega, where George had set a rhinoceros horn viper to guard his gold in the thirties, a cobra was flushed when the grass was cut around her tent. Joy then looked up at a flock of chattering birds and saw they were mobbing a deadly mamba camouflaged in a branch just above her.

The elements were equally threatening but she shrugged off these hazards as a small price to pay for a uniquely privileged view of this savage and esoteric way of life, doomed to change like much of the spectacular landscape that supported it.

It is ironic that the inspiration for the enterprise had come not from the true people of Kenya but from the colorful Arabs on the coast and that the tribal sketches that first won attention were made not for formal portraits, but for the chess set she never completed. *The Geographical Magazine* printed the sketches in early 1948 and a month or two later Sir John Ramsden, a trustee of the Coryndon Museum, bought them privately.

However, Joy still lacked official support and her early sitters were chosen purely on their suitability as subjects for striking portraits. It was not always easy, but with the help of Sandy Simpson and Griff Griffith she found some superb subjects among the Nandi above the Rift Valley and the Turkana to the west of Lake Rudolf. After that she ran into serious trouble.

Anywhere near a town the old traditions were fading or forgotten; sitters turned up in gaudy modern fabrics and vulgar beadwork. Elsewhere elders were reluctant to reveal to a stranger—especially a woman—their more arcane rituals and regalia. The long-established missions were well placed to help, but some were loath to risk resurrecting the old beliefs they were trying so hard to stamp out. Fortunately the Church Missionary Society—evangelical Anglicans—did decide to help her.

Joy's greatest stroke of luck was when the colony's Commissioner for Social Welfare casually asked to see her paintings and immediately promised to show them to the Governor in the hope of obtaining a commission.

In January 1949 she was offered, and signed, a contract with the government. Under it, she was to cover between 15 and 22 tribes (out of a total of 74); paint five large portraits, and three small full-length figures from each and deliver them by the end of the year. She was to receive £7.50 each for the larger pictures and £3.50 for the smaller and she was also allowed £350 for traveling and other expenses; in all she stood to earn about £1,150. Every provincial and district commissioner was instructed to help her.

Although Joy made it quite clear she was no anthropologist, ethnographer or even professional artist, she was enthusiastically supported by Louis Leakey at the museum. She undertook to make detailed notes of her subjects, and unless a ritual or costume was authenticated by at least two elders, she refused to paint it.

Knowing what would be involved, George thought her fee was derisory, but to her it was princely. She rushed out to buy her own car: the first almost burst into flames on its test run, the second disintegrated at the end of its first safari but the third—a pristine one-and-a-half-ton Morris Commercial—served her purpose.

It was rather the same with her cooks. The first, Daniel, invited her to watch a Malakoti *ngoma* (dance). While the warriors were gripped in a characteristic frenzy or fit he, too, rolled on the ground, swiveled his eyeballs and bubbled at the mouth. But when she rose to leave he leapt to attention and asked: "Do you want pancakes or banana fritters for supper?" She was impressed.

Sadly he did not keep it up. He soon ran into debt wherever they camped and Joy had to get rid of him, as she did his replacement, Isaiah, who was still smiling when she dropped him at the gates of the prison.

On the other hand Kifosha, the Kikuyu who had shared her ordeal on Mount Kenya and now joined her again, withstood the tests of time and her temper, like the Morris. "Kifosha is a gentleman," she wrote in her diary.

Cooking for Joy on safari cannot have been rewarding. Money became so tight she lived on the cheapest food she could buy—eggs, vegetables and fruit—and was so engrossed in her painting that often only a headache at sundown reminded her she had not eaten since dawn. She allowed two days for each portrait, working from eight in the morning until five in the evening.

Her quarters were usually her own tent, but the Morris had a box body, caged in, so that she could set up a camp bed inside it if necessary. She improvised a studio wherever she went—in the shade of a tree, a veranda, or some makeshift hut. She also carried a specially high tent in which there was room for the most exotic headdresses, long spears and the elaborate paraphernalia frequently fancied by witch doctors. It was designed to open on all four sides in response to the wind, rain and shifting light.

Joy decided watercolor was the best medium since it dried fast and was less affected by the fine dust that blew everywhere. If dust did settle on a damp surface she could wash it off and repaint it.

> In order to convey the rich pigments of the African complexion I developed a technique of my own. I usually started with the highlights and went into darker tones by putting one layer of paint on top of another layer until I achieved the effect I wanted. I almost modelled in paint to get the strong contrast of the bone structures.

If her sitters spoke Swahili she tried to put them at ease and keep them animated by asking about their families and admiring their jewelry and weapons. As a man she would never have won the confidence of the women, as a woman she was careful not to overdo the flattery of the men. Even so an Igembe witch doctor made such obscene suggestions and gestures that George reported him to the DC!

Pippin, and later Pati, helped to entertain her sitters. The hyrax also lit sparks of cupidity for her flesh and fur.

Korani Elmi, a Somali and one of the very few Africans to be appointed an honorary game warden, had shot thirty lions with his bow and arrow at point-blank range by lying stock-still for hours beside a kill. He told Joy, very politely, he much preferred ambushing a pride of lions to sitting for her.

Often inducements were essential to persuade her subjects to sit or produce their most sacred treasures; she also offered recompense, usually in cash or tobacco, at rates set by the local DC. Occasionally a surreptitious tot of gin or whiskey succeeded where other blandishments failed.

Joy was determined that the costumes and artifacts should not distract her from catching the likeness and character of her subjects; she wanted to create a collection of living people.

> I tried to achieve this by holding the attention of my sitters with my eyes and thus automatically, but unconsciously, I believe I was able to convey the spirit of my models. In our "silent eye language" we both communicated in a far more direct way than words could have achieved.

The eyes of a Maasai, Konei ole Sendeo, ringed in white paint, exhausted and nearly defeated her. Because he was a *laibon* or spiritual leader, she felt he was out to mesmerize her and assert his authority as he did among the Maasai. Perhaps he succeeded; when his portrait was recently shown to members of the tribe they instantly recognized him.

2

"In the beginning was the word."

Quite apart from its allegorical significance, this assertion may be literally true. It is now considered by many that it was the power of speech rather than the ability to stand up and walk on two legs, or to make and use tools, that proclaimed the arrival of man.

Whether or not this is the determining factor of our species, anthropologists sometimes use language rather than other aspects of our culture, our physical appearance or geographical connections to trace our roots. It was the principle used to differentiate the seventy or so tribes then thought to be represented in Kenya—an arbitrary figure since the borderlines between tribal groups and their divisions were so imprecise. Asked to paint about twenty in a year—an impossible task—Joy finally covered nearly sixty in five years.

Checked against two recent books, whose contents pages list an average of forty principal tribes each, her coverage can be seen to be admirably representative: only two populations of any size, the Iteso and Sabaot, both in western Kenya, were omitted. Considering that her painting safaris were made virtually alone, underfunded and had to be completed in the days of increasingly active Mau Mau revolt, her achievement was astonishing. When color photography was still so uncertain, there was no other way to capture so effectively the rituals and traditional regalia before they dissolved into legend and dust—or were entirely forgotten.

The history of the Kenyan tribes is a bewildering tangle of speculation, contradiction, ignorance and constant renaming. In 1948, when Joy started her record, Kenya was inhabited by about 5,250,000 Africans, 120,000 Asians and 30,000 Europeans. Of the more than 5 million Africans there was no community, however tiny, whose direct antecedents had remained on home ground since representatives of *Homo erectus* left it a million years ago. Every inhabitant of Kenya was therefore an immigrant.

The Africans broke down into five currents or groups. Each spoke a different basic language that could be used like a dye marker to distinguish one stream from another. Where they became neighbors they fought, intermarried and made exchanges of language and culture. Simplistically the five main streams may be called "Aboriginal," Cushitic, Nilotic, Bantu and Coastal.

The "Aboriginals"—for instance, the Dorobo and the Boni—were not truly so. Their ancestors were probably Bushmen, related to those in southern Africa and the Kalahari, who lived by hunting and gathering and who were driven into the forests on the mountains by more aggressive tribes with whom they later interbred.

The Cushitic tribes—among them the Somalis, Rendille, and Boran—came from the Horn of Africa and had been pushing into northeastern Kenya from Somaliland and Ethiopia for millennia. At one stage they were known as Hamitic, but this term was frowned upon since it implied that their culture was of Middle Eastern rather than African origin. Be that as it may, some, like the Somalis, were Muslims. The Cushitic people are among the toughest in the world. Their way of life, with their camels, cattle, sheep and goats, is perfectly adapted to the thankless conditions of the desert—a biblical pursuit of its meager grazing and water, or battles for its wells.

As their name implies the Nilotic people—who include the Turkana, Luo, Njemps, Samburu and Maasai—had pushed up the Nile and occupied western and parts of central Kenya. Joy was thrilled to find one Luo dressed for a funeral in the apparel of a pharaoh. Basically the Nilotes were pastoral but only seminomadic.

The Maasai lived for their cattle, would not cultivate for fear of upsetting the grassland and disdained to hunt—except to destroy the arch enemy of their herds, the lion. Their tall, godlike and often arrogant young warriors hunted lions single-handedly to prove their virility and when they speared one adapted its mane as a headdress.

The Bantu people belonged to the great human reservoir that over the centuries had slowly spread through western and southern Africa and finally north into Kenya. Their tribes, especially the Kikuyu, Embu and Meru, were concentrated around Mount Kenya, the Aberdare Mountains and Nairobi. Together with others in the west, near the lakes and on the coast, they made up two thirds of the African population. Most of the Bantu were not blessed with the magnificent physique of the Nilotes but enjoyed instead particularly agile minds which the Kikuyu, for instance, put to excellent use. They also had green fingers. Settling on fertile and well-watered land, they made the most of their fields, plantations and gardens.

Just before Joy returned from her year in Europe a Kikuyu who then called himself Johnston Kenyatta also made his way back to Kenya from Europe. He had spent more than fifteen years there preparing himself to win for his tribe equal rights with the white man and to recover the land he believed to be theirs.

At the London School of Economics he read anthropology, often attending lectures by Professor Malinowski, and sharing a table in the lunch break with another student, Elspeth Huxley. In 1938, Kenyatta published a book on the Kikuyu, *Facing Mount Kenya.*

The longer he stayed in Europe the more widely his ability and potential stature were recognized. Visiting Moscow, he learned the tactics of revolution and also the fundamental lesson that communism could not feed you: he therefore studied cooperative farming in Scandinavia. He became friends with two other future African presidents—Hastings Banda of Malawi and Kwame Nkrumah of Ghana. Their company broadened his intentions into not merely securing proper rights for the Kikuyu, but wresting power in Kenya from the British. Nevertheless, he returned to his country in 1946 with a British wife and a will tempered with wisdom.

There were more than a million Kikuyus, the largest of the Bantu group. With their intelligence, explicit aims and willingness to work hard, they constituted a formidable power base.

Joy's personal experience of the tribe was a happy one. Kifosha became not only her cook but her houseboy, interpreter and gun bearer as well. She trusted him completely, but when the first Mau Mau murderer was caught near Taveta, where she was painting, Kifosha took her completely by surprise.

> One day Kifosha came to me with a letter and 10 shillings which he wanted to send to the editor of the *East African Standard.* In it he confessed deep shame at how his tribe was being degraded by Mau Mau methods—how they had twisted the good tribal traditions for evil purposes. He wanted to donate the money to a campaign to help other Kikuyu to fight the menace.
>
> I warned him of the possible consequences of a signed letter like this: that he and his family might become victims of Mau Mau bestiality too. He only replied that no compromise was possible and he would have to take the risk.

Joy was able to make her sequence of Kikuyu paintings only with the help of Chief Njiri, who was totally staunch to the best traditions of his tribe, refused to speak English and always wore African dress. At the same time he supported the government throughout the emergency, for which he received a medal and was happily spared the grisly fate of some other loyal chiefs.

The Coastal people of Kenya never had to undergo the horrors of Mau Mau. In breeding and culture they reflected the mixture of Bantus, Arabs and Asians who, over the centuries, had settled on the seaboard. One of the groups, the Swahili, spoke the language alloyed with Arabic that has become the lingua franca of the whole of East Africa.

With the salt of the sea in their lungs, the Arabs, Indians, Swahilis and Bajun islanders manned the dhows that carried maritime trade up to the palm groves at the head of the Persian Gulf and down to the clove-scented island of Zanzibar.

The first spark of the tribal project had been struck on the coast when Joy painted Sheikh Azan, at Malindi. The real work began when Sandy Simpson introduced her to the tribes on the western wall of the Rift in 1948. In January 1953, her main task ended back on the coast, and she set off for Isiolo to plan with George their overseas leave.

On the way home another strand of her life reached its final conclusion. In recent months Simpson had dropped in on her from time to time, but he had become increasingly impersonal; when she discovered he had driven past her camp one day without stopping she felt bitterly insulted. She wrote *finis* to both him and her tribal enterprise after a meeting on January 13.

Five years since I started my work with him—and now as indifferent as only a man without a heart can be. So ends the great climax in my private and public life. Funeral?

3

Whatever George's shortcomings, Joy could never complain he was heartless. Apart from his Sunday letters he usually remembered anniversaries and other special occasions. One year he sent her a thermos filled with ice cream for her birthday via a Miss Sleepingwell.

George was always concerned for her and urged her to see the best doctors in Kenya. She suffered not only from malaria and tick fever but also from her teeth, her eyes and her tonsils.

He was also particularly alarmed by her continued habit of taking long lonely walks through the bush and had once tried to cure her when she had gone off to commune with nature and refused to move on.

George had taken the only course to bring me back to reality and had returned to camp.

Finding myself suddenly all alone, I almost panicked.

The lesson did not work, even though George also wrote to the local DC and asked him to dissuade Joy from the practice that finally led to her death.

From the very beginning George's feelings about the tribal project were mixed. He respected Joy's talent and ambition but was hurt when she was away for so long.

I am very pleased indeed that you have been given the painting commission for your sake because you so much wanted it. But I do feel that the government are being pretty mean. £800 seems damned little for a year's or eighteen months' work.

As it became clear Joy would never complete the project in eighteen months his anxiety about money grew increasingly emphatic.

I am beginning to hate this commission of yours and believe it will wreck our marriage more surely than any Peter, Simpson or Griffith could. Do you think it right or fair that for the next year we may be with each other for a bare fortnight? I don't want to spend my next leave in a place like Vihiga, with you working the whole day and then us going out for an evening's walk among a lot of filthy villages.

I just do not care two hoots in hell whether Kenya gets your collection of paintings or not. If you had an atom of common sense you would sell the paintings to an American or European museum, where they would be seen by people (millions) who appreciate them.

He tried a lighter touch at the end of the letter in which he had recounted the antics of the Mexican hunting party that caused so much trouble.

I am quite sure if relations had been friendly, I would have been able to persuade Pasquel to make a donation of £3,000 for your paintings! The man is fabulously rich. It is said that he offered £200 to any woman of his choice who would sleep with him.

A party of important Egyptians have arrived at Isiolo. There you sit in this dreadful place Vihiga throwing drunken Vermouth parties with penniless DOs when you could be drinking champagne and getting thousands of pounds out of Egyptian princes and Mexican millionaires.

Your, full of love, George.

A few weeks later he was at the end of his tether again.

I am not going to insist on you giving up this commission, because I think that would be too much to ask, and also I am proud of your work and am willing to sacrifice quite a lot for your sake.

But I must make it clear that I am not willing to send you money in order to enable you to continue the commission and stay away from me for an indefinite period.

In his eyes every penny he earned belonged to both of them and he supported Joy—and paid her taxes—throughout their marriage, except during the first few months in England in 1946 when she had the money from her flower paintings to spend.

She, on the other hand, banked everything she earned in her own name, and expected him to support her while her tribal painting continued after her government funding ran out. He struggled to sort out the financial implications.

I have just filled in the income tax form and our joint income comes to £2,162. After deducting all allowances and your expenses except the car, which I do not think they will allow, our chargeable income is still £1,568, on which I shall have to pay tax of £232! I am enclosing a copy of your expenses as sent to the commissioner of income tax. My salary of £945 per year sounds marvellous but by the time income tax has been taken off it amounts to £536 plus another £180 (about) allowances. Still, in spite of the depressing picture don't worry, I will always see you through.

Here is an extract from George's return to the Commissioner.

My wife's income derived from the sale of paintings
Watercolor paintings of flowers and natives   £1,217
Expenses   £ 143
During 1949 my wife got a commission from the Kenya government to paint the native tribes of Kenya. She is continuing with
this work, in spite of the fact that the government may not be
willing to put up any more money. Idealism of the highest order!
Very difficult for an underpaid government official like myself to
live up to. But there it is and I hope it will influence you in the
assessment of my tax.

From odd notes in diaries and letters it is clear that Joy made a
worthwhile sum of money each year from selling her paintings of
flowers and sometimes of tribespeople. George would occasionally
borrow from Joy to buy a new shotgun, a camera or safari equipment
but she required him to repay all his debts in full. She also expected
him to pay every one of the household bills and her living expenses
on her safaris. Yet both of them were infinitely less concerned with
making money than with living each hour or day as if it were their
last, as many days might have been.

By 1951, Joy had accumulated many more paintings than had been
commissioned, at far greater cost in money and peace of mind than
George, or even she, had bargained for. After buying nearly 400 the
Kenya Treasury ran out of funds, and Joy began to stalk the corridors
of power on the warpath.

A retired Treasury official described the impasse like this.

Eric Davies, the Chief Native Commissioner, was caught between
two immovable objects: Joy's determination to extend her record
and the Treasury's unwillingness to pay out until a new contract
had been approved. He used to lock his door and pretend to be
out when warned that Joy was coming to visit him.

She even called on the Governor. In a bid to arouse public interest
and attract donations he suggested staging an exhibition in Nairobi,
which was done in August. Warriors in tribal regalia stood at the
entrance for the opening, and Joy spent time there each day, as she
described in her much later book *The Peoples of Kenya*.

I talked for a long time to one of the African visitors and stressed
that the purpose of my work was to help to preserve the knowledge

of fast disappearing tribal cultures. I spoke too of my hope that it would lead others, whose help was needed in the struggle to develop the country, to a better understanding of the peoples of Kenya. After he had left I learned that it was Jomo Kenyatta to whom I had been speaking.

But despite the exhibition and appeals to every possible source, no money was forthcoming. In the end it was George and Joy who put their hands in their pockets to finance her final year on the coast and complete her priceless collection.

4

Anyone who actually witnessed the life illustrated in Joy's paintings marvels at their accuracy, although to western eyes her figures are the dramatis personae of fantasies, mysteries and nightmares.

In circumcision, awestruck boys stand plastered with ashes and ocher, or slung with bows, arrows and the sunbirds they have shot as a prelude to the ritual. Girls wait in seclusion, entirely concealed in tentlike constructions of rustling reeds, or sheaths of blackened leather with slits for their eyes.

Warriors kneel, swagger and crouch in challenge, plumes swaying on their heads, leopard skins draped down their backs, their spears and painted oxhide shields raised to strike or parry a blow. Brides-to-be and married women in beads, bangles, earrings and brief cowrie-shell skirts modestly lower their eyes or boldly gaze back at the artist. Bodies are patterned with scars; ears are pierced with the holes that have been gradually stretched by the insertion of increasingly large bones or wooden disks.

Witch doctors clutch the tools of their art—tortoise shells, curving horns of magic powders, monkeys' paws and oddly shaped lyres. An elder is off to a funeral in a leather mask, its macabre features marked out with lucky beans and rodents' teeth stuck on with honey.

Tribal society was virtually classless, without kings or chiefs—the latter were colonial appointments. Authority was vested in the elders and precedent. If decisions were drawn out by prolonged debate, time in those days was seldom of the essence.

The progression from infant to elder was one of slow graduation in which groups of contemporaries took a step up the ladder of life every seven years or so. The measured ascent provided a set of steady expectations, a division of labor, and sense of responsibility that ensured the tribe remained stable, fed and protected from its enemies. By means of body decoration, jewelry and simple or elaborate costumes, everyone's place in society was defined with precision.

Ceremony, dancing and ritual prepared men and women for the battles of life, occupied their leisure, or gave expression to different forms of religious belief. It was a sensual world for people who lived through their eyes and ears, by smell, touch and speech, but for whom words and numbers on paper meant nothing. They did not write down their laws or their history, they knew them by heart; they did not count their cows or goats at night, they watched as the animals passed into the fold and matched them with the pictures in their heads.

The first great step for a boy was the day he found himself in charge of the family's goats; by far the most significant event in his whole life was his circumcision. He could conceivably be as young as seven, or possibly as old as twenty-one, but if he betrayed fear by so much as the flicker of an eyelid, his standing was ruined forever.

The circumcision of girls, though even more personally daunting, was perhaps less tribally significant. At its simplest the operation entailed the removal of the top of the clitoris with an implement not always sharp. In a more elaborate variation the lips of the vagina were also removed and the aperture made smaller and tighter by infibulation, at first with thorns or stitches and then by the scarring that followed. After marriage and in childbirth the tearing or cutting, and the pain and dangers of infection, were very considerable.

Male circumcision is said to have originated in the desert to avoid the irritation and sepsis arising from sand in the foreskin. Clitoridectomy and infibulation were claimed to encourage chastity and fidelity by reducing the pleasure of sexual intercourse or making it impossible. Strangely it was carried out by women, and Jomo Kenyatta, in his book *Facing Mount Kenya*, holds the view that it was so deeply embedded in his tribes' social evolution it would be worse to forbid it than to allow its survival.

Once circumcised, and then a *moran* or warrior, a young man's duties were hunting, looking after the cattle and camels, stealing someone else's, or fighting. He might not marry but was encouraged, in some tribes, to explore the delights of lovemaking without carrying it through to consummation, which Kikuyu girls prevented by tucking their skirts between their legs.

In George's day it was still possible to come across men in the NFD sporting scars or teeth denoting the number of men they had killed. Others wore their enemies' navels or testicles as trophies. But in the days of *pax Britannica* many *moran* found too little to occupy them and sublimated their energy in other directions; forbidden to hunt, the Samburu sometimes won their spurs hooking a sandal on a rhino's horn. Joy believed they and the Maasai diverted their energies into beautification.

Even so, while she was painting a Maasai *moran* he suddenly threw away his headdress and shield, grabbed his spear and flung himself into a melee that had broken out in the manyatta. Several men received alarming slashes and wounds but her subject quickly returned unconcerned to the sitting.

The effects that some Maasai or Samburu achieved with their finery were strikingly attractive. Their tightly plaited hair glistening with red ocher was drawn forward in a fringe held with a clasp; it was also gathered on top of the head and allowed to fall to the shoulders. The contours of brows, cheekbones and lips were emphasized in clay, and the face framed in an oval of ostrich feathers or topped by a high helmet of lion mane. The *morans'* throats, arms and wrists were set off with bands of beads; their earrings glinted in the sunlight.

The second great initiation, the transition from warrior to elder, was marked by the ceremonial stripping of their finery and shaving of their heads. As a senior warrior, or junior elder, a man was allowed to marry.

The traditions of marriage varied all over the country according to tribal beliefs that ranged from the most archaic and pagan to the strictest Muslim observance. Custom frequently allowed for a trial period; during this only part of the price for the bride might be paid—in head of livestock—and only at the end would her father hand over the balance of the dowry. Polygamy was widespread, but the greatest care was taken to avoid inbreeding.

Each milestone of betrothal, marriage and childbearing was reflected in a woman's dress and ornamentation, usually incorporating cowrie shells, the natural symbols of womanhood. No man was therefore in any doubt about her status, which was just as well in view of the excitement generated at the height of an *ngoma*, for which she decked herself out as carefully as the men did. Some of the Turkana women went so far as to cover their breasts with large water boatman bugs which bit them and made them swell up.

Joy described several dances. This is a Kurya *ngoma*.

With almost military precision the women and girls lined up in a circle until each was in her proper place, the women in the centre and the girls on the periphery. First they jumped in slow rhythm, but gradually they worked themselves up to a frenzy faster and faster, twisting their abdomens vigorously until the greased back-aprons skipped from side to side at each jump, making a fascinating counter-movement to the jumping bodies.

When they were all in full swing, a procession of giants appeared, walking stiffly on large wooden blocks more than a foot high, which were tied to their feet. These were the young men come to join in the dance. Covered with colobus monkey capes, and heightened not only by the blocks but also by tall headdresses of ostrich plumes, they towered over the girls by several feet and slowly they encircled them.

Having walked around them, they too started jumping, lifting their heavy wooden clogs with astonishing ease, and twisting their bodies at the same time until their back-aprons decorated with metal, swung in rhythm with those of the girls. Soon there was one mass of glistening, wriggling people leaping to the sound of drumming, oblivious of time and fatigue.

It was undoubtedly a man's world in which the women rowed and the men did the steering. Women dug, planted, milked, collected the firewood and built the huts in the manyatta. But a woman also had the protection of custom under the scrutiny of the elders—in case of an illegitimate pregnancy, sterility, widowhood or her husband wishing to set her aside.

The tribes had a reverence for elders, not only because of their experience. The peoples who believed in a god expected that as the old approached death, and therefore their god, they would absorb some of his wisdom.

Not all the tribes believed in a god or gods as did the Maasai and Kikuyu. Some worshipped the earth, the sky or the sun; some were pantheists; some animists; and others had no religion at all. But virtually every tribe boasted its medicine man or witch doctor who—

for a fee—would prescribe a cure for an illness, make rain, prophesy the future or cast good and evil spells.

Some certainly possessed effective herbal remedies; Jomo Kenyatta testifies to witnessing four cases of successful rainmaking when he was a boy; and there were famous stories of *laibons* and others foretelling the appearance of strangers, with skins like a pale frog's, plague and lethal fire sticks. European settlers, smallpox and firearms duly arrived.

Joy was skeptical of most claims, including those of this witch doctor she painted.

He told me happily that he was the best-known witch doctor in the area, earning between 200 and 300 shillings' worth of cattle for every successful treatment. When I inquired about the secret of his witchcraft I was told he owed it to his diet which consisted of cats, dogs, leopards, hyenas, lizards, geckos, chameleons, tortoises, snakes, crocodiles, and other delicacies. As he recorded this menu, I could not help feeling very worried about Pati.

On the other hand, she recognized that powders applied externally or internally were psychologically sound for detecting a nervous culprit who was sweating with anxiety or whose mouth had dried up. Two delicately balanced dik-dik horns might also tremble like a lie detector when touched by a guilty suspect.

One of the most impressive accounts of these mysterious powers was published in General Sir Frank Kitson's book about the Mau Mau, *Gangs and Counter-gangs*. Serving then as a major in Kenya, he consulted an old witch doctor about a murder of which the old man could have had no previous knowledge. The old man not only gave him—and the petrified suspect—a detailed account of the crime, but finally led them to the hut in a wood where it had taken place, and even showed them the hiding place under a fire where the murderer kept his gun.

While Joy was compiling her record of sorcery among the other tribes, Mau Mau leaders began to resurrect the most hated form of Kikuyu black magic.

Orogi was a poison so sinister that long before the arrival of the British its use was punishable by death, for it was a compound of toxic herbs and powder ground from dried human, animal and reptile flesh. Notable ingredients were eyes, ears, noses, hands, feet, blood, breasts and male and female genitals.

Kikuyu elders commanded great respect and did not hesitate to deal with offenders against the taboos and traditions of the tribe with appropriate strictness. Sadly, the zeal of the missions and the interference of the administration did much to undermine their authority.

With a god of their own and their belief in spirits and the mysteries of sacrifice, with their love of rhythm and desire for education as a means to their political ends, the Kikuyu were fertile ground for the missions. The Gospels and the Creed, hymn singing, reading, writing and arithmetic, were eagerly embraced at the expense of the Kikuyu's traditional beliefs. In the same way, their old secular disciplines lapsed when government officials usurped the role of the elders.

The leaders of Mau Mau struck at their people just before the missions and government had completed these conversions and just before the deepest forces of tribal memory had dissolved. All over the Kikuyu reserve secret meetings were held to recruit under oath, administered with a potent amalgam of perverted Christian ritual and the spirit of *orogi*, rebels to the cause.

Later, when the fight against the revolt was reaching its climax, Joy was asked to paint a prisoner captured from a Mau Mau gang in the forest. It was only long afterward she was told he had been taken out the next day and shot.

As with their migrations, settlements and lifestyles, it is impossible to generalize about death in the Kenyan tribes. Some believed in the survival of the spirit in this world or another; in some the dead were mourned with wailing and their garlanded cattle driven back to the homestead; in others the dead were buried with solemn ceremony, their bodies composed in a variety of positions according to their status and sex. Graves were marked with a cairn, an effigy, a post, or simply forgotten. The Maasai would not disturb the grass to bury the dead and the Turkana left theirs out in the open for the hyenas.

5

By the time Joy and George went on overseas leave in March 1953, she had completed a total of about 560 paintings: 150 had not yet been paid for.

At the back of her mind she still hoped to find a publisher for her record, and she planned to hunt one down in Europe to which she and George had decided to drive by way of the Sahara.

Louis Leakey persistently badgered the Governor, the Treasury, the local aristocracy, the Colonial Office in London and the Aga Khan for funds, but with no further luck.

It was not until 1957 that his persistence paid off, when, with the backing of some of Joy's friends and supporters, now well placed in the administration, the government stumped up £10 each for the balance of the pictures, bringing the grand total to 580.

Dear Louis,

Here—at last—are all the paintings I have at present of the tribal collection. Unfortunately I sold a few of the Samburu and was also not able to get the circumcision pictures of the Samburu, as the Circumcision was not on during the last years. So I will try to do these missing pictures with the first opportunity and hope they will be bought later on?

Louis, I want to thank you very much indeed for all your very kind help about these pictures. I know they gave you lots of trouble—but I hope all was for a worthy case, as I wanted these pictures to remain unsplit in Kenya and I could not do more personally as to refuse them to sell abroad—but you did a very great deal in helping to raise the money to secure them for Kenya. Well—at last—here is the collection complete and where we all want them and that is all that matters.

Again—very many thanks!

Yours, Joy.

The light was fading when Joy recorded the last scenes of this tremendous pageant. It takes only a few moments of honest reflection to recognize that it represented the natural activities and concerns of mankind, whereas it is the distorted life of urban civilization that is the stuff of fantasy and nightmare. Perhaps in the coming centuries Joy's pictures will be allowed out into a wider public gaze for, like the rock paintings of the Lascaux caves, or the Bayeux tapestry, they are the arresting and lasting images of sights no human eye will ever see again.

THIRTEEN

Across the Sahara

1953

1

George was reluctant to spend his leave in Europe and hated the prospect of being cooped up in a ship to get there. Joy's idea of driving through the Congo and across the Sahara was therefore a clever solution.

It was also brave, not just because a five-thousand mile drive anywhere in Africa in 1953 was extremely hazardous, but also because it meant that for two months, in the humid heat of the rain forest and the burning oven of the desert, they would be almost entirely alone.

In fact for the first time they were about to spend eight months continuously together. Joy would not even have the distraction and consolation of a Pippin or a Pati, whom she left in the care of a trapper outside Nairobi. The journey could finally make or break their marriage.

George planned a route that would take them through Uganda, the Belgian Congo, French Equatorial Africa—that included Chad and the Cameroons—and Nigeria. There they would turn north through Niger and Algeria—both French again—until they reached the Mediterranean at Algiers.

Long familiar with the history and practice of British colonialism, a hybrid of trade and paternalism, they would witness at firsthand the last late flowering of Belgian and French imperialism. Within ten years the European flags that had been flying over all three Empires for more than half a century would be hauled down and the deeds handed back to their African owners.

George acquired ample containers for water and forty gallons of fuel, and metal-link mats to get them out of the loose sand in which they were certain to flounder. To stretch their money they would

183

often have to camp which meant towing a trailer for their tents. The
trailer, like the rifle and shotgun he insisted on taking, aroused the
suspicions of every customs post north of the equator.

Leaving a locum in charge of George's Game Department territory
they set off at the end of March, and the trouble began on the very
first day when they crossed from Kenya to Uganda. Seeing all their
ready cash disappearing on a bond against the guns, Joy burst into
tears. George roughly reproved her for her emotional outburst, but
the officious customs officer relented, and whenever they had similar
trouble later George nudged Joy and told her to get on with her
act.

They spent the night of March 26, their last in Uganda, with a
splendid view of the glaciers on the Ruwenzoris. While they slept,
the Mau Mau revolt in Kenya flared into greater violence with a
murderous attack on the Naivasha police station and a massacre at
Lari.

No fewer than a thousand Mau Mau were mobilized to attack the
Kikuyu families living at Lari, about twenty-five miles northwest of
Nairobi. Their orders spoke of oaths, blinding, castration and death
for anyone resisting them or helping the whites. The target area was
a plain, about seven by three miles, whose inhabitants living in grass
huts were loyal to the government. Some of their menfolk had joined
the Kikuyu Home Guard and were actively fighting the Mau Mau.
On the night of the attack they were patrolling the forest.

At ten o'clock the assault, planned in every detail, was unleashed.
The first wave of attackers swiftly bound wire cables around each of
the two hundred or so huts, ensuring that escape through their doors
was impossible. The second wave then went in carrying cans of petrol
that was flung onto the walls and the roofs.

Suddenly the whole plain erupted in balls of fire from which flames
curled up into the darkness. Screams of indescribable panic and pain
mingled with the roar and crackle of the fires. Here and there women
with their children, and a few of the old, managed to force or grope
a way through the smoke and burning walls of their huts. They
staggered out into the flickering half-light.

As they did so the third wave of attackers emerged from the surrounding night. This was the moment they had been waiting for with
their sharpened pangas and *simis*. The elderly were mutilated or
chopped up like pigs. Chief Luka and his eight wives were finally
burned in the flames, but before he died the chief was mutilated;

then he was cut in two and his skull crushed. Women had their breasts lopped off; mothers were forced to watch their children's throats being cut and their blood drunk; and the stomachs of the pregnant were slit open. One woman escaped into the bush with her baby strapped to her back, unaware that its head had been cut off.

The exact total of casualties was never known, but a hundred people died and others were left horribly burned or disfigured. The atrocity by Kikuyus against Kikuyus was so unspeakable that its effect was the opposite of its intention; it forfeited the world's sympathy with the rebels and strengthened the resolve within the tribe to resist the Mau Mau movement.

Because they crossed into the Belgian Congo early that next morning George and Joy were totally unaware of what had occurred in the night or they would have certainly turned back to fight the emergency.

They would never see again the Kenya in which they had settled so long ago and that they had so recently left. Nevertheless, the evils of the Mau Mau were remarkably circumscribed. The fundamental sense and goodwill of the rest of Kikuyu and the Kenyan people stood them in excellent stead for the next thirty years, in marked contrast to the demoniac schism and bloodshed released by the withdrawal of the Belgians from the Congo—now Zaire—in 1960.

2

George and Joy took less than a week crossing the Congo; they would have spent longer had they not visited the country together three years before. At the end of 1949, Joy had persuaded George to take two months' leave there. They had struggled up the steep slopes of the volcano Nyiragongo and, defying its poisonous vapors, perched on the treacherous rim to gaze down 600 feet at the living inferno.

> We were deafened by the raging magma boiling below us. The spectacle was overpowering and George and I sat speechless as the light faded and the pulsating fire clouds rose above us into a black infinity . . .

Beautiful and dangerous, the volcano epitomized everything she and George relished and that held them together.

The gorillas at Lubero were also a magnificent sight, and only dangerous if threatened. In the days when few people were able to see the largest of the apes in the wild, George and Joy were lucky enough to catch glimpses of two mothers with young in their arms and a large silver-back male who launched a screaming charge but stumbled on a branch just before he reached them.

Less dramatic but moving, because they stirred memories of George's childhood, were the elephants at Gangala-na-Bodio that had been trained like their Asian counterparts to work in the fields and forests.

Joy broke the rules of the oldest national park in Africa—then known as Albert, now named Virunga—and picked several plants she wanted to paint, including a rare begonia and a ruby-red orchid. The authorities confiscated the pictures but a few years later she received a deluxe copy of volume 3 of *Spermatophytes en Flore du Congo Belge* with her sketches as a frontispiece.

In 1953 they had no time for more than a quick look at a station breeding okapi, a rare black-and-white striped cousin, though much smaller, of the giraffe. They simply drove for hundreds of miles between the walls of trees that lined the road through the Ituri Forest, home of the Pygmies.

Despite the Belgians' enlightened view of conservation, the exploitation of the Congo, initiated by King Leopold, was as callous as any in colonial history, costing millions of African lives. In places there was virtual slavery, and if a tribal plantation or forest failed to produce its quota of palm nuts, rubber or ivory, the punishments included torture, mutilation and death. The ultimate colonial legacy when the Belgians pulled out, despite the intervention of the United Nations, was equally costly in lives.

The main reason for George's awkward insistence on bringing his rifle was to shoot in Chad, the largest, rarest and most handsome antelope in Africa, Lord Derby's eland.

Joy's great delight in Chad was the acquisition of a young banded mongoose in Fort Crampel. He had an extraordinarily endearing character and both she and George fell in love with him. In the overpowering heat of the Land-Rover he always found the coolest spot in which to sleep, but he was quick to wake up and make conversation in a series of high-pitched squeaks whenever they stopped. And he never failed to respond to their gestures of friendliness.

George had suffered from dysentery ever since leaving Kenya, and his patience became exhausted by the constant breakdowns. Six times he had to repair broken springs or the linkage to the trailer. He grew increasingly silent and morose which inevitably exasperated Joy who was already demented by the damp heat, the discomfort of the Land-Rover and the minute sweat bees that constantly swarmed around her with the persistence of midges.

For two days they stopped at Fort-Archambault whose towering white walls were surmounted by battlements. There George was allotted a white hunter of dubious experience to take him out into the dense woodlands in search of the eland. Even with an expert his quest would have been forlorn; in the hands of an incompetent charlatan, it was hopeless. Today Derby's eland is almost extinct in the wild and in retrospect George may have been glad he never got a shot.

On this trip, as on her tribal safaris, Joy took many photographs, noticing every nuance of the changing scene: huts shaped like bottles and melons or camouflaged as boulders high among the rocks; miniature ceramics and beautiful shoulder-high pots; naked men armed with bows and arrows or girls dressed for circumcision.

Before long Crampel, the mongoose, began to show signs of serious distress. When they reached the large town of Kano in Nigeria, Joy rushed him to a vet, who thought he must have eaten a poisonous beetle.

While Crampel grew increasingly pathetic, George and Joy, unable to help, went about their last-minute preparations for the Sahara. George stocked up with necessities and double-checked their arrangements with the *Société Africaine des Transports Tropicaux* (SATT) which controlled almost every aspect of transport between Kano and Algiers.

Joy photographed the ancient walls, the vats used for indigo dyeing and the deep wells in which the freshly dyed cotton was rinsed or the unfortunate were thrown to their death. She bought herself a traditional desert robe—a double length of lightweight cotton with a hole for the head that covered every part of her body including her outstretched arms. Above it she wore a strong straw hat with a wide brim and tall conical crown.

On their last day Joy took Crampel back to the vet who gave him an injection and told her to return in three hours. When she came back the mongoose was convulsed with fits. He calmed in her hands but soon died.

Both George and Joy were heartbroken, and George went so far as to say that neither of them had ever become so attached to a wild animal. In the stifling heat of the overloaded Land-Rover, while George suffered from his upset stomach and Joy her pent-up irritation, the mongoose's cheerful and inquisitive energy, and above all his affection, had been a substitute for much that they were unable to offer each other.

On April 23 they crossed from Nigeria into the French colony of Niger. They had been traveling a month and their most critical test was about to begin.

3

The southern approach to the Sahara is deceptively gentle and green. Pasturelands of tall grass stretch away across the unfolding plains, dotted with goats, donkeys, horses, camels and, occasionally, the smoke of fires. A line of wells follows the road. The earth is red; houses and mosques are red; and two pillars of red mud mark the entrance to the first town, Zinder.

On the second day the desert began and Joy put on her toga of floating cotton. For the next 1,700 miles they would be driving continuously across the Sahara, the largest desert in the world. It is still growing southward and stretches 3,300 miles from the Atlantic in the west to the Red Sea in the east. During the days there would be no respite from the relentless glare and furnace heat of the sun until they reached the Hoggar Mountains in the center, that rose to 9,800 feet and offered a more temperate climate.

Flat sand stretched to the horizon and as it cooled toward evening timid gazelles nibbled at the struggling bushes. The first night out in the Sahara was one of glorious moonlight and perfect stillness but Joy felt a sharp pang of pain at the loss of Crampel, blaming herself for his death.

In the morning they stopped to photograph the veiled Hausa with their stock and wander through the town of Agades, the last outpost of greenery. In the gardens, palm groves and orchards of tropical fruits, crickets chirred and doves purred; swallows and martins circled around the minaret of the tall mosque.

For the hottest six months of the year, which were fast approaching, the Sahara was closed to all but essential traffic—late April was running things fine. At night the temperature could drop to freezing, and at noon rise to about 136°F (58°C). An American millionaire who crossed the Sahara with a refrigerator and his wife in 1936 filmed her frying an egg on a rock beside the route, from which it was all too easy to stray.

Some stretches were marked by white posts or rusting petrol drums, sometimes thousands of yards apart. The only constants were the tracks churned into the sand by the massive tires of the SATT lorries. Even those could be fallible guides for in places the route disappeared over crests of bare rock, and the tracks were entirely obscured by *barkanes*—dunes that shifted with the wind. Most teasing of all, the tire marks occasionally fanned out in different directions where cars had foundered along one route and latecomers had pioneered others; but which were which?

George was still silent and Joy had plenty of opportunity to wonder how his mind really worked. When they were first married he would take only one bed on safari—she assumed she was to sleep on the ground. Once he had loaded every piece of equipment and set off without her. She wrote in her draft memoir:

> He almost treated me as a man, which I might have interpreted as a compliment, but I never knew if incidents like this were due to absent-mindedness or if George had lived too long alone to think of anyone but himself.
>
> He was the ideal man for his job, respected and liked by all his staff and friends, but as a husband he lacked the slightest understanding of the nature of a woman, leave alone a woman as complicated as I was.

It is difficult to imagine a better companion in the Sahara than George. Quite apart from his experience of safaris and deserts he was an indefatigable mechanic, able to restore any part of the vehicle to working order. The springs and trailer continued to give trouble and there were frequent punctures for the going was frightful.

They were blinded by yellow clouds of grit and enshrouded by sandstorms, and they slalomed or skidded down tracks in the dunes. For miles they ground and juddered over loose stones, sharp ridges of rock and huge corrugations created by the juggernaut tankers and freight lorries.

It was still three years before oil was discovered in the Sahara and there was no allowance, except at the forts and oases, for private civilian travelers. The landscape offered no shade and every year two or three people perished from hunger or thirst on this stretch of the route, or out in the desert, having lost their direction.

They averaged 100 miles a day. When he came to loose sand George nursed the Land-Rover over the patches, but five or ten times a day they were *ensablés*—sunk into graves of soft sand—and had to dig down and lay out the metal-link mats that gave the tires a grip. By the evenings they were exhausted, but usually found water in a well or gully.

Stopping for lunch one day they were approached by a fine-looking Tuareg on a magnificent white camel. Like so many of the others they encountered in the next two weeks, he was swathed from head to toe in an indigo cloak. A visor of dark cloth over his nose and mouth left only a slit for his eyes. He offered them milk in an engraved copper bowl and Joy was ashamed she could respond only with food from a tin.

Joy registered everything—the little mice emerging from nowhere to harvest their crumbs; the exhaustion of a sandgrouse that flopped into the shade of the Land-Rover and lay quivering on her lap for half an hour while she spread its wings and sprinkled it with water to cool it; and a dried bush that was lifted up in the wind and waltzed across the moonlit desert by a dust-devil.

After a week they came within sight of the Hoggar Mountains which seemed to rise like a range of blue camel humps out of the haze. When they grew closer the foothills turned into an inferno of coal-black rock. By then they were well into Algeria, climbing toward the modern military and administrative headquarters of Tamanrasset that stood in the heart of the Hoggar at about 4,500 feet.

For three nights George and Joy took advantage of the coolness of the mountain town. Once again, the larger buildings—the barracks, a long thin dwelling like a frigate, and the fortress or Casbah—were plastered in the Saharan style with red clay. The blacks, whom the French had liberated from slavery by the Tuareg, now never worked and were happily passing the time stretched out in the shade. They clustered around the Land-Rover as soon as it stopped.

The French officers, in command of the Tuareg troops, received George and Joy very courteously, and they were also immediately befriended by two missionaries; one was the only English resident, a woman of 78, Dr. Wakefield. For three nights while enjoying the coolness of the mountains George and Joy discovered some of their curious past. Human occupation dated back to prehistory, and Joy found one or two rock engravings not far from the road. In addition their hosts were eager to show them three more recent memorials.

The first was at Cottenest, where the French army, carrying its campaign to conquer Algeria into the Hoggar, was confronted in 1902 by the Tuareg on their camels. Each attack was mown down as it charged the French guns. Pillars and plaques marked the graves of the French, while the noble Tuareg were remembered only by fragments of bone still bleaching in the sun.

The other two sites were rapidly becoming places of pilgrimage inspired by Vicomte Charles de Foucauld, an officer in the army whose life in Paris became so dissolute that he was posted to Algeria as a reprimand and for his own salvation. There, the grandeur of the Sahara and the qualities of the people transformed him into a holy man and hermit. Calling himself Père Charles de Jésus, he never made a convert yet from 1902 until his death was devoted to the Tuareg. In 1916 he led the defense of the Casbah against a siege by brigands, but was lured out and shot at its gate. This was his first memorial.

After his death, a religious order, the Little Brothers of Jesus, sprang into being, and for them Père Charles's hermitage at Assekrem became the principal goal of their pilgrimages. Noticing that Dr. Wakefield, who lived entirely alone in a tiny hut furnished and crammed to the ceiling with books—they provided her chair, table and bed—seemed to be ostracized by the French, Joy invited her to visit the shrine with them.

Assekrem is high in the mountains at about 8,500 feet. The view from it is sensational as the rounded humps of range after range recede into the distance, their colors constantly changing behind the moving veils of dust and sand, and with the shifting angle of the sun.

On the way back to Tamanrasset Joy let slip the word *damn*, whereupon Dr. Wakefield loosed off a diatribe revealing such aggressive intolerance that Joy immediately understood her neighbors' distaste for her.

When she went on insulting me because I never went to church I gave her my ideas in full.

I told her that God is present in every sunbeam lighting up a tree, in every song of every bird, in every rustle of the wind; and when the last flicker of the setting sun turns the country into pure gold it is for me far superior to any candle light in a cathedral. I further told her that I do not have to dress up to meet God on Sunday in church and when I talk to him at any moment I speak to him in my simplest language as to my closest friend.

This is probably the nearest Joy ever came to writing down her personal credo. In a more lighthearted moment she once wrote this to a friend.

I am not a Christian Scientist and try to dodge them as tactfully as I can as they are all such nice people. But I would rather find my own way of coping with religion (and going to hell as heaven seems taboo for people like me). I always prefer those who are not dripping with goodness but have to fight their mischievous side to try to be "good."

Nevertheless here and there among her letters are hints that she really did try to grapple with the need for a code of personal morality, and the library she left suggests a serious search for some form of faith.

There was still nearly a thousand miles of desert to go before they reached the Atlas Mountains—and it was probably the toughest part of the journey. The quicksands were formidable; five-foot-high *bark-anes* crept along the tracks; inches of sand settled on their tents at night; and the wells needed twice the length of rope advised in the Michelin guide, for by now the summer heat was really beginning to build up and the water had sunk to a hundred feet beneath the surface.

For miles on end the desert was strewn with the bodies of swallows and other small birds that would never complete their migration to Europe. Caught in the whirlwinds of flying grit, their eyes and beaks were fatally crusted with sand.

For several days George coaxed the Land-Rover through these hostile conditions, frequently stopping for repairs. Then, on the fourth day, they ruptured the engine so badly, twenty miles from the next oasis, that he was defeated: only heavy welding equipment could save them, and they had none.

At each stage of the journey SATT or the army had sent word ahead so that a search could be made if they did not reach the next station, but at this time of year they were unlikely to be rescued by any other travelers. They had not met a single car since entering the desert. Then, incredibly after only a few hours, four Land-Rovers and a large Dodge came into view. It was a party of government geologists and Shell prospectors, who towed them into In Salah and were actually able to replace from their spares the part of the engine that had fractured.

The journey ahead, across 150 miles of the Tademaït plateau, was as demanding as ever, although there were signs of stirring life: birds of prey soaring in the clear blue sky, a few Barbary sheep and tattered specimens of the three trees hardy enough to survive in the Sahara—palms, acacias and tamarisks.

May 7   Camped in a sandstorm in a sand dune. Too tired to bath. G. wants a naked photo of me again. Breakdown: too much mental strain.

Happily for both of them their ordeal was nearing an end, and they spent the next night in the most beautiful oasis of the Sahara—El Golea—famous for its oranges. "Lovely flowers—my only joy. Gardens, fountains, roses," Joy wrote in her diary. She woke to the singing of birds.

Anyone who has slept out in the Sahara speaks of the sublime quality of the nights, from the spectacular sunsets to the exquisitely subtle mother-of-pearl dawns, in such movingly gentle contrast to the furious blaze of the midday sun. The galaxies glitter with extraordinary strength in the darkness and when the wind drops the shifting sands continue to sing. On their last night in the desert Joy looked up to see a shooting star whose sparkling tail hung in the heavens for at least an hour.

By then the Atlas Mountains were visible in the distance, a purple backdrop to a world that had been brown for so long and was now growing green. On May 11, two and a half weeks after leaving Kano, they slept in the Hotel Transatlantique in Ghardaïa, a richly fertile oasis in the foothills of the mountains.

The following morning the telegraph poles, the tarmac and the traffic brought home to Joy that the adventure had come to an end: "The Sahara is over—suburban Europe begins."

It was not literally so because they spent a week in the mountains and Algiers, and another one exploring Morocco—driving up into the High Atlas range and camping beside the Atlantic.

Before they crossed into Tangier on June 1, George hid their excess cash in the spare tire. The next day they changed it: Joy bought some shoes with hers, while George decided to keep his for whiskey and beer.

June 2 was an emotional day. Queen Elizabeth II was crowned; the news broke that Edmund Hillary and Tenzing Norgay had conquered Everest, the first men ever to do so; and in the evening George and Joy listened to the Queen and Churchill on the radio.

> Stroll through the town, dinner at Spanish restaurant. George will keep all his money from now on for drinks. He timed it as well as Mt Everest. That's the end of our marriage.

Next morning they caught the ferry to Algeciras.

4

Joy's artistic and mental appetites, like her physical energy, were so prodigious that she planned a four-month tour of Europe from which few significant creations of God or man—the natural and aesthetic, the secular, sacred and profane—were to be omitted.

While they were still looking at the paintings and palaces around Madrid, they heard for the first time about the Mau Mau massacre at Lari. George immediately cabled Nairobi, volunteering to return and enlist in the army, but was told to complete his leave.

He and Joy stayed with friends and relatives, in castles, country houses and inexpensive hotels, and they camped in such romantic and bizarre places as Toledo, the hills above Avignon, a cul-de-sac in Monte Carlo and the aerodrome in Geneva.

In pursuit of nature they spent nights in the Sierra Nevada and below the highest peak in the Alps, Mont Blanc; days riding through the Gredos mountains to see the herds of ibex, and watching an old chamois guarding her kindergarten of kids in a valley of the Karwendel range; and mornings picking edelweiss and alpenrosen in the Dolomites for Joy to paint. They discussed tropical fish and the sex change of crabs with the curator of the Monaco aquarium.

Joy's dedication to the arts led them to look at the prehistoric cave paintings of Altamira and at the Mas d'Azil in the Pyrenees, visit six of the great galleries and churches in Florence on a single day, and tick off the Prado, the Louvre, and the national galleries in London and Edinburgh. They went to operas by Mozart, Verdi and Wagner—and of course to *Der Rosenkavalier*.

Joy's architectural tastes were eclectic. She admired the Romanesque in Avila, the Moorish of the Alhambra, a string of Gothic masterpieces from Burgos Cathedral to Kings College Chapel in Cambridge and a medley of the classical, baroque and rococo when they saw eight churches on their second day in Venice. On her secular list were Roman aqueducts, arenas and Hadrian's wall; the fortified town of Carcassonne; the Doge's Palace; Versailles; and the castle at Windsor.

Despite Joy's profession of pantheism they stayed in Cadiz to witness the Corpus Christi procession, visited Bernadette's grotto at Lourdes and went to Canterbury Cathedral. Arguably profane were the bullfights they watched in Spain and Provence, a night in Goebbels' old lodge near Berchtesgaden, and an evening at the Folies Bergères.

Joy allowed a month for relaxation with her friends in Austria, but felt no closer to her mother and her sister Traute. When she saw Dorle, who had moved to England, she felt even cooler toward her—perhaps because Dorle had just had a baby while she herself had failed to conceive again.

In Britain, Joy felt most at home in a crenelated Norfolk country house owned by a family named Birkbeck where they were invited to make their base. They arrived there with sand still spilling out of the Land-Rover. After a week they set off to see George's uncles and aunts in Scotland. On the way back George called at his old school in Cheltenham, Dean Close, and talked to the boys. It was, for both of them, a journey into time past.

Joy revisited, with obsessive faithfulness, the places she had been to with her first love, with Ziebel von Klarwill—she even went back to the village where they were married—and with Julian Snow. In London they looked up Jack Swain who showed them his excellent film featuring George, *Stronghold of the Wild*, which was then on release.

George had not met Tony Ofenheim since 1935. She came up to see them in London, and on his last night in England they dined at her house near Greenwich. Joy visibly prickled and nervously monopolized the conversation, sensing that George and Tony continued to derive particular pleasure from each other's company.

Throughout Europe, as across Africa, tempers had smoldered and occasionally a fire broke out. In Paris Joy leapt into the middle of the traffic leaving George, who had forgotten the name of their hotel, with no means of finding it again. Later she pulled out a tuft of his hair and he struck her, according to his diary, for the second time in his life.

Nevertheless, their marriage still held, and despite Joy's fury at George's apparent indifference to her cultural marathon he sometimes surprised her. He was much impressed by two pictures by Rubens in Vienna, not for their voluptuous flesh but because of the exquisite and accurate painting of a tiger and her cubs threatened by a crocodile and of a boar hunt. He also told her that one of the madonnas in Florence was the most beautiful thing he had ever seen in his life.

In November 1953, he left Joy in London so that she could look for a publisher for her tribal paintings. They parted at the customs barrier on a misty and very cold night. When he boarded the *Durban Castle* for Mombasa, he never expected to see England again.

FOURTEEN

The Law of the Jungle

1953–1955

1

In later life, as in his books, George always gave the impression that he played no effective part in fighting the Mau Mau. In fact he did.

He came back to a country at war. There was evidence of it everywhere: men in uniforms, military vehicles, abnormal numbers of police and roadblocks. Everyone carried an identity card. In hotels and bars the younger and more extroverted white Kenyans of both sexes, never averse to attracting attention, decked themselves with gun belts.

Up-country such precautions were essential. Doors had to be locked; windows protected with barbed wire; and sirens installed and houses organized with alarm rockets that could be set off at the touch of a button. No Kikuyu, Meru or Embu employee was to be fully trusted; all personal weapons had to be attached with a lanyard.

If the face of Kenya had suddenly changed, so had George's. He had decided to appear at the fancy dress ball, when his ship neared Mombasa, as half-primitive, half-civilized man. It entailed cutting his dinner jacket down the middle, which did not distress him, and shaving off half his beard, which did—especially when he realized he would have to get rid of the other half in the morning!

On Christmas Eve he was asked to report to brigade headquarters in the Aberdare Mountains with his game scouts, and to supervise tracking in a sector of the forest patroled by two British regiments.

While he had been on leave, Jomo Kenyatta and a number of other Kikuyu political leaders had been tried, convicted and imprisoned for sedition. To many people the trial was a travesty, for although few people doubted Kenyatta's complicity in Mau Mau his guilt was never proved beyond doubt.

Ten to twenty thousand Kikuyu, in the Active Wing of the

movement, had taken to the forests from which they launched their vicious and unnerving attacks on isolated European and peaceful Kikuyu victims, leaving herds of mutilated cattle bleeding to death in the pastures.

A further thirty thousand, in the Passive Wing, mingled with the majority of the Kikuyu living in Nairobi or on their tribal reserve between the capital and the forests. It was said that trying to identify them was like hunting for needles in a haystack of needles.

Three quarters of a million members of the Meru and Embu tribes—cousins of the Kikuyu—who lived on or near the eastern and southern foothills of Mount Kenya were also riddled with activists.

The keys to Mau Mau recruitment were the oathing ceremonies, perversions of the old tribal rituals. They usually opened with the initiates passing seven times through arches of thorns or banana leaves.

The magisterial official report on the Mau Mau by F. D. Corfield says this: "The full physical details of the ceremonies can hardly be printed in a public document. It is sufficient to record that for one of the more notorious concoctions semen produced in public was mixed in a bowl with menstrual and sheep's blood and drunk while repeating the oath."

A friend of Joy's in London at The Voice of Kenya, the colony's broadcasting and information service, collected the details and circulated them discreetly in duplicated form. Joy received a list of various oaths in January 1954. Here is one.

This is the platoon, or forest, oath; once a man has taken it, he is on call to go to the forest at any time to join the gangs. It is being widely administered at the present time (resulting in a sharp rise in the price of donkeys).

A male donkey is taken into a hut and castrated. The testicles are put on to the fire, and when they have swollen up they are skinned and cut in pieces, each piece being lightly scored seven times. Then a naked prostitute who has her monthly period, sitting on a three-legged stool, inserts pieces of the testicle into her vagina and puts them on sticks. The oath-administrator lays these pieces six times on each candidate's lips, and on the seventh time the man eats them.

The oath-administrator says: "You are eating the Batuni [platoon] oath. This is a man's oath. You are to destroy everything.

You will be sent to do anything we may tell you by day or by night, at any time, in any weather. If you are told to get a man's head, or to steal cattle, or any other thing, you will obey. When you have killed a man you will eat his flesh, you cannot refuse. If your father or mother or brother or sister refuses the Mau Mau in any way, you will kill them. You will obey all Batuni orders."

The Governor, Sir Evelyn Baring, had mobilized a considerable military force to fight the campaign of atrocity, and a decisive and energetic Commander in Chief, General Sir George Erskine, was appointed to put down the rebellion.

By the time George returned to Kenya sixteen Europeans had been murdered and a thousand innocent Kikuyu killed or wounded. Although on the other side of the balance sheet, three thousand Mau Mau had been killed and a thousand taken prisoner, the battle was far from over. In this kind of warfare the initiative lies too often with the guerrillas.

The official strategy was to order most of the Kikuyu to return to their tribal reserve; to cordon off the reserve, Nairobi—whose population was one third Kikuyu—and the forests on Mount Kenya and the Aberdares; and thus to inhibit the Active Wing from receiving food supplies from the reserve or money and orders from the Mau Mau command in Nairobi. At the same time the army was to probe the forests.

George immediately spotted how unsuited the army was for the task of sweeping the forests.

It was an interesting experience, not unlike hunting buffalo, although made more difficult by handicaps inseparable from military operations, the greatest being noise in infinite variety: clicking and clanking mess tins, coughings, cussing (it is said that the Aberdare parrots now prefix everything with a soldierly adjective), and the hacking of bamboos when making camp.

The Mau Mau gangs fighting under Dedan Kimathi—in the Aberdares—and General China, once a lance corporal in the King's African Rifles—on Mount Kenya—were as sensitive as animals to the whereabouts of their enemies. Seldom washing, and wearing skins when their clothes disintegrated, they became as one with the creatures of the forest and made a point of never killing game if they could possibly help it. As a result, elephants, buffalo, antelope, deer, monkeys and the birds not only ignored them but became useful scouts, alerting them to the movement of army patrols.

In fact the forest gangs could smell the army's toothpaste, hair oil and cigarettes up to two miles away. Despite this, and despite the skill with which they concealed their tracks, George's scouts led the patrols to several hideouts. They captured a terrorist and George had a sentry in his sights when one of his men inadvertently gave him away.

After five weeks in the forest George was withdrawn and went back to Isiolo. His real contribution to the battle against the Mau Mau, which he never mentioned later, was about to begin.

2

Just before the operations around Isiolo got under way, Joy returned from Europe.

When left alone in London she had given a series of lectures around England under the auspices of The Voice of Kenya, which was anxious to reassure the people of Britain that the majority of the tribes in Kenya were peaceable. Her talks were illustrated with slides of her tribal paintings and her photographs.

Despite her Austrian accent she found she could hold the attention of audiences of up to two hundred people. Her greatest success was with a gathering of women to whom she began to explain male and female circumcision. It was a topic none of them would have liked to discuss in private before, and still less in public, but there were so many questions that Joy found it difficult to get away at the end.

Encouraged by her reception she had redoubled her efforts to find a publisher in London, and in Sweden, where her friend Ake Holm promised to help her. She spent a month among the snows of Uppsala and Stockholm—where she lectured too—but, as in London, she failed to find a publisher; and whatever her relationship was with Ake Holm, who had married, she gave it one of her metaphorical "funerals" (her shorthand for the coup de grâce at the end of an affair).

In March 1954, George went down to meet her on the quay at Mombasa. Once again her first glance seemed to cut him dead, for she simply did not recognize him without his beard. At her insistence he quickly grew it again.

When they reached Nairobi, Joy was thrilled to find that her little hyrax Pati recognized her after a year's separation. However, on the drive up to Isiolo a corpse on the road brought home the sinister world to which she was returning.

Although Isiolo was well outside Kikuyu territory, the Meru tribe, who were closely related to them, lived just to the southeast of the town, occupying land known as the Northern Grazing Area, and it was very much part of George's responsibility. He and everyone in the *boma* were aware that the forest fire of violence could easily blow their way and set them alight.

The administration and police had been considerably strengthened and their staffs of Goan, Indian and Kikuyu accountants and clerks had also expanded. To supply their needs the Asian, Somali, Kikuyu and Meru traders and shopkeepers had multiplied too. Their doyen was the rotund and turbaned figure Hadji Abdullah Farah, a natural son of the late Sir James Kirkpatrick and therefore a first cousin of George's colleague Alick Kirkpatrick, who regularly dropped in on George and Joy for a drink. Unknown to George or the police, the *boma* was teeming with potential informers.

George and Joy lived three miles outside the town, across a river. It was usually dried up, but when the new DC, Robert Nimmo, arrived in the rains his car became hopelessly stuck in the mud until he sent for fifty prisoners, who lifted it bodily onto firm ground again.

Nimmo was tall, slim and good looking. Joy took to him almost too warmly at first, but thanks to his firmness, tact and sense of humor, he and his wife became close friends and confidants of both Joy and George, and he helped sketch this picture of their life in Isiolo.

One evening George planned to go down to Limuru to spend a convivial evening with Alick Kirkpatrick, still Assistant Chief Game Warden, but because of a Mau Mau alarm had to call it off. That night Kirkpatrick was shot and killed. His private affairs, like his father's, were never entirely straightforward and although at least one lady was present at the time of the accident the magistrate decided it was suicide.

George and Joy gave almost nightly, and very good, drinks and dinner parties on their meager income. Beer, whiskey and wine flowed, and Joy matched the best with her vermouth. Dinner might not begin until midnight or end until 3:00 A.M. George was a brilliant raconteur, and their guests included naturalists, sportsmen, generals, writers and wandering filmmakers.

Since Joy still resented George's preprandial sundowners, he and his fellow game warden Gerry Dalton devised measures to elude her. George would leave a message for Joy at the end of the day to say he had gone on business to the Daltons—where he kept a clandestine bottle of whiskey. The first time Joy telephoned for George she was told he had not arrived; the second time that he had just left. When Joy began to grow suspicious of the routine and would come up in person, Dalton had to conceal a game scout halfway along the track. If he blew his whistle Dalton and George withdrew to the shamba with their bottle and glasses.

This is from Joy's 1954 diary.

June 3 Ramadan party at DC. George off with Dalton. Came home drunk—again. I rang Dalton to stop that.

Harry Benson, a friend of both George and the Daltons, put it like this: "He liked a sip in the right company but was no boozer." Dalton's wife, Merrell, thought the same and wrote in 1991: "George was a moderate drinker only." An officer billetted with Joy at the time also confirmed this.

Merrell Dalton's appreciation of George and Joy brings out precisely the uncomfortable admiration that Joy's friends and acquaintances felt for her.

We saw him frequently, especially when Joy was making life intolerable for him. They were like oil and water, he so quiet and gentle, she so energetic and temperamental. She was greatly gifted and could outswim, outwalk and outclimb any man was the saying. Between them, perhaps, the tie was a deep, true love for and affinity with Nature and all that is wild. She was utterly fearless.

A local DO and his friends were especially impressed when her car broke down one night and she walked through the darkness alone, disregarding the elephants and the Mau Mau, to arrive two hours late for a gathering.

Always conscious that she was an outsider in the *boma*, set apart by her talents, nationality and temperament, Joy was further tormented by her inability to conceive. She told Robert Nimmo's wife she was still determined to have two or three children. In August she planned carefully to start a baby, monitored the dates, remained in bed at the critical period—but failed again.

As always, she picked herself up and went off to paint the Samburu. She could not bear to be idle, and when these pictures were completed she began to go out with George again on his game department safaris and even on his new anti-Mau Mau patrols.

3

After George had arrived back in Isiolo, stories had come in that bands of Meru and Kikuyu were working around parts of his territory to forage and extort money. There were cases where men had their noses or ears cut off if they refused to cooperate. Mau Mau agents were also buying arms from the Somalis, who were willing to do anything to get rid of the British.

George was asked to arm his twenty game scouts with service rifles and to help the police and Home Guard in tracking the gangs. In April, Adamson Force, as it came to be called, took to the field for the first time and a week later it followed up a typical local skirmish. At first it was unable to keep up with the elusive and fast-moving gangs—with practice it did better.

This growing Mau Mau activity in the north was directly due to setbacks in the south, as a result of three new army initiatives, employing tactics not unlike those used by the Americans in Vietnam. One operation was to screen 30,000 Kikuyu in Nairobi and intern half of them. The second, when the oaths began to lose their superstitious potency, was to hood members of the Passive Wing, who were then prepared to act as informers at identity parades.

Third, after breaking the power of the Passive Wing—including the high command and fund-raisers in Nairobi—the army turned its attention to the Active Wing in the forests, taking many prisoners. Intelligence officers discovered that by applying Kikuyu psychology they could sometimes persuade even the most hardened cases, in return for their lives, to go back into the forest with European officers disguised as Kikuyu. Before long these pseudo gangs succeeded in meeting the genuine rebels, who were either won over or destroyed.

After the new strategy began to take effect there were some desperate reactions among the Mau Mau. For instance one gang leader, Mwangi Toto, set out to divert resources intended for General Kimathi and for Meru to his own ends. An eyewitness described how his gang had literally chopped up the children of a family who would not cooperate. Shortly afterward an army officer found the corpse of an old man from which the same gang had just removed the eyes and testicles for further oathing.

As the scope of operations shifted north the police received a tip that one of their targets was the Adamsons' isolated house. Its defenses were strengthened and for a time Joy moved in with the Provincial Commissioner and his wife.

In June Joy went on safari with George to the Tana, where a gang was said to be recruiting. They spent two weeks on the river, just across from Kora. They saw no trace of any Mau Mau but George found and plotted the falls that today bear his name.

It was hardly surprising that it took George and his twenty men some time to come to grips with the gangs, since he had perhaps 30,000 square miles to cover, and often had to rely on donkeys for transport. However, in July they demonstrated their growing competence. George never mentioned the incident; Joy did.

She had been away for the day and returned to Isiolo with a film producer. Her diary entry is brief.

July 24   Catlow and cameraman back with me to Isiolo. Destiny? George all day Mau Mau: 6 shot, 20 captured, on Wajir road.

It was a surprise to find the extent of his active involvement in fighting the gangs, and his growing prestige. The Game Department had recently promoted him to Senior Game Ranger, a rank devised to acknowledge his long and exceptional service and to raise his salary. He was also given a platoon of twelve Tribal Police from Moyale, mounted on Somali ponies, to strengthen and speed his response to calls from the police and the army.

The successes of Adamson Force were toasted with gin in the *boma* and immediately followed by Joy's most intensive efforts to have a baby.

As if he were not busy enough already, George temporarily took over the local screening center.

Very soon it was discovered that there had been an active Mau Mau committee in being in Isiolo since 1952. Its Kikuyu and Meru members included many Government employees, traders and even some of the local prostitutes. Probably at least 90 per cent of all Kikuyu, Meru and Embu in the Northern Province had taken one or more of the Mau Mau oaths!

The best account of George's work with the security forces, and light on Joy, come from Brigadier Percy Blake of the Royal Inniskilling Fusiliers, whose battalion was moved north to Meru and Isiolo in September. Then a major, his company was actually posted around the Adamsons' house.

George agreed that his team should split up and act as guides to the soldiers on their intensive patrols: Blake's admiration for him was unqualified. On the first day George sat down cross-legged on the ground and talked to the men with the relaxed and friendly authority that characterized everything he did. His influence helped the soldiers to come to terms with this harsh and foreign world, far tougher even than the jungle. They could have achieved nothing without him and he quickly led them to their first success.

These extracts, condensed from George's diary, vividly convey the ups and downs, twists and turns, of a hunt that had already gone on for four days.

September 12   Started off this morning with full safari. Found the gang had headed SE. Followed up. Off saddled and away again about 3.00 pm. Found another boma recently vacated, part of freshly killed ox and a little posho [maize flour]. Hard ground, difficult spooring.

September 13   Sent 4 men to local chief. No news of any value. Put out ambushes.

September 14   First ambush party to return was Sgt Ryan's: they brought 2 Meru who told us that a gang of about 50 had come on Saturday and taken an ox. Second nothing seen. Third said 5 men had appeared at about 3.00 pm. The Bren gunner had fired a full magazine and the scouts followed up without result! I set off with Sgt Ryan and 8 men to follow up the spoor.

September 15   Ibrahim Abdi spotted 3 men in the distance coming toward us. We crouched down and waited. They saw us when still about 250 yards off and started to run. We opened fire, including the Bren gun, but did not hit.

September 16   Sent 5 men along the west side of the stream to look for tracks, while the main safari took the eastern side. About 10.30 when crossing the plain, heard shots from the far side of the river, saw figures in the distance running to the west. Sgt Ryan, one soldier and Kikango, Godana Dima, and myself gave chase. After about 2 miles Kikango killed a Mau Mau.

We followed the remaining three to within five miles of Isiolo. Their spoor showed them to be tiring as we found three or four places where they had sat down. Finally they reached a lugga and turned south up it, thick bush and rocks.

Together with Ryan I went along the bottom while the rest followed the spoor on the east bank. Suddenly I came across them crouching behind some rocks. They saw me and started to climb up the bank where they were met by the scouts.

I killed one and the scouts got another. The third got away.

According to Blake, George excelled his own trackers when they had difficulty with the spoor and he remained unruffled, decisive and wise throughout the chase. In a report later George said the men would have inflicted three times as many casualties had their shooting been up to a reasonable standard.

However intensive the patrols, there was still time for relaxation— particularly bird shoots organized by George and much appreciated by the senior officers. Joy frequently went out with the guns, not to see the sport but for the company; she had no women friends so far as Percy Blake could see. Otherwise she had Pati to look after, played the piano quite beautifully for hours in the middle of the day and continued to paint. In November she started a portrait of Blake and worked at it every day for a month.

He was immediately aware that she was attracted to him and that he would have to be very careful for he had seen her set her cap at a young brother officer—and several other men too.

One of them, Charles Chenevix Trench, was obliged to escort Joy out to dinner up-country at a time when both his wife and George were away. He said the evening ended like this.

I was looking forward with considerable apprehension to the drive back with Joy under a full moon. At last I could delay our return no longer—but just at that moment salvation arrived in the shape of Hadji Abdullah Farah, all nineteen stone of him, lumbering through the moonlit bush. Lorry broken down—could someone give him a lift into Isiolo?

"Yes, Hadji, I will give you a lift into Isiolo. I'll drive, Mrs. Adamson will sit in the passenger seat, and you sit between us."

Toward George, most women, and her African servants, Joy was hard. She also became aggressive if she drank too much at dinner.

On the other hand, Blake found she was a wonderfully lively and intelligent companion; she was observant and amusing, if caustic, about other people; toward men, and anyone in difficulty, she was both kind and ready to volunteer help. She never indulged in luxuries and although elephants terrified her, walked boldly past them when they raided the garden at night.

Blake managed to tread the tightrope stretched between his friendship with Joy and his grateful admiration for George with only one slip. Joy thought he cut her in the mess one evening, walked out and miserably sat alone with a sherry bottle, listening to records until 3:00 A.M.

When the Inniskillings left, she gave him a painting of a bouquet of NFD flowers and a drawing of himself set in a decorated circular border. The full-scale portrait remained in Kenya and was only sent to him forty years later, after both Joy and George were dead.

The departure of the Inniskillings in December signaled more trouble as George described in his report.

I felt certain that as the troops had moved, the gangs would be back in the Northern Grazing Area. Sure enough, on December 23, I took a patrol of my scouts and the dubas [tribal police] and encountered a gang in the Muka Hills. We killed five, including two leaders. On this occasion, the mounted dubas caught three of the terrorists in the open and rode them down. The other two, part of a gang of twelve, were caught between two parties of scouts, who ought to have annihilated the lot, but again through their woeful shooting, only got the two.

Joy refers to the action in a letter she wrote to Louis Leakey in January 1955, and adds this.

George and his men killed five on Christmas Eve, and a short time ago three more. He is permanently out either on foot or horse, or in a Land-Rover or plane, and I hardly see him.

In a year that had seen countless atrocities—among them the murder of two honorary game wardens and Louis Leakey's elderly cousin, who was forced to watch his wife being strangled and was then buried headfirst in the forest while still alive—George had helped account for sixteen terrorists.

His efforts were widely appreciated. A little later his chief, Willie Hale, turned in his regulation annual reports on his staff and sent George a handwritten note about his.

I have given you an excellent report as one of the most beloved persons in Kenya. The country owes you a great debt of gratitude for the great and untiring services you have rendered during the past year, both to the preservation of wildlife and in combatting the terrorists.

The following June the Governor, Sir Evelyn Baring, wrote to tell him that he had been awarded a medal in recognition of his "outstanding service"; the citation for the award was written by Percy Blake.

4

Everyone in Kenya was aware how the Emergency, at a moment's notice, could suddenly demand all their energy or dominate their thoughts and emotions. Long, sweating and exhausting days were spent in the saddle or scouring the dust; at night the senses twitched at the snap of a twig or a scratch on the window and the mind worked out new tactics. There were too often new horrors to absorb.

Joy found the normal picturesque drive to Nairobi could suddenly become a nightmare. The undergrowth had been cut back on either side of the highway—as in medieval England—to reduce the risk of ambush, and there were still mornings when she saw smoke rising from smoldering huts, and bodies left lying by the road.

Everyone, from the Governor to the humblest private or game scout, needed some form of recreation, and the Inniskillings were always welcome at the shoots George organized. The provincial and district commissioners usually turned up, and it was difficult to keep the high command away once they got wind of the sport. The Commander in Chief and his deputy—and on one occasion, six brigadiers—would arrive with their twelve-bores.

There might be a dozen guns and fifty or sixty beaters—brought out from prison, or provided by the Samburu and Turkana headmen—who drove the birds over the guns carefully placed behind bushes or ridges. The game included sand grouse, francolin, which flew like partridge only more slowly, and guinea fowl, which came at a cracking pace if the wind was behind them. Bags might run to two or three hundred birds and were eaten with pleasure by both the guns and the beaters.

Forever restless, despite her painting expeditions under the strict protection of the local DCs, Joy wrote a letter to Louis Leakey in January expressing her perennial wanderlust and still unfocused ambition.

I feel rather imprisoned here in Isiolo, as I cannot go on my own safaris at present. I kill time as best I can by painting flowers and natives, and have started carving native types in wood, which is easier than painting when one is so often interrupted. But on the whole I feel I could do something much more useful or important before I am too old.

I have written to Nepal and asked for a permit to paint the mountain flora there but have never got a reply.

Now to come to the thick end of this letter—have you any idea what I could do useful and within my abilities until travelling alone becomes possible again?

Even Leakey's fertile brain, taken up by more urgent affairs, failed to offer an answer. His father had been a missionary to the Kikuyu, and as a result Louis had become their blood brother and totally at home in their language. He had been official interpreter for most of Kenyatta's trial, written two cautionary books on Mau Mau, and was once more doing intelligence work for the government.

In July, Sir Evelyn Baring, on whose shoulders the burden of Mau Mau weighed heaviest of all, and who had nearly cracked under it, decided he too should take time off with his family and make a fishing safari to the halcyon shores of Lake Rudolf. He planned to stop on the way for an official inspection of Adamson Force. Baring also

asked that George come to Rudolf to show them the birds and game
and to organize the fishing.

George, in whose character there was a strong streak of obstinacy
mingled with cunning, saw that the fishing trip offered the perfect
chance to fulfill his twenty-year-old but illicit ambition to visit South
Island. To ensure the safety of the exalted fishermen he would
have to get a suitable boat with a powerful engine to the lake. Once
there it would be ideal for the crossing to the island, from which
Dyson and Martin had vanished in 1934, leaving the mystery he was
determined to solve. Since this adventure had already been forbidden by the PC it would have to be planned and undertaken in
secret.

A past master at such enterprises, George ensured that the Governor's inspection, fishing trip and safari, as well as his own private
preparations, went off without a hitch. Baring's handwritten note of
appreciation started:

By far the best time we have either of us had in Kenya was our tour
of the north. From beginning to end we enjoyed it enormously . . .

Joy joined George near the El Molo huts on the shore of Lake Rudolf.
For two days a southeasterly gale kept whipping up waves crested
with white horses and a crossing to South Island was impossible. By
the time the wind swung around to the west and dropped, Joy was
physically sick with apprehension and scribbled her will in pencil on
a scrap of paper and handed it to their faithful driver Ibrahim.

July 26, 1955

In case anything happens to me, my will is that my PO Savings,
about £900, and Barclays Bank Savings, about £700, should go to
my sister Miss Dorothy Gessner, Leamington Road, (exact address
is in my green address book in the top drawer of my writing desk,
Isiolo).

All my paintings go to the Museum, Nairobi (about 80 at Isiolo,
the rest at the Museum).

Please find a *good* home for Pati Pati, my hyrax, perhaps Gilbert
Sauvage who had her while we were in Europe.

All photographs, mostly tribes, go to the Museum.

Joy Adamson.

Gloriosa virescens, a fine example of Joy's skill as a botanical artist. She painted several hundred flowers from 1938 to 1946 and received the Grenfell Gold Medal from the Royal Horticultural Society in London.

In 1947 Joy moved on from flowers to other subjects.
Left: A young jackal and (*right*) a Regal sunbird hanging from a spray of hypericum. *Below left:* A crowned
crane and (*right*) a Jackson's chameleon.

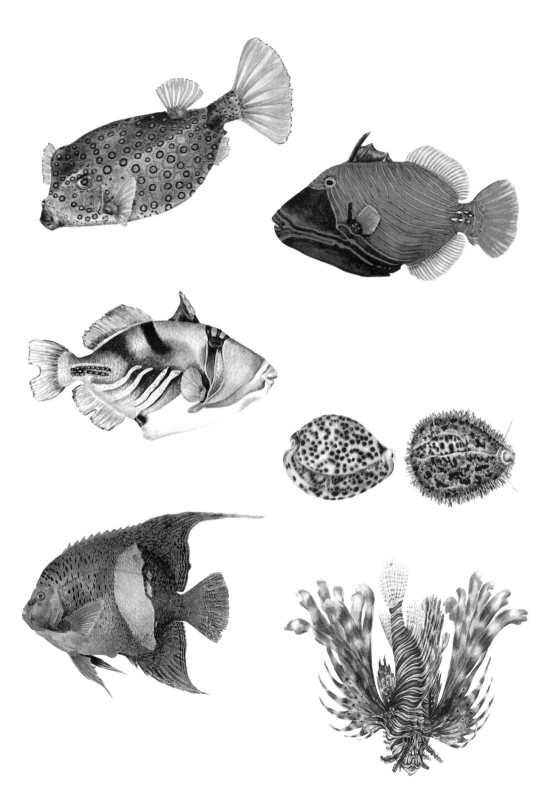

A few of Joy's eighty paintings made on the coral reef at Kiunga in 1946.
Left, from top: Ostracion tuberculatum, Balistapus undulatus, Pomocanthops maculosus.
Right, from top: Rhinecanthus aculeatus, Cypraea Tigris, Pterois volitans.

OWUOR
NYAHERA, K
LUO

A Luo elder in his dancing headdress fashioned from feathers and hippo teeth, 1950.
The majority of Joy's tribal portraits were painted from 1947 to 1955.

Turkana portraits, 1948. *Left:* A married woman and (*right*) a warrior of the Leopard group.

Next page: A rare, if not unique, photograph of George and Joy together with Elsa in their camp on the Ura River in Meru, 1959.

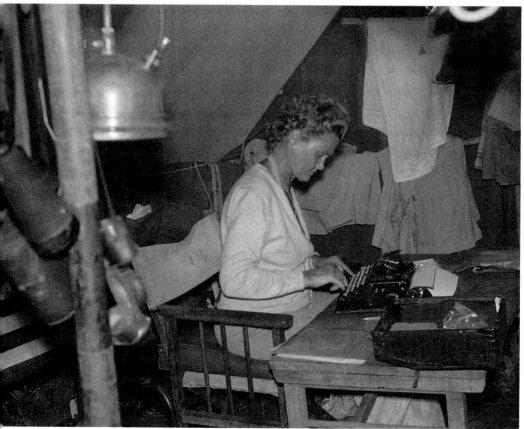

Above: George with Boy in Meru, 1965. Six years later George shot the lion after he had killed a man at Kora. *Below:* In Meru, Joy typed in her hut or, when the roof leaked, in her truck.

Colobus monkeys at Elsamere, Joy's house on
Lake Naivasha. She painted them after she had
damaged her hand in 1969.
Below: Three cubs from Pippa the cheetah's
second litter in Meru in 1967.

Virginia McKenna and Bill Travers with Christian, John Rendall and Anthony Bourke, who bought the young lion at Harrods in London and flew with him to George in Kenya.

Above: Penny, Joy's leopard, after her release in Shaba. *Below:* One of Joy's few sketches of Penny that survived the fire in her camp three months before her death in 1980.

MIRELLA RICCIARDI

Previous page: George with his pride. Several of these lions were born in the wild, including Shade who bit Terence in the face. BILL TRAVERS

Kora. *Left:* Terence Adamson, who built George's camp and the roads around it. *Below:* Boy with Katania, a little lioness who was taken by a crocodile when only a few months old.

George's last three lions at Kora, 1989. A tussle between Batian and Furaha while Rafiki looks on.
Below: The School for Errant Young Ladies throws a birthday party for George by the Tana River.

George, in the mess hut at Kora. Snakes hunted in the roof, hornbills demanded to be fed at mealtimes and naked mole rats undermined the bookcase.

After the fuel, food, guns and rods were loaded onto the 14-foot flat-bottomed boat, with a 4-horsepower outboard, there was only two inches of freeboard at the stern. When they reached a calm beach on the island just before dark the largest crocodile George had ever seen slipped off it into the water. George quickly fired a flare from his Very pistol that was answered by flashed headlights from the land—a pre-arranged exchange that became a nightly routine.

Their bedroom was a crevice in the rocks; their bed and bed clothes simply a blanket for Joy and a cotton *kikoi* for George.

The next day they started to explore the island which is ten miles long, with a spine of volcanic hills rising to 1,500 feet above the lake and covered in knife-edged outcrops of lava which literally destroyed their shoes. There were tough, spare acacias and sterculia trees, frankincense bushes and squat tufts of grass, perniciously spiky.

George described their discoveries in a letter to Gerry Dalton who lent him the outboard.

I had intended to spend two nights on the island, but the weather became bad and we were stuck. Hell of a gale all night, the wind dropped soon after noon, but before the sea had time to calm down it started up again, and so it went on.

Plenty of crocs, some enormous brutes. They seem to come to the island to breed as we found nests wherever there was a patch of sand.

A very unpleasant feature is the abundance of snakes. Two kinds, one the striped sand snake which I believe is fairly harmless, the other the spitting cobra. I found a young one in Joy's bed in the morning. It spat at me as I killed it. I did not tell her about it until we got back.

George was struck by finding 200 goats on the island in small herds and by the huge perch cruising along the shoreline among vast numbers of tilapia which jostled each other to gnaw at the pink algae sliming the rocks.

Although he and Joy discovered cairns on the tops of some of the hills, presumably left by Dyson and Martin, it was only on the fourth day that George spotted a whiskey bottle sticking out of the sand a few yards from where they were sleeping.

We found the remains of the camp of Dyson and Martin. All that was left was an empty bottle and a few rusty tins. Near the north end of the island we found a steel petrol drum and an inner tube. I should imagine the two men started back, and probably near the shore hit a submerged rock which tore the canvas bottom out of their boat. Then the crocs got them.

By their sixth and seventh days George and Joy were so eager to get back to the mainland that they stayed near their boat in case the wind dropped. Joy copied her diary entries into George's diary and left her own in a cairn, in case they suffered the same fate as the scientists. She felt "trapped by the gale on this island of death, while the merciless sun sapped our endurance."

Today, when a small plane can land on this barren little island, it is even more desolate. The wind, searing at noon but so chilling after dark, still sweeps down its length for day after day; but the goats have all gone from the hills, no doubt to feed the El Molo or the hungry Turkana. The layer of pink algae, too, has vanished from the rocks along the waterline—and hence the fishes and the crocodiles have deserted the shores.

On their eighth day they made it back to the mainland, where Ibrahim, Godana Dima and the El Molo chief were waiting. A blind Rendille girl, gifted with second sight, had told them where and when the boat would return. It was a pity she had not sent a message to the local DC. George ended his letter:

Unfortunately our prolonged stay on the island created the most absurd alarm, search parties, aircraft and Christ knows what else were organised and I was pretty well in the dog box: thought I would have to pay enormous bills for aircraft, etc. But I went straight away to the PC "hat in hand," almost on my bended knees, and sent abject letters of apology to everyone I could think of. Twenty-one years ago I went to the lake, crossed it in a tarpaulin, disappeared for four months. No one cared a curse!

So much did they care in 1955 that Joy was told the PC in Isiolo had actually reserved two graves for them in the cemetery at Nyeri.

5

However inadequate Joy's English, she was still determined to see some of her African exploits in print. While George wrote an official report on South Island for his department, Joy worked on an article and carefully selected the photographs to illustrate it.

Then, in October, protected by the local DC, she went to Wajir to photograph and paint portraits at a rare Boran circumcision ceremony. At last her long drawn-out task was complete.

The latest recruit to George's bird shoots, accompanied by the Chief Game Warden, Willie Hale, was the new Commander in Chief, Sir Gerald Lathbury, who quickly struck decisive blows at the Mau Mau by ringing the forest with wide ditches, fences and strong points, and by strictly enforcing a forbidden zone outside it that denied the rebels both supplies and escape.

By the final months of 1955 the fighting was virtually over, apart from the defiant struggles of a few gangs like Dedan Kimathi's in the Aberdare forest.

The toll of the Emergency was a tragic one far beyond the numbers set out in the table below. The many wounded and maimed still suffered, as did the families divided and scarred by the bloodshed that so many of the Kikuyu never wanted.

	Civilians	Forces	Mau Mau
Europeans	32	63	
Asians	26	3	
Africans	1,819	101	11,503
Total	1,877	167	11,503

As far as George and Joy were concerned the Mau Mau Emergency ended at the close of 1955 when the gangs could no longer extract food from the manyattas or escape across the Meru plain to seek sanctuary in Somalia. Adamson Force had served its purpose.

On Remembrance Day in November the annual parade was arranged in Isiolo. All the units that had been active in the field— the army, the police, the Home Guard and George's patrols—were to be represented, which led to an unexpected contretemps.

This is from a letter George received just before it.

Kenya Police Headquarters, Isiolo

OCTOBER 25, 1955

Dear Adamson,

As you are no doubt aware I have been posted to Isiolo and am likely to be here for some time.

Our work will inevitably bring us together and we will be expected to meet socially. For this reason I would like to arrange a meeting with you so that we can possibly clear up some misunderstandings.

You will realise that when you wrote to me in Turkana in 1949 [sic] you had heard only one side of a story and that I was given no opportunity to say anything in extenuation.

If you agree, I suggest we arrange to meet either at my house, or at yours in the near future.

Yours sincerely,

A. L. Griffith.

There is no mention of Griffith's unwelcome arrival in either George's or Joy's diary, but hers does include one cool reference to a "Mr. and Mrs. Griffith," with a list of other guests at a party in the *boma*.

When all the men were assembled for the parade Griffith suddenly marched the police off because the Inniskillings were given precedence on the right of the line. His protest was thought particularly petty since the Provincial Commissioner had chosen the occasion for the official disbandment of Adamson Force and to thank George for his collaboration with the Inniskillings by presenting him with a specially carved shield.

Like almost everyone else in Kenya, George and Joy could now return to their normal lives, although theirs were anything but conventional. In *The Searching Spirit* she wrote this about their visit to South Island: "who has not dreamed of living on a desert island, or like Adam and Eve? For us this dream had come true."

Robert Nimmo saw her a week or two after their return from South Island and asked how she had come by two bruises on her face. She replied that on the island George had removed all her clothes and behaved like a caveman. When I pressed Nimmo about this, and Joy's other allegations of George's violence, he said he found them impossible to believe.

Whatever the truth, she was still desperately trying to have a baby by George right up to the end of the year, when she would be forty-six.

In December her latest adopted orphan, a baby zebra, died. A tragedy also befell another of her protégés. She told the story only in an unpublished book she called *Waifs and Strays of the Bush,* but it expresses in miniature the concern for wild creatures that made her and George famous all over the world.

The bright red and purple bougainvilleas she had planted around the house had now reached the roof, and in December a pair of shimmering little Hunter's sunbirds built their nest among their flowers under her window. They had emerald caps, scarlet chests and long curving beaks for sipping nectar.

After seventeen days, by the time their two chicks hatched, they had come to accept Joy's constant surveillance. In a further twelve, when the larger chick was fledged, the parents tempted it out of the nest with tidbits while all four birds kept up a constant twitter. Joy put a cushion below in case the fledgling lost its precarious balance.

Returning from lunch two days later, Joy noticed an ominous silence outside the window. Fearing the worst she rushed into the garden, calling for George, and began to search the ground for the missing baby. The mother darted back to feed the younger chick, but the father sat in a thorn tree singing a lament.

When George arrived he immediately started peering too, not down but up into the branches of the tree. Then he pointed to the little bird's body, dangling from a thorn on which it had been spiked.

"Shrike," he murmured, getting his gun.

Sure enough a red-tailed shrike returned to its victim some minutes later. The parents immediately mobbed it and George had to wait for his shot. After a few more days the younger bird took to its wings and flew away with its chattering parents.

Christmas Eve that year was celebrated in style. Kifosha, the cook, decorated the table, the cake and himself to everyone's delight, including his own.

During the day Joy posted off, with appropriate photographs, five different versions of their South Island adventure. Having fulfilled her talents as an artist, just as George had fulfilled his as one of the two most respected game wardens in the country, she was within touching distance of seeing herself in print at last. What is more, both she and George were only five weeks away from the safari that entirely changed the course of their lives. Their conflicts, military and civil, public and private, had exposed them to almost every kind of hazard that Africa and marriage could throw at them. There could hardly have been a better preparation for raising a lioness.

Part II

THE LION
& THE LEOPARD

1956–1989

Sir George Davis was English consul at Florence at the beginning of the 19th century.

One day he went to see the lions of the great Duke of Tuscany. There was one which the keepers could not tame; but no sooner did Sir George appear than it manifested every symptom of joy. Sir George entered its cage, when the lion leaped on his shoulder, licked his face, wagged its tail, and fawned on him like a dog.

Sir George told the great duke that he had brought up the creature; but as it grew older it became dangerous, and he sold it to a Barbary captain. The duke said that he had bought it of the very same man.

Brewer's Dictionary of Phrase & Fable

FIFTEEN

Born Free

1956–1960

1

In January 1956 Godana Dima, the Boran who had rescued Olo from the lion with no more than his blunt spear, came to George in tears. His brother and four friends had been sleeping in a thorn *boma* with their goats when a lion broke in and took his brother. In the morning the friends could find only his hands and feet.

George immediately set off in pursuit of the man-eater, taking Godana Dima, Kikango, who had killed the Mau Mau, and Makedde, a Turkana. He was also joined by Ken Smith, one of the newly appointed wardens who, from then on, were periodically attached to him to gain experience.

While they were following fresh lion spoor on to some rocks they were suddenly confronted by an extremely hostile lioness. Ken Smith fired and hit her. For a few moments she disappeared, leaving a trail of blood, but when she charged again it took a shot from Kikango to turn her and another from George to finish her off.

Hidden in the rocks, and possibly sired by the man-eater they never found, were three tiny cubs whose eyes were still covered by a film. There was nothing unusual in George feeling remorse at killing the lioness and rescuing her cubs, or in Joy, who had nursed many baby animals, in adopting them; in a few days, when their eyes were fully open, they would imprint on her.

Other colleagues in the Game Department had also taken on young lions. Lyn Temple-Boreham, George's peer as a warden, had raised two in the Mara, Brutus and Caesar, until they were fully grown— which means until they stood over three feet tall at the shoulder, were up to six feet long, excluding their tails, and weighed more than 400 pounds.

A fully grown lioness is rather smaller than the male but since females usually do the killing, her teeth, claws and muscles are just as lethal. For these reasons the cubs' adoption had to be reported to the DC, Robert Nimmo. George hesitated, Joy did not. William Hale, as Chief Game Warden, also had to know.

The cubs quickly attracted a series of distinguished visitors, first among them a party from Government House. Lady Mary Baring arrived with William Percy, the seventy-year-old brother of the Duke of Northumberland. Joy wrote this about the visit.

We have had Lord William Percy with us for 10 days and we enjoyed each other's company tremendously. He is one of the most interesting and versatile creatures I have met for a long time. He just loves this outdoor life in Africa and watches the birds and everything around him in a most stimulating way.

Percy's enthusiasm for the cubs especially endeared him to Joy. He became the first honorary godparent.

Next to inspect the cubs were William and Morna Hale. William, quite reasonably, made it clear he thought three lions would be too much of a handful, even for Joy, and that she must get rid of at least two. Furthermore he did not want George's staff wasting government time as their keepers.

Joy was furious. ". . . William, you are no friend of ours!" she blurted out at the beginning of lunch. The Hales promptly rose from the table and left while George calmly went on drinking his soup.

A week later his sangfroid was again put to the test when Joy protested against leaving the cubs to join a safari with him and Robert Nimmo.

"If you try to make me come I will shoot myself!" she stormed, striding to her room with a revolver and slamming the door. A few minutes later there was a shot. George raised his eyes to the ceiling and went to investigate. He postponed the safari for twenty-four hours.

During the next few months Joy—and Pati—took over the cubs. George simply helped with their practical needs—wire netting to keep them on or off the veranda, bedding, and tires to swing on. The hyrax was their self-appointed nanny, and like all good nannies maintained her ground and her dignity—even when the cubs grew large enough to put George's donkeys to flight.

Nuru, the gardener, was the African chiefly responsible for the cubs, but Makedde and Ibrahim, still George's driver, also helped. In July, when the time came to part with two of the little lions to Blydorp Zoo in Rotterdam, all the staff agreed with Joy that the two larger and bolder ones should go; they would keep the smallest, gentlest and plainest. Because of a resemblance between them she named the cub after her first mother-in-law, but never mentioned it publicly for fear of hurting Elsa von Klarwill's feelings!

For eleven hours Joy bumped about with the two cubs in the back of the truck that took them to the airport in Nairobi. When she returned to Isiolo after five days Elsa was sitting at the gate. George had not known when she was coming back, but Elsa had, and refused to budge from her post.

The departure of Elsa's two sisters to a zoo concentrated Joy's mind on what should actually be done with young animals damaged in the wild or orphaned. It brought home to her the fact that there were no proper holding facilities for animals trapped for export to zoos and circuses or whose ranges were needed for farming and forestry.

She therefore devised the idea of a national "orphanage" which was reported in the *East African Standard* on August 17. Both the PC at Isiolo and Robert Nimmo supported her request for fifty acres near the town to pioneer the scheme, but the authorities in Nairobi preferred somewhere less remote. The proposal was therefore put to the Director of National Parks and Louis Leakey, one of the National Parks' trustees.

A few months later Joy asked Leakey about the progress of her brainchild.

> What was decided at the meeting about the wild animal orphanage? Webb [Director of the Dublin Zoo] is coming out in the middle of January and I hope very much he may help to stir up things— not a zoo but an orphanage-cum-research-cum-animal-supply perhaps.

Nearly fifty years later the Nairobi orphanage still cares for damaged and orphaned animals, under the supervision of Louis's son, Richard, Director of Kenya's Wildlife Service.

At the end of the year Elsa was visited by a second honorary godparent, Elspeth Huxley. Mrs. Huxley noticed particularly Joy's habit of slipping out for an hour or more at a time to sketch Elsa or to commune with her. Elsa would then suck Joy's thumb and knead her thighs with her paws as if hoping for milk. One evening Joy emerged with some quite nasty scratches which she dabbed with disinfectant, and Elspeth declined, she hoped not too hastily, several invitations to join these sessions. By then Elsa had attacked a cow and given one of the game scouts a nasty gash.

Before long Elsa was bored with chasing the donkeys and tried to stampede giraffes and trip up an elephant that was browsing in the garden. It would take more than fifty acres to contain her once she was fully grown.

George's thoughts of returning Elsa to the wild had also gathered impetus. Since his last visit to England he and Tony Ofenheim had continued to exchange news. Always forthright, she told him he must either set Elsa free or shoot her; if he sent her to a zoo she would never speak to him again.

2

In January 1957, Joy's friend Herbert Tichy came out from Vienna. By then a well-known photographer and travel writer, he hoped to produce a book on East Africa. George and Joy saw a chance of combining safaris with him to their two favorite places—Kiunga on the coast and Lake Rudolf—and the next phase of Elsa's education.

The journey through the Boni Forest to the coast was exhausting, for the weather was far hotter than usual, and Pati went into a coma from heatstroke. The night before they reached Kiunga she died. A year earlier Joy would have been distraught, but Elsa demanded so much of her time and affection that not a word of emotion slipped into her diary.

On the beach at Kiunga Elsa tirelessly leapt after a coconut George swung on a string for her, splashed with Joy in the surf and enjoyed playing tag with the plucky pink crabs that tried to pinch her nose.

Joy was disappointed that Tichy was less enthusiastic and responsive than in the past, but he instantly rose to the occasion when needed. To quote George:

February 15 Joy went up the beach with Elsa. About 6.30 pm. I was feeling definitely queer in the head. I imagined Elsa attacking

Joy. Suddenly a terrible fear gripped me that I was going mad.

I had the sense to call Herbert who was lying on his bed. I told him that I might do anything—anything! Asked him to stay with me and not leave me for a moment—told him to remove all guns, knives, everything with which I could injure myself or another.

I knew I was sinking into darkness, I went through the most terrifying mental anguish, I cried for help, I wanted something to clutch on to like a drowning man. Herbert held my hands which were ice cold and he urged me not to give in.

I felt myself going colder and colder—I started to cry out for Joy because I knew that I was going into the limbo of insanity or death. At length I heard Joy come up from the beach. It was like the sound of a faint voice at the end of a mile-long corridor. I urged her to hurry because there was so little time left. She came and at once I felt a great relief as if a great burden had been suddenly lifted from my head.

All the time the cold kept creeping relentlessly up and up, up from my feet, up to my knees, and it grew ever faster and faster until, like the bursting of a dam, it flooded over me and I *knew* I was dying.

The last feeling I can remember was of immeasurable peace.

Ibrahim had raced off for a doctor, who ascribed the hallucinations to the latest brand of antimalaria pills. George told Joy afterwards that he believed she had saved his life. His delirium revealed both the sensitivity he so effectively hid from her and his longing for reconciliation.

Joy's diary is also revealing. She was now frequently trying to have a baby by him, talking peacefully with him in her tent during the early morning or late into the night, and enjoying happy evenings with him and Herbert Tichy around the campfire. Yet the next day or within hours, she writes: "George just bloody minded and so smug." "*I hate him*. He is crude, morose, lazy and inefficient." "Terribly hurt. *I do not want to die in George's dependency*."

George, Joy and Herbert Tichy all published accounts of their safari with Elsa to Lake Rudolf in July. Since George wanted to check the state of the game and any possible poaching between the lake and the Ethiopian border, he took his new assistant, Julian McKeand, whose version too has appeared in print.

The shore of the lake was like a sauna and because lions hate heat their progress was infuriatingly slow. The walking larder of goats for Elsa soon expired from exhaustion, and she strained every day to get at the donkeys; George had to discourage her with his hide whip, a *kiboko*. Even so she mauled one donkey which George had to shoot, and he only saved a second by rugger-tackling Elsa in the nick of time. Joy nagged him about everything: the smell of his tobacco, his handling of Elsa, and the state of their marriage. And when they reached the far end of the lake, there was not a head of game to be seen.

Everyone, including Elsa, was relieved when George turned back. Nevertheless Joy provoked George once too often; according to McKeand, who had seen her constantly needle him about Elsa and even toss his pipe into the bushes, he hit her. "He had a stick in his hand. He struck her across the face and she gave a terrific howl." Rushing out of camp, she disappeared for several hours.

Joy's diary for that day suggests that some remark about divorce was the cause. She goes on:

August 11 He beats me with rifle butt, kiboko, and fist to my neck. Askari stopped him.

In view of the fact that both McKeand and Tichy were there, Joy's account seems exaggerated. Years before, one of Joy's doctors—a woman—had told Peter Bally that to slap her face might be the best, or only, way to bring her back to her senses at the height of a tantrum.

The drama by Lake Rudolf reached another crisis when Herbert Tichy woke up from his siesta to find Elsa standing over his camp bed and blood streaming down his face from his scalp.

George had the lioness chained up in a flash, while Joy started swabbing Tichy's face; by then he was in a state of severe shock.

"Don't worry about that, woman," George said gruffly. "Give him this," and he thrust the whiskey bottle at her.

According to Tichy, it took several large doses before he was willing to let George cut back his hair and look at the damage. When George did this his jaw dropped. "So much whiskey for such a tiny cut," he bellowed in disgust!

Joy would do anything for Elsa on safari. She once persuaded George Low to climb up a hill in the bush to give the lioness an enema; Nuru and Makedde had to carry her down on a camp bed.

By the lake she greased Elsa's paws to protect them from the scorching lava. Nights on one mountain trip were so cold she took Elsa into her tent and under her blanket.

It was all the braver after two terrifying experiences. Once Elsa had come up behind Joy and taken her whole head into her jaws. Later, when Joy was going for an evening stroll with George and the Lows, Elsa raced down a hill toward them. While the others got into the Land-Rover, Joy walked back to the house, but on the way Elsa knocked her over three times and "playfully" roughed her up.

George drove Elsa off with his *kiboko* and Lois rushed the sobbing Joy into a bath to disinfect the deep bites and scratches on her shoulders and the back of her head. Despite these incidents, when George looked back, at the end of his life, on more than fifty lions he had known as well as if they had been his own children, he considered Elsa one of most friendly, intelligent and restrained of them all; yet Joy had good reason to be afraid of her sometimes. Nevertheless, she criticized George for hitting Elsa on her muzzle with his stick when he wanted to control her, believing it was the most delicate part of her body. Of course, it was not; a lion leads with its nose when it pushes through a *boma* of thorns or slams into an eland or buffalo during a kill.

During the next six months Elsa's voice deepened to a growl, she began to consort with wild lions at night and there were too many people living around Isiolo to let her permanently loose there. The decision about where to release her was finally brought to a head in 1958 when George was once more ordered to take his quota of leave. This time it was a mere 220 days that had to be spent away from the Northern Frontier.

Lyn Temple-Boreham, warden of the Maasai Mara Reserve, came to their rescue. He offered Elsa a permanent home, under the Siria escarpment, on the strict condition she learned to look after herself in the first three months.

This first attempt to return Elsa to the wild did not work for two principal reasons. One was her breeding. Born in northern Kenya, she belonged to the subspecies *panthera leo somaliensis*, which are used to high altitudes and the dry country. Three hundred and fifty miles to the south the lions at lower altitudes and in the hotter and lusher conditions of the Mara and Serengeti belong to the subspecies *leo masaica*. Elsa quickly became sick and nearly died of tick fever: she wasted away, her coat grew dull and her face went ash-gray.

The other reason was that although George and Temple-Boreham probably knew as much about lions as any two men in Africa, they could not find a way of persuading the local prides to accept her.

Happily, the DC at Meru, close to where Elsa was born, agreed she could be transferred to an area near the Tana. This is George's account of their departure for Elsa's new—and final—home.

July 4 Joy had the foolish idea of trying to drag Elsa by chain into the car! When it didn't work, Joy behaved like a lunatic. I went off to shoot meat, got a kongoni. Finally, after much abuse and ill temper from Joy, Elsa came along and without demur jumped into the car.

Apart from this Elsa traveled without protest, which is remarkable since they covered more than 400 miles, drove for more or less 24 hours on end, lost the oil in a gear box, broke two springs and had half a dozen punctures.

When they reached Meru and arrived in the area that is now a National Park, they quickly decided to set up a camp by the Ura, a small tributary of the Tana. George described the setting.

This was truly a corner of Africa where, as Joy put it, "even the foxes say goodnight to each other." The river banks were lined with luxuriant green undergrowth above which rose doum palms, acacias and tall fig trees. A little way back from the water the bush quickly thinned out, and apart from the thorns, only the big baobabs had been left standing by the elephants. Looming over this pictur-esque African landscape was a long ridge of reddish rock, which provided ideal lairs and look-outs for lions.

The scene was set for the lionization of Elsa. At two and a half years old she was theoretically ready to fend for herself, join a pride and mate. The only drawback was that because of her upbringing she was unable to do any of these things. George therefore had to devise an elaborate plan for her rehabilitation.

Even young lions descended from several generations in zoos inherit instinctive techniques for hunting and killing, but they need opportunity and practice to apply them. By shooting warthogs and waterbuck in front of Elsa's eyes and encouraging her to take pos-session of them immediately, George provided this training.

Her social life was more difficult. Young males learn to look after themselves on their own; females usually remain in a pride, bonding with their sisters and contemporaries so that when they have cubs they can share the roles of suckling and hunting.

From time to time a new male will take over the pride by force; the females will cling to their familiar territory while he will defend it against potential usurpers. On the other hand, if an interloping lioness tries to insinuate herself into his favors, the females quickly send her packing.

Elsa's situation was therefore hopeless unless George could find a way of helping her to ingratiate herself first with a local male and then with his females. Since he still had four months' leave due to him, George was reluctant to leave her even for short periods until he had solved the problem.

The strength of Joy's love and respect for Elsa continued to deepen with her growing conviction that the lioness understood and reciprocated her feelings. "I sketch Elsa happily on her kill in the tent. She understands *everything*—George not!"

A month later she notes after a reference to Elsa: "Darling—I love you so much."

Elsa's most remarkable demonstration of understanding and restraint occurred when she knocked over a buffalo in the Ura and was efficiently drowning it. While her blood was still up, Nuru, a Muslim, rushed down to cut the animal's throat before it died so that he and the other Africans could eat some of the meat. For a second Elsa turned on him, but suddenly realized he had come to share, not steal, her kill.

At last patience began to pay off and it was clear Elsa had mated, although there was no evidence she was pregnant. George did not want to leave; Joy knew they must make the break.

November 13   Took Elsa to Elephant Lugga. She knew everything and kept close to me on the way—leaving her for good. She licked and hugged me for the last time in my tears!

It was the first, not the last, of many partings. Against the odds, Elsa managed to look after herself but whenever George or Joy returned to their camp, every ten days or so, and fired a shot in the air or let off a thunderflash, the lioness rushed to greet them, rubbing her head against their knees, or wrapping her paws around George's shoulders and licking his face with her rasping tongue.

Joy's plan to loosen, and then break, Elsa's dependence was a profoundly unselfish resolve—perhaps the first of her life. But as sacrifices sometimes do, it was to bring her both release—from a sense of isolation and sterility—and reward beyond her imagining.

3

Joy had built herself a log table and bench under a fig tree beside the river. She called it her studio and began to type and sketch there, with Elsa stretched out at her feet and baboons mocking them from the rocks across the stream. Her determination to write regularly for publication had been strengthened when her South Island story was accepted, with her photographs, by all five magazines.

While Joy typed, George fished or lay in the shade reading. She frequently begged him to help her tell Elsa's story but he foresaw only disaster if they attempted to collaborate.

After the success of *Born Free* Kenya was rife with rumors that Joy, whose command of English was famously imperfect, had not written it. It was attributed to the ghostly hands of Elspeth Huxley, Cecil Webb or her publishers, with substantial help from George's diaries. Gossip was mistaken, although Joy did use some material of George's and drew on his diaries for two later books.

Joy asked Elspeth Huxley if she would write a book about Elsa, but she declined on the grounds that the story would make more impact from Joy herself. Joy then wrote to Hamish Hamilton, who had used one of her photographs as a frontispiece for *No Room in the Ark*, a bestseller by Alan Moorehead. Joy's diary puts the outcome in a nutshell. "H.H. accepts. Ghost writer. All off!" Joy simply would not contemplate a ghost.

After she began typing her script she and George saw Cecil Webb at Isiolo, possibly in connection with the animal orphanage. Having written a successful little book about a hare, he offered to help her. He was given a barely legible carbon copy of the story Joy had typed on discolored, and almost transparent, flimsy paper.

She had no need of George's diaries for the book. She had recorded every detail of Elsa's life with her camera and hoped that the three large albums of photographs, sent to London without captions and with only a résumé of the story, would find her a publisher. They did not.

In February 1959, satisfied that Elsa could now cope on her own with only occasional visits from George, Joy therefore set off for London. There she was quickly turned down by three publishers but left batches of photographs with half a dozen more.

"The world *shall* hear of Elsa," Joy told her cousin Mary Pike. Then she suddenly remembered Marjorie Villiers of the Harvill Press.

The Harvill Press owed its name to its founders Manya Harari, a Russian married to an Egyptian banker, and Marjorie Villiers, an English widow. They had met and become friends in the intelligence section of the Foreign Office during the Second World War and started to publish together when it ended. Manya Harari's great coup had been to discover and help translate the best-selling Russian masterpiece *Doctor Zhivago*.

Passionately devoted to literature and ideas, the two partners were also extremely sympathetic to animals—they both owned dogs—and to personal introductions. Not long before they had published *Animals in Africa*, a pioneering book of photographs by Ylla with a text by Louis Leakey, and Leakey had given Joy an introduction to Marjorie Villiers as a possible publisher for her tribal book.

Harvill had declined that book on economic grounds but Joy now called at their tiny office in Belgravia, without an appointment, and refused to leave the waiting room until she was seen. When Marjorie's four poodles could contain themselves no longer and burst out of her office for a walk, Joy pounced.

Marjorie Villiers listened to her story and looked at her snapshots—she did not have her albums with her. Next day Marjorie wrote to William Collins—always known as Billy—chairman of the very large and successful British publishing house that had recently bought the Harvill Press. He was in New York on business.

APRIL 8, 1959

My excitement is this: there is a woman called Mrs. Adamson whose husband is a game warden. She came to us some time ago, but yesterday she reappeared with a totally different, and to my mind extremely exciting, proposition. The Adamsons adopted a lion cub . . .

Mrs. Adamson has written a text of 30,000 words. As she is an

Austrian she did not feel that her own words were sufficient. She has therefore given her notes to Cecil Webb, who was the head of the Dublin Zoo, to process. He has now retired and is living in Kenya, and we have not yet seen the text. But whatever form it may be in I cannot imagine that it could not be got into a wonderful story.

Billy Collins's characteristic response was a telegram.

APRIL 10

Adamson book very exciting. Please arrange publish. No difficulty selling America.

Joy had taken a gloomy room near Harrods—she never stayed in a hotel if she could possibly help it—and Marjorie went there to look at her massive photograph albums, bound in lion skin. Afterward she wrote to Collins:

APRIL 13

I am keeping Mrs. Adamson very warm indeed. I cannot do more than that at the moment because her text, which was sent to Cecil Webb, has not yet been returned with his amendments. So far, therefore, we only have her verbal story and a short introduction by Lord William Percy.

I have seen her 5,000 photographs and by the end was nearly unconscious. She is not a born photographer, but obviously amongst so many there must be a lot of good ones.

While I was writing this the lioness appeared in the office to announce to me that she had sold the first serial rights to the *Daily Mail*, who had suggested that they should immediately provide her with an agent. I didn't like this at all.

After this meeting, Joy went into top gear and reported progress to Marjorie.

APRIL 14

There are 21 pages already typed, 51 pencil corrected and the remaining 20 or so easy—just to copy my draft. I went to a typist to whom I have talked before and he can do these remaining odd 70 pages only in 7 days!

By the beginning of May, Billy Collins was back from America and after a meeting that to Joy seemed a game of poker her agent was offered £1,000, then a large sum of money. In two minds about accepting it, Joy consulted Elspeth Huxley over lunch, who told her to leap at it and ordered champagne to celebrate.

The arrival of an agent on the scene to negotiate the contract for a book that had already fallen into Marjorie's hands, the world rights of which Collins felt they could handle better themselves, was an irritating fly in the ointment.

Part of the arrangement with Collins and the Harvill Press was that anything suitable of George's would be included in the book. On May 4 he sent a batch of pages and followed these on May 23 with an article he had written for *Reader's Digest* that they did not want, telling Joy that she must revise it as if written by herself.

George also wrote Joy a series of letters about Elsa's progress while she was away and agreed to their inclusion, provided it was made clear that he helped Elsa by shooting game only if it was essential and never in excess of her normal needs.

Marjorie described to Billy Collins how she edited this material.

MAY 12

First I have to scramble her text and his together, taking bits of both. Then I send her the first draft. She comes in and pulls it to pieces, some very necessary criticism because I've unwittingly made the wrong chronological sequence in sewing up the manuscript. We get this typed out and then send it to Lord William Percy who comments on it very sensibly and then we have the third and last version typed.

There was no question of Marjorie introducing anything that was not Joy's or George's. In fact Joy went over every word of the edited version of the script with a German-English dictionary to see that no nuance had been improperly lost or introduced. By the time Cecil Webb's version reached London it was no longer relevant.

A former chief game warden of Uganda, C. R. S. Pitman, had agreed to write a foreword to the book, and Lord William Percy, who had become Joy's astringent mentor while she was in England, contributed a preface and had suggested the title *Born Free* from St Paul's boast ". . . .But I was free born." He and Marjorie Villiers saw eye to eye about the qualities and perils of Joy's writing, especially her proneness to sentimentality. He wrote:

> Had I been her ghost writer many things in the book would have been different but I was never asked to do that. Indeed if I have made any contribution to it I have been more successful in persuading her to leave things out than in affecting its style, phraseology or judgment.
>
> It is a thousand pities that her husband did not write the book or at least help her with it, but I know why that was past praying for. One can only hope that the facts of a unique animal story have an intrinsic interest which compensates for any failure of the style.

It was not only the unvarnished story of Elsa that carried *Born Free* into the ranks of classic and best-selling animal stories. Its eighty pages of photographs were an essential aspect of it. They were selected, enlarged and arranged to make the greatest impact or, as a sequence, to tell the best story. It was a laborious process. Joy would hurry into the office each day, excellently preserved by her life in the sun and fresh air, her blue eyes alert. As we worked they flickered from concentration to laughter, doubt or displeasure. Satisfying her vision for the book was stimulating and fun; curbing her excesses sparked off rows of greater intensity than I had witnessed with any other author.

One other factor led to the book's impending success—the character of its publisher, Billy Collins. Joy was so taken up with the details of her book that by the time she returned to Kenya in July she had not taken a proper look at the man on whom her fortunes depended. His enthusiasm and charm, combined with the informal style of his Georgian office, and family life in a comfortable flat above it, concealed his ruthless professional skill.

4

One letter George wrote to Joy in London was particularly optimistic about Elsa's progress.

MAY 12

From your letter you seem to think that Elsa is still half way between being tame and wild. This is not the case. She is a wild lioness in every respect except one, and that is her easy friendliness toward Europeans. I feel that she looks upon us as some kind of lions, not to be feared.

It is curious that all the lions George was to adopt and release in the next twenty years made this distinction between white and black skins—presumably because lions have a basic aversion toward all humans that is only modified by their familiarity with their foster parents.

MAY 31

On Thursday morning when Asman brought me my tea, after putting it on the table outside, he came into the tent where Elsa had deposited her meat during the night, to pick up my sandals to clean. Elsa was off the roof of the car and into the tent in a flash and before I could do anything had Asman down. But she was amazingly good in spite of growling in a frightening manner, she gave him a slight nip in one leg. I managed to get between them and while I calmed her made Asman crawl out over my bed. Afterward, as if in apology, she was particularly friendly toward him.

From another letter one may question if Elsa was so color-conscious after all. René Babault, a white hunter, had been warned to keep away from Elsa's range but failed to do so. He good-naturedly recounted the consequences to George.

On a recent safari to the Ura river we came across your pet, Elsa. She joined the party after dinner one night, much to the clients' astonishment.

She is in good health, though a little thin, and obviously terribly excited at seeing people again. So much so that she insisted on greeting everyone individually and later climbed into bed with me. At one stage of the proceedings she playfully bit my arm when I tried to take away a mosquito net from her. This, however, has now quite recovered.

This and a similar episode were left out of *Born Free* at the insistence of William Percy, who was aware that Elsa's exploits were beginning to unsettle the authorities. Behind their backs George and Joy came in for considerable criticism, most of it irrelevant and ill-natured. Percy, who had no doubt learned a thing or two about Kenyan proclivities when staying at Government House, summed them up like this.

> No one who is not a resident in Kenya should dare to suggest any co-operation between any two people in the atmosphere of personal dislikes, enmities, jealousies, and backbiting which bedevils it, and is more rife than in probably any other British community in the world.

Perhaps the most telling charge that informed critics leveled at the Adamsons during the first months of Elsa's release was that she must be suffering great stress, having been cast out by her human pride without being accepted by one of her own in the wild. George's answer was "better that than bars or a bullet."

So far as George could see, the only local lions in the area were a pair—male and female—without a full pride; almost certainly mated, they had no interest in Elsa. George therefore took one of the most questionable decisions of his career. He asked a trapper to bring in a young male from outside as a mate for Elsa.

This was the result, as relayed by Joy to Marjorie Villiers. It was of course omitted from the book.

SEPTEMBER 4

We got a terrible shock a week ago when a report came that a lion had mauled 3 tribesmen. G. went at once to investigate.

18 miles away at a trading centre, the people told him that on the 25th evening a young lion killed 6 goats but was chased off before he could eat one. Then he mauled a woman in the cheek, but she was rescued. Then he went to the headman's place where 5 men slept outside. He grabbed one by the leg and dragged him away, but the others rescued him and the lion went away.

Early next morning a man passed about a mile away and heard a lion's growl inside a bush. The lion came for him, but the man rushed off and gave the alarm. The war horn was blown, which meant that everybody in earshot came rushing along with whatever weapon they could find—spears, axes, bush knives, etc.—and a huge crowd surrounded the lion.

He charged out several times, defending the dog he had inside the bush, killed and half-eaten at last. He was greeted with a hail of weapons, and finally literally hacked to pieces by the mob.

It is such a ghastly story and is like a nightmare to me as we are to blame for his terrible end.

The tragedy was especially distressing because very soon after the death of the young outsider Elsa seduced, or was seduced by, the local lion—not without protest from his mate who fought Elsa and left her badly scratched more than once.

A month later the story took another extraordinary twist as Elsa's wild instincts began to assert themselves.

NOVEMBER 10

George found the place where Elsa had left her buck. A lioness had dragged it some 400 feet away, eaten the head and legs. He thinks that our good-natured Elsa had deliberately given it to this lioness in order to help her when she was handicapped by having to look after cubs.

Elsa's own cubs were due around about Christmas and her mate remained extremely attentive to her; so much so that when George and the kitchen *toto* walked within six feet of a bush in which he was waiting for her, they were nearly knocked over when he finally bolted.

DECEMBER 21

I had nothing to give her for the last two days. She and her lion were roaring their voices out two nights ago, each of them about 50 yards on either side of my camp; the baboons were also doing their best. It was a really grand concert.

I expected the party to join me in the tent at any moment and as I had nothing to entertain them with, I was rather worried. Indeed, I am very concerned that if we stay too long the lion is going to get fed up at sharing Elsa with us. So now we have decided to leave her alone for three days.

Christmas Day was celebrated in camp and was memorable for the silver tree that Marjorie had sent Joy from London, for Kifosha's lapse in serving Worcestershire sauce with the pudding and for Elsa's arrival in the middle of lunch no longer carrying cubs.

It was several days before George was able to sneak up on her lair in the rocks while Joy was feeding her in camp. He confirmed there were three cubs. So sure was Elsa's instinct that she waited another six weeks before she brought the cubs to see Joy. By then their eyes were clear and they were firmly imprinted on their mother.

Together Joy and George had achieved something unique. They had raised a lioness until she was mature, successfully released her into the wild and retained her affection, even after she had mated and borne cubs.

For anyone who did not believe them they had the photographs to prove it.

5

The news of Elsa's cubs was cabled to London, printed as a postscript in the book and provided a keystone for its promotion.

Good publishers sometimes acquire the books they deserve. Billy Collins certainly received his deserts with *Born Free*. Since 1945 he had built up a formidable list of bestsellers, but was always looking ahead at what people might want to read next. One day he told his editors: "We may have got one of the best lists of war books in London, but the public will grow bored with them soon, and will want some other form of adventure. What we need is a really good animal story—like *Jock of the Bushveld*." He was therefore ready for *Born Free* and well placed to handle it because he had specialized in publishing natural history with the help of advisers like the eminent zoologist Julian Huxley.

Few men in London were more dedicated to publishing than Billy Collins. Tall, athletic and handsome, he liked to win at whatever he did. He had played tennis for Oxford and in the Wimbledon championships. By 1958 he had given up everything else for the business, in which his family joined him. His wife, a Roman Catholic and close friend of Marjorie Villiers and Manya Harari, was his religious editor and had been instrumental in buying the Harvill Press. One of his daughters helped lay out the plates of *Born Free*, and the other sold the foreign rights to it. His two sons worked in other departments. Collins had also recruited a team of top-class salesmen and a publicity director of genius, Ronald Politzer, who pioneered modern book promotion which included the first major serials in the *Sunday Times*.

Politzer and Billy Collins were especially intrigued by the Adamsons' cine footage of Elsa and saw a chance to use it when a well-known producer, Harry Watt, wrote to ask if Elsa could be recaptured to play in the film he was making of *The Lion* by Joseph Kessel.

George wrote back:

Elsa is now a completely wild lioness ... it might make a very thrilling film to see the heroine eaten, but it would be distinctly uncomfortable for her. Besides, I could not possibly risk Elsa getting indigestion, if the heroine is anything like the book.

Risking a snub, Billy Collins immediately wrote to Harry Watt asking if he would edit and present a ten-minute documentary on Elsa. He sportingly agreed.

The promotion campaign—which involved a massive circulation of brochures and photographs, and life-size posters of Elsa—nearly received a serious setback when the *Sunday Times* declined serialization on the grounds that the *Daily Mail* would be using extracts, and also in the belief that an animal story would have little appeal to their readers.

Ronald Politzer, sat up the whole of one night laying out a double spread of the photographs and intimated to the paper that if they did not carry the story of the lioness it would receive no more field marshals for serialization. The blackmail worked, but the *Sunday Times* refused to pay a penny for the rights.

By then the buzz about the book—publishing thrives on epidemics of rumor and infectious enthusiasm—had begun to spread abroad. In America it was accepted by an extremely gifted publisher, Helen Wolff of Pantheon Press—a friend of the Collinses, and of Marjorie and Manya, from whom she had taken other books, including *Doctor Zhivago*. In Europe imprints were also quick to snap up *Born Free*.

Another of Billy Collins's assets as a publisher was his control of a large printing factory. He was able to run off 28,000 copies of *Born Free* before publication—an enormous number for an unknown author. Early copies were rushed to the great and the good whose commendations might influence public opinion. The first two replies were prophetic.

Elspeth Huxley wrote:

Elsa's story is quite extraordinary. I hope your book will do an enormous amount to change—or at any rate to push hard at—the

237

whole way of looking at lions. No longer as ravaging, savage beasts but gentle or friendly so long as they are not frightened or harmed.

Peter Scott—the naturalist, broadcaster and outstanding bird artist—went further.

> This book is in every sense a masterpiece. As a study of animal behaviour it has a great importance, as an example of near perfect relationship between man and animal it is unique. Sensitively written and superbly illustrated I cannot see what can prevent it from becoming a classic.

The *Sunday Times* came out with its extract two weeks before publication. The response was overwhelming and it demanded a second.

Outside Hatchards bookshop in Piccadilly I watched customers tear the wrapping paper from their copies of the book to look through it in the street. They could scarcely believe what they saw.

Within a week the entire first printing was sold out and Joy's book was on its way to selling five million copies in more than a dozen languages.

SIXTEEN

Running Wild

1960–1962

1

Four hundred years before Joy wrote *Born Free*, her namesake Konrad Gesner, the flower artist, published his *Historia Animalium*. It is strange that Joy never mentioned him or his description of the lion: "King of the four-footed beasts ... bold, beautiful and gallant." Gesner quotes Pliny as saying that "the lion alone of all wild beasts is gentle to those who humble themselves to him and will not touch any such upon their submission."

Joy's book appealed to her millions of readers, many of whom had never owned an animal, because it was a love story with a twist. The love that had been lavished on Elsa as an orphan and that had prepared her for freedom, was reciprocated, astonishingly, after she was wild. Only one other man, Norman Carr, in what is now Zambia, had successfully released lions in the wild—two males—but he had never kept in touch with them once they were free, and he never knew if they had mated.

At another level the book evoked a long history of archetypes and legends. One of the living creatures guarding God in the book of Revelation resembled a lion; Aslan, the lion in *The Chronicles of Narnia*, personifies divine omnipotence; throughout history monarchs have chosen the lion as their emblem; and the prophet Isaiah promised that one day the calf would be able to lie down with the lion.

For many people *Born Free* was not just a marvelous story but an inspiration—they suddenly felt how important it was to bridge the widening gap between man and the natural world.

In a letter to Billy Collins, Joy herself said:

I am really proud that Elsa trusts me so completely that ... she always comes to me when she has a thorn to be pulled out.

To repay her trust Joy was impatient to launch an appeal to help animals in danger.

> About the leaflet. Please, Marjorie, help me get it published at once or tell me that it will not be possible—and then I will forget about it and give my March royalties to the game department to help with the animal removal teams.

As a result of the book, the newspaper serials and a condensation in *Readers' Digest*, Joy sometimes received fifty or even a hundred letters at a time and had to advertise her apologies in the papers for not answering them immediately. The studio became an office.

Joy and George were never more in need of their exceptional energies. Quite apart from her fan mail, Joy had to approve plans for a children's book, send almost weekly batches of a script on her previous orphans to Marjorie and write Billy long letters about Elsa and the cubs in case they all had a second bestseller in the making. She asked her lawyer if she could dispense with her agent and she also consulted accountants about the huge royalties she was likely to earn. They advised her to steer them into a company and a trust.

George was equally hard put to deal with his own fan mail, keep watch on the Ura when Joy was away and cover his duties as a game warden.

Life beside the river was far closer to most people's idea of Eden than the barren little island on Lake Rudolf. There were times when even the troop of fifty baboons on the far bank were peaceful and Joy noticed that a bushbuck family—the ram, his doe and their fawn—would join them for a sense of security. She made a point of feeding tidbits of banana and papaw to the fishes.

The setting of Elsa's camp in the Meru reserve was idyllic, among fig trees, acacias, gardenias and scented henna bushes. When the rains came buds swelled and burst, weaver birds slung their nests from the branches, and as soon as the chicks hatched the carpet of flowers was strewn with hundreds of eggshells.

A family of screeching parrots, brilliant in their orange and emerald plumage, took up residence in a large baobab. The bush babies, who lived in a hole just above them and slept by day, looked bewildered by the hubbub. They were small enough to sit in the palm of a hand, their long tails dangling down, and their wide eyes gave them a comically human expression.

At dusk there was a hush when the birds had settled to roost and before the evening concert began. A great belt of light, some ten feet wide, bridged the shoulder-high grass with green phosphorescence, and flickered on and off as tens of thousands of fireflies perfectly synchronized their messages.

During the rains insects streamed to the lamps, and frogs hopped out of the darkness to feast on the bodies that were scattered below them. One used to jump on to Elsa's back and pick off the flies there; others joined Joy in her canvas tub.

But the Ura, like Eden, was a dangerous idyll, threatened by serpents. Pythons occasionally left their perfectly cast skins in the bush, and their tracks often marked the banks where the cubs went to drink. For a time these physical dangers were more apparent than the moral.

2

No one ever seemed to arrive at Elsa's camp without passing a party of elephants. Joy was chased by a rhino, and George had to fire at one to stop it charging him and then his Land-Rover. Joy and the kitchen *toto* were both bowled over by a buffalo that stepped on Joy's ribs. More seriously, Elsa and the cubs found themselves harassed by her mate and his original consort. Far from befriending Elsa, they were quick to steal any meat George left for her.

Realizing Elsa would have to be fed if she were not to leave the cubs unprotected, and reluctant to go on shooting game, George introduced a herd of goats in the care of an aged Meru, Toitonguro, who joined Joy's retinue for the next ten years.

In a letter to Tony Ofenheim, George sketched a picture of his life and Elsa's.

You are certainly my oldest correspondent and the only one I *like* writing to.

I was supposed to retire in July. Fortunately this has now been put off until the end of next year. By then I think it will be time to go. Not that I am any less keen on trying to preserve the remnants of the wild life of Kenya, or that I feel too old. But I have had enough of government service and want no part in aiding "progress" at the expense of nature.

I have no intention of leaving Kenya as it is my home and will stick it out until the end, whatever that may be.

Elsa is sitting with her three cubs a few feet in front of my tent, finishing off the remains of a goat. The cubs are nearly three months old and perfect specimens and little devils. They give their mother no peace. One seizes her tail, another jumps on her back, and the third pulls her ear.

From the beginning Elsa seemed to have a precise view of how familiar she was prepared to allow the cubs to be with George and Joy. At first they were not to go into the tents or to get too close to people; later they were not allowed to wet the tents or the paths. Like human children they were trained in the etiquette of eating and drinking; if they didn't pay attention to her vocal instructions they were cuffed.

Very soon their different characters emerged. Jespah, the most adventurous and assertive, adopted the role of eldest son. He poked his nose into everything, cuddled up to Elsa whenever he could and was also protective. Little Elsa, the only female, was the shyest: she was a replica of her mother in looks and equable temperament. Gopa always kept his distance; he grew the largest and his wildness developed into sturdy independence.

If they approached too close to Joy, Elsa would interpose herself between them, and if Jespah persisted in stalking her Elsa would spank him hard. Joy wrote this.

> She also dealt firmly with me if she thought I was getting too familiar with her children. For instance, several times when I came close to them while they were at play, she looked at me through half-closed eyes, walked slowly but purposefully up to me, and gripped me round the knees in a friendly but determined manner, which indicated very plainly that her grip would become much firmer if I did not take the hint and retire.

Despite this Joy was incapable of controlling her impulse to "flirt"—as she called it—with Jespah. As a result, while Elsa was dozing with her head on Joy's lap, Jespah clawed her foot and nipped her hand when she tried to push him away—to him it was play. On another occasion, when he was eight months old, he rose on his hind legs, put his paws on her shoulders and licked her face.

Feeding Elsa and the cubs near the camp to help safeguard her "kills" from the wild lions sometimes meant that battles with them were fought close to home; and there were other contenders too. At night crocodiles hauled themselves out of the Ura and Elsa was not always successful in protecting her supper. George and Joy both had to shoot crocs a few yards from camp. A five-foot monitor lizard— like a small dragon—took to raiding the larder.

In the small hours, if Elsa was replete and asleep on the roof of the Land-Rover, hyenas, jackals and genets would come and squabble over the scraps, or a civet cat would creep along the branches above the tents and set off a panic-stricken protest from the weavers.

Joy found little rest at Isiolo, either, when she took a few days off there. More waifs were wished on her, but she was unable to save the lives of an impala or two baby elephants, while a young cheetah escaped and disappeared into the bush.

Her most frightening experience occurred when she was alone in the house. She was awakened by heavy footsteps going into the room next to her. Seizing the revolver from under her pillow she followed them. There, in the bathroom, she was confronted by a porcupine!

3

Having done her best to ensure that the whole world heard about Elsa and her cubs, Joy was extremely reluctant to allow anyone near. However, on the recommendation of Billy Collins she let David Attenborough film them.

> Their visit was, I think, a great success. They had incredible luck as Elsa did something different nearly every day—on the rock, playing with the cubs, or walking back to camp (Jespah stalking David constantly and David sneaking or dodging round bushes). We did nothing but laugh all day and enjoyed every minute.

Attenborough's version is rather different. Elsa had just been badly clawed in a fight with her rival lioness, and Joy was extremely upset. It caused her to be embarrassingly unpleasant to George, and Attenborough noted in his journal that Joy said, by way of explanation, "You see I love Elsa more than any man."

When the new Chief Game Warden, Ian Grimwood, flew Sir Julian and Lady Huxley to Meru, Joy did her best to keep them away from Elsa's family. George, however, just bundled them into his Land-Rover and took them back to the camp for the night.

As a result Juliette Huxley became a staunch and affectionate friend. Huxley himself wandered around the camp before breakfast in a red dressing gown, clutching his binoculars, enthralled by the monkeys and parrots. He was so impressed by Joy's relationship with Elsa that he wrote an introduction to Joy's next book *Living Free.*

In this he dwelt on the way in which Joy's understanding love had elicited from Elsa what he called "an organized personality" out of her individuality and set of instincts, strung on the thread of her memory.

> It is important for the progress of science. It means that in the young science of Animal Behaviour or Ethology the investigator will only obtain his most valuable results by supplementing his scientific objectivity with an understanding or even affectionate approach to the animals with which he is working.

With a prescience that it took most ethologists more than twenty years to accept, Huxley rejected the view that the attribution of emotion to animals was automatically anthropomorphic.

Billy Collins always relished the chance of seeing his authors and their subjects in their natural habitat. When he reached the Ura at 9 o'clock at night there was no sign of Elsa but he found the beauty of the camp intoxicating. Then, as they sat around the fire with their drinks, Elsa rushed through the long grass, followed by her cubs. They were formally introduced.

Afterward Billy described in a broadcast what happened that night. His tent was pitched between George's and Joy's and surrounded by a thick circle of thorns with a strong wicket gate.

> About 3.30 I had a sort of feeling; it was twilight outside and I could see Elsa looking at my boma—and all of a sudden she was alongside me. My idea was to get out of the mosquito netting as quickly as possible but we got all entangled and she was on top of me—she weighs some 300 lbs—20 stone. I had the experience of keeping bees and I knew the great thing was to be quiet, so I talked away to her "Good Elsa, nice Elsa ..." Some five minutes later George Adamson appeared and got her out.

Nipped and scratched but apparently unshaken, Billy spent the day with Joy in her studio by the river, talking about her work. That night his thorn defenses were reinforced.

> So another beautiful night—the usual noises of Elsa and other animals. About three o'clock I hear Elsa at my gate. Within a few minutes she was in and all tangled up in the mosquito net on top of my bed. So far as I could tell my head seemed to be in her mouth and she was all over me.

Again, calling to Elsa and swearing at the thorns, George struggled to the rescue—only just in time. Elsa and Billy were swaying, upright, on the camp bed. Her paws were on his shoulders, her jaws around his cheeks, and trickles of blood ran down his neck and shoulders.

With exemplary calm and detachment he shrugged off Joy's apologies and reflected:

> The interesting thing is why she should have been so determined to enter my tent. It might have been jealousy. She obviously realised that I knew the Adamsons pretty well and she just did not want a stranger butting in.

Perhaps Elsa heard the voice of the serpent whispering to her from one of the trees, for she briefly succumbed to temptation, but she did not go very far, unlike Joy who did.

There is no doubt that during this visit Joy and Billy became lovers. She was fifty, he was sixty, both had kept their looks and their figures, and were swept away "without any of the normal preliminaries," in the words of a discreet friend in whom Joy confided.

Billy had a profound respect for his wife, Pierre, but she had never fully recovered from a serious illness in her forties, after which she had converted to strict Roman Catholicism and joined the business in order not to lose Billy to his publishing. Intelligent and amusing, she had a flair for sensing which authors and books were going to prove important or fashionable, and she had initiated the acquisition of Harvill. She engaged in the politics of the office with Byzantine skill and tenacity.

If Pierre kept Billy's superego in trim, Joy gave his libido a holiday in Africa. He adored the adventure—spotting new birds, or being held up by elephants, threatened by a rhino, and put in his place by a lion.

On the day he left Kenya he wrote an inscription in Joy's copy of *Born Free* that began:

To Joy. In memory of one of the happiest weeks of my life . . .

No doubt she had told him exactly the same stories about George as she had told George about Peter Bally; and she was so transparent in her deceptions that George must have guessed what was happening, particularly when Billy came back a few months later "to discuss *Living Free.*"

His visit coincided with a telegram from her agent, asking her permission to sue Billy for allegedly withholding some money due to her. The telegram was burned on the camp fire and the agent discarded for her future work.

On Billy's last day Joy took him up into the Aberdares, where they had a picnic by a waterfall, surrounded by wild delphiniums and gladioli.

I have always felt that George was neither very angry nor really hurt by Joy's infatuation. In fact he may have seen Billy as a convenient lightning conductor, capable of absorbing her combined creative, romantic and sexual charges. She never took another serious lover.

It is difficult not to see the serpent's influence in another of Joy's attitudes to George while they were on the Ura with Elsa and her cubs. She categorically refused to make over to him any share of the royalties from *Born Free*, although she knew they would amount to at least £100,000—the equivalent of half a million dollars today. It all went into a company she had formed. Her main pretext was that he had refused to collaborate on the book. Apart from the fact that he was responsible for the whole framework of Elsa's existence, many of the words and photographs were his and her claim was patently disingenuous.

Only two explanations of Joy's decision seem valid. Either she was overpowered by a desire to wound him or she was terrified that if they both had adequate means, once relieved of his Game Department obligations, he would feel free to leave her.

Years ago I noticed a photograph of a wardress in a German concentration camp that reminded me of Joy when she was in one of these unrelenting moods. I was therefore electrified when I came across this entry in her diary while she and George were commuting between Elsa's Camp and Isiolo.

George tells me I am the "dead spit of the woman in charge of Belsen." I return my wedding ring.

This crisis was followed by two months of extreme tension for Joy, during which she tried to save the life of Pampo, a baby elephant, at Isiolo, while still visiting Elsa on the Ura. When her truck broke down at the start of a journey back to Isiolo something inside her snapped. Irrationally, she raged off into dense bush, alive with lions, rhinos and snakes, unarmed and without an askari. Alarmed for her safety, George called her but she ignored him. He wrote this in his diary:

> After about ten minutes she crossed the river and set off through the rocky outcrop. On reaching the track to Tharaka she started along it. Had to use force to stop her. Tried to get her to return to camp but after going a short way she lay down and refused to move.

George fired a shot which brought some of his men, who in turn fetched Ibrahim with a truck. During the fracas George slapped Joy's face and accidentally hurt her ear. Back at Isiolo they both saw the doctor and explained what had happened: although temporarily damaged, Joy's ear completely recovered. The bruises on her body were noticed by John MacDonald, the vet attending Pampo.

George remained philosophical in the face of all these difficulties with Joy and wrote a characteristic letter to Tony Ofenheim about his life and the lions'.

DECEMBER 22

It is funny—by the end of the year Joy will be worth at least £30,000, yet I who have done quite a lot and made it possible for Joy to produce her book, am just about broke and am not even a shareholder in "Elsa Limited"! In fact I have good reason to think that Joy has cut me out of her will, knowing b—— well that I am much too fond of Elsa and her cubs ever to abandon them.

The cubs were a year old a couple of days ago. In spite of warnings from Joy and others, I never feel the least uneasiness sleeping in my tent with Elsa, Jespah and Gopa surrounding my bed, lying stretched out on the floor, Little Elsa always just outside.

But like a lot of things in this world, it was too good to last.

Recently there has been much agitation among the Tharaka tribe, who live near Elsa's domain, to get her removed.

By this time the new Governor had declared an end to the State of Emergency in Kenya, and within the next three years Britain's Prime Minister let loose "the wind of change" that freed her African colonies, Jomo Kenyatta walked out of his prison and Uhuru—the independence of Kenya—became a reality.

Tremors of the new order had reached the Ura, and at every level Elsa's presence was becoming resented. Herdsmen were no longer able to graze their cattle in the area. Tharaka hunters—in fact poachers—were harassed by George and his scouts, who shot their dogs and called in the police: in revenge the Tharaka burned down his camp. It was unfortunate that Joy was particularly vituperative to a Meru on her staff whose brother had been a Mau Mau general.

The area around the Ura had recently been declared an African District Council reserve and there was further friction between the Adamsons and its European warden. He thought George was after his job and Joy accused him of inefficiency. To make matters worse, he released a lioness too close to a village and she killed a man, and his death was attributed to Elsa. Almost simultaneously a woman filming in Tanganyika was killed by a tame lion.

On Christmas Eve Elsa and her cubs came into camp and sat around Joy's candle-lit tree. On the table was a letter from the District Commissioner ordering Elsa's removal.

4

In January 1961 Joy had to leave camp on business, knowing that Elsa was unwell. A few days later George sent a telegram to Nairobi saying she was very much worse. At 7:30 the next morning Ken Smith, who had originally found Elsa and her sisters with George, called at Joy's hotel to tell her the situation was desperate.

Unlike Joy, George seldom gave expression to his feelings for Elsa. However, in a letter to Tony Ofenheim he did:

I slept with her in the bush as I was afraid she might be attacked by hyenas or wild lions. In spite of her weakness Elsa came up to me twice during the night and rubbed her face against mine with all her old affection.

Next morning George found Elsa half lying in the water, and when she could not drink from his cupped hands sent Ibrahim for a vet: he was not back by dark.

During the night Elsa became restless, walked down to the river and into the water, then crossed to a half-submerged mud bank and lay on it until about 4.00 am, I suppose to cool her fevered body. Her breathing was very laboured and I knew the end was near.

I roused the camp and got my three boys to improvise a stretcher and we carried her back to the tent. I lay down beside her and started to doze off. Suddenly she got up, walked quickly to the front of the tent and collapsed. I held her head in my lap. In a few minutes she sat up and uttered a great and agonised cry. Elsa was dead.

It may seem absurd but Elsa meant more to me than any other living creature has ever done.

Although Joy quotes George's diary account of Elsa's death in *Living Free* she omits these last few lines:

My Elsa gone. Gone the most wonderful friend and part of my life which nothing can replace. Why should it be? Something which has created nothing but good will and love in the world.

John MacDonald, the vet, arrived soon after Elsa died. With considerable hesitation George asked him to remove various organs in order to carry out a postmortem; they then quickly buried her body to spare Joy the sight of Elsa's disfigured remains. Three volleys were fired over her grave.

Ken Smith arrived with Joy an hour or two later, and even in the distance, he could tell from George's demeanor that they were too late. He stopped the truck some way off and watched as George and Joy slowly walked toward each other, embraced and shook in their grief.

MacDonald sent the organs for analysis in a laboratory at Kabete, but they were held up on the way and decomposed. With this evidence destroyed, a rumor spread that Elsa might have been poisoned. However the Adamsons had sent blood samples to Nairobi, which proved conclusively that Elsa died of *babesia felis,* a tick-borne fever.

Her death was reported all over the world and brought letters of sympathy from the most remote towns and smallest villages.

Distraught and tearful, Joy fell on a tree stump and gashed her leg so badly that it had to be treated in hospital and dressed every day for a month. Nevertheless she did not let the accident deflect her from finishing *Living Free* and helping George with the cubs.

For a month the cubs remained near the camp, behaving impeccably; then they disappeared. By painstaking work George found the spoor of three youngsters with two adult lions and assumed that the cubs had been adopted by the wild pair that had given Elsa such trouble. His relief was short-lived. In March some young lions moved into Tharaka stock country, about fourteen miles away from the camp.

The cubs have played merry hell, killed and mauled 3 cows and 27 goats! It has cost us £75 in compensation, apart from having to engage a gang of 30 labourers to cut tracks to the scene of the cubs' activities.

I was able to identify the lions which had been raiding stock as Elsa's cubs only just in time to save them being killed with poisoned arrows. In fact a game scout had been sent from Meru to shoot the lions, and the Tharaka told to use any means to deal with them.

I sat up over a goat close to the Tana and in the course of the night there was a bleat from it. I switched on my light and there was Little Elsa with her jaws clamped around the wretched goat's throat. Soon she was joined by Jespah and Gopa.

For the next nine nights the cubs raided bomas along a stretch of about 8 miles of country. Twice they broke into huts. In one there was a woman who let out a piercing shriek which scared them out. Another was occupied by a man who woke up to find a lion with its head under his bed trying to rake out a goat. He yelled and kicked and the lion (probably Jespah) left the hut.

It has been a real nightmare, but the cubs have never attempted to hurt anyone.

Poor Jespah has an arrow head sticking in his rump which has been there since 26 March. Fortunately it was shot by a toto and was not poisoned, but it will have to be cut out.

It was now certain that the spoor of the three young lions George had first seen belonged to cubs of Elsa's rival, whose existence near the camp explained the intensity of the battles between the two mothers who had both regarded it as their exclusive territory.

In this latest crisis Joy was desperate again.

Oh, Marjorie, I am so out of my depth—still, what can I doooo? I promise I will try to get the cubs through, unless anything happens to me. Then there will be George—he must always have access to money needed to help the cubs.

George knew he could no longer simultaneously manage his job, catch the cubs, take them to the Serengeti where they had now been promised a home, and watch over them until they had established themselves or died in the attempt. After nearly twenty-five years as a game warden he resigned on April 23.

Having done so he promptly achieved the impossible. Although he had recently helped a clever young vet called Toni Harthoorn develop tranquilizing darts for the capture of animals he was unable to get hold of him now. He therefore used the seven miles of newly cut track to bring in three traps, which he set out side by side.

Each had a sliding front attached to a rope that ran over a pulley on a horizontal branch above. The ropes ran back to George's truck and were joined so that with a single slash of his panga, he could bring down all three doors at once.

Every night the three crates were baited with goat meat and the cubs grew increasingly confident of eating inside them. Close by Joy was nearly drowned in her sleep when her tent was swamped by a flash flood; but a few nights later she was woken by a thundering crash. Jespah, Little Elsa and Gopa were caught.

5

It was a six-hundred-mile journey to the Serengeti and took two days, driving almost without a break, often through freezing rain. Near Mount Kenya a vet tried to remove the arrowhead from Jespah's flank, but the lion was so restless he had to give up after three hours and predicted the arrow would soon work itself out.

The small convoy was met at the gates of the Serengeti by John

Owen, Director of National Parks in Tanganyika, who had offered the cubs sanctuary with the approval of his trustees.

The golden grass of the Serengeti plain stretches over 4,500 square miles, occasionally broken by kopjes—hillocks strewn with large boulders, fig trees, acacias and undergrowth, ideal cover in the heat of the day for leopards and owls. An escarpment rises along one border, below which a stream runs through a gentle valley shaded with trees and grazed by gazelles. This was the home John Owen had chosen for the cubs.

Only ten miles away one of the greatest migrations on earth—in those days perhaps two hundred thousand wildebeests, zebras and topi antelope, with a predatory escort of lions, hyenas and vultures—was slowly approaching.

The cubs were bruised, rubbed, scratched, bleeding and dirty at the end of their ordeal. George let them into one crate where they huddled together for reassurance and affection. He was able to twiddle Jespah's arrowhead under the skin, but although he had brought a scalpel to cut it out, Joy would not let him.

After forty-eight hours, when the cubs had calmed and settled, George raised the trapdoor. Gopa was the first to recognize freedom and headed for the river. Jespah watched and hesitated then he followed. Finally Little Elsa set off in pursuit of her brothers.

As a special concession Owen allowed George and Joy to camp out in the valley for a month and to kill for the cubs under the eye of the park wardens, Myles Turner and Gordon Harvey, both of whom George knew well.

But the grass was very high and wild lions trying to steal George's kills frightened the cubs; it was almost impossible to keep track of them. Joy grew hysterical and begged Owen to let her stay on longer, catch Jespah and bring a vet to remove the arrow. Even George seems to have lost some of his judgment, though not his sense of humor, in this letter to Ken Smith, written during a brief return to Isiolo.

The Tanganyika National Parks have been bastards. They insisted that Joy should camp at a public camping place near Seronera, 25 miles away from the cubs. Not allowed to sleep out near the cubs in her car. Only allowed to travel back and forth in daylight. Naturally the cubs, being NFD lions, spend the day in thick cover and only appear at night.

Joy has not seen them since I left. She goes out every morning and spends the days looking for them, alone and unarmed. Myles Turner, who is in charge, took away the rifle I left for Joy, and even a revolver! (Park rules, no firearms!). They are too bloody mean to let her have a game scout.

The whole set-up is a bunch of petty bureaucrats. The Director, Owen (son of the notorious anti-settler Archdeacon) will not make decisions without consulting the Trustees. Myles Turner dare not fart without asking Owen!

Reluctantly the trustees bent the rules to allow them one final week, at the end of July, to camp out in the valley. They slept in the car with a lamp burning all night. On their last morning the cubs appeared and took cod-liver oil but not meat. They were clearly not hungry.

Jespah did not limp and looked perfectly healthy. All three young lions were ready to take a chance in their new world where a pride was a pride and no longer half human. If their future was unknown, the happiest end of any wild animal story is a mystery.

A few weeks later Billy Collins arrived in the Serengeti. He brought news of rocketing sales of *Born Free,* and the children's book of photographs, *Elsa.* His advance sales of *Living Free* were 100,000 copies. To add to Joy's elation her publisher in America, Helen Wolff, had moved to Harcourt Brace which offered sixty thousand dollars— today worth ten times that sum—for *Living Free.* What is more, both she and Billy were ready to realize Joy's long cherished dream and publish her book on the tribes.

Billy's visit began with a romantic safari through the spectacular Tanganyikan parks. He and Joy stayed at Lake Manyara with its flocks of flamingos, families of elephants drifting between the lake and the forest and lions dozing along the branches of the trees.

Next they went up into the stupendous green bowl of the Ngorongoro Crater. Within its two-thousand-foot slopes they watched thousands of animals—elephants, buffalo, rhinos, antelope and zebras— peacefully grazing. Then they headed toward the great migration.

The history of Africa has been determined by insects, notably mosquitoes and tsetse flies. While mosquitoes have spread malaria, tsetse flies have disseminated trypanosomiasis, or sleeping sickness, among men and domestic stock, leaving much of the continent free for its multitudes of game that are either immune or survive on account of their numbers.

One kind of tsetse does not necessarily carry sleeping sickness but has a poisonous bite to which some people, Billy included, are allergic. He was so badly bitten that before they reached the migration they had to turn back. It was another turning point too.

Despite their shared delight at the success of her books, their feelings for each other, and the dazzling beauty all around them, Joy overplayed her hand. Billy, like everyone else, began to feel oppressed when too long alone in her company, especially as she repeatedly badgered him to support her against the Tanzanian authorities.

Something else nagged Billy too. Ever since his second visit to Kenya his wife, Pierre, had gone into a decline. "She is a lot in the country now, and when she is in London, mostly in bed. She has no temperature or pain but generally feels awful," Marjorie Villiers told Helen Wolff. Billy's conscience must have pricked.

Feeling ill, irritated and possibly guilty, he failed to respond to Joy's hopes.

September 10   Terrible drive back—Billy killed all. Arrive 7.00 pm. Manyara. Little execution. Just one week ago utter climax—now at bottom of abyss.

The following day there was a conference of international conservationists in the Serengeti at Arusha—among them Julian Huxley and Peter Scott. Billy tried to moderate Joy's emotional demands for their support but Peter Scott felt she was not being truthful about the conditions she had agreed on with the trustees and they refused to intervene.

This was a very difficult time for George. Although he had been happy to hand over his duties to Ken Smith, he still had to come to terms with retirement, Joy's refusal to share her royalties and her intemperate crusade against the authorities.

In December he wrote again to Tony Ofenheim.

I am retired, with 800 days of accumulated leave due! We continue to live at Isiolo where I have rented a house. I would just love to ask you to come and stay with us, but Joy makes that impossible— any friend of mine is an enemy of hers! She will be going to the UK probably late January. Could you stop on your way back from South Africa?

In fact, Joy was too busy to leave Africa. She and George went back to the Ura to repair and protect Elsa's grave. Otherwise they commuted between Isiolo and the Serengeti, where they continued to search for the cubs in the daytime.

Despite her setback with Billy, his colleagues in London helped Joy plan a lecture tour in America, discuss the film rights of *Born Free* with a Disney director, and set up a conservation committee to make grants from her royalties. Marjorie Villiers began editing her third book, *Forever Free.*

For both business and personal reasons Billy decided to come back to the Serengeti. Unfortunately an inoculation in London against tsetse bite gave him a serious thrombosis and added to the tensions at home. His reception in Kenya was no more relaxed, but Joy agreed to launch her new book in Britain with a nationwide lecture tour.

When she and George said good-bye at the airport in September, she parted not only from him but also, forever, with her privacy.

SEVENTEEN

Reaping and Gleaning

1962–1964

1

Joy's arrival in London in September 1962 was her first real chance to reap the reward of her lifelong efforts to excel. Her books had won golden opinions and Collins's publicity director believed that *Forever Free* was the best and most dramatic of the three.

Such was her public appeal that Noel Gay, an agency who specialized in popular music, had agreed to organize her tour and edit her film footage for it. She was faced with a schedule of twenty cities in England and Scotland, and friends were alerted all over the country to nurse her through the ordeal. Marjorie Villiers explained to Lady Reece, then living near Edinburgh, why.

> She has had rather a bad time with an eye poisoned by a thorn, a septic arm, a smashed nose, concussion and other oddments.

One of the oddments was whiplash trouble in her neck, caused by a Land-Rover crash, which was being treated by the Queen's osteopath.

No one could ever have accused Joy of vanity in the bush, but when she had to put on a show in Europe or America her Viennese taste and her own sense of style asserted themselves. Her letters bubbled over about long and short evening dresses, luncheon and cocktail dresses, all from the best Belgian couturier in Nairobi. Only once did Joy's judgment falter: she arrived in London to champion wildlife in a leopardskin coat. The Collins representative in central Africa, David Bateman, confessed its origin.

> One day Joy came to me and said: "I have a secret passion. I have three leopard skins and have always wanted them made into a coat.

I dare not go into a furrier, being who I am. Would you do it for me?"

She handed me the skins and her design in a bag, and a week or so later I collected the coat. It was very beautiful and when she put it on she literally purred and said: "I don't suppose I shall ever be able to wear it, but I have always wanted it and will always treasure it."

Joy was so aware of her Austrian accent that she was easily prevailed upon to take a crash course in elocution. As a result, her audiences were just able to understand her lecture before she showed her forty-minute film of Elsa and the cubs. It was a pattern she was to use all over the world.

Elspeth Huxley said that this lecture tour was Joy's bravest achievement. She was racked by both pain and nerves, and nearly always broke down when she spoke of Elsa's death.

October 4   Leicester. I cried at lecture. Had to stop. Applause!

Quite apart from the story Joy told, people responded to her sincerity, and to her developing faith that she was being guided by Elsa's spirit, a belief that was supported by two remarkable letters she received from unknown admirers. The first was from the distinguished author of a field guide to South African animals, C. T. Astley Maberly, who wrote:

My contact with nature and wild animals has constantly impressed me with the kinship of all Life: differing only in degree of what I think the mystics call "consciousness." Not only man, therefore, but everything has "soul" or "spirit": in differing degree being linked to the Divine. In this respect the more highly developed animals come close to man and no doubt, as with us, some individuals are more advanced than others.

The second was from Una, Lady Troubridge, the intimate friend of the well-known authoress who wrote under the name of Radclyffe Hall.

My husband's cousin adopted two orphaned lion cubs, reared them in Norfolk for two years, and then, one evening, the lioness failed to recognise him and charged him.

While he was dying he kept saying: "Don't blame Mitzie—she did not know me!" and his sister sat with the lioness's head on her knee, picking out with a penknife the shots with which the gamekeeper had driven her off. But they sent the two lions to Dublin Zoo (I would sooner have shot them).

I happen to be a Catholic and St Thomas Aquinas in his *Summa Theologica* admits the right of belief that animals have *souls*—so that we are the more culpable in treating them as though they hadn't.

Joy's evocation of Elsa's spirit during her crusade was therefore not purely idiosyncratic. She might also have cited the German rationalist philosopher Leibnitz, who allowed animals souls. The proposition that they, like humans, possess them added an extra moral dimension to her case against their maltreatment.

If some scientists balk at this line it is worth remembering that it was Einstein who wrote: "I maintain that cosmic religiousness is the strongest and most noble driving force of scientific research." It is also, of course, one of the most powerful forces governing human attitudes to their fellow creatures.

Even Joy's harshest critics speak with respect of her generosity to conservation and wildlife. Apart from making over the greater part of her royalties she formally launched an appeal for the protection of wild animals. She invited contributions wherever she spoke.

Her friends were also aware of Joy's private generosity. For several years at Christmas, Marjorie Villiers and others who had helped with her books received sets of handsome German glass engraved with animals. Her sensitive kindness was especially appreciated by one of the families she stayed with on her way round England who had a handicapped son.

You were so sweet to him; it made him enormously happy. He got great pleasure out of using the oil paints. It was a great inspiration and very generous.

Joy's greatest triumph came at the end of the circuit. On New Year's Eve her talk to 300 women in the chapel of Holloway prison, where she spoke from the pulpit, roused them to cheers and at the end they tossed her coins for her Appeal. And in early January, on a snowy Sunday night, she filled all three thousand seats in London's Festival Hall; Peter Scott was the chairman. Behind the scenes he managed to persuade her to discard her leopard-skin coat, but not to merge her appeal with his own fledgling charity—The World Wildlife Fund.

Her whole tour pushed up the sales of Joy's British editions to nearly a million copies and netted a handsome sum of money for her charitable work.

From the minute she had landed in London Joy had been on tenterhooks about Billy Collins. Very soon it was plain that however far she had come with her painting, her books and photography, she had learned nothing about men. She grew frustrated and then infuriated by his lack of attention. If she had listened for a second to Marjorie Villiers, she would have realized Billy was under the strictest constraints. He had to maintain in the office a façade that betrayed no more than friendship and professional concern for a best-selling author. Every minute of his evenings was scrutinized by Pierre—"the Dr.agon," as Joy quickly dubbed her—with whom he lived in the flat above.

It did not help that in Kenya Billy, an eternal optimist, had promised Joy more time in England than he could give her. They had also planned a week in Sweden together to promote her books. This Billy was able to fulfill, and the Collins sales representative in Scandinavia was startled when he knocked on Joy's hotel door early one morning and it was opened by his chairman. It is probable that only a row had been going on behind it. This is Joy's diary entry.

November 15 Sleepless. Morning final break with Billy. Moral coward. Liar. He says that he did not love me because I did not want it. First business and family. Joy does not exist. He only uses me—so. *Finis. By God it hurts.*

Perhaps what hurt most was this. She had told him in Sweden, as she had told no man before, that he could call the tune—only to find that behind the scenes Pierre was calling it.

In December Joy flew to America for a month to meet her publishers and promote her books. She discussed her plans for the tribal book with Helen Wolff, as she had done with Marjorie Villiers in England. She also exposed to her the anguish in her heart.

I feel like a sick animal who wants to hide itself until it is fit to join the herd.

2

While Joy was reaping Elsa's harvest in England and America, George had been left to glean straw in Africa. He had known setbacks, defeat and despair in the past but had quickly recovered; now his spirit was drained. From part of a long letter he wrote to Tony Ofenheim it is easy to see why.

> When I got your letter the relationship between Joy and myself was at its lowest ebb and that is saying a lot. I think Joy had been reading some of your letters behind my back and I was subjected to the most poisonous and constant nagging, day after day. This was in the Serengeti while searching for Elsa's cubs.
>
> There were times when I was very close to murder. I do not suppose you have experienced anything like it and it is difficult to describe. But imagine my self control as a fairly solid body suspended by a number of fine strands which under normal circumstances can stand a lot of stress, but constant buffeting wears them thin until one by one they start to break. At the end I think there was one strand left.

Joy not only read George's letters but sometimes impounded them before they reached him. If she hoped to find "love letters" from Tony she was disappointed. To George they were just as valuable — serious but humorous expressions of her deep and evergreen friendship. He told Tony how, soon after Joy left, he had come across Little Elsa, but not her brothers.

> I saw her six times more and then she vanished. Always she would come to meet me when she heard the car and I would give her water, a dish with some cod liver oil and, let me whisper, the carcase of a Thomsons gazelle which I had shot illegally with a .22 (for the love of heaven don't tell anyone this).

George's habit of shooting gazelles to tempt lions into the open was not the wisest practice. Once he was caught red-handed by one of the Serengeti wardens, Myles Turner, who had taken to spying on him from the air.

He did not intend, though, to spend all his time in the Serengeti.

For the next few months I am going to live a life of peace, I hope, at my house at Isiolo. I have the vague idea of writing a book. There is plenty of material collected over the years, if only I can put it all together in a readable form.

His hopes of finding a little peace at Isiolo were short-lived, for the political scene was erupting again. The British government had recently appointed a Governor, Malcolm MacDonald, to hand over power to Jomo Kenyatta, now Prime Minister, who had packed his government with his own tribe, the Kikuyu. As George explained to Tony, this spelled trouble in the north.

> The political situation is what can be described as explosive. The Somalis want to secede to Somalia, half the Boran want to, the other half don't, the Rendille want to, the Gabbra not, the El Molo (all one hundred of them) want to be completely independent from everybody. Perhaps I could get a job as financial adviser to the El Molo. But I don't think I could take it, their women put me off.

George confided to Tony, as he did to no one else, his bitterness that Joy had monopolized the entire book royalties.

> I, who made it possible for her to do all this, have not had a ha'penny out of it. In fact, a lot of my own resources have been swallowed up in Elsa. In a few months when I go on pension I will have to find some sort of job to keep me going. A tourist guide probably.

Considering the terms on which he and Joy parted in September, a letter George wrote to her in January 1963 is extraordinarily magnanimous.

> I am very sorry to hear about your difficult relations with Billy. You have to remember that no one is perfect and all have a weak side to their characters which shows itself in different ways. Always look for the good side, which in most cases outweighs the bad, and makes a normal human being.

When Joy returned to Isiolo in March it must have been difficult for him to restrain his resentment any longer. His annual income was little more than £1,500 a year: Joy had been earning £1,500 a month on her tour. On top of this, three film companies were angling for the rights to *Born Free*, and Columbia was behind one that would bring her $45,000—worth ten times that today—and 7½ percent of the profits.

Joy had already begun to hand out money from her company, Elsa Ltd., and the Elsa Trust, both of which were Kenyan. She was also registering the Elsa Wild Animal Appeal as a charitable trust in England.

Scrupulously advised by her committee in Nairobi, Joy immediately approved a large grant to help establish the Samburu Reserve on the Ewaso Ngiro River, which has proved one of Kenya's most attractive and popular parks ever since. She had also agreed to fund a trapping control officer and an animal rescue team.

Joy's other preoccupation at this time was her tribal book that was taking shape as *The Peoples of Kenya*. Working like a fury she somehow managed to complete 140 pages within a few months. She planned to end the book with a circumcision ceremony she had painted with the help of a Boran named Dabasso, who had studied anthropology in England at Cambridge. He had since been promoted to DC in Isiolo.

At the end of June, following violent attacks on two European DCs and the murder of nine officials by Somalis demanding secession, Dabasso was ambushed and shot in his Land-Rover.

The extraordinary beauty and resilient vitality of Africa seem to be matched by an equal prevalence of danger and violence. Serious accident and sudden death are met with a degree of acceptance rare in the West.

On an early visit to Kenya I witnessed a total eclipse of the sun at midday from a small spit of sand with half a dozen other people. It was an enthralling and eerie experience. I learned only afterward that I had watched the sun disappear with a friend who had cut short the life of his dying mother, a couple whose son had been murdered two miles down the coast, a girl whose mother had been recently electrocuted and a boy whose father had been blown up in a small plane by Idi Amin in Uganda.

George and Joy, like all the other Europeans who made their lives in East Africa, were perfectly happy to chance these odds for the exhilaration they derived from this extraordinary world.

3

From the day *Born Free* was published Joy began to keep copies of her letters and to file anything significant she received.

In August she set off around the world to lecture again—in South Africa, Australia, New Zealand and America. The format of her talks was always the same and wherever she went she appealed for donations to Elsa at the end of the performance.

Many people who have achieved worldly success in their chosen objective among the five principal human goals—honor, fame, money, power, and love—nevertheless find themselves still unfulfilled. However, some of them discover that if they can identify with a new and altruistic aim they can finally experience satisfaction.

Joy's heart was in the African bush, where her fame was of no account, while she took no pleasure in money for herself. She had failed to find love and had never sought power. Chronically dissatisfied, she instinctively sought relief in a disinterested cause.

The grit in this ointment was her ego: her identification with her Appeal was not truly selfless. She expected others to give their money or time, George to forgo a share of the Elsa royalties, and normal rules of behavior to be broken because her end justified such means.

Her lectures in South Africa were not well attended since her film had been shown to saturation promoting her books, but she still raised over £2,000 in a month. The most touching tribute of the tour was paid to her by one of her former husbands.

In the aftermath of the Mau Mau uprising and with the approach of Kenyan independence, many white families had emigrated or returned home. Peter Bally had gone back to Switzerland with his wife and children, while Ziebel von Klarwill—who now called himself Rufus Klarwill—and his wife had joined the flow from Kenya down to South Africa. It had meant abandoning his Mount Kenya safaris which had flourished after the Mau Mau emergency, for he had been able to ferry mountaineers up on to the moorlands along the tracks through the forest cut by the army. He built a hut in Teleki Valley at about 14,000 feet.

Joy never saw von Klarwill in South Africa, but he saw her. He stood in a line in Cape Town for her to sign his copy of *Born Free* but she never looked up, and he never declared himself. Afterward he sent her an enchanting photograph he had taken of her on skis in 1935. He wrote on the back: "It is a long time ago—but *that* is what you still are in my mind."

Joy's month in Australia raised another £1,500, but the breakneck schedule and punishing distances destroyed even her stamina. She collapsed on the plane to New Zealand and was carried off on a stretcher.

Her month in New Zealand ran into two, to allow her to recover before she went on to the United States. The saga of those weeks began in style, when she was received by the Governor-General, Sir Bernard Fergusson, and then swept off to see a kiwi, the national bird of New Zealand, in South Island with an escort of four police on motorbikes—an honor previously afforded only to the Queen.

The Lord Mayor of Auckland, an enthusiastic conservationist, invited Joy to tea and offered to introduce her to a number of millionaires, although he carefully warned her that he did not know if they shared her ideals.

"In that case tell them I will be quite happy to sleep with them if they give Elsa enough," she said as a joke. Auckland is Presbyterian and she received not a penny.

After a month Joy's whole body seized up again. She suspected her neck was the cause, but a wise old woman to whom she went for manipulation refused to treat her, telling her, "Your whole system is poisoned. You must have all your teeth out."

When a dentist confirmed the diagnosis Joy agreed to the drastic solution on condition the operation was done on a Saturday morning and that a full set of new teeth was ready for her evening lecture. The country's top dentist whipped out the old teeth, and presented the new set to Joy as soon as she came around. That night she took the stage. By her last day her Appeal was £1,500 the richer.

Joy spent Christmas alone in Fiji and went on to Honolulu for two days, where her bag was stolen with her passport, air tickets, money, lecture notes and 1963 diary—"So I flew to America almost naked."

After her celebrity treatment in New Zealand and Honolulu, where her loss was broadcast on radio and television within a few minutes, she was brought back to earth in New York. There was no one to meet her.

Her lecture agents, Colston Leigh, were the biggest in the business and drove her hard. Each week, for more than three months, the pattern of her days was constantly changing but always the same: a Monday breakfast flight to one more new place; a reception committee and coffee; TV and radio interviews in a hotel or a broadcasting station; perhaps a morning lecture; a knife-and-fork lunch with politeness, questions and a talk at the end; more interviews, tea in some immaculate home, and too little time to change before cocktails; an evening lecture; possibly supper on another plane, another reception committee, another hotel—and bed.

A psychiatrist who went to one of Joy's lectures at the end of her tour noticed she sometimes stood rigid from stress or pain for minutes on end. Nevertheless she was overwhelmed by kindness and although Colston Leigh forbade their speakers to solicit money Joy took no notice and calculated that she had earned for her Appeal at least £2,000 a month—the equivalent of about $40,000 today—by the end of her tour.

At her lectures she was most touched by gestures, however small, from members of her audience who owned a cat, a dog or a canary—with whom they could probably communicate more easily than with other people—and who understood perfectly what Joy was trying to tell the world about Elsa. During her few private evenings and on weekends she was taken under the wing of the famous, the rich and the generous, some of whom became friends for life, visiting her and George in Kenya on frequent safaris.

Twice Joy met young Kenyans. One was a Luo, who asked at the end of her talk how game conservation could be reconciled with the agricultural needs of a soaring population. She explained that because of their specialized feeding habits game animals could yield more protein per acre in an arid environment than domestic stock, without degrading the land as cattle and goats would. Since they also attract tourist revenue they offer a better economic investment in many places than agriculture.

In Michigan she met the other, a postgraduate student, Perez Olindo, with whom she appeared on television one evening. It was the prelude to a productive partnership when he returned to Kenya.

The most exhilarating moments of her exhausting journey around the world were with the dolphins in Natal and Miami. She put on a brave face when a chimpanzee bit her hand at a tea party in New Zealand, and a wolf bit her leg in California. For all her courage, imagination and sympathy with animals, she seemed to lack the natural affinity with them that George instinctively possessed.

Some zoos raised her spirits, particularly when she was feeling frantic from overexposure to strangers, or from the aftereffects of air-conditioning and cigarette smoke. Many more broke her heart, as when she saw the caged lion in Central Park in New York. She began to note those that fell short of tolerable standards and to work out a code for the practice of zoos in an ideal world. Above all, she believed, they should not acquire animals born in the wild.

One of the most acute observers of human and animal behavior, Desmond Morris, author of *The Naked Ape*, published evidence that *Born Free* had changed a generation's attitude to the lion. After he discussed the book in a children's broadcast, the BBC repeated a poll of its listeners who had previously voted it high among the most-hated animals. Three thousand cards then placed it among the most loved. Desmond Morris goes on:

> Elsa had also done something else. She had made people start to query the morality of keeping animals in captivity—in zoos, and even more so in circuses.

Morris was in a position to know: at the time he was curator of mammals at the London Zoo.

Before she left America Joy had meetings with two people who became very important to her. One was Carl Foreman. She had decided to accept the film offer backed by Columbia and he, with successes like *High Noon* and *The Guns of Navarone* to his credit, was to be the executive producer. He promised the picture would be true to the book, the contract was signed and they toasted each other in champagne.

The other was Helen Wolff, her American editor, who became her close friend and mentor at a critical moment, for Joy's relations with Billy were entering an ice age.

An émigrée from the Nazis, with an Austrian mother, a sympathetic heart and a mind addicted to excellence, Helen summed up Joy quickly: she had never before met anyone with "such concentrated will power and intensity. During even a short meeting she used up all the oxygen in the room."

With patience and chocolates Helen managed to neutralize Joy's urge to establish domination. Then she sent her off for a month to the MacDowell Colony for writers, artists and composers in New Hampshire, to have her neck treated again, to commune with the chipmunks and porcupines and to work on the text of *The Peoples of Kenya*.

Helen had hoped Joy's retreat would act as a sedative, but she flew to England intent on a confrontation with Billy Collins. Even when

Helen joined her there and together with Marjorie Villiers tried to effect a reconciliation with Billy, Joy refused to be appeased. She left for Kenya two weeks later, still tormented by her mixture of feelings for Collins—"the love of my life."

4

Although George never received a share of the Elsa royalties, Joy did steer one or two benefits his way.

For instance he had helped the vet, Toni Harthoorn, experiment with his new technique of tranquilizing animals before translocation with darts fired from specially adapted guns. They had moved Thomas kob from farmland, Rothschild's giraffes from an army range and oryx and the rare Hunter's antelope from danger to safety. Early on a number of animals died before the right dosages were established, but the method was more humane than the old one of stampeding a rhino or giraffe and dropping a lasso over its neck from a long pole.

Because of this unique experience Joy and Ian Grimwood, the Chief Game Warden, asked George to head an animal rescue and translocation team, and he accepted.

Joy had also made it a condition of the *Born Free* film contract that George should be offered the job of technical adviser on the handling of lions, which he agreed in principle to accept.

However when Joy had left for South Africa, at the beginning of her second triumphal tour, he felt he had to make one more attempt to find Jespah and wrote to her reproachfully.

> You well know that the best chance of finding the cubs is now. In two or three months the grass will be long and the rains starting, when the task would be hopeless. I do not grumble about paying for the last safari. It has cost me over £200 and now I am left with £30 in the bank and still a number of heavy bills left to settle. So with the best will in the world I cannot do any more on my own resources.
>
> If you want Jespah found you have got to do something about it now.

Joy wrote back no less tartly from Cape Town.

I will pay the same rates as the Game Department. You will then have three months left to look for a job.

But go NOW if your intention is true and you really want to help Jespah more than yourself.

George had certainly meant what he said: others could manage the rescue team, only he could hope to locate Jespah. From then on in his life there was nothing he would not do for a lion in trouble.

During the last three months of 1963 he labored to find Elsa's offspring in appalling weather conditions and under the suspicious eyes of the wardens. There were times when the Irish maverick in him surged up and he raged against "petty bureaucracy," his ultimate term of abuse.

As a result he sometimes could not resist taking liberties, with unhappy consequences, as he had once told Ken Smith.

Came on a lion in the most shocking and pitiful state. His lower jaw was broken and hanging down on his chest. I do not think he had eaten for a month. It was too late in the day and too far away to call one of the wardens so I took it upon myself to put a bullet into his brain. Poor old lion, I truly believe he knew what was coming and welcomed it. He sat in front of me and looked me full in the eyes as I pulled the trigger.

Now the bureaucrats have taken my rifle away—the next lion I find in a similar state, I shall have to get out and cut its throat!

It was all very well taking Joy's, and then George's, guns away, but even in the approved camping sites lions twice came into their tents at night and a leopard drank from their washbowl.

Myles Turner had to wake them in the middle of another night to borrow morphine. A farmer camping three hundred yards away had been taken from his sleeping bag by a lion, which dropped him only when his courageous African staff chased it with pangas. The man died before he reached hospital.

George never found Jespah, and before the end of the year suffered further disappointment. He felt obliged to withdraw his agreement to work on the film because he realized it would conflict with his rescue team work. No sooner had he done so than he was told his Serengeti searches were taking up so much time that another man had taken over the rescue operation.

Penniless as he was George had no real regrets when his final break with the Game Department in December 1963. He had, for some time, seen the writing on the wall.

> At one time we game wardens used to be treated more or less as gentlemen. Now the Ministry appears to look upon us as a bunch of crooks, out to do Government out of every half crown and sixpence we can lay our hands on. It all means more paperwork and less time to do one's proper job out in the field!

George was even more apprehensive about what would happen to the country when the Duke of Edinburgh officially handed it over to Jomo Kenyatta in December.

> Our Prime Minister has released all the Mau Mau prisoners and invited the Field Marshals, Generals and other leading lights of Mau Mau to attend the Uhuru celebrations, dressed in special uniforms. At least I am glad not to be present when the old flag is hauled down for the last time. Lord Delamere's statue has been removed from near the Stanley and there is the suggestion that it be replaced by one of Dedan Kimathi!
>
> The Firearms Bureau has ordered me to hand all my guns into the police, which means that when I get back to Isiolo I will not have even a pistol for self-protection, let alone to shoot the odd bird for the pot.

It was uncomfortable to be left without a gun in Isiolo or anywhere near the Somali border. In March the ex-DC at Lamu heard a Shifta raid was in progress and at the age of seventy-seven went to investigate—and was killed. A few weeks later the DO at Mandera was shot. One of the Somali chiefs painted by Joy was a ringleader, as was Ken Smith's assistant in the Game Department.

Just before Joy excommunicated the entire Collins organization I received a letter from her with this spirited suggestion for dealing with the Shifta.

> MAY 2, 1964
>
> Grimwood needs urgent money for training Game Department Officers to fly as all the wardens in the NFD have had to be withdrawn because of Shifta trouble. I have suggested we buy a

plane with Elsa money, hire pilots until the Game staff can be trained, and chase the Shiftas from the NFD at once. They can only operate during the rains, when water is available, and we can hit them from the air. Government cannot do this without getting into trouble internationally—but the Game Department can, under the excuse of protecting the game from poachers. Shoot around the Shiftas of course, but frighten them away. We may be able to hold the NFD in this way before the Somalis can take it over completely.

Some of Joy's royalties certainly went to train several of Kenya's ablest game wardens to fly and their skills were used with outstanding success for the next ten years—but not to fight shifta!

George, however, was left without a penny saved, on a pension of £990 per year. Having no new job yet, he continued with his hunt for Jespah on a shoestring, remonstrating with Joy for her indifference.

Since you left on your lecture tour I have not had a single word of encouragement from you in the search. As far as you are concerned "George is having a wonderful time at Elsa's expense." I have no bad conscience at using Elsa's money for the purpose which should come first before all others.

Perhaps you have forgotten that when Elsa died we both vowed to look after her children to the uttermost of our ability? At the time you told me not to worry as you would see that I did not lose by it. Well, I have been the loser ever since.

Now broke, he took the only course open to him while he looked for work. He and Terence, who was helping Ken Smith with game management in the Isiolo area, decided to sell the family farm at Limuru. There was so much uncertainty about the future of property under Kenya's first African government that they were selling at the bottom of the market—and the market was still falling.

Then, at long last, George saw a straw that was worth clutching at. The film contract for *Born Free* had been signed and he was asked once again if he would work on the movie.

EIGHTEEN

A Moving Picture

1964–1965

1

All successful films about real people are confidence tricks. Actors have perfected the art of delusion and moviemakers the craft of suggestion. But how do you make a film about real lions? One man thought he knew—the director, Tom McGowan, who had made a number of pictures for Walt Disney. "Lions are no problem," he assured everyone. "If properly treated and trained they are just like large dogs."

He was so plausible that he had prevailed on two producers, Paul Radin and Sam Jaffé, to join him. Together they had persuaded Carl Foreman to lend his formidable talents, energy and vision to the project as executive producer. The four men had then convinced Columbia that a movie based on such a runaway bestseller was a gilt-edged investment.

The truth is that lions were not just like dogs, nor could they be trained to perform, with actors in front of cameras, the whole range of activities required by the script.

In April 1964, George was one of the first people to set eyes on the make-believe world where his and Joy's life with Elsa would be re-enacted—a 750-acre farm at Naro Moru. Under the towering peaks of Mount Kenya an army of carpenters were starting to transform the farmhouse into sets, to build a village that would house a community of 160 people, and to put up compounds or holding pens to accommodate the cast of animals from two hyraxes and two cheetahs to an elephant—and of course the lions.

One by one the producers, the director, the lions and their trainers turned up under George's skeptical gaze. He was shocked when he saw the first two lionesses arrive—large, surly and ungainly creatures from a circus. Their trainer, an attractive girl who had once been mauled, would not go into their enclosure without a pointed stick in each hand, wide leather straps on her wrists and—usually—a guard standing by with a loaded rifle.

Because the film was to be shot in less than a year, would show Elsa as a cub and finally as a mother with cubs of her own and because it also featured her mate and a couple of man-eaters, more than twenty other lions would be needed. Wisely the company used George in helping assemble the rest of this cast.

At the beginning of June the stars, Bill Travers and his wife, Virginia McKenna, arrived at Naro Moru with their three children. George wrote to Joy:

> I am very much impressed with them both and do not think there could have been a better choice to act the parts. They are absolutely without affectation and genuinely anxious to do justice to the spirit of Elsa. Neither of them will stand for anything bogus.

The Traverses moved into a house a mile along a track from the main farm; George was camped with the lions halfway between them. Rather like the prophet Daniel, he was perfectly at home in a lion's den and preferred it to life among the power struggles, intrigues, drinking and lechery at the court of Nebuchadnezzar.

There were frequent dramas at night. An emotional girl stood naked on the roof of her hut in protest against her lover's behavior; and the owner of one of the lions, convinced his wife was committing adultery, followed her to a tryst and slipped into the lion's compound to conceal himself—only to find that a strange lion had been installed there. Later he caught pneumonia carrying out his surveillance from the depths of a pond.

The producers, if not the director, saw the writing was on the wall for their entire production when they tried to film a circus lioness chasing a warthog. She was ignominiously put to flight by the outraged pig. It was then that George, Bill and Virginia came to their rescue.

George carefully assessed the characters of the additional lions that were brought in from all over Africa during the next two months. Ugas, a superb young male, and Mara, an attractive but difficult lioness, both came from the Nairobi orphanage, now a going concern; Boy and Girl, two six month-old mascots, were loaned from the Scots Guards stationed in Kenya. Mothers and cubs were acquired from

Marchesa Bisleti at Naivasha, and from the Emperor Haile Selassie in Ethiopia.

Bill and Virginia had made it a condition of their contract that there would be no doubles to play their scenes with the lions. They were determined to re-create the Adamsons' relationship with Elsa. In fact their task was far more difficult and dangerous—for they were working with not one lion but many, and were having to do it against the clock. The director and camera crew always worked from inside wire cages. Any false move could result in accident or death to the actors outside.

The making of *Born Free* therefore became an extremely sophisticated experiment in animal behavior, something that escaped those who later dismissed the film as giving a misleading impression of lions. The truth was it revealed an aspect of lions they knew little about.

Each evening the Traverses and George worked out how to induce the lions to cooperate in the next day's shoot. They examined minutely their general behavior, male and female, old and young; the quirks of their varying characters; and how their moods changed at different times of day, in sunshine and rain, and in fluctuating temperatures.

One of the most basic problems was how to persuade a lion to move from place to place in front of the cameras at the right moment. George discovered he could induce this by lying down; it could not resist walking, or rushing, over to investigate. By sitting in a concealed pit and twiddling a shaving brush on a stick, or by dangling a hen in a coop from a branch, George could persuade a reluctant lion to sit out in the sun or to climb up a tree. He also realized it was vital to anticipate the lions' reactions to different people—men or women, black or white—and to each other.

George had learned more about lions from Elsa than he had discovered in the whole of his previous career. Now he picked up more in one year's filming than in his five with Elsa. Girl seemed too ill to play on the sand at Malindi until George realized she was pining for her brother: as soon as Boy arrived she polished off glorious beach scenes in a moment. Mara, a born actress, then had to plunge into the sea because Girl hated the water. By careful study of their territorial instincts and by inducing two lionesses to regard the same patch of ground as their own, he was able to stimulate animosity between the two chosen to re-create Elsa's fight with her rival.

273

George and the Traverses each had their favorite lions. His were Ugas and Mara. But one of his assistants nearly disappeared into Ugas's enormous jaws—he was no respecter of women; while Mara, overtired at the end of a long day's work, flung herself petulantly at Bill and dislocated his shoulder.

As an old soldier, Bill, who had served with the Gurkhas behind the Japanese lines in Burma, made immediate friends with Sergeant Ryves, whose deep love for his mascots Boy and Girl had developed their faith in humans. It was a wrench for the sergeant to leave them but he knew they were in good hands. Every morning the Traverses would walk alone with the two young lions on the plain between the camp and the mountain. The devotion between them became so great that when Girl caught a gazelle she carried it to Virginia and laid it at her feet.

Virginia McKenna brought to Joy's part the delicate beauty and skill as an actress for which she was already widely admired. Until she played in *Born Free* no one could have known how much courage she possessed. Handsome and equally brave, Bill was perfectly cast in George's resolute and quizzical character, although he was a good head taller.

The performances the Traverses gave were so precisely those that were called for that they established for twenty-five years the public's image of the Adamsons. In Joy's case the image was far from reality.

Both actors responded to the lions with great intelligence and, more important, with their hearts; perhaps only a married couple totally confident of each other would have been prepared to take such astonishing chances. As a result they elicited the widest possible range of behavior from the lions.

Everything else conspired to confound the producers. The rains were the worst for thirty years; the cloud around Mount Kenya constantly interrupted the shoots; morale sank to rock bottom; and there was a revolt against the director's insistence on using the circus lions. To add to the frustration, Boy bounced on Virginia one morning, snapping her leg in two places, and Joy flew in to Nairobi, determined to pounce on Carl Foreman, who had also arrived on location.

Joy's legitimate quarrel with Foreman was that he intended to distort the end of the film so that in the final scene "Joy" scooped up "Elsa's" cubs in a maternal embrace. A past master of blarney, Foreman found flannel got him nowhere with Joy, but he was a subtle negotiator and decisive producer. He undertook to shoot two endings of the film and to choose between them in the cutting room; he sidelined the circus lions; and he appointed a new director from England, James Hill, who immediately established his authority. The prospects improved.

While George was happy among the lions, enjoyed the company of the girls in the unit, was respected by the crew and kept busy all day, Joy felt insecure and unwanted. When shifta activity obliged her to leave Isiolo, she moved into George's camp but was allowed on the set only as a courtesy. She soon grew jealous of Sieuwke Bisleti's official role in helping look after the lions, became furious when reproved for interfering with them herself and was unluckily clawed on the arm by Mara while watching a scene in the sea at Malindi.

It came as a much needed fillip when, with the other key members of the production, she was invited to tea with President Kenyatta at State House. There, on the walls, were more than seventy of her portraits representing all the different tribes in the country. Malinowski's old pupil was proud, not ashamed, of his people's traditions.

Joy's life was brightened further when a Major and Mrs. Dunkey asked her to take over their seven-month-old cheetah, which they had found as a cub near Wajir and brought up in the family, because they had been recalled to England. Although the cheetah, whom Joy re-christened Pippa, had grown used to sleeping in the house, traveling in the car and even going out to restaurants, they agreed Joy should release her like Elsa.

Despite Pippa's company Joy spent many introspective evenings alone in her tent while George was with the Traverses or in the mess. She knew that Elsa had drawn them together as only a child might have done, but the gap was widening again. She dreaded his silences as much as he did her verbal assaults. "I am so frightened to live with George—where, how, can I live alone with Pippa?" she wrote in her diary in February 1965. They still had a few more months at Naro Moru before she would have to decide.

However smoothly, if slowly, the filming progressed, there were still crises. Animal drugs were an inexact science: the hyrax playing Pati, dosed for her death scene, actually died in Virginia's arms, and Girl, drugged to feign sleep beside "George's" camp bed, failed to recognize Bill and clamped her teeth on his arm.

On another morning, Girl suddenly took Virginia by the arm and inexorably forced her to the ground. Slowly, quietly, firmly, George distracted the lioness while Bill intervened to extricate Virginia. The first rule was never to move quickly in the presence of the lions.

One of the most striking and beautiful scenes in the film was Elsa's courtship, played impeccably by Ugas and Mara. The most exciting, and one of the last to be shot, was the battle between Elsa and her rival. The two lionesses had each been led to feel that the setting of the duel was the heart of her own exclusive territory. Fire hoses were brought in to separate them if the fighting grew too vicious. It didn't, and a convincing scene was secured, simply by playing on their natural instincts.

When the filming was finished Joy took Virginia on a moving visit to Elsa's grave and wrote this letter to her and Bill when they left.

APRIL 5, 1965

After you left I found it difficult to move, feeling such pain and emptiness inside me. What can I say to describe how I feel? You will know it without my going into superlative thanks.

But you will not know a strange coincidence. When I wrote the words on Elsa's photograph I had an impulse to add "God Bless You"—I hesitated, and then did not write it. But after you had left I read my little guide, *Daily Light*, which has a few quotations from the Bible for each day. There I read "I will not let thee go, except thou bless me."

So Elsa is there all the time and watches and acts.

Love, lots and more for everything you have done, love also to your cubs please—and their nanny,

Joy.

Joy was amazed and delighted that a couple like the Traverses, who had never been in Africa, let alone played with lions, could establish a rapport with them similar to hers with Elsa. She told me in a letter, "This film could revolutionize the whole approach of man to animals."

Revolution or not, there is no doubt the film did help to alter our view of the natural world. It also had a profound effect on Bill Travers and Virginia McKenna: his career soon took on a new direction, and later they both began to devote their energies to the protection of animals. Perhaps the life most radically affected was George's.

2

From the day that the first lions arrived at Naro Moru, George began to care about them because they were lions. Lions had always been part of his life as a warden, but Elsa's special place in it had grown out of her adoption and total dependence on him and Joy. His long search for her cubs in the Serengeti, and his close scrutiny of more than five hundred other lions there, seem to have changed something inside him.

By Christmas, his fondness for individual lions—especially Ugas and Mara—had really taken root. He began to think about what would become of them when the filming was over. He therefore wrote to Stephen Ellis, once the DC at Isiolo and now warden of the Nairobi Park, who had brought up Ugas in his house, to ask if he would give his blessing to the lion's release. He also told Tony Ofenheim about his hopes for Mara.

> When she first came she was a bit of a problem child, however I took it upon myself to cultivate her friendship. Now, most nights she sleeps inside my tent. I have proved in the case of Mara, and two other fifteen-month-old lionesses who have also shared my tent, that given personal care and the right treatment they will respond with affection and trust as Elsa did. In fact I would go so far as to say that any lion, given the right treatment from the start, can become a friend.
>
> I am hoping it will be possible to release some of the lions after a period of training. It would be horrible to see them go back to a life in captivity in zoos and orphanages.

George's hopes, which were shared by Joy, rose a month later when Ted Goss, the new warden at Meru, offered them and any lions they could muster a warm welcome there, for with the help of a large donation from Joy's trust it was now a National Reserve. Apart from Goss and Bill and Virginia, the Adamsons appeared to have very few allies.

The film company, whose costs had soared over budget, needed to get back every penny by selling whatever they could—tents, under-clothes, lorries and lions. They had therefore committed all their animals to zoos or to the Marquess of Bath for his new park at Longleat. George's gloom at this setback was at last relieved by a letter from Sergeant Ronald Ryves in England.

2nd Battalion Scots Guards

MARCH 21, 1965

At this moment of writing I am sitting deep down in the centre of the Bank of England, doing my duty watching the lolly, and as I have a few moments off I am taking the time to write to you.

Sgt Major Graham sent for me the other morning and showed me the letter you sent him asking for Boy and Girl. I put it to him that it was unfair to bring them back to a climate that even I hated. There wasn't a zoo in this country fit to give any animal the type of surroundings that I would be happy to see them in, let alone Boy and Girl (and believe me, I have visited quite a few zoos since I have been back).

So please, George, let me know straight away should anything go wrong at your end. I do have the last word in this case. I love Boy and Girl so much and have missed them more than I can say. It's so hard for me to part with them, but after knowing you and Joy I know what is best for them.

Bill Travers and Virginia McKenna fought as hard as the Adamsons—with whom they had become very close friends—for the other lions. Consequently the producers grew increasingly bitter, protesting that the agitation would damage their movie. The pressure, on TV and the radio, and in the press, spurred Carl Foreman to fire off an outraged letter to Joy, while George put to Carl his own point of view.

I find it difficult to believe that you really consider our lions would be better off in zoos than in the wild. It is like telling a young man on the threshold of life that for the sake of his personal safety and comfort he must remain at school for the rest of it, rather than go out into the world and take his chance.

Foreman responded with a long and characteristic letter.

As you well know, there is considerable difference of opinion on the part of experts in the field on the whole question of the feasibility of training lions for release in the bush. Many respected people, known to you personally, are entirely convinced that release is highly dangerous to both lions and human beings who might encounter such lions in the reserves.

This was perfectly fair comment and the basis of the criticism George was to face for the rest of his life. However, toward the end of the letter Foreman postures on a moral platform, only to sink into something like blackmail.

And George, let me take the liberty of reminding you that truth has many faces. No single person has a monopoly of it, or a monopoly of all the virtues.

For example, as you know, I am holding Joy's leopard-skin coat for her in my apartment in London, and I have had to hide it away, for otherwise I should be in the awkward position of having to tell people that it belongs to Joy Adamson. There are many people who would not be able to understand how Joy could countenance the shooting of leopards for a coat, in view of everything she stands for.

Foreman would have been dumbfounded if he had known exactly what Joy believed she—and he—stood for. As the textbook says, the subjects of histrionic personality disorder dramatize themselves as larger than life characters. Joy wrote this in a letter.

I know that all those who have raised the development of the human mind to a higher level—Akhenaton, Christ, and so many leaders in philosophy, art and religion—were inspired by ideals. They often died hardly recognised, while their materialistic opponents not only caused disaster but setbacks for the evolution of the human race. Still, it is damn hard to see our Elsa being torn to pieces by these money-grabbing people.

The Columbia door was closed. The first two little cubs George had wanted to save were to be shipped off to Lord Bath with their mother. The fate of Ugas and Mara lay in the hands of their owners and the Director of National Parks, Mervyn Cowie. Aware of Cowie's adamant disapproval of everything he and Joy stood for in their attitude to lions, George asked the Secretary of the East African Wildlife Society, an American named Frank Minot, to act as an intermediary. His reply was pessimistic.

The greatest problem seems to be to get people to come together and reason. The bitter and childish personal hates and feuds between persons has a very serious result on getting anything constructive with conservation done.

George therefore tried two last personal appeals to the owners of Mara and Ugas. He lost Mara, for her owner had reluctantly come to the conclusion that the safety of Whipsnade Zoo, near London, was preferable to the hazards of the bush.

The letter he wrote to Stephen Ellis, which included this passage, was more successful.

> Ugas in particular was my favourite. He was the most sensitive, intelligent and good natured of all our lions, and when I got to know him well he was never rough with me and I could walk out on the plains with him without fear of being knocked for six.

A few months later he was asked to collect Ugas from the orphanage as he was getting too frustrated and rough for his keepers. Both he and Mara, in the enclosure next to him, leapt in delight to greet him. It wrung George's heart to leave the lioness to her life of imprisonment at Whipsnade when she might have joined the others as a member of the first man-made pride he was setting up in Meru.

There is no doubt that both ignorance and narrowness of mind prejudiced the game world about the nature of lions. This limitation was crystallized in the attitude of many zoos.

Harold Tong, the Director of Whipsnade, a rural satellite of Regent's Park Zoo, the grim penitentiary in London, was interviewed on the radio about the wisdom of his accepting film lions from Africa. He claimed that he could offer them a much better future than freedom in a national reserve, where successful release was impossible; that bonded lions in a pride were not unhappy to be separated; that lions in captivity were safe from violent squabbles; that hand-reared lions had little immunity from disease; and that Elsa had died as a result of her upbringing. On all these counts he was demonstrably wrong.

His most revealing boast was this: "Lions do extraordinarily well in small places, probably best of all in circus wagons." It is little wonder, with this tradition behind them, that zoos and circuses are still prepared to perpetuate the callous confinement of so many animals which are quite clearly suffering, or have have been driven literally to madness by it.

I feel that Ronald Ryves understood animals, and the way we should relate to them, better than Tong. This is what he wrote when he heard that George had safely moved Boy and Girl into Meru.

I cannot find the words to tell you just how grateful I am to you in being so helpful to Boy and Girl. You understand the love that one must give to animals to receive their love and trust in return. If only it were possible to show just half the world, I am sure we humans would be able to live much more in peace together. This film may help.

3

George left Naro Moru with Boy and Girl in the back of his Land-Rover at the end of April. Ted Goss met him at the gates of the Meru Reserve and took him to a campsite they had chosen together. Joy had agreed to cover the expenses of the release, and for the time being at any rate George would be fully occupied and not need to take a job as a safari guide or white hunter, or go back to India, as he had seriously considered.

A week later Joy arrived with Pippa and settled into a camp near the reserve headquarters at Leopard Rock. The lions and the cheetah could not be too close, and since the shifta were still very active in the NFD the site was picked for security.

While the film was being edited in London the battle to save the last few lions from captivity was still raging. Nevertheless Carl Foreman, who was now deep into his next film, *The Young Churchill,* saw the error of his ways about the ending of *Born Free* and in the final scene Elsa's cubs were spared a human embrace. The producers also made another valuable decision: they commissioned a score from a young composer named John Barry, who produced theme music for Elsa, as he had for James Bond and *Doctor Zhivago,* which remains memorable after twenty-five years.

The first hint that the film might follow the book into history came when it was chosen for the Royal Command Performance, an annual charity première in the presence of the Queen, on March 14, 1966.

Joy left George in charge of his lions and her cheetah and flew to London for the premiere without a stitch of suitable clothing or a single brooch—her tent at Naro Moru had been robbed. The safari through London to find a couturier and a jeweler who could satisfy her demands was almost as fraught as her hunt for Elsa's cubs.

At last, feeling guilty at the expense, she crept into one of the Queen's own dressmakers, Norman Hartnell, who in only four days produced a creation in gold fit for the occasion. The goldsmith John Donald made for her, on the actual day of the premiere, striking earrings, a ring, and a magnificent pendant, all of gold, set with pearls and tawny citrines. She literally glittered when she was presented to the Queen.

That evening crowned every one of Joy's youthful ambitions, except that she had no man at her side. Billy Collins was there, but although their relations were less chilly, she still had not fully recovered her faith in him. Since she stayed in England for another ten days George went alone to the premiere in Nairobi.

A kindly American lady chartered an aircraft specially to take me to Nairobi so I felt I had to go. I chased all the moths out of my dinner jacket and practised tying a bow tie round an old tin can.

In April, Joy went on to America to help promote a series of openings in Washington, New York, San Francisco and Boston. Most of the audiences, like most readers of the book, were amazed that lions and human beings could live together on such intimate terms. For some people the picture was too sentimental, but the majority were both gripped and moved by it. Accepting the illusions of the medium, few spotted how many lionesses performed the part of Elsa, and still fewer can have realized that they, and the other lions too, were all acting spontaneously, and the risks this involved.

Joy did. She wrote to the Traverses:

This wonderful success is entirely due to you both and the lions— nobody else could have done what you did together and it is impossible for me to thank you enough.

By word of mouth, as much as by any other means, the film became a box office hit all over the world and its music won an Oscar.

NINETEEN

The Spotted Sphinx

1965–1968

1

George and Joy were unbelievably lucky to be offered a home for themselves, their lions and their cheetah in the seven hundred square miles of Meru. The reserve offered Joy the perfect answer to her prayer "Where, how, can I live alone with Pippa?"

After a few months she moved away from the heat, dust and traffic of Leopard Rock to camp under a tamarind tree beside a stream called Vasorongi. She was within a mile or so of Kenmare Lodge, where tourists could stay, and about fifteen miles from Elsa's camp on the Ura. Like a leopard marking her range she set up notices on the tracks approaching it: "Experimental camp—no entry."

George's camp was fifteen miles to the west on Mugwongo Hill, a distinctive feature with twin humps like a Bactrian camel. It was one of several hills, a ridge and a series of rocky outcrops, that rose from a plain intersected by a number of streams flowing across it to the Tana. The tall trees and thick bush along the streams, and the swamps scattered across the plain, provided an ideal habitat for game of all kinds, great and small, including lions and cheetahs.

A creature of changing manners and moods, a cheetah or hunting leopard, with its long legs, deep chest, narrow waist, and curving tail, has the delicate line of a greyhound; for Joy it was "the quintessence of elegance." It moves and rests, or surveys the plain from the branches of a tree with the poise of an aristocrat. As soon as it has spotted a victim, perhaps weaker, less healthy, smaller or slightly apart from the rest, it maneuvers into position.

A cheetah's sudden attack is launched with an explosion of energy that propels it at up to 70 miles an hour. Nearing a gazelle, it steadies, to zigzag with it and knock it off-balance in a cloud of dust. It is the fastest animal on earth—20 miles an hour faster than a thoroughbred horse. Its performance sets the pulse racing. Going straight for the throat, it throttles its prey in less than five minutes. Pausing to recover its breath, the cheetah then drags the carcass to the shade of the nearest bush, out of sight from the vultures. It kills six days out of seven, and only wild dogs have a higher success rate.

Extraordinarily little was known about cheetahs in 1965, considering they had been domesticated by the ancient Egyptians and the Arabs, and were bred and trained for hunting black buck in the sixteenth century by the Mogul Emperor Akbar, who owned more than one thousand of them. More recently, cheetahs were raced by Raymond Hook in the 1930s, were exterminated in India in the 1940s, and one was successfully released in Transvaal in the 1950s.

The cheetah is by far the oldest of the three large African cats. It found a niche hunting smaller game on the plains 25 million years ago, while competition from the biggest predators, now extinct, prevented lions and leopards from evolving until about two million years ago. When they did appear they became instant rivals of the cheetahs, driving them off their prey, and destroying their young whenever they discovered them. Together with man they have just about snuffed out the cheetah.

In exploring the mysterious nature of the cheetah, which had proved almost impossible to breed in captivity, Joy would again be breaking new ground.

By the time she reached Meru, Pippa was two thirds grown. She would stand just over two feet tall, stretch six feet from nose to tail, and weigh about a hundred pounds. The background of her coat was sandy-colored with the firm texture of a dog's; her black spots were softer, like cat's fur. More cat than dog, cheetahs do in fact have a number of canine traits and cannot, for instance, retract their claws. Joy was several times nastily scratched.

Cheetahs must be constantly on their guard against the larger predators, since lions, leopards and hyenas not only kill their cubs— a practice they all employ against each other to reduce competition— but also steal their prey. It was for these reasons that George had to camp separately with Boy and Girl.

Joy kept her friends in touch with Pippa's progress.

Experts told me that no cheetah will ever leave its human foster parent for good, Pippa has already proved them wrong! For the first 12 days she kept close to my camp, where I had a compound to protect her at night. During these days she learned how to keep clear of baboons and elephants, to climb ant hills and trees to see over the shoulder-high grass, and to drink from the river.

Since June 5 Pippa has found her own territory 4 miles away near a swamp and never returns to my camp. We visit her at intervals of 4–5 days and feed her if she gets too thin. She has twice been seen together with a mate. I watched her tossing a jackal into the air when he tried to pinch her meat.

Six months later she wrote:

Yesterday when out with Pippa I had a wonderful experience. We saw a hippo cow with her tiny calf in the Rojoweru. Pippa growled at this huge creature.

The Shifta kept everybody busy during Christmas to the extent that all bookings in the lodge were cancelled. They looted a village across the river and killed 6 people. 29 Shifta were killed during the holidays. There is a permanent platoon of the security force now at the lodge, as well as police and game scouts.

In March 1966 Pippa had lost her first litter of cubs and Joy was therefore worried about her second.

On August 24 Pippa took a game scout and myself all the way back to the plain. She had four tiny cubs, all blind and not able to move except wriggling themselves in a position to suck. To be trusted by an almost wild animal to see such newly born babies is something I cannot explain. Even Elsa concealed her cubs from us most cunningly until they were 6 weeks old and had established their instinct to know that they were different from us.

A fortnight later all was still well.

Two days ago we found Pippa in the morning on a freshly killed duiker—the first time I have witnessed her kill. But the skies were instantly full of vultures and, fearing they might invite any predator in the area to the feast, we spent all day close to Pip to protect her cubs.

Her first litter was very likely killed under such circumstances, as my assistant found them on a kill with their parents when they

285

were 6 weeks old. 300 yards away he met 8 lions. That day was the last time he saw Pippa's first cubs.

On December 1, Joy wrote:

The cubs are now 3½ months old, absolutely wild, but tolerate my presence. Pip sometimes kills a small antelope; sometimes I carry meat into the bush; and between both our efforts the cubs are thriving.

Recently I was most worried as all were missing for 8 days. I searched 5–7 hours daily and had nightmare visions of disasters, when Pip finally turned up in camp. She was empty—but not thin—and asked for meat, which she promptly carried across the stream near my camp to her cubs who waited half a mile away. She had made a long detour to avoid coming near camp with the cubs.

There are 3 girls and 1 boy, all full of life, fun and so attractive. They climb trees like monkeys and chase each other all the time.

However much Joy adored the cheetahs, one tiny orphan crept even closer to her heart in these first two years at Meru—a two-day-old leopard cub given her by a Father Botta of the mission at Tigania. Everyone in camp found it irresistible, including Pippa; but after six weeks it died of *babesia felis*, as Elsa had. It left Joy with an ache and an ambition that she was determined one day to assuage.

She could never have managed her exhausting study of Pippa without practical help from three directions.

First there were several Africans attached to her camp. Old Toitonguro, with his crinkly face and smiling eyes, kept a small herd of goats to feed the cheetahs: he had a way of knowing "in his heart" where to find Pippa out on the plains. Another, Stanley, a Meru boy, though he had to lug meat and water for miles through the sweltering heat, also became very fond of Pippa's family.

Second George, who was allowed to shoot game for his lions outside the reserve, frequently brought Pippa haunches of wildebeest, zebra and kongoni. Otherwise there was little he could do right in Joy's eyes.

Joy's third and principal source of support was Ted Goss, the warden of Meru. Tall and relaxed, a typical Kenyan in his broad-brimmed khaki hat, he had joined the Game Department specifically to set up the reserve. His plans were imaginative: he introduced a boat and water safaris on the river, set aside a wilderness area exclusively for safaris on foot with an armed ranger and brought in seven white rhinos from South Africa—the first in Kenya for centuries.

Since both the reserve and the Game Department were bankrupt, Ted Goss's relationship with the Adamsons became a form of symbiosis. They provided the reserve with excellent publicity and Joy's Trust largely bore the costs of running it. In return George and Joy enjoyed sanctuary, while she received almost daily help from Goss with her cheetahs and business correspondence—to the point of dependence.

It was, however, a precarious world in which the rules were constantly changing as the independent government began to sort out its priorities.

2

Joy had been so preoccupied that she had not yet come face-to-face with the brave new Kenya.

> I have been living out of suitcases for almost four years now and have lost all my roots and sense of security, however spiritual my idea of security is.

Elspeth Huxley said of Jomo Kenyatta that his prison at Lokitaung had proved to be "a chrysalis from which the demagogue pupated into a statesman." He made a famous speech to an audience of white farmers at Nakuru, calculated to reassure expatriates who had remained in the country after Uhuru.

> All of us, white, brown or black can work together to make this country great ... Let us join hands and work for the benefit of Kenya. We are going to forgive the past and look forward to the future.

Important as it was to reconcile the different-colored skins, Kenyatta also had to modify the historic traditions that divided the tribes in his country, without dissolving the social and personal values that were rooted in these very traditions.

Change was inevitably in the air and very soon Joy had firsthand experience of the new society at its highest and lowest levels. She sought, and was granted, an interview with the President—the *Mzee* or Old Man, as he was respectfully known by his people—to petition him on behalf of his wildlife.

David Bateman from Collins came with her. Kenyatta sat hunched wearing a fezlike cap behind a beautiful desk, on which lay his ebony walking stick and famous fly whisk. His piercing, red-rimmed eyes bored into Joy as she spoke for fifteen minutes. By the time they were shown out he had said not a word. Perhaps he remembered her monologue about tribal traditions at her exhibition many years before; certainly he absorbed what she said.

It was not long before Joy saw Kenyan democracy working at the other end of the spectrum. One day an African policeman turned up in her isolated camp and ordered her to come with him to face a driving charge. He had no papers and she sent him away with a stinging dismissal.

His incensed colleagues were back a few days later and Joy found herself heading, in a crowded lorry, for a night in Nanyuki jail. They refused to let her out when they stopped at a police station, but pleading personal necessity, she darted into the office of a surprised superintendent. She avoided the cells, but not the courtroom.

I was charged with driving without a licence, to which I pleaded guilty, and for not attending court although the police had only given me nine days to attend instead of the legal minimum of ten.

To watch an Indian magistrate, an African prosecutor, and an Austrian accused interpreting the meaning of "within ten days of the offence" in legal English was just too comic; finally the Irish lawyer solved the problem and the magistrate had to admit a mistake by the police.

In addition to looking after the cheetahs, Joy managed her business affairs and continued her writing with equal determination.

Her hut, either stifling with heat or dripping with damp, became her studio and office complete with typewriter, filing boxes, sketching blocks, photograph albums, cine equipment, store cupboards and shelves. For radio contact with the outside world she had to drive fifteen miles to George's camp or to the reserve HQ.

By now the income from the *Born Free* trilogy, several derivations from it and the film, amounted to £250,000—close to $4,000,000 today. She had therefore engaged international accountants to minimize her taxes, the prime responsibility falling on the Nairobi firm Gill and Johnson. Peter Johnson was the rocklike partner on whom Joy depended for financial and every other kind of good sense for the rest of her life.

It was her good fortune to have discovered a man of saintly patience and total integrity. His wife, Mary, was as shrewd as he and had an excellent sense of humor. Together they kept Joy in perspective, pulled down the shutters in a storm and during her frequent times of distress gave her unfailing support and affection.

In order to hold the tax level on Joy's income at 25 percent or less her royalties were channeled into Elsa Ltd. (Kenya), Elsa Trust (Kenya), and The Elsa Wild Animal Appeal (a UK trust). Joy was a director of Elsa Ltd. and held 51 percent of its shares.

In the early days of independence the government had to meet the urgent demands of its rocketing population for land and food, if necessary at the expense of the game. Conservation was therefore in crisis, and Peter Johnson foresaw that Joy, with characteristic single-mindedness, might give away everything and be left with literally nothing for her old age. He persuaded her, much against her will, also to set up a trust in the Channel Islands that was purely her own. By 1965 it was worth £25,000—about $400,000 today. At 4 percent it would bring in the equivalent of George's pension.

By now both George and Joy recognized that the shifta were still so active around Isiolo that they would have to abandon any thought of living there, and when Peter Johnson heard of a house for sale at Naivasha he took Joy to see it in January 1966. It was a ravishing site—fifty acres of indigenous forest on the shore of the lake with a compact stone house overlooking the water.

Three weeks later Joy, or rather Elsa Ltd., owned it and she only then began to discover its treasures: the eagle owls and the colobus monkeys in the trees, the otters, bushbuck and hippos on the lawn at night. Hell's Gate, the dramatic gorge in the hills just behind it, was teeming with game and haunted by leopards.

The next house along the lake was the most notorious in Kenya, a Moorish extravaganza named Oserian, but commonly known as the

Djinn Palace, where Lord Erroll had lived and held some of his most decadent parties.

It took Joy two years to move into her new property, which she called Elsamere.

It is truly lovely. I have designed the house with lots of verandas and wide glass doors and windows, and have made the rooms as spacious as possible, in order not to feel cluttered after living for so long in the bush.

There was no service great or small for which Joy did not rely on Peter Johnson. He wrote:

We have your leopard coat and colobus monkey cape and six jars of face cream. What would you like to have done with these?

It was he who organized the committee controlling Joy's conservation funds. Although it included some of the country's most senior figures in wildlife management—like Frank Minot, now the resident U.S. representative of the African Wildlife Leadership Foundation—Joy significantly influenced its grants, which amounted to £50,000 between 1959 and 1968.

The Peoples of Kenya was much the most elaborate of Joy's books and it required superhuman concentration to complete it in her camp. She was deeply concerned that an independent Kenya might find her work offensive; and to reassure her, Malcolm MacDonald, now the British High Commissioner or Ambassador, agreed to obtain unofficial government approval and did so.

Despite this, Joy told Helen Wolff, "I expose so many secret rites in this book that either it becomes a bible fit for the Africans or I am sent to hell." She deferred moving into Elsamere until the book had circulated in Kenya for a year without a fuss.

It was a handsome quarto volume whose illustrations—her photographs and portraits, reproduced in monochrome or color—were interspersed with the text. It was finally published in September 1967: like the portraits themselves it is a unique record and has been reprinted several times since.

Joy also managed to write her first book about cheetahs, *The Spotted Sphinx*, in Meru. It was longer than her lion books but in the same format and there were 12,000 black-and-white photographs and

1,900 color slides from which to choose. Marjorie Villiers labored to translate the script into readable prose while her new assistant, Ernestine Nowak—like Joy an émigrée from Czechoslovakian Austria—selected and arranged the photographs.

Apart from all this, Joy had to approve Columbia's treatment of a second film about Elsa and her cubs, *Living Free.* Two further film projects arrived on her table.

The disputed fate of the film lions had so undermined relations between the Traverses and Columbia that neither party was enthusiastic about working together again. Bill Travers therefore suggested a film about the life of the Adamsons, the lions and the cheetahs since the filming of *Born Free.*

3

It is difficult to imagine circumstances more perfectly fitted to Pippa's and Joy's natures than those in Meru. Yet even there Joy could not change her spots and suffered both physically and psychologically.

There was little or nothing she could do about her recurrent malaria or kidney stones—or about the incessant pain in her neck. After the leopard cub died, she had fallen on a crate and broken two ribs, and after one of Pippa's cubs damaged a leg, she developed shingles. She constantly suffered from insomnia and a fluttering heart. Above all she was tortured by a loneliness that stemmed from her chronic compulsion to strike out at anyone who was close to her.

When her stepfather died painfully of cancer in 1965 she wrote to her sister Traute reminding her of their mother's "egoism" and "gross neglect" of her children. After their mother had a stroke Joy told Traute:

> I do not like to embarrass you but you lead a far more extravagant life than I do. Meanwhile neither you nor mother ever found it necessary to send me the smallest, inexpensive birthday or Christmas present just to show that you CARE for me.

Her thoughts and feelings about her sister Dorle were no friendlier and seem to have been reciprocated. Even so, Joy struggled with her conscience and occasionally sent her mother and her sisters presents of money.

In the same way, Joy grudgingly supported George's work with his lions, and if he was ever in physical trouble or danger, she went straight to his rescue. But she stridently disapproved of his insistence on feeding the lions long after they had learned to kill and made clear her distaste for his friends and assistants. When he began to invite his cousin Pam Carson to stay in his camp, Joy took exception to their happy but proper relationship and wrote to their friends accusing him of disloyalty, cunning and lies.

From the start, Joy took Ted Goss's daily visits for granted, and turned against him when he became engaged, brought his fiancée to Meru and called at the camp less often. Her trust was financing the reserve and she required first option on the warden's time, whatever the hour or his other commitments.

An American girl, Netta Pfeifer, whom Joy employed to help with her books and correspondence, was dismayed by the difference between the woman who had emerged from the pages of *Born Free* and the autocrat of Meru. Her own book contrasts the atmosphere in Joy's camp with that of the ashram in India where she recovered from her experience in Africa. Yet she still admired all Joy stood for and hoped to work for her Appeal in America.

Joy wrote a letter to their committee about her that Frank Minot branded as a "form of character assassination"; he warned the committee it was useless to continue their search for a scientist to work with Joy since her interference would soon prove intolerable.

Joy was equally autocratic with her camp staff. George's godson, Jonny Baxendale, arrived just in time to save her from being stabbed by her cook with a carving knife. Her execrable Swahili had been totally incomprehensible to the man; her manner had not.

In another sphere of her life Joy insisted Helen Wolff in America should control publication of *The Peoples of Kenya* purely as a retaliation against Billy Collins for his lack of affection and failure to make a contribution to her Appeal. Just before the book came out Joy wrote to her.

I feel worried that there are now so many intrigues going on in London that threaten my frail relationship with Collins.

I feel lonelier with every such experience and realise how very few people are reliable friends. I know of course that I am no angel, but at least I hope that I am honest and loyal—two qualities I expect also from my friends.

As soon as *The Peoples of Kenya* was successfully published, and when *The Spotted Sphinx,* with its far larger commercial potential, was nearing completion, Helen received this astonishing letter.

> When you first asked me if I would agree to let Harcourt have 40,000 copies without paying royalties I agreed as I naturally wanted to help to get this book to as many readers as possible.
>
> Since all my royalties are donated to the Elsa Appeal nobody can accuse me of wanting to get rich personally from this book, but I simply cannot afford contracts like these. Naturally I am more than grateful for all the superb work you and Marjorie have put in to get this book so beautifully set up and therefore I feel terribly embarrassed to have to tell you that I may have to look for another publisher for my cheetah book.
>
> I will not ask Harcourt to revise the agreement as this goes against my honour.

Helen Wolff's reply reveals much about her character and Joy's.

> I certainly did not ask you to let Harcourt have 40,000 copies without royalties, but you offered this in one of your characteristic bouts of generosity. You did this because you wanted this book to be published as cheaply as possible.
>
> Harcourt does not need to be blackmailed into decent contracts. For any normal book you would get maximum advances and maximum terms, and they generously contributed to your Elsa Appeal.
>
> I am sorry you think you have a grievance against us, but I am equally firm in telling you that you have no cause for it. It would be insincere to pretend that I am not rather shocked by your letter.
>
> Dear Joy, you cannot do this to your friends—think it over.

Virtually all who had close dealings with Joy sooner or later found themselves faced with a situation like this. Her determination to get her own way, coupled with her power of self-deception, especially where her Appeal was concerned, too often led to trouble.

She could precipitate a breach with her most loyal advisers. Her lawyer in London had proved a brilliant buffer between her and Columbia during the making of *Born Free.* She had given him power of attorney and told the Traverses, "I have absolute faith in him."

When he decided to bring his wife on safari in East Africa he accepted Joy's invitation to show them the Serengeti and the Rift Valley lakes. Joy chose the route, decided the timetable, talked without a break, lost the way, took over the wheel and damaged the rented car.

Remaining silent for the whole of one day, the lawyer remonstrated quietly with Joy that evening. "Bloody, bloody man," she wrote in her diary, "he treats me as a safari driver." She immediately appointed a new lawyer.

It was symptomatic of the disorder in her personality that she was gradually alienating herself from each of her closest long-standing allies. Peter Johnson was the sole exception. Ken Smith also kept in touch, although he was really George's friend.

Despite all this, George was still there. On his birthday she baked him a cake and gave him a fridge for his lions' meat; he made her a table for hers. At Christmas they gathered with their assistants in her camp and toasted each other in whiskey or vermouth.

4

During her third and fourth years at Meru, Joy's hopes for her cheetahs were totally vindicated.

There were, of course, setbacks. She had to send Pippa's male cub, Dume, to Nairobi for treatment when it broke two legs. It contracted distemper in the orphanage.

It was torture for me not to be able to explain to Pippa why I had interfered. I hoped by giving her daily the good news of Dume's progress, which I heard over the radio, she might feel that he was well— as she always licked my hand when I talked to her about him.

The day the vet hoped that I could collect Dume I woke up with a heavy feeling that something had gone wrong. He had died that night. When I had to tell Pippa that her son would never return she did not lick my hand but got up and quietly walked away. Next day she left, with her three remaining cubs, the area where they had spent the last weeks together with Dume.

When a second cub, whom she had named Whity, damaged a leg, Joy consulted Toni Harthoorn, who flew in with his wife, Sue, also a vet. Catching and sedating the young cheetah was difficult and dangerous. She vigorously resisted capture and several times broke free. Happily she both responded to treatment and appeared to bear no lasting resentment. This second accident left no doubt in Joy's mind that cheetahs suffer from a serious genetic weakness in their legs, possibly because they have taken late to tree climbing. Their total numbers are so few it is unlikely the flaw will ever breed out.

Joy wormed Pippa's family, dosed them and fed them with vitamins, but on advice she refrained from medicating Pippa when she suffered symptoms of *babesia canis*, so that she could build up her own immunity.

As with Elsa's cubs Joy was unable to live up to her precepts for Pippa's, yet she was honest when she broke them. She admitted in her book she had wrongly handled the cubs and had even hit Pippa when she hungrily took meat from their mouths. Needless to say she endlessly photographed and filmed them.

Despite all this, within eighteen months they were killing for them-selves, and in the way of any wild family were led by Pippa to the extremities of her territory and chased away if they tried to return to the center. Pippa had long established a territory, demarcated by spraying, scraping and the deposit of faeces. Other females would not contest it, and wandering males would loiter in it only if she was ready to mate.

For a time her daughters consorted with each other before they separated in search of mates and to adopt their own territories on the fringe of Pippa's. Sons would have remained together longer, hunting and searching for females.

By now the Kenyan parks and some reserves were under the control of their new Director, Perez Olindo, the young zoologist Joy had met and broadcast with in Michigan. He was quick to visit her, eager to secure her continued financial support. He also backed her work with her cheetahs, too often dismissed as a sentimental hobby that devoted money and time to a species that was not endangered.

In fact Africa's cheetah population was already in a state of drastic decline. A few years before there had been more than 25,000; today there are fewer than 10,000 left. Loss of habitat, disease, fragile leg bones and the thoughtless harassment of young families by tourist operators—whose drivers often crowd around a hunt or a kill—are all contributing to their plight. Their survival in the wild can no longer be taken for granted.

Joy's critics were mistaken in other ways. Admittedly her emotions were engaged but she was serious, and in 1968, when George Schaller, a highly respected ethologist, came to visit her at Meru, he wrote out a checklist of the precise details of the cheetah's behavior she should record.

Joy was particularly interested in their communication. Her sensitive ear quickly picked up the nuances of their whole range of sounds from hisses and bird whistles to moans, growls and yaps like those of a dog. They came when she called them.

Other aspects of their perceptions so baffled Joy she thought of them as "extrasensory." Toitonguro knew where to find Pippa, and she anticipated his unscheduled arrivals with goat meat. She ceased waiting for Dume in camp as soon as he was dead, and found a new mate within twenty-four hours when she lost her first litter and again when she had weaned her second.

Joy discussed her belief in Elsa's and Pippa's ability to receive and transmit awareness by telepathic means with one of the world's experts on parapsychology, Dr. J. B. Rhine of Duke University in North Carolina. He asked her to record and send him the fine details of her observations but I can find no trace that she did so.

She probably received more enlightenment from the distinguished gynecologist Dr. H. De Watteville of Geneva, who helped her to understand the phenomena that led Pippa to a mate, or a mate to her, as soon as her second litter grew up and her third litter was killed by hyenas. There is an interaction between the hypothalamic centers of a cheetah's brain and hormones secreted by its pituitary gland, which prepare the whole body for mating—testicles or ovaries and uterus, according to gender. Eyes, ears, nose, skin, urine and so on are all susceptible to these changes.

Once she was released from her role as a nursing or caring mother Pippa's brain sent out its messages, and a male picked up the end results. Since she was primarily a cat, the act of copulation then triggered ovulation.

De Watteville speculated that an animal as sensitive as a cheetah would react violently to any abnormality in its environment so traumatic as confinement in a primitive compound or cage. The affront to its system could well account for the failure to breed in captivity.

Joy's methods were never scientific, but no one has ever known cheetahs in the wild either better or longer, and her observations are still quoted in standard books of reference twenty years later.

TWENTY

A Pride of Stars

1965–1968

1

What George and Joy set out to do in Meru and what they ended up doing several years later were quite different things. If asked to explain this Joy would have replied that after successfully "rehabilitating" Pippa she stayed on to extend our understanding of the cheetah and to explore some of the animal's enigmas. George was frequently pressed to give his reasons for remaining with the lions; they changed, for good reason, from one month to the next.

He made his camp more accessible than Joy's. Mugwongo Hill was a beacon. It was possible to land a small plane quite close, and there was a grove of acacias to provide shade for a camp in which visitors were welcome. The rocks and ledges on the hill provided ideal lairs and lookouts for the lions.

When George arrived in April 1965 with Boy and Girl, and his cousin Pam Carson, the camp had already been carefully set up by his assistant on the film, Giles Remnant. There was a six-foot fence to keep the lions in at night and interlopers out. Boy and Girl, eager to explore their new home, were over it in a flash on the first morning and thereafter came and went as they liked.

Pam Carson worked with police intelligence at Isiolo and was very good company. Joy's waspish resentment of her and groundless threat of divorce proceedings drove George to a rare display of passive retaliation. According to Remnant he exaggerated the mannerisms that he knew got under her skin. He rattled his tea spoon, puffed out clouds of thick pipe smoke and strung miniature bottles of whiskey round his camp. When he heard her Land-Rover approaching he whistled up the lions and disappeared into the bush with them, half-heartedly responding to her calls while leading her in circles through the rocks and thorns.

He always felt he could pour out his deepest feelings to Tony Ofenheim.

> Age has not made Joy any easier to live with. In fact the only reason we stick together is our shared love for the animals, otherwise we would have parted long ago. Also there is the consideration of presenting a united and loving front to the public so as not to damage the image created by the books and now the film, not that it makes any difference to me as I do not get a ha'penny out of any of them, but at least it helps the animals.

There were at least five hundred elephants in the reserve and plenty of game for the lions—a thousand buffalo, four hundred zebras, herds of eland and scattered giraffes, waterbuck and other antelope. George gave Tony a vivid account of the lions' daily, and nightly, exploits among them.

> They have hunted everything from elephants down to dik-dik. Their powers of scent, hearing and sight have sharpened.
> At least six times they have encountered wild lions close to camp. At first they were very frightened and I would have to let them spend the night inside my tent. But on the last occasion, I went and found Boy and a wild lioness quite unconcerned about each other.
> Seeing Boy and Girl, as they are today, who could say that they would be happier in a zoo?

His rhetorical question was soon answered by a letter from Virginia McKenna about Mara and another of the film lionesses.

> I went to Whipsnade last Saturday. I won't talk much about it as it is too distressing, but they recognised me at once, rushed over to me and jumped up at the wire, moaning and rubbing it. Mara had a running eye—caused by a fight with the male (4 lionesses and 1 huge lion in the compound). She has had lots of fights apparently.

On the brighter side George had been able to collect Ugas.

> The people in charge of the orphanage at Nairobi warned me that Ugas had become a dangerous animal and had not been handled

since the filming. The second day he was just the same loving and affectionate animal I used to know.

George's approach to his lions was empirical. It had been wrong to release Elsa alone, and a disaster to bring the young male to the Ura as a mate for her. At Meru he had to balance his pride.

Although male lions always take precedence at a kill, it is usually the females who lead the hunt and bring down the prey. Males reserve their killing for battle with another lion, to take over his pride or territory. Having obtained only one lioness, George accepted an offer from Sieuwke Bisleti to send him a litter of four cubs, three of them female.

The National Parks of Kenya had agreed to release Ugas to George only on elaborate conditions that he quietly ignored—careful scientific observation must be maintained continuously . . . the lion must at all times be prominently marked or tagged . . . no reporters, photographers or visitors were to be admitted to the area without previous authority from the Ministry of Natural Resources and Wildlife.

Meanwhile, Joy was incensed that George intended to accept the cubs from Sieuwke Bisleti, first because she had become increasingly resentful of her, and second because it would mean prolonging contact with his pride. She tried to reinforce the stipulations laid down by the National Parks with threats of withdrawing the Trust's financial support, but she succeeded only in rousing the maverick in George.

For the next few years Meru became an extraordinary arena. While his lions were forced into a battle with their own kind for survival, George was obliged to engage in political jousting for his.

2

George thought it would be the best part of a year before Ugas, the oldest and largest of the lions, could lick his pride with four young cubs into shape, although by now Girl had demonstrated her prowess as a hunter—she had killed zebras, a young giraffe and finally a large eland.

On the other hand, progress was delayed when Ugas damaged his eye so badly that George had to call in Toni and Sue Harthoorn. They recommended injections of penicillin and George, who had already inoculated Boy against sleeping sickness and taken his temperature with a thermometer in his anus, administered them. However the antibiotic did not work.

> Toni and his wife, both clever vets, have spent an immense amount of time to help Ugas, free of charge. It was agreed that the only course was to take out the eye. It was a ghastly performance, carried out under the shade of a bush, and took an hour and forty minutes.

Ugas soon came to terms with having only one eye and began to engage with the local lions in love and war. When he went "whoring after wild women," George knew it would land him in trouble, and sure enough a posse of wild lions began to invest the camp at Mugwongo, "uttering low moaning noises that might sound friendly but which experience had taught me were a deadly challenge to a fight." George christened their leader Black Mane.

Life in the bush can be brutal. In June Ted Goss was trampled by an elephant he was attempting to tranquilize with a dart. It smashed his thigh and he was lucky to pull himself from under its belly before his game scout dropped it with a bullet. He was in hospital for months.

George also ran into trouble. While hunting meat for his lions he wounded a buffalo and followed it up.

> It suddenly charged from behind long grass, six feet away. As I put up my rifle to shoot, the muzzle was jerked by the buffalo and it bashed me in the ribs, knocked me down, tried to hook me with its horns, trod on my left foot and banged me on the side of my face, giving me a black eye. It then left me and went and lay down some 40 feet away. The Meru came and helped me up and gave me my rifle, which I reloaded. The buffalo got up again and I thought it was going to have another go at me, but it lay down and died.

He was in such pain that Joy sent for the Flying Doctor, who flew him to hospital in Nairobi, but the main damage was no worse than a fractured rib.

While George was recovering, Girl gave birth to two cubs by Boy, with alarming consequences that taught George some fundamental facts about the basic dynamics of lion society. Girl first lost one cub to a leopard, abandoned the other and—to George's surprise—immediately went into heat again. George therefore took over the unaccustomed role of foster father and fed the young cub, whom he named Sam, from a bottle.

There was, however, violence in the air. For one thing Black Mane and his confederates were growing increasingly offensive. For another Girl's condition had suddenly stimulated rivalry between Boy and Ugas.

> He and Boy had a real set-to, standing on their hind legs and taking terrific swipes at each other with both paws and claws extended. Any one of the clouts might have removed half the face of a human but, surprisingly, there was little or no damage on either side.

Believing that peace was restored, George and his Indian assistant, Arun Sharma, walked off, but as they did so Boy suddenly lashed out and clawed Sharma on the arm.

> Luckily I had a stick which I seldom carry and managed to beat him off while telling the Indian to make for the car.
>
> Then Boy came for me, I hit him on the nose, checking him for a moment, next he had another try, looking really nasty, and I thought I was for it but I hit him again with all my might between the eyes which seemed to bring him to his senses and he retreated.

A second drama occurred a few nights later. Sam, the adopted cub, was sleeping in a box by George's bed.

> About 3.00 am. I was woken up by a noise outside. I could hear the wire rattling. I glanced at Sam's box and saw that it was empty.
>
> I went to the back of my hut and in the light of my torch saw a lion a few feet away, standing on his hind legs against the wire, trying to force his way out. He had Sam in his jaws. At first I thought it was Boy. I shouted at him, and he looked around with a loud growl. It was Black Mane!
>
> I rushed to get my rifle and by the time I got out again Black Mane had forced his way out, dropping Sam. The poor little chap was lying in a heap gasping, in a few seconds he was dead, bitten through the neck.

Red hot anger arose in me and I determined to kill Black Mane for this most unnatural murder.

George later confessed how the night ended.

I got in the Land-Rover and dashed towards some roaring coming from the hill. There I found Black Mane and Girl together— mating. They disappeared at once into the darkness.

I therefore quietly followed Girl and Black Mane until dawn. When Black Mane wandered away I shot him through the shoulder to the heart and hid his body from the tell-tale vultures.

Some may find the execution of Black Mane unforgivable. But once he had felt so much at home in my camp that he dared to climb into my compound and take Sam, neither my staff nor I would be safe again. What is more, no young cubs born to our lions at Mugwongo would be safe either.

As George was later to learn, neither Girl's coming into season when her cub was so tiny, nor Black Mane's murder, was unnatural. A lioness cannot afford to waste energy raising a litter of only one or two cubs; three or four is the norm, and statistics show that only 25 percent of lions born ever reach maturity. Like Pippa's, her system therefore lost no time in preparing to breed again. It is also usual for a male who has taken over a pride to kill off its young cubs; it is the certain way of ensuring that his own offspring avoid competition.

The tragedy occurred two days before Christmas, and on Christmas Eve Joy invited George over with Arun Sharma and Terence, who had arrived to lend a hand in camp. On New Year's Day Bill Travers and a film crew of three were arriving to make the documentary. In case they needed to stay at Mugwongo, Terence was extending the enclosure.

3

The atmosphere in George's camp was as relaxed as it was tense in Joy's. Although he was shy, often silent, and happy to spend weeks alone in the bush, people always seemed drawn to him and he became increasingly sociable.

George's domestic arrangements were in the charge of his eccentric cook, Korokoro, who had to contend with a plague of snakes and scorpions in wet weather. He consoled himself by playing a weird homemade flute, fashioned from a hose pipe, and with the occasional swig. He had taken to sporting as gaiters the corrugated sleeves that arrived around George's White Horse whiskey bottles.

Thanks to the help of Malcolm MacDonald, Bill Travers had obtained permission to film in the reserve from the Minister of Tourism and Wildlife. Bill had convinced him that a documentary portraying what had become of the Adamsons and the film lions, as well as the country's incomparable scenery and game, could only benefit Kenya. He would produce it for television and finance it himself; George and Joy were each to receive 25 percent of the profits for their contributions. Bill expected no problems, for Joy had recently written:

> You can always rely on me that I will be loyal to you and back you up in whatever I can do. There will be lots of big difficulties as well as positive links between us in consequence of the film, so we have to know where we are with each other. I truly love you both.

By the greatest misfortune the start of the filming coincided with the death of Pippa's cub Dume. Joy was therefore off-balance when she realized that she and Pippa would be overshadowed by George and his lions. As a result she proposed that since "Elsa" was funding George's lions, "Elsa" should take over the production and adjust the film's content to throw more light on her and Pippa. It was a presumptuous and impractical suggestion. Bill inevitably declined it—although he offered to make a second film devoted to her and Pippa—just as George refused her demand that he should pull out.

Joy then handed down a verdict. She would have nothing to do with the film; she would never speak to Bill again; and George must return his Land-Rover from "Elsa" and forfeit all future funds from the trust.

Fortunately Bill managed to make up the lost footage on Joy and her cheetahs in other ways. He took the cameras to Whipsnade and once again the film lionesses rushed to Virginia when she called them.

Some time later Bill and Virginia both came back to Meru with James Hill, who had joined them in producing the film, to see George and call on Joy as a courtesy. When James left the car to announce their arrival, Joy said, "I will talk to you and Ginny, but not to Bill unless he apologizes." Bill therefore walked over and offered to apologize if she would tell him what for. She could not, or would not, explain and, her face contorted with fury, she said she would never speak to either of the Traverses again. Nor did she.

Despite Joy's withdrawal from the documentary, Bill and James produced a one-hour film and sold it to two of the principal networks, NBC and CBS, in the USA where it was shown three times on prime-time television from coast to coast, earning $375,000. The film *The Lions Are Free* was thus shown to an audience of 35 million and George received an avalanche of letters full of impossible questions, mostly from children wanting to become game wardens, lion tamers or his secretary. In years to come he became a connoisseur of fan mail and from it chose some of the ablest young assistants for his camp.

George's share of the profits of *The Lions Are Free* eventually amounted to more than £50,000 (about ten times that amount today) or the equivalent of his pension for fifty years.

He was also due to receive welcome income from another source. He had been struggling to get to the end of his autobiography that Joy predicted would never be finished. He had been much encouraged when Billy Collins offered him a contract—on the strength of an article about Boy and Girl he had written for the *Times* in London—and sold the rights to a major American publisher, Doubleday.

Although he had kept a diary for so many years, George found writing laborious. Occasionally Joy looked over his shoulder and sometimes insisted on changes. For instance, his account of their decision to marry was altered from "we felt that we could not live without each other" to "I felt that I could not live without her."

George reflected, with some irony, on Billy Collins's and Marjorie Villiers's reaction to the script.

> They were quite pleased with it but pointed out that a large part infringed the copyright of Joy's books which of course is true as quite a lot of her writing was based more or less word for word on my diaries and notes. It is a frightful bore, I now have to rewrite a large portion of the manuscript.

Bill Travers helped him to make up the lost pages by recording anecdotes that added appreciably to the book's charm. *Bwana Game* sold 28,000 copies in the British edition, which with foreign editions and the paperback rights brought in £10,000. George's half share of the family farm had finally netted him £2,000, so that altogether, for the first time in his life, he had real money in the bank.

It was probably this new degree of financial independence that underlay Joy's irrational anger with Bill Travers and spurred the campaign she now waged to have George's lion project closed down by the authorities. In a letter to Ken Smith, at about this time, she gave vent to her animus against George.

> He now betrays Elsa quite blatantly for money, while I am left to defend her spirit and turn her money into something more beneficial than whisky or to help loafers who cannot make a success of their own lives.
>
> You may join others in saying that poor George never had a financial share of Elsa—which I can contradict. When I learnt from his own relatives that he had inherited from his parents a complete inability to handle money I decided to give George his share in a form other than cash, financing his search for Elsa's cubs in the Serengeti and, until recently, his camping expenses here. Now, since he has turned our trust into a farce, we have withdrawn the money.

Joy here reveals "the capacity for self-deception that can at times reach astounding proportions," attributed to histrionic disorder. Quite apart from the fact that her subvention to George amounted to only a few thousand pounds, she had never taken any notice of his mother and brother, nor had he ever enjoyed enough money to mismanage it.

The likely truth is that she was terrified George could now afford to cut adrift and leave her lonelier than ever.

4

Joy argued, with complete justice, that George had taken on the lions to give them their freedom, including freedom from dependence on man. She objected, wisely, to his allowing the lions to sit on the Land-Rover roof. Twice they had climbed onto visiting Land-Rovers, and both times fallen through weak or rotten canvas—once on a party of startled rangers, and once on a family of fourteen Indians who good-naturedly laughed it off.

Joy also maintained that the lions' familiarity with people could breed contempt and easily lead to an accident. George had, in fact, returned one day to find a party of eight young men playing football with Boy and Girl. He could not think why the lions had accepted the strangers so quickly, until he learned that they were on leave from the Welsh Guards and must have triggered memories of their cubhood as mascots.

In Joy's view George ought to make a break with the lions as soon as possible and join her with the cheetahs. He replied that he had certainly achieved his original objective—the lions were free and had learned to feed and protect themselves—but he felt there was still more to be achieved by keeping in touch with them. For one thing it would demonstrate that Elsa wasn't a freak in maintaining their friendship once she was free—for another it was proof to the world of just how much we can discover about animals if we treat them with care and affection.

He argued that the first thing everyone asked to see on coming to Meru was his pride. The reserve—soon to become a National Park—desperately needed income from visitors, and the publicity his lions were generating had certainly increased the numbers. He also wrote this to the Game Department.

> Another aspect deserves careful consideration. In my opinion the seven lions, owing to their friendliness towards man, offer a unique opportunity which may never occur again of a thorough and intimate scientific study of these animals in their natural life, impossible of achievement with wild lions.

The Minister, the Hon. Samuel Ayodo, accepted the argument and took a broader view still. He was persuaded that the curiosity aroused by George's continued relationship with his lions would, like the film, stimulate worldwide interest in both the attractions of Kenya and the need for conservation.

Joy also failed to obtain the backing she expected from her committee and trustees, partly because they felt she had never been justified in monopolizing the Elsa money in the first place, and partly because they saw some force in George's case.

On the other hand, she did receive rock-solid support from Perez

Olindo as Director of National Parks, and from the temporary warden of Meru. Olindo held firmly to two principles. From the point of view of the lions' welfare he believed in the words of the song: "If you want to learn to love, you must learn to let go." As to the visitors' welfare, safety had to come first, and he could not guarantee it unless the lions were discouraged from approaching strangers.

The warden was unequivocal in clinging to the axiom of his service—a park is a park. It made no sense to have resident naturalists camped out in Meru for years on end, feeding half-tame cheetahs and lions when it was no longer necessary, and licensed to disregard many of the other regulations too.

It was a ticklish situation for Olindo, who had to take into account political and public opinion on the one hand and his hopes of obtaining a further £8,000 from Joy on the other. He resolved it by declaring that Mugwongo would become the site of the park's new headquarters, with a camping area around it—in fact a no-go area for lions. It looked as if George had been outmaneuvered on the ground if not in high places.

At that moment some heavy artillery opened up in his defense. The great conservationist, Bernhard Grzimek, champion of the Serengeti, Director of the Frankfurt Zoo and founder of one of the most effective conservation agencies in Europe, who had stayed in George's camp, wrote to the Minister emphasizing the scientific potential of George's work and recommending its continuance with the aid of a biologist.

George Schaller, whose reputation as an expert on animal behavior had been secured by his study of gorillas in the wild and was gathering momentum with his work on the Serengeti lions, also wrote in support to the Minister. Later Schaller spent several days with George, recognized he knew "lions as individuals better than any living person" and tried to find a young scientist to work with him.

Toni and Sue Harthoorn, with their high professional standing in Kenya as vets and their personal knowledge of George's lions, lent further weight to George's case, and Sue arranged for him to see the Minister. Such a formidable barrage proved effective. George was allowed to stay on with his lions at Mugwongo.

In December he joined Joy on a visit to her new house at Naivasha and agreed that it was lovely. They spent Christmas in her camp and the hatchets seemed to be buried. She gave him a very handsome watch.

5

Early in 1968, a new permanent warden, Peter Jenkins, was appointed to Meru. He belonged to the crack regiment of the National Parks staff, and his sister Daphne was married to the warden of Tsavo, David Sheldrick, also a man of considerable caliber.

To them the perimeter of a park was inviolable. Its interior, immaculately managed, was their show and they were the showmen. Jenkins's arrival with his wife, Sara, a young son, Mark, and a baby, called for diplomacy on all sides—a requirement more easily met by George than Joy.

George's relations with the wardens depended greatly on tactful liaison by his assistants. He felt obliged to turn down one applicant who had owned two pet baboons and a cat; but Arun Sharma had won a place at a game management training college. His successor, Hans Oppersdorff, had been trained as a ranger in Natal. He had an excellent instinct for animals, but although his months with George were as happy as any in his life, Joy took against him and he left for Australia.

By a stroke of luck George was able to replace him with a young man on whom he could completely rely, and who would also get on with Peter Jenkins—his own godson, Jonny Baxendale. Fair, good-looking, and almost as well built as his giant of a father, he also had a way with the lions. On a very hot day, dressed only in sandals and exiguous shorts, he lay down with the pride while they took their siesta in the shade of a tree. Disturbed by a noise he slowly stood up to find himself being watched by four incredulous Dutch tourists.

Peter and Sara Jenkins were frequent visitors to the camp, calling for a drink or a meal, and bringing the children. Because lions are peculiarly intrigued by the young, Jonny urged Sara to take Mark and his sister into a hut if they began to make a noise, since one of the lions was certain to start pacing the wire with a glint in its eye.

Halfway through the year the Traverses came out to Kenya to show George *The Lions Are Free*, which he thought "really excellent," and to invite him to make a brief appearance in a film about one of Daphne Sheldrick's orphan elephants at Tsavo. Named Pole Pole— the Swahili for slowly—the young elephant was to be a gift from President Kenyatta to Regent's Park Zoo in London.

She was destined for fame, not only as a star in the film *An Elephant Called Slowly* but also, through her tragic death in the zoo, as a martyr to ignorant management. Her memorial is Zoo Check, the successful and growing movement founded by Bill Travers and Virginia McKenna to monitor, and where necessary to press for the closure of, zoos.

At the end of the year, in order to bring some regularity to George's position, he was appointed assistant warden at Meru. He and Joy were also invited to celebrate Christmas lunch that year with Peter and Sara Jenkins.

December 25   Got back to camp at about 5.30 to find Korokoro drunk. He had finished a whole crate of beer and a third of a bottle of meths!

As an epilogue to the year George wrote in his diary:

It would seem that Boy and Ugas are dominating the country between here and Leopard Rock.

In other words, George had discovered how it was possible to introduce a group of hand-reared lions to the wild, there to establish their life as a pride. The four Bisleti lions were fulfilling the role for which they had been taken.

The full-blooded roar of a lion, reverberating off the rocks, is the most thrilling sound of the African night, lifting the spirit and prickling the spine. It begins with a long drawn-out, throbbing, bellow of thunder—imperiously repeated once or twice, though a shade less loudly. Then follows a series of gruff but diminishing grunts.

Listening to a bravura performance one night, George asked Korokoro what he thought Ugas was proclaiming to the world. This is how, on the last page of *Bwana Game*, he translates Korokoro's reply.

WHO IS LORD OF THIS LAND? . . . Who is lord of this land? . . . I AM! . . . I AM! . . . I am! . . . I am! . . .

TWENTY-ONE

A Season in Purgatory

1969

1

Mornings in Meru break like the dawn of creation. Blocks of black lava looming in the mist turn into buffalo; birdsong swells with the light; elephants peacefully browse among the acacias, their tusks gold in the early sun; a herd of startled impala float through the bush, leaping like a corps de ballet in full flight.

But twice a year, in March and October, the skies darken, thunder rumbles and curtains of rain pour down on the plain. Joy, typing by a dim lamp, late into the night, wrote:

> The rain is drumming on the roof and drizzling through it too. As my only companion for the last week I have had a red cobra, and wherever I go I have to look out for this damn wriggling creature. I am really scared since a friend was bitten by a puff adder here.
>
> Cut off by rising streams we have no escape if any of us has an accident. Still, in a few weeks time there will be sun again—then the dry and hot season, followed by the grass fires.

Joy was not exaggerating. When the flood came halfway up the walls of her hut she took to typing in the back of her truck. The filmmaker Alan Root, who has lost parts of his body to a hippo, a leopard and a gorilla, very nearly died when he was bitten by the puff adder in her camp and ended up losing a finger.

When the hot weather came it was very hot indeed. The undergrowth and dead grass were then burned to encourage fresh shoots for the grazers and improve the game viewing. One year a gust of wind carried the flames to Joy's camp and destroyed a truck.

By the beginning of 1969, although the cubs from Pippa's second litter had dispersed and were looking for mates, and her fourth litter was thriving, Joy still hoped to stay on to see Pippa's grandchildren grow up and mate themselves. Yet she knew she must make a break one day, as she told Helen Wolff, who had recovered Joy's confidence because Harcourt Brace had bowed to expediency and agreed to pay a small retrospective royalty on *The Peoples of Kenya*.

> Sooner or later I will have to make a sadistic cut through my love for these darlings or I will handicap their future.
>
> Living would be impossible without love, and if we feel for animals and try to understand them love automatically takes over. Why must I always lose it again?
>
> It's losing one's deepest self that produces incurable injuries. I am frightened of the next, which I know is inevitable.

In the middle of January Perez Olindo offered Joy two small leopard cubs from the orphanage in Nairobi, and since Pippa was keeping her family well away from camp she believed she could raise the leopards for a time in the enclosure next to her hut. They would cushion her coming separation from the cheetahs, and it had always been her ambition to bring up and release one.

The trip to Nairobi would also give her a chance of seeing Billy Collins again. He had just spent five days with her on a safari around Meru that had restored something of their former intimacy but left her uneasy.

Since her success he had acquired a number of other talented, attractive and younger authors in East Africa. They included Daphne Sheldrick, author of *The Orphans of Tsavo*; Jane Goodall, who had collaborated with her first husband, Hugo van Lawick, on *Innocent Killers*, about hyenas, jackals and wild dogs, and was now leading a very important study of chimpanzees in Tanzania; Mirella Ricciardi, whose photographs in *Vanishing Africa* carried on where Joy's tribal record had left off; and Sue Harthoorn, who described her adventures with Toni in *Life with Daktari*. Sometimes Joy feared that one of them might supplant her in Billy's affections and desperately wanted him to dispel her anxiety. Perhaps it was this sense of insecurity that had so often precipitated and then ruined her relations with men.

According to Jonny Baxendale, whom Joy asked to follow her in convoy to Nairobi, she set out in a rage. She had told Peter Jenkins about the leopards and he had warned her that he would not have them released in the park.

"Then I shall ask Perez Olindo to sack you," she retorted.

"If he agrees, fair enough," Jenkins is said to have answered, and walked away.

Always a bad driver, Joy was worse when she was angry. Jonny Baxendale was therefore alarmed but not surprised when he came around a corner to find a crowd on the road, some looking over a precipice and some surrounding Joy who was covered in blood.

She dictated this letter from hospital.

I have no idea how this accident happened, as I was driving up hill, suddenly lost control of the car and rolled down a steep escarpment. When I regained consciousness I found myself next to the shambles of the car, which is a write-off, and close to a thick bush, otherwise the car would have tumbled down another hundred feet into the river. Luckily I was driving in convoy with George's assistant, who soon arrived and took me to the Nairobi Hospital, another five hours drive, where they operated on my right hand. All the tendons were cut through, the bone partly destroyed, and after stitching everything up they grafted from my thigh a new cover on my hand. It will take about five months before the fingers will move again, and up to two years before the hand is completely healed.

Billy Collins rushed around to see her in hospital and told both Marjorie Villiers and Helen Wolff that his five days with her had been immensely enjoyable, adding, "She was very cheery when I spent the last evening with her in hospital."

In fact she made an effort to be cheerful with everyone.

i am getting treatment for my hand and have drawn the enclosed cheetah. the physiotherapist forced a pencil between my fingers, around which a rubber foam was tied so that i could get a grip. i personally regard this as a masterpiece only equalled by rembrandt. i am inundated by journalists here who want photos of the dying j.a. in hospital, which is of course of world importance. i refused, put a blouse over my nightie, and pretended to be on safari. these photos are to be used—but merely a memento of trying to make fun of something too serious to think about.

i will try to free myself of this mental cage in which i am at present.

From that day on her letters and scripts were typed exclusively in lowercase or capitals. On flimsy and discolored paper, frequently duplicated with carbon paper long past its prime, they became even more of an obstacle course to decipher.

In May she went to England for treatment that entailed prolonged physiotherapy, an operation at East Grinstead and another in London. Billy Collins met her at the airport and she stayed for much of the time with her old Kenya friends, Robert and Pat Nimmo, in the country.

There she found that Ziebel von Klarwill had left South Africa and was living nearby. She told George she had been to see him. "He owns a grocer's shop in a tiny village. He and his wife sell sugar and cigarettes to make enough money for their needs. He asked me to help him find French and German books to translate." The only emotion she expressed afterward was embarrassment.

Typically, Joy packed a prodigious amount of work into the hours not spent in treatment. She lobbied Sir Hugh Elliot, head of the International Union for the Conservation of Nature in Geneva, and Peter Scott, chairman of its Survival Service Commission, to back a program for restocking India and parts of East Africa with cheetah; promoted the publication of *The Spotted Sphinx*; prepared a children's book on Pippa; started her autobiography; negotiated with a dozen film producers in England and America for her cheetah story; and opened an exhibition of her tribal paintings at the Ceylon Tea Centre in London. About twenty original portraits had been loaned from Nairobi, and another forty had been reproduced for sale by a firm called Arts Unlimited. A little later the Tryon Gallery reproduced a few of her animal and fish paintings as limited prints.

As always when she was in England, she fumed against Billy Collins, who still never gave her the time she thought due to her. Taking the bull by the horns, she actually suggested to his wife, Pierre, that since Billy was hers for a lifetime she should let him off the leash to take her, Joy, around the world for a month. It is amazing that Pierre ever spoke to her again. On her return to Kenya Joy wrote this to Marjorie Villiers.

I WAS DEAD RIGHT WITH BILLY ON VERY LAST EVENING HE OFFERED TO HAVE SUPPER WITH ME AND WHEN I ACCEPTED HE EVEN THEN

BACKED OUT AND I HAD A SHERRY IN HIS FLAT WITH PIERRE AS WELL. I WILL NOT WRITE PERSONALLY TO HIM ANY MORE.

HE ORDERED A LEATHER-BOUND COPY OF PIP FOR ME AS PRESENT FROM HIM WHICH I REGARD AS THE BUNDLE OF HAY IN THE STORY WHERE A WHITE STALLION WAS NEVER FED UNTIL HE DIED. THEN THEY PLACED A BUNDLE OF HAY NEXT TO HIM SO THAT PEOPLE COULD NOT SAY THAT HE HAD DIED OF HUNGER.

THESE MONTHS IN LONDON WERE GRIM TO SAY THE LEAST AND I HAVE AS ONLY VIVID MEMORY OF BILLY AND MY FRIENDSHIP A USELESS HAND WHICH IS ALSO AN ANALOGY OF HIS BEHAVIOUR.

2

George had now been living and working with full grown lions for more than ten years without a serious accident, but during the next twenty he would have to live through several. The most lamentable, because the victim was a young child, and totally unaware of any risk, occurred in March while Joy was in hospital.

Returning to camp one afternoon Jonny Baxendale came across Boy on the road, some way from home, and stopped to greet him. Boy hopped on the Land-Rover roof. When he would not get down Jonny decided to sit on the bonnet and have a beer in the sun until the lion changed his mind.

What happened next is taken from *My Pride and Joy*: it tallies precisely with George's letters and reports at the time, and I have cross-checked it with Baxendale.

Peter Jenkins drove up in his new Toyota with half doors and open windows. With him were Sara and the baby; Mark sat on the front seat between them. Peter drew up some yards away, and switched off the engine. They began to chat as Jonny went over to collect his mail and the children grew a little restless.

After a few minutes Boy stepped down on to the Land-Rover bonnet and peered into the Toyota. Jonny felt a sudden twinge of apprehension and murmured something about backing off. Peter replied he did not think he would wait for the lion to scratch his paint. Just then, as silent and effortless as a shaft of light, Boy shot off the bonnet, passed Jonny and was thrusting his head through Peter's door of the Toyota.

Somehow, with his head and body forced back against the seat by Boy's massive shoulders, Peter managed to switch on the engine and, as Boy's paw stretched out to pull over Mark's head, the car jerked into gear. Meanwhile Jonny, who had punched Boy in the ribs and pulled at his tail without any effect at all, ran for his rifle. He saw the car leap forward in a spurt of dust and Boy's hind legs dragging beside it. When Boy's forequarters fell out of the Toyota, seconds later, he expected to see Mark pulled out too, and his telescopic sights were already on the lion, only twenty yards away.

Jonny was reluctant to shoot Boy without finding out what harm had been done, and he therefore drove straight to Peter Jenkins's house. Mark had only been scratched on the head but had a deep and unpleasant bite on his arm. George goes on:

> The next morning I went with Jonny to apologise to Peter and Sara, to enquire about Mark and to ask Peter if he wanted me to shoot Boy. Peter answered that the decision was not his: he would refer this episode, and the whole issue of my lion rehabilitation, to the Director of Parks, with the strongest possible recommendations. He and Sara displayed the most admirable courage, calm and courtesy, both now and later, in everything to do with the accident.

I have twice tried to speak to Peter Jenkins about the episode, but both times he has declined. However, an account attributed to him broadly confirms this one, except that he says the two cars were farther apart than Baxendale implies.

Mark's arm, after an early setback, healed satisfactorily, but he was left with headaches and nightmares that recurred into manhood.

It may have been unwise of Jenkins to stop so close to Boy when he had children in the car, but he had been right in maintaining there were inevitable risks in having lions in the park whose behavior was not entirely natural. From the time of his arrival he had warned George and Joy that he wanted to close down their rehabilitation projects as soon as he could, since they had both achieved their original purposes.

Joy was equally right about the danger inherent in letting lions climb onto cars.

Unfortunately—for everyone—the authorities in Nairobi were unable to give quick, clear instructions about what should be done. In a succession of orders and counterorders Boy was to be shot; Girl and Ugas were to be shot too; none of them was to be shot for fear of a worldwide public outcry; George was to remove all three lions from Meru immediately.

When it was discovered that the lions did not belong to the National Parks, which had issued these contradictory directives, the case went up to the Minister. He decided that it was in the best interests of Kenya to play the accident down, for the time being George and his lions were to stay on in Meru.

In the light of later events the most judicious decision would have been to shoot Boy and ask George and Joy to leave within the next few months. Although the cheetahs created none of the problems that George's lions did, Joy's presence inevitably interfered with the management of the park.

In the circumstances Olindo and Jenkins decided to exercise such powers as they had within their department. Joy was given notice to leave by the end of the year, and other tactics were employed against the lions and George.

First, Jenkins decided to put an end to Boy's trust in people—so carefully nurtured by George for five years—by throwing thunder flashes at him and twice he charged the lion in his car. Second, Olindo sold Sandie, a second little cub that George had adopted when abandoned by its mother, a Bisleti lioness, to a dealer. Third, the Game Department withdrew George's special license to shoot game for the lions. Finally, he was posted to the Marsabit reserve two hundred miles away.

Both Boy and George saw red.

When Jenkins charged Boy the lion simply charged back. He also went further.

May 9 Peter much exercised about Boy. Apparently last Saturday he appeared in the Rangers' lines in the afternoon and frightened the people. That night he, or another lion, tore open the window frame of the guardroom where there were two men asleep. They woke up and shouted, whereupon the lion sprang away. What is Boy up to?

Meanwhile George made sure Sandie "escaped" from her enclosure the night before the dealer was due to collect her; he took to shooting gazelles surreptitiously around Mugwongo to maintain touch with his pride; when the camp was again haunted by two wild lions he peppered them with bird shot; and he resigned as Jenkins's assistant.

By early September George had nearly had enough and began to explore the possibility of rehabilitating tigers in Nepal. "There are only about 2,000 left in the whole of Asia," he told Joy. "Before India received independence there were estimated to be somewhere in the region of 50,000."

Only one thing held him back. He could never desert a lion in trouble; Boy was on the blacklist, and the wild lions had driven him and Ugas away from Mugwongo.

3

While Joy was in England, George and Brian Heath, who had come to look after her camp and the cheetahs, sent regular bulletins and long letters with the news and gossip from Meru. Like Oppersdorff, Heath noticed that often Joy tried to press her unwanted affections on Pippa, who was making regular kills of Grant's gazelles and a number of young and half-grown waterbuck.

In the first week of September Joy was unable to stand any longer the mental and physical constraints of her physiotherapy course in England and flew back to Kenya. A few days later Pippa strolled into camp and, when Joy walked up to her, started purring, licking her hand, and rubbing her head against Joy's leg. The three cubs had grown so much that Joy hardly recognized them; the female was as large as Pippa and the two males slightly bigger.

About ten days later Pippa dragged herself to within 300 yards of camp dangling a broken foreleg. She was very hungry and must have limped for miles to get back to Joy, for there had been no sign of her or the cubs for a week. Joy caressed her, hoping to comfort her, but she only growled in pain.

The Harthoorns were abroad; and when another vet was flown in from Nairobi, he diagnosed a fracture so serious that he thought Pippa should be put down. Joy of course refused, and Pippa was flown to the orphanage for an X ray and treatment.

On October 10 Joy wrote to Marjorie Villiers.

There is a tragedy. I have lost Pippa. For four days she did well, after which she got gangrene, and from her shoulder downward her whole leg was a terrible septic wound. The Harthoorns—just returned— did their best to clean it all up and give her heavy sedatives but after two weeks on these powerful drugs her heart failed.

I stayed with her all the time and slept within a few inches of her at night. We did all we could but on the 7th she died.

The Harthoorns helped me to get her to their home where we kept her on dry ice and next day I drove her back to her home, here, at my camp.

In her second book about cheetahs, *Pippa's Challenge*, Joy speculates that if the leg had been set in a light metal or plastic splint, instead of plaster of Paris, it could have been easily examined and the gangrene spotted earlier, or possibly avoided. She wrote to the Harthoorns:

I do not know how I can thank you enough for all you have done for Pippa and myself. I am so sore that I can hardly think clearly, but want you to know how deeply grateful I am and feel so much closer to you now than before.

George had already dug the grave at my camp where Pippa always rested. Now she will rest there for ever.

Before earth was shoveled onto Pippa's coffin, Joy placed three small stones on it, symbols of her cubs, hoping they would bring her comfort.

Billy Collins had written Joy two letters on the day he received a cable about Pippa's death, one to Nairobi and one to Meru. Three weeks after the cheetah was buried the leather-bound copy of *The Spotted Sphinx*—"the bundle of hay"—arrived. Joy felt rather different about it now.

This morning your leather-bound Pippa arrived. I broke down when I saw her head on the cover. How very, very kind of you to choose this lovable sketch to place on it. I had no courage to look inside—it is too painful at present. But thank you, dear Billy, for sending this beautiful book. It means more to me than you may imagine. I am so busy that I have no time to think deeper and whenever Pippa comes into my consciousness I cry and cry.

Joy was certainly sentimental about Pippa and her cubs, as she was about every other animal in her life, but she was profoundly serious and rational about the welfare of their species. Cheetahs may lack the majesty of the lion and the ferocity of the leopard, but having hounded these exquisite creatures to the verge of extinction we have no right to leave them there. Joy provided an example, an inspiration and the data we need for bringing them back.

4

The acacias under which George pitched his camp at Mugwongo have all died and fallen now, but close by a sterculia, on whose twisting branches the young lions loved to lie to catch the breeze, still stands. There is no trace of the huts where so many people shared the long African evenings with him and his pride in utter contentment. They included older men like Bernhard Grzimek and Billy Collins; younger ones, Bill Travers, George Schaller, Alan Root, the New York photographer Peter Beard, and John Aspinall, who has spent the fortune derived from his casinos in breeding elephants, tigers and gorillas in England; George's brother, Terence, their cousin Pam Carson; and a succession of assistants.

There was plenty of activity, for the two wild lions having driven Ugas, Boy and the Bisleti lion to the farthest corners of the park were mating with their lionesses. George had no heart to shoot them in cold blood, was tired of discouraging them with his shotgun, and simply confronted them eyeball-to-eyeball—when they reluctantly withdrew.

There were confrontations with Peter Jenkins too. George's life-long loathing of interference had raised his blood to boiling point: he continued to shoot game in defiance, and went further still. "Brian arrived with a party. Against all the rules, walked about among the lions and finally allowed several members to come and pat Girl."

Peter Jenkins, aware of what was happening, retaliated as he had to. The result hurt George.

On October 17, my camp at Mugwongo was demolished and burnt by order of the Gestapo, leaving the enclosure intact.

All George's kit had been moved over to Joy's camp where together they stood and watched five years of his life rising to the clouds in a column of smoke.

Joy had not seen Pippa's cubs since her death, and their reappearance after forty-four days coincided with the culmination of George's battle for his pride, recounted in a long letter to his Canadian friend Alan Davidson, who had recently stayed with him.

On October 29, Joy was out looking for Pippa's cubs when about a mile from the new Park HQ she came upon a lion which appeared to be injured and had a porcupine quill sticking out of its cheek.

I had been summoned to the HQ by Jenkins, who wanted to know why I was still camping at Mugwongo. At this moment Joy arrived with the news about the lion. We went to investigate.

It was poor old Boy. He was very emaciated and with a bad limp in his right foreleg. He was so pleased to see me and made no protest when I pulled the quill out. While I stayed with Boy, Joy went off and got a goat which Boy finished within half an hour. We got him another. I stayed beside Boy during the night as he was in no shape to defend himself against wild lions or other animals.

Next morning Dr. and Mrs. Harthoorn came to have a look at Boy. I gave him an injection of Sernylan. When this took effect, the Harthoorns gave him an anaesthetic and made an examination. Boy had a deep wound in the front of the shoulder and his humerus was fractured. Evidently he had had a battle with a buffalo. The Harthoorns thought that an operation could be performed.

Rather reluctantly Jenkins agreed.

That night Boy would try to sit up and then fall over again, so I got myself one of your bottles of White Horse and my pipe, and sat with my back against him, propping him up. As the night wore on Boy became steadier, myself possibly less so!

Next morning, with the aid of another goat, I got Boy into the back of the old Land-Rover and took him to Mugwongo into the enclosure. I rigged up an old tent as shelter and three camp tables for the operation, it took three and a half hours. A thirteen inch steel pin was hammered along the hollow of the bone. I had to hold the end with a large pair of pliers, while Toni hammered. At the same time it was necessary to pull Boy's leg with a block and tackle to get the fragments in line. In spite of the anaesthetic it must have been a terrible ordeal for poor Boy.

Never before had a major operation like this been performed in the bush.

It was agreed that George would fly Boy to Joy's house at Naivasha, as soon as he was fit enough. In the meantime, Jonny Baxendale and Brian Heath would put up a cage for Boy and a shack for George in the garden. Sue Harthoorn promised to come and see him through the journey. But a few days later the rains broke as never before and it looked as though she would never get through.

Then came a night when all Boy's family—including an old bull elephant that had become George's familiar around the camp—gathered near his enclosure. Apart from the original seven in the pride there were eight surviving offspring, including little Sandie whom George had saved from the dealer. She seemed especially eager to get closer to Boy, so George let her in and she spent the night huddled up to him.

In the morning, without any warning, a small plane slipped through the clouds. Sue had come for Boy, and the pilot warned them they had to leave in the next half hour before the weather closed in again.

A cavalcade escorted the comatose lion to his plane. Joy insisted on bringing a goat for him. Bill Travers had sent a camera team. Girl clearly meant to come too; nothing would dislodge her from the roof of a truck until she saw a young giraffe, gave chase, brought it down and started to eat it.

George's letter to Davidson finished:

Once again Boy was heavily anaesthetised. We had much difficulty getting him into the aircraft. He must weigh all of 450 pounds. Over the Aberdares Range, the aircraft had to climb to 12,000 feet. The combination of altitude and drugs nearly killed Boy. There was no oxygen available. It was touch and go. Mrs. Harthoorn gave him a shot of adrenalin. Just in time the plane went down over Lake Naivasha, landing on a private air strip near Joy's place.

So, with only twenty minutes' notice, George gave up his existence at Meru. He never said a word, but such was the look on his face that, next to the adrenaline for Boy, Sue Harthoorn put out a sedative and a stimulant for *baba ya simba*, the father of the lions.

5

Purgatory is a state of suffering after death through which souls who have not earned immediate entry to heaven, or deserved consignment to hell, may pay off the debt of their worldly sins before final acceptance in paradise. It is a Roman Catholic concept but has parallels in many other religions.

If purgatory does in fact exist, some people seem to experience a foretaste of it in this life, and perhaps Joy was one of them. To many believers, and to some philosophers and psychologists too, life is a challenge to keep our egos in proper control. Too often Joy's was apt to lash out at anyone who failed to comply with the demands of hers. She did much good in the world, through deeds great and small, but she had much to atone for.

To her credit she knew this. The interjection in her letters "I am no angel" was a genuine, not flippant, disclaimer. Her library at Naivasha contained a number of books on faith and devotion, in English and German, many of them published by Collins and sent to her by Billy. Possessing an uncomplicated faith, and a regular Anglican churchgoer, he may have hoped that Joy, like Pierre, might find reassurance from religion. Joy also made a brief attempt to learn yoga and discuss Eastern philosophy with Sue Harthoorn. But at the end of 1969 she wrote to Marjorie Villiers in despair.

> I do not like to cry to you but I was never so low in all my life. Since January I lost Billy and through him my right hand. Now Pippa and finally George. What is the next move?

This is a very good example of the way in which she would sometimes refuse to face facts or would rearrange them to suit her convenience, and would also project on to others emotions, motives, folly or blame that were really her own.

It was not true that she had "lost" Billy: he had simply refused to behave toward his wife the way Joy had toward George. He frequently wrote, came once or twice a year to Kenya and made no attempt to sever their connection.

It was true that she had virtually lost the use of her hand as a result of her own reckless drive to Nairobi to see the leopard cubs and to meet Billy. But he was not the cause of the accident. She had been delighted when he had come to see her in hospital and he had given her no reason to feel jealous. It was only later in England, when her mind was tortured by his coolness toward her, that she projected on to him the sense of provocation that caused her to crash.

Pippa was a true cause for grief. Her slow death from gangrene was peculiarly harrowing, and Joy's ordeal was made worse by the fact that she had painfully scalded her hand at the time.

It was probably true that she had "lost" George, but not in the last twelve months. It had been five years ago that she had so damaged his feelings for her while they were in the Serengeti.

As if to seal her alienation Joy chose this moment to end relations with Sue Harthoorn on the grounds that she had organized publicity for the operation on Boy purely to promote herself. Joy was also angry with her for planning to collaborate with George on a children's book.

It was a further setback still for her morale when the Survival Service Commission told her that they could not support her plan to breed and restock cheetahs in Africa or India because no suitable locations remained. A quarter of a century later, Whipsnade—which has successfully established a cheetah breeding program—is appealing for funds to support an identical project. But is there any suitable habitat available in which to release the cheetahs?

It was the ultimate blow to Joy when her final plea to stay on in Meru was rejected; her generosity had, after all, helped to set it up and kept it going for a number of years.

Toward the end of December she collected stones from the Tana and built a large cairn over Pippa's grave. It is still there, guarded by the bees that have swarmed in a crevice of the stonework.

On Christmas morning she and her African staff listened to a recording of "Silent Night" in Swahili, given to her by the Austrian embassy. The landscape had been transformed by a heavy dew, sparkling in all the colors of the rainbow. Cobwebs hung on the branches of the trees like glittering decorations. Around her, Pippa's cubs jetted on the bushes, gamboled in energetic love play and purred in the sun.

Before George came to collect her from her "spiritual home" on New Year's Eve she had a final meeting with Pippa's daughter Whity, whose damaged leg the Harthoorns had successfully treated. She was pregnant. The cheetah accepted some milk, allowed Joy to take photographs and then slowly disappeared into the bush.

TWENTY-TWO

Each Man Kills

1969–1971

1

George was deeply in love with Joy for the first few years of their marriage. After that I believe he had only one passionate love.

His later attachment to Joy, despite their many battles, remained much closer than a mere formality. It is true that he took great pleasure in the company of such cheerful, attractive and intelligent women as cared to spend time with him; Pam Carson, for instance, came to make curtains for his shack at Elsamere, and Sue Harthoorn looked in on him and Boy. But his passion was reserved for his lions.

Elsa had been a child to him and Joy; Ugas, his favorite during the film and for the first four years at Meru, was like a ward; and Boy, once he was under threat of being shot, and especially after his accident and operation, became a wounded son in need of protection. At Naivasha George's devotion grew deeper.

Boy's progress was slow at first, but when Paul Sayer, a friend of the Harthoorns, removed the pins from his shoulder, his spirits rose, and at night he let out great bellowing roars followed by as many as fifty grunts at a time. Neighbors in between heard a lion belonging to the Bisletis at the far end of the lake returning his compliments.

Stanley, the Meru who had carried meat and water to Pippa, came to look after Boy, but even so George was far too busy with the house and grounds to enjoy the beauties of the lake with its broad fringe of pink water lilies. Unlike many of the birds—from the tiny malachite kingfishers and little white egrets to the goliath herons, the rafts of pink-backed pelicans and the fish eagles, screaming their cheerful and imperious challenge from the tops of the lakeside trees—he had no time to fish.

The omens from Joy were not propitious. She sent scratchy little notes with officious instructions about the house, making it perfectly

324

clear he was there on sufferance. When her time at Meru ran out and George went to collect her at the turn of the year, she was certain she had been ordered to leave only because of his provocative behavior with the lions.

Her frustration grew worse at Naivasha. She discovered that while she now had time to paint and play the piano, the injury to her hand made both impossible. She slammed down the piano lid in tears. Refusing to be defeated she booked herself into the hospital in Nairobi for a third operation, but the mood at Elsamere was baleful.

Unfortunately Boy's shoulder refused to heal and the Harthoorns came out with Paul Sayer to secure the fracture with a permanent plate. The operation was another pioneering surgical feat and lasted five hours. Boy would have died a few nights later had George not rung up Sue for advice. She recommended relays of hot water bottles, squirting brandy down Boy's great throat, and stirring his adrenaline with recordings of lion roars!

During one of her visits Sue noticed that Boy gave Stanley several menacing looks and once even growled at him. She asked George what was the matter between them.

"I think it's because when he was poorly Stanley didn't always treat him with the respect he deserved." He and Joy had always noticed that their big cats were more suspicious of black than white skin, presumably because they had all been nurtured by Joy or him.

By now Joy was in hospital for her hand operation and another storm was brewing. She had told Billy Collins that she regarded him as responsible for crippling her hand and he therefore kept away when he came out to East Africa in February 1970. Instead he went up to Naivasha to see George and Mirella Ricciardi, whose family had a farm on the lake. Mirella, in Joy's eyes, was mistakenly under suspicion of having designs on Billy. Joy told Helen Wolff:

> Billy Collins was here. He never called or sent flowers and instead drove to my home at Naivasha with Sue Harthoorn. He spent five days with Hugo van Lawick and Jane Goodall in the Serengeti. I take this as the end of our friendship as well as our publisher-author relationship.

"End of the Collins era" was George's succinct comment in his diary: Mirella now joined Sue Harthoorn and Sieuwke Bisleti on Joy's growing blacklist.

A few days later, when Joy was home again, it was nearly the end of the Adamson era too. Coming in late one evening, Joy refused to give George food, so he found the key to the larder and helped himself. Joy strode into the kitchen and started to push him around; he slapped her face and reminded her that the house belonged to the Elsa Trust, not to her. Joy took it as a declaration of war and sent for her lawyer next morning.

It was probably no coincidence that this new outbreak of hostilities coincided with Tony Ofenheim's first visit to Kenya since 1935; she stayed at the Lake Naivasha Hotel a few miles down the road. Soon after she left George sent her a bulletin from the battlefront.

They gave me your letter with the traveller's cheques. It is very kind of you to spare a thought for Boy. I did not buy him oysters, but a dish of bone marrow, which is the leonine equivalent!

We could easily have looked in on Boy on Monday on the way to Nakuru as Joy had gone into Nairobi that morning, as I found out later. Relations between us have reached a crisis, final this time I think. She is suing for divorce on the grounds of cruelty. So long as I do not have to pay alimony or her lawyer's fees, I will not contest it. Life might be much easier for me!

The present arrangement—quite amicable—is that I can stay in my shack for as long as I want to, which will not be for very long, as I want to take Boy away as soon as possible and restore him to his natural life.

Now I am trying to persuade Terence, calling upon his brotherly love, to help me out and look after Boy while I go on reconnaissance. It remains to be seen whether "brotherly love" will overcome fear of Joy. Terence has no illusions!

In spite of the fact that our married life has not been exactly a bed of roses, we have gone through a lot together and it is sad that it should break up after 26 years.

It was grand to see you again after all these years. I think you have worn better than I have! I treasure the few days we spent together.

Joy mobilized her doctor and lawyers and started proceedings in earnest. Someone has removed the files that recorded a long list of grievances—some genuine, some embroidered, and some fabricated—from the archive at Elsamere, but it is clear that before long friends like Ken Smith and the Elsa committee urged her to take a clear look at the consequences. Divorce would put an end to the image of Adam and Eve in the garden of Eden, she would have no man to handle her staff with whom she had problems as always and she felt desperately alone if George was away for even a night.

She therefore went into reverse and tried "to soften" him: one evening she played him Beethoven's violin concerto; she left him three eggs on Easter morning; and in lieu of a public divorce she asked him to sign a private code of behavior.

But marriage is a vehicle that runs best on four cylinders: affection, reliability, a common roof and shared income. Joy had taken out the spark plugs once too often and vital parts had corroded.

The threat of divorce merely concentrated George's efforts to find some corner of Kenya in which he could release Boy beyond interference by Joy and the wildlife authorities, without danger to human inhabitants, but with reasonable access by Land-Rover. Needless to say, Joy hated his plan, for it would leave her alone and prolong Boy's human dependence.

At this critical moment George's future was decided in a basement of a London furniture shop, to be precise at the World's End in Chelsea. Bill Travers wandered in there to look for a desk and found himself staring at a three-month-old lion cub. The two young Australians running the shop had bought it for Christmas at Harrods. Recognizing Bill as "George Adamson," they asked him what they could do with it when it grew up.

"The lion—called Christian—is very beautiful indeed," Bill wrote disarmingly to George. "Do you think he could be rehabilitated with Boy?"

Since they had worked on the two films together an extraordinary synergy had developed between George and Bill; between them they could achieve the impossible. So far George had failed to find anywhere suitable for Boy and was dubious about accepting the young English lion, but as the weeks went by the picture gradually changed.

Ken Smith—once more in the role of a benign wizard—suggested that Kora, on the Tana, might fulfill all the criteria for which George was looking; he was warden of the area and would recommend it. George became convinced there would be no more difficulty in releasing Christian than Ugas. And Bill persuaded the government that a film about translocating a lion from London to the land of his forefathers would provide unusually attractive publicity for Kenya.

While approval of this pipe dream was hanging in the balance the wizard was suddenly translated to the Ministry. There he was able to give his recent proposal official assent with a pass of his wand.

Terence survived Joy's wrath while George and Bill went to prospect the country around Kora and choose a campsite under two rocky hills, about twenty miles below Adamson's Falls. As soon as they returned Terence hurried off to open up the old tracks from Garissa to Kora and to start building the camp.

In August George went to meet Bill Travers, Christian the lion, his two young Australian owners and the film crew at the Nairobi airport. They caused quite a sensation, not least because the Australians, Ace Bourke and John Rendall, were dressed in the best Chelsea fashion of the 1960s—if Christian's mane was not fully grown, theirs certainly were. From that day on, George's hair noticeably assumed the respectable length of an Old Testament prophet.

He escorted his exotic party to Kora, then returned to Naivasha for Boy and Stanley—and also Katania, a little orphan cub he had been asked to release with the two other lions. Joy saw this moment as her last chance to place a stumbling block in his path.

She insisted a vet should attest that Boy was in a fit state to travel and, fearing that the Harthoorns were biased, arranged for Paul Sayer to come too, planning to intercept and influence him as soon as he arrived. But she failed and the three vets pronounced Boy recovered and humored her with a formal-looking document. I wonder if they showed her this one too?

University College, Nairobi
Head of Department of Physiology & Biochemistry

13.8.70

CERTIFICATE

This is to certify that we have this day examined a 64-year-old male:- silver mane, good appearance, ribs well sprung, vigorous gait and sunburnt skin.

In my opinion the above named is sound in wind and limb, and free from diseases and defects.

George certainly looked good for another twenty years, but nobody guessed that he would spend them all at Kora.

2

George sent Tony Ofenheim a description of the new home he had found.

> Kora is about 75 miles upstream from Garissa. The area might aptly be described as a waste of dense thorn bush, very hot. Country which no one wants. That is of course why I finally got it, at a price. Probably the remotest place left in Kenya, which suits me fine. Also, a big advantage is that my lions and myself are out of the clutches of the National Parks. The area—about 500 square miles—comes under the Tana River County Council. The members seem well pleased with the arrangement, as they might well be at a rental of £750 per annum!
>
> I chose a camp site at the base of a huge towering rock, about three miles from the river. In order to get to the place it was necessary to cut a track for 25 miles through the bush. Fortunately Terence joined me and did the work.
>
> Joy finally decided not to go ahead with the divorce, possibly because I failed to show much concern at the prospect! Well, I am quite happy to be left in peace at Kora with my lions for the next two years at least, away from the dramas and problems.

The Kora area is shaped like a V, with the Tana running across the top as its northern boundary. Terence's 25-mile track, roughly following the river, joined the camp to Asako on the road to Garissa. After it was completed he leveled a small airstrip near Asako and opened up a network of tracks linking the camp to points on the river and to the road that eventually led to Nairobi.

The Tana, with its riverine forest, winds like a bright green snake through the gray thornbushes growing in an arid wasteland of reddish earth and rocks. It took seven hours to reach the camp from Nairobi by road; by air, and then Terence's track, it took two and a half; either way four-wheel drive was essential.

The camp was enclosed by a twelve-foot-high fence of strong wire mesh, with double gates opening on to the track. On the opposite side its huts faced north toward the tall pink mound of Kora Rock and its smaller companion, with a single boulder on top, Kora Tit. Beyond the hills was the river.

Because Kora is only three miles south of the equator and 300 feet above sea level, the rainfall was sparse and very unreliable and temperatures in the dry season rose to 100°F in the shade by the middle of the day. The camp, on a slight rise, caught the occasional breeze and looked down on a forum of open bush between it and the hills. George had permission to shoot the odd zebra or antelope for the lions and it was here that Stanley put out their meat. There was also a water trough that the lions shared with a jackal, a pair of white-tailed mongooses, a porcupine, an owl and a magnificent martial eagle which George watched killing a guinea fowl.

In addition to the airstrip and Terence's tracks, George's other means of communication, indispensable to many operations in the African bush, was the radio set that Joy made him bring. It was tuned to two different frequencies. One, the Laikipia Security network, was a relic of Mau Mau days, whose controller and subscribers—including farmers, wardens and Joy—came up on the air at regular times in the mornings and evenings. The other was connected, through control in Nairobi, to the national radio and telephone network.

George resented the radio as an intrusion on his privacy, but to Bill Travers, with his film crew to manage, it was an absolute godsend. It kept him in touch with his close friend and anchorman in Nairobi, Monty Ruben.

A trained zoologist and able businessman, Monty Ruben was the resident guru of every famous movie shot in East Africa from *The Lion* and *Born Free* to *Out of Africa* and *Gorillas in the Mist*. He had first met George and Joy at Naro Moru, after which he had constantly given them support from Nairobi and had helped with the negotiations to move to Kora. He had a way of solving any problem that was put to him, technical, diplomatic or personal. Very soon he was the radio godfather of Kampi ya Simba—Camp of the Lions.

George had deliberately brought Christian to Kora a few days before Boy and Katania so that he would have a chance to get over his flight and sudden translation to an environment as different from London as it is possible to imagine. He would need all his poise with Boy.

Christian was exactly a year old when he arrived in Kora. His father had been born in Rotterdam and his mother in Jerusalem, but his African instincts had survived several generations of foreign captivity. During a break in the journey George had to rescue a cow that Christian was expertly stalking.

A few days later, when George arrived with Boy and Katania, Christian's reactions were tested more critically. Boy had to demonstrate his dominance and charged the wire of Christian's enclosure with incredible ferocity—so much so that before George dared let Christian out he used little Katania as a peacemaker, allowing her to consort with both males through a hole in the wire.

At the end of the week George staged the crucial confrontation between Boy and the lion from World's End on a face of bare rock. In a flurry of aggression and dust Boy hurled himself at Christian, who rolled on his back in submission, letting out a howl that ended in a cross between a whine and a rattle. Another of his instincts had survived.

George's routine for introducing new lions to Kora was nearly always the same. For the first few nights he slept in or next to their enclosure, so that they knew his scent and his voice. When he got up he would go and talk to them, taking them a bucket of fresh water as a pretext.

After breakfast he would lead a party on a slow walk to the river so that the lions grew familiar with the smells and excitements of their new world—in Christian's case rather different from the London graveyard where he, Rendall and Bourke had played football. Here Christian had to get used to balls of elephant dung and a pricklier ball that suddenly turned into a porcupine. One morning he pushed his nose into a strange-scented bush while Boy stood well back. Seconds later Christian leapt literally eight feet into the air when a rhino charged out.

George never hurried—unless it was a matter of life and death— and at the end of the stroll he would unhitch his rifle from one shoulder and a leather case from the other and settle down by the river. There he handed around gin and orange from the leather case. All the time, as he chatted and drank, his eye was taking in the messages on the sand, in the trees and from the water.

He could tell how recently a party of elephants had been down to drink. As soon as he saw the storks take off from the *lugga* on the opposite side, and the baboons set up a jabber in the trees, he guessed that a family of Somalis were bringing their camels for a drink. If what looked like a gray-green log drifted toward one of the lions a little faster than the current he reached for his rifle.

When Katania disappeared it took him a day or two to find the right page on the sand to tell him the story. She had followed the other two lions to the river; Boy and Christian had swum across and back again, safely; Katania had followed them into the water but never emerged from it. A crocodile must have taken her in midstream.

By September the main filming was finished, and Ace Bourke and John Rendall went off on safari to look at the Maasai Mara and Serengeti plains. They returned unexpectedly to say good-bye. Christian, by then, had begun to roam far and wide, but within a few minutes he turned up in camp.

"He *knew* they were coming!" George wrote to Joy.

3

George was going to be sixty-five on his first birthday at Kora, a respectable age at which to retire in peace with his lions, far removed from the strife of the everyday world.

He had traveled three thousand miles in search of somewhere as remote as this tract of *nyika*, the wide belt of thorns, commiphora bushes, flat topped acacias and myrrh and frankincense trees, that stretches from Kora to the coast, and from the Sudan in the north to Tanzania in the south. It had kept maritime invaders out of Kenya for a thousand years and even George's neighbors still found it uninviting.

There was little to tempt the Wakamba in the west to encroach on the triangle. Best known for their wood carvings that crowded the markets in Nairobi and Mombasa, they were also respected as seers; one of their elders had predicted the arrival of the "Iron Snake," the East African Railway. They were basically cattle people now, though they had a strong urge to hunt and made regular forays to the Tana for ivory, rhino horn and antelope meat.

The Orma, to the east, around Asako and Mbalambala, an area on the opposite side of the river, were also cattle people, but less enterprising and therefore less trouble.

The only real threat were the Somalis, who violated the old "Somali Line" of the Tana at every opportunity. In the dry season they drove their stock to drink in the river and, although it was forbidden, liked to cross into Kora for the excellent grazing and browse along the banks.

At the end of 1970 the rains failed, the river was scarcely knee-deep and hundreds of goats, sheep and camels made their way over. It was a foretaste of the future, but so far the invasion did not offer serious temptation to the lions.

Rather than spend Christmas alone at Naivasha, Joy decided to inspect the progress at Kora, just as Boy had begun to take possession of at least one local lioness. At night he lifted up his voice and let out his distinctive roar of loud growls followed by a series of grunts— once George counted as many as ninety. As at Meru, the excitement of courting set him on edge. One afternoon when Joy walked past him into camp he gave her a nip on the arm.

Surprisingly she was neither cross nor alarmed, perhaps because she had been thrilled when he had recognized her with a rub of his huge head, and perhaps because she was delighted by his recovery. Yet something had changed in his character and behavior.

Bill Travers, who carried a steel rod in his leg, which had been badly broken during the filming of *Duel at Diablo,* had recommended caution before Boy's release at Kora.

> I have no real sensation below the knee. I certainly can't run as well as I could, nor do I have much control. If this is the case might not Boy eventually become disabled and therefore in danger of becoming, in spite of himself, a man-eater?

Soon after Joy left, Boy suddenly bit Stanley, though not severely. A few days later there was yet another incident. Just before dawn Muga, a laborer, left the compound, against standing orders, to defecate in the bushes. As he squatted his face was seized by Boy.

George rushed out with an electric cattle goad. Boy backed off as soon as George yelled at him but crouched in the bushes looking extremely dangerous. With great presence of mind Simon Trevor, the brilliant cameraman who was shooting the last of the footage for *The Lion from World's End,* drove out in his car with the headlights blazing to rescue Muga, who was taken to hospital with a hole through his cheek.

There is no doubt that sometimes George loved his lions not wisely but too well. To go on treating Boy and Girl like two large dogs as he had at Meru, after the warnings from Joy and Peter Jenkins, and the incident with Mark, smacked of hubris. Now George was led into a sense of false security when Muga quickly recovered and asked to come back to Kampi ya Simba. George told Joy:

> Boy is just the same friendly, good-natured creature as before. He shows absolutely no hostility toward the Africans, greets Stanley the same way as he has always done.

Boy continued to pay court to the lionesses in the neighborhood, much to the displeasure of the local males.

> On most nights we would be woken by the roars of the wild lions and in the morning could trace their movements from their spoor. They usually went around in twos and threes. In this thick bush, where game was difficult to catch, the prides were small, and young males would hunt together, after they had left their family. Lions everywhere adapt to the prevailing conditions.
>
> Christian showed considerable pluck when he went out with Boy, he was too young to be of real help when it came to a serious fight—which it soon did. Boy came in, just as it was getting dark, bitten or slashed on his head, hind legs and scrotum, and with a deep wound on his back—a bite on the spine is one of the lion's most effective techniques to paralyse or cripple its adversary.
>
> I sprinkled the wound with sulfanilamide powder, covered it with gentian violet and tried to confine Boy to the enclosure after dark. The second night he refused to come in, so I parked my Land-Rover close to him and went to sleep on the roof. I woke with a frightful start, an hour later, as the car suddenly swayed under the weight of a lion which had leapt up beside me. As soon as I could find my torch I saw it was Christian. I did not quickly forgive him for the shock—particularly as he refused to leave me for the rest of the night.

Paul Sayer flew up and removed two large splinters of bone from Boy's vertebrae while George and Simon Trevor constantly swabbed the gaping wound with hot water and Epsom salts.

The war took on an even more unpleasant turn when George was sent a series of five more young lions, all of which had been trapped or orphaned and were in need of a home. Christian welcomed them immediately; Boy granted them grudging acceptance; two wild lions offered no quarter at all. Very soon George found one of his new young lionesses dead in the bush, bitten through the back of her neck.

It was a repetition of the scenario at Mugwongo, and George followed it to its logical conclusion. He reached for his gun and finding the two wild males in the bush, shot one of them. He was not prepared to give up and return the remaining lions to captivity, so until Christian was mature and Boy fully recovered, he would have to level the odds.

He hated to kill, and applying the doctrine of minimum force he refrained from shooting the second lion. He also very much reduced his killing of game for his pride. At the most he had shot an average of one waterbuck, antelope or buffalo each week—no more than a pride of the same size would have killed on their own. From then on he started to buy camels and cows from Mbalambala. It was expensive, but one day it saved his life.

4

By the beginning of June 1971 an atmosphere of tranquillity descended on Kora for the first time since George and Boy had arrived there.

Simon Trevor had taken all the footage he needed and vanished. Terence had temporarily completed his roadwork, paid off his labor force and gone back to finish building his house at Malindi. George was alone in camp with Kimani, his cook, and Stanley to help with the lions—though he told Joy the Meru was now "scared stiff of them."

In fact Boy was sufficiently recovered to look after himself and stay away from camp for a week at a time, especially if there were lionesses at large to engage his attentions. George therefore felt he could concentrate on the education of Christian and the other four youngsters, and the events of June 6, the worst day of his life, took him completely unaware. He described them to Joy.

All that happened is like a bad dream. At times I imagine I will wake up and find everything normal.

Boy had been away for the night, and in the morning George took Christian and the others to a ridge below Kora Rock where he left them and went back to breakfast. While he ate he heard Boy drinking from the water trough.

> Just as Kimani had come to clear the table we heard cries behind camp. I jumped up and for an instant was undecided whether to take the rifle or the electric cattle prodder. Then I knew that I would probably have to shoot Boy and took the rifle.
>
> As soon as I got out of the back gate I saw Boy with Stanley in his mouth about 250 yards away. As I rushed at him he dropped Stanley and moved away about twenty yards. Stanley was sitting on the ground, covered in blood. I ran on past him a few feet and shot Boy through the heart.
>
> In a matter of two minutes I was back with Stanley and shouted to Kimani to help. The two of us supported Stanley and started to walk back to camp. After only a few paces he collapsed. I ran for the station wagon and we got him into my hut, by which time he was unconscious. As I started to examine his wounds, he died.

Once Boy had bitten him, Stanley never had a chance. A tooth had severed his jugular and he was dead in less than ten minutes.

George went straight to the radio. He had been advised that in an emergency he should contact the police at Garissa, nearly eighty miles away, via Nairobi control, but he was now told that since it was Sunday they would be off the air till the following morning.

Determined that the other lions should not find Boy dead by the road George heaved his corpse into the Land-Rover, drove to a *lugga* a few hundred yards from camp, dug a grave in the shade of a tree and lowered the lion into it with a block and tackle.

His diary ended that night:

> Lions very quiet. They know something has happened. Boy my old friend—farewell.

"It was terrible to do this to my old friend and to part from him in such dreadful circumstances," George wrote in a letter. Years later, on separate occasions, Pam Carson and I noticed he could not speak of Boy's death without a break in his voice.

When he could not raise the police early the next morning George started to dig a grave for Stanley. But by 10:30 he got through to

Nairobi and was emphatically ordered not to touch the body. During a ghoulish day he waited impatiently for the police to make the five-hour journey to Kora, was roughly cross-questioned and, with Stanley's body beginning to decompose in the heat, obliged to dig up Boy to prove he had shot him. The police did not leave until nine o'clock at night.

Neither George, nor Joy, nor the police in Meru, could trace any of Stanley's family, and at the age of 28, he was buried in a common grave at Garissa. George felt profound distress at the young man's death. He made a clear written report of the accident for the police, the District Commissioner and the Wildlife Ministry.

He never really understood what had happened. It is possible that Stanley was sitting or squatting at the time of the accident. In the end George came to the conclusion that Stanley must have ignored frequently repeated orders and, believing all the lions were well away from camp, had gone out to look for honey. Unexpectedly he had encountered Boy and, instead of holding his ground, had run for the gate. His flight would have brought Boy after him.

George's subsequent letters all reiterate Boy's good nature and his remarkable tolerance—of strangers, film crews, battle injuries, operations and transfer from one habitat to another. But although he refers to the episode with Mark Jenkins, he makes no mention, either in his letters or reports, of the earlier incidents with Arun Sharma, Joy, Muga and Stanley himself.

I feel certain this was a form of blindness rather than dissemblance, but his disregard for other people's warnings contained an element of hubris which—in the pattern of Greek tragedy—was followed by nemesis or retribution.

Among his papers I found some lines from Oscar Wilde's *The Ballad of Reading Gaol*, written out in an unknown hand, ending:

> Some do the deed with bitter tears,
> And some without a sigh
> For each man kills the thing he loves
> Yet each man does not die.

George had to live on through his nightmare, but there were others to share it.

Bill Travers had been planning to come back and make a second film about Christian but was advised to keep away for the time being. He wrote to George:

> The saddest part is that it happened to Stanley and not one of us. Both Ginny and I felt personally involved and that we should be there to answer for our responsibilities and support you.

He and Ginny had, after all, seen George off on the road to Kora when they helped rescue Boy and Girl from captivity, and again when Bill brought Christian to Africa.

Much more unexpected, though she never failed George in any acute crisis, was Joy's reaction. When she first heard the news over the radio her response was frantic concern for her reputation and George's, which he calmed with a few quiet words. Her considered position, in the light of all that had passed between them, I find very moving.

> When I read your letter I cried, and wish, like you that it were only a dream.
>
> Should it come to the worst, consider Elsamere: we could enlarge the compound and you could live with your lions here. Of course it would be ghastly to come to this end, but please do not destroy the lions.
>
> I will help you as much as I can. I feel so upset for you, knowing how you loved Boy and the whole Kora idea. But should you have to leave, don't despair. We can afford to feed the lions and keep them, in your company, away from zoos and orphanages.

So unshakable was George's faith in his lions, even after this catastrophe, that he recorded his wishes about what should happen if he himself was killed.

> My current occupation of rehabilitating lions carries with it a certain amount of risk, not from my own lions, but rather from situations which unwittingly they may lead me into. Should such an eventuality arise, resulting in my death, I earnestly request that my remains be interred alongside Boy, without any fuss or bother whatsoever.

Joy with Elsa and her sisters at Isiolo in 1956.
Right: Marjorie Villiers, a founder of Harvill Press,
who in 1959 spotted that *Born Free* would be a bestseller. *Below:* George and Elsa at two years old.

Left: Pati, the rock hyrax adopted by Joy. She had a weakness for spirits but became an excellent nanny for the three lion cubs.
Below: George and Elsa on the beach at Kiunga.

"I love Elsa more than I have any man," Joy said, but she insisted that she be set free and not kept in captivity.

A bath and a siesta on safari with Elsa in 1958.

Above: Elsa threatened Nuru when he went to cut the throat of the buffalo she had brought down until she realized he was helping her. *Below:* Elsa and her six-week-old cubs.

Above: Joy with Billy Collins, her publisher, beside the River Ura in 1960.
Left: Elsa's cubs take their chance of freedom in the Serengeti, 1963.

Above: Virginia McKenna and Bill Travers, the stars of *Born Free*, photographed with George by Joy, 1965. *Below:* Joy, Virginia and Bill, with the Queen at the Royal premiere of the film in 1966.

Above left: "*That* is how you still are in my mind." Joy's first husband sent her this 1937 photograph after she signed his copy of *Born Free,* without looking up, in Cape Town in 1963.
Above right: Joy's notorious leopard-skin coat.
Left: Pippa, the cheetah, before she was given to Joy in 1965.

1969. *Above:* Two of Pippa's last cubs in Meru; the cheetahs are nearly full grown. *Right:* Joy nurses the dying Pippa.

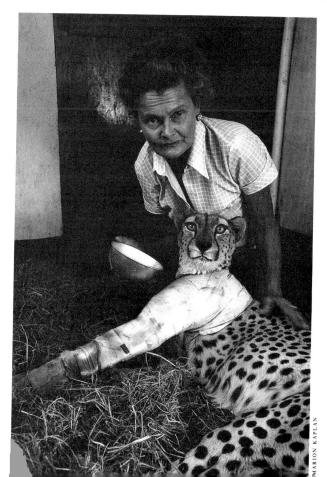

JONNY BAXENDALE

Above: George with Ugas, George's largest and favorite film lion after his release in Meru.
Below: The sedated lion Boy is taken to the plane to be flown to Naivasha after the operation on his foreleg.

Above: Elsamere, Joy's house on Lake Naivasha.
Below left: A Verreaux eagle owl displays, and (*right*) two colobus monkeys scrap together.

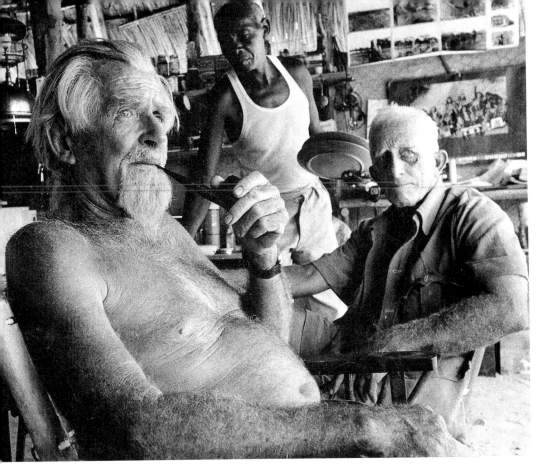

Kora in the 1970s.
Above: George, his brother,
Terence, and Hamisi, their
cook. *Left:* Tony Fitzjohn,
George's companion and
assistant for sixteen years,
with Christian, the lion from
London.

Kora. *Right:* George with Christian. *Below*: Kampi ya Simba. The Tana River is to the north, beyond the top of the photograph.

Left: George, Tony Ofenheim
and Christian at Kora in 1972.
Below: Joy at Shaba in 1977 with
(*left to right*) Jock Rutherfurd,
Martin Clarke, Makedde and Kifosha,
who first joined her in 1943.

Shaba. *Above:* Penny the leopard and her two cubs in July 1979. *Right:* the last photograph of Joy with Penny, taken shortly before Joy was stabbed to death, January 3, 1980.

Kora. George in his Land-Rover, nick-named the Nightingale. He was shot and killed at its wheel, August 20, 1989.

TWENTY-THREE

Alone by the Lake

1971–1976

1

The authorities made no attempt to close down George's camp at Kora after Stanley's death; his presence contributed too much to such a remote and impoverished corner of the country. Joy therefore realized she must face life alone at Naivasha.

"He sits in the bush, sleeping half the time because of the heat," Joy wrote petulantly of George. It was untrue although he certainly relished the peace, seclusion and slow rhythm of life on the Tana.

Joy, on the other hand, started to throw herself into concentrated bouts of correspondence and writing, hectic worldwide promotion tours and entertaining the stream of visitors she encouraged to call on her at Elsamere.

You can still see the house, much as it was, and even stay there. Inside and out there are lively reminders of her presence. The noisiest and most exotic are the black and white colobus monkeys swinging through the stand of tall fever trees along the lake. There was only one pair left when Joy arrived and but for her they might have been the last.

The colobus monkeys were quick to produce a son, and Joy watched them teach him the acrobatic skills of survival. But one day the father disappeared and Joy found his mummified body, peppered with shot, high in the fork of a tree. She was heartbroken by the mother's forlorn and terrified expression but gradually restored her confidence with fruit and vegetables, and the baby began to flourish.

To give them company Joy released a young orphan into the mother's care but it died in torrential rain after two nights of freedom.

However the son grew up to sire a baby by his mother, and Joy released two more orphans rescued, in the nick of time, from illicit export by the Game Department. Together they established a troop, and today their leader lords it over the garden and forest, letting out his thrilling roar, a curious rattling whoop, in the middle of the night or just before dawn.

The Verreaux eagle owls Joy discovered nesting by the lake also provided entertainment and drama. The largest owls in Africa, they sport ear tufts and striking pink eyelids, and emit a lugubrious baritone hoot. When they virtually wiped out the population of mole rats and snakes in the garden, Joy fed them chicken heads, to save the small birds from a similar fate.

As soon as the chick hatched the parents had to fight a continuous battle to protect it from the fish eagles and auger buzzards. In the following season a second chick was born and curiously tried to drive away its sibling which was as conscientious as the parents in feeding and protecting it.

Before long, during one of George's rare visits, he found another eagle owl in the forest: it looked as if it were dead, but George was not convinced. He wrapped the motionless bird in a sack, put it in a cage with a pigeon he had shot and disappeared. When he returned an hour later the inert owl was alone in the cage.

It had put on a masterly act for it only had a damaged eye and a broken wing. After it had recovered Joy watched it frighten a large genet cat off its meat one night. A Verreaux eagle owl once put a rhino to flight.

Joy next befriended the wildest waif she ever took in—a jackal from Kora with a swollen and gangrenous leg which George thought had been bitten by a puff adder. She nursed it and agonized over its precarious recovery for five months. It was so shy she had to give it a protective screen of sacking; it scarcely ever let her touch it, and refused to play with a pye-dog puppy she found to amuse it. The leg healed but remained permanently stiff; nevertheless the jackal finally broke out of its cage near her veranda and was not seen again.

Joy sketched the jackal—as she did the monkeys and owls—for she found that with tremendous effort she could paint again, though with none of her former delicacy.

Her most powerful urge at Elsamere was to adopt a leopard cub and introduce her to the wild, as she had Elsa and Pippa. It was ambitious, for she was now over sixty and leopards are notoriously farouche and peculiarly secretive during the early life of their cubs.

In September 1972, Father Botta, who had given her the leopard cub at Meru, suddenly offered her a second. She again fell wildly in love with the tiny kitten, which she named Taga, and suggested to George that they might collaborate over its release. "I desperately need help as I have three full-time jobs and it takes a heavy toll on my health."

After ten days she had to drive the cub into Nairobi to obtain medication for it prescribed by a vet. George heard from her again.

> Since I wrote to you I killed the darling leopard by sheer stupidity. While I went to buy prescriptions I locked Taga inside the car. I had put her into an airline bag with the zip open, closed the windows for security, and left the car under a shady tree.
>
> When I returned one hour later there was no movement inside the bag. I found Taga dead—suffocated. I cannot tell you my remorse. I keep too busy to have time to think, but the nights are hell.

She had to wait another four years to redeem the disaster.

2

Joy's three jobs were running Elsamere, carrying on her writing and film work and managing the business of the Elsa Appeal.

During her years at Naivasha from 1970 to 1976 she wrote the greater part of four books. *Pippa's Challenge* (1972) included Pippa's death and ended with Joy's departure from Meru, to which she went back at least once or twice a year. Sometimes she was lucky and found one of Pippa's cubs. In 1976 she spent a day watching Whity with her sixth litter; she was now ten years old. Joy also always made time for tending Elsa's and Pippa's graves, where she unfailingly experienced reassurance and peace.

At the end of 1972 she published her sketchbook *Joy Adamson's Africa*. Attractive examples of her paintings, drawings and doodles were reproduced with short commentaries on the various types of subject she had attempted. Her landscapes were limited to two, for they lacked perspective, like her view of life as a whole.

The third book was the autobiography she finally called *The Searching Spirit* (1978). In her foreword Elspeth Huxley said there was not a dull page in it. Always economical Joy only touched on Elsa and

Pippa, but made considerable use of her unpublished scripts going back to 1944, including those about her safaris, adopted animals, travels abroad and life at Elsamere—none of which stood up as books in their own right.

The main drawback was that Joy had set herself an impossible task. She could not tell the full story of her life without including her marriages and she could not be honest about them while all three husbands were still alive.

> I tried to keep my shortcomings balanced with my positive qualities, but the experiences which influenced my character most are for the confessional or a psychoanalyst only.

Marjorie Villiers had to eliminate many inaccuracies, and there were others, which she could not check, that remained. She also removed cryptic references to Joy's emotional relationships—occasionally quoted in this biography—because they made no sense without their background. As a result Joy told George that "it's no longer my book." Marjorie's task of wrestling with the script was made no easier by the side effects of Joy's fluctuating feelings for Billy Collins, whom she saw once or twice a year in Kenya or London. A few extracts from her diary reveal them.

> Some terrible foreboding. Collins has all he needs—I can die? . . .
> Billy 6.00 pm. Music. Nice dancing—he is so young . . .
> Billy is so old. He escorts me to Piccadilly—2 kisses—we still love each other—only our eyes talk . . .
> Billy never looks back—wants to go up Mt Longonot at 73! Does not smoke, little drink, loves walking, good brain—so stimulating.

Their snatched romantic interludes, alone together in Kenya, were interspersed with months when his refusal to demonstrate his affection in London aroused all Joy's old anger. This led her to demand impossible terms for her books and even accuse his firm of "shady play."

The fourth script was published posthumously as *Friends from the Forest* in 1981. It is a short book telling the full story of the monkeys and owls.

Much of Joy's time at Naivasha was taken up with films. In 1971 Carl Foreman and the producers of *Born Free* returned to make *Living*

Free, which included the story told in *Forever Free*. Nigel Davenport and Susan Hampshire played the leads, but this time there was no genuine interaction between the actors and the lions, and although the film was largely shot along the lake near Naivasha, George and Joy took no part in its production.

Despite the film's failure to make an impact the same producers came back yet again in 1974 to shoot a TV series for Screen Gems "based on" *Born Free*. Gary Collins and Diana Muldaur played George and Joy. Although Joy had the right to comment on the scripts Foreman persuaded her to accept that 80 percent of the material might be fictional. After five episodes production was summarily halted. The truncated series was broadcast all over the world but bore no resemblance to the life that George and Joy had been leading for the last thirty years.

There were, however, three documentaries that offer glimpses of their real world. The first, about Pippa in Meru, was made for television and shown by London Weekend in 1970. The second, financed by Joy with the encouragement of her trustees, was about her own life. It contains revealing interviews with her and members of her family. At one point she remarks, "You see I had to marry George because of Elsa." To her this was a matter of destiny; she had married George twelve years years before they adopted the lioness.

The film was broadcast by the BBC and is frequently shown at Elsamere today. Finally, in the United States, Benchmark edited for educational distribution the original 16-mm footage of Elsa, in whose name Joy had launched her worldwide appeal.

In January 1977 the Austrian Ambassador to Kenya presented Joy with the Austrian Cross of Honor for Science and Arts. It was the highest distinction of its kind the country of her birth could bestow on her.

3

The Elsa Wild Animal Appeal was originally set up in London in 1961. Similar appeals were established in other countries during the next fifteen years. Behind the Iron Curtain Joy gave her local royalties to swell the donations she and others succeeded in soliciting.

The structure of her company, trusts and Appeal, all interrelated through their share holding, boards and committees, enabled her to spread the burden of deciding what to do with her money while retaining control of it.

In effect the Appeal gave her an armor of light in which she felt confident to spend, give, withhold (from George), ask for more and travel the world, promoting her books and films and passing on the message she had received through her relationship with Elsa. Increasingly lonely, she also found the Appeal was a bridge to other people.

Her generosity and vehement belief that in order to survive man must radically alter his attitude to the natural world were both utterly genuine. Reflecting this, the two principal activities of her international appeals were grant making and spreading the word. Her devoted boards and committees threw themselves energetically into fund-raising, but it was often uphill work.

In Great Britain the secretary of the Appeal, Jean Aucutt, is the only officer to have served it continuously for thirty years. Trustees have come and gone and only once did the majority all feel inclined to go together, when Joy refused to contribute to George's work at Kora. For professional advice about applications for grants, they relied on Mark Boulton, the Director of the International Centre for Conservation Education in Gloucestershire. Increasingly they have supported his courses for game management trainees from all over the world.

The Elsa Appeal got off to a shaky start in the United States. Joy primed its initial expenses with £20,000 but saw no return until the early 1970s, when a group of devotees in California appointed a teacher, Leo Lobsenz, as their executive officer. He was greatly helped by Peter Rasmussen as general manager. Funds were raised in Elsa's name by a variety of means for a variety of ends.

Tippi Hedren, the actress, gave the Appeal her full-hearted and valuable support, which included lending lion cubs for fund-raising occasions; an aspiring volunteer arrived for a meeting with a full grown tiger; Margot Henke, who shared her New Jersey apartment with her husband and twenty cats, handled most of Joy's American fan mail; Marlin Perkins, presenter of *Wild Kingdom* on television, and his wife, Carol, initiated the foundation of the first wolf sanctuary in the United States; and Carleen Flannagan originated the idea of Elsa Clubs in schools—there were eventually five hundred.

As a result of these efforts donations were made to create imaginative teaching kits and to help, among other causes, those of grizzly bears, dolphins, sea otters and bald eagles.

At the heart of the Appeal was an almost electrical, person-to-person, transmission of enthusiasm for the protection of wildlife. In fact, the dedication of Carol Perkins—who saw Joy two or three times each year over eighteen years—Margot Henke, and Leo Lobsenz stemmed from the personal impact Joy made on each of them when they met her in Kenya for the first time.

This is how Betty Henderson, another teacher, who met Joy by chance birdwatching in Hell's Gate, volunteered to become the moving spirit of the Appeal in Canada. She was musical—like Margot Henke, who trained as an opera singer—and played the piano beautifully, which forged an immediate bond with Joy when she first called on her at Elsamere. Like Leo Lobsenz, she was unmarried; and since they were in Kenya at the same time Joy engineered the meeting, though not the wedding, she hoped for between them!

The Canadian Appeal continues to raise money today with the help of one of its founding directors, the distinguished wildlife artist Robert Bateman, and among other causes it supports the fascinating owl research and rehabilitation center near Niagara, where all seventeen Canadian owl species are treated and studied, from the great white snowy owls to the tiny gray saw-whets. Projects to conserve the Northern swift fox, cougar, Vancouver Island marmot and common loon have all received grants from the Appeal.

There were occasions when Joy's uncontrollable urge to dominate any enterprise with which she was connected, and the inevitable backlash from this, nearly caused terminal crises in both the United States and Canada.

During Joy's seven years at Naivasha, her travels to support her books, films and Appeal also took her to Europe, Russia, Thailand and Japan. In Russia they rolled out the red carpet for her at the ballet, led her up into the mountains in search of wild boar and bears and proudly showed off their herds of zebras, eland, buffalo and bison, incongruously roaming the steppes. They asked her to add a graft to the Friendship Tree, a citrus tree that commemorates among others, Darwin, Pasteur, Tolstoy, Tchaikovsky, Pushkin and Gandhi, either with grafts of different fruits made in their names or with soil on its roots from their graves. Joy inserted her graft in the name of Elsa. Friederike Gessner had come a long way from Troppau by an exotic and improbable route. On her return to Kenya she was met at the airport by the Soviet Ambassador, Dimitri Gorunov.

As Joy had always intended, the bulk of her money was spent in Kenya, where she was in demand as lecturer at the Museum and as a celebrity at fund raising events. Each of the Elsa projects was appraised by her committee. Much went to the Wildlife Clubs of Kenya: most young Kenyans, certainly most children in the country, have never seen a lion, and until they do they cannot be expected to care about the animals' future. The large sum of £40,000, left to the Appeal by an American, Beatrice Lehman Hill, was committed to securing Hell's Gate and the splendid hinterland behind Elsamere as a National Park, at a time when the government could not afford to acquire them without help.

The creation of this park, among other factors, decided the Elsa trustees to establish Elsamere as a conservation center after Joy's death. The forest, the colobus monkeys, the unsurpassed bird life around the lake and the hippos on the lawn at night are living memorials to one aspect of her questing spirit. Evidence of others, her easel, sketches, carvings, photographs, typescripts, library and trophies—even the tall and broad-brimmed straw hat she bought in Niger to see her across the Sahara—is on display in the large room where she used to sleep.

4

Joy's habits were as Spartan at Elsamere as they were on safari. She slept on a truckle bed, her meals were simple and monotonous and she wore bush clothes except when at home to a party of visitors. Her only indulgence was her evening Cinzano, of which she sometimes had too much when angry or morose.

Letters were her only sure means of communication with the outside world. The radio was either faulty or permanently jammed with farmers and missionaries chattering in English, American, Italian or Swahili. A single line served all the telephones round the lake so that too was either engaged or unanswered by the exchange.

Joy's neighbors Kitchener and Millicent Morson were old friends of George and after a time scarcely a week went by without Kitch spending hours on the drains, cables, roofs and cages at Elsamere. Theirs was a friendship in the classic tradition of the Kenyan pioneers. Her neighbors on the other side, Hans and June Zwager, owned Oserian, the exotic and notorious Moorish house known as the Djinn Palace, relic of the Erroll scandals. They were generous hosts and often exchanged visits with Joy.

The twelve-mile stretch of road into Naivasha was one of the worst in the country. During the rains a car slid about on the mud and water rose above the axles; in the dry season it foundered in dust and oncoming traffic was hidden in a cloud of white powder. In any weather the cruelest section was two miles of tarmac cratered like a battlefield. Always impatient, Joy once overtook a dawdling car with perfect mistiming, collided and seriously hurt her right arm.

Her awareness of what she called "the mind-body act" never prevented her from damaging herself when she was particularly on edge. Quite apart from the car accident, she broke her elbow and an ankle and had two more operations on her hand.

She could not be bothered to take her broken plate to a dentist and had it glued together in the local garage. She even resented the time it took to go into hospital to have an arthritic hip replaced with a steel one.

Finally I got so "breakdownish" that they released me a few days early to stop me bolting.

I have a woman to bath me but she and I don't fuse and I have to help her more than she helps me, although she is five years younger. There is so much to catch up on, but all the time this irritating old lady screeches at me not to overdo things while she knits and does nothing.

Joy's attitude was typical of the way she regarded almost all the women, young, middle-aged or elderly, whom she employed to help her. They were apt to be branded as incompetent, cold, neurotic, egocentric or senile. One was "a crank, bogus and dogmatic. I can't quite put my finger on it but I have a feeling she would have turned Elsamere into a brothel without difficulty!"

Her life might have been easier if she had retained a dependable African staff, but unlike most Europeans with sizable houses she appointed no responsible *mzee* to manage it for her. As a result a constant procession of house servants, gardeners, drivers and night-watchmen accused of idleness, insolence, drunkenness or theft left Elsamere in defiance, confusion or under arrest.

One of the burglars was sentenced to five years. We found Elsa's milk tooth mounted on my wedding ring—the only thing I had really mourned. My model evening dresses had been used as rags.

It is amusing to see the difference between the cultures when the things one person values are treated like junk by another.

After a very old game scout had called in search of George and a handout, and had whispered that her staff was planning to murder her, Joy had nightmares. Aware that she was growing increasingly isolated, she needed, and sometimes took, sedatives or sleeping pills.

She had not trusted anyone completely since the wounds inflicted by her first love and her parents' separation had never healed. In December 1973, two weeks before her mother died, she wrote this to Joy.

I am sorry that you can only think of us as enemies and that you do not want to visit us.

Joy willingly waived her share of her mother's small legacy in favor of her sisters' children—Traute's son and Dorle's son and three daughters. But her animosity against her two sisters continued to fester. In October 1974, she wrote to Traute: "I never had the feeling that you were fond of me. On my last visit I was left with the impression you hated me." By the end of the year Traute had died, too, of cancer.

Joy's correspondence with Dorle was little different. All three sisters found problems in relating to one another as they did to men.

On the other hand, Joy received unfailing encouragement in a flow of letters from the wise women who had helped guide her fortunes for so long—Alys Reece, Elspeth Huxley, Marjorie Villiers and Helen Wolff. She tried in vain to persuade them to come and stay at Elsamere, and Ernestine Nowak declined her invitation to come and live in George's cottage.

There were, however, good friends from America who regularly visited her in the course of their safaris in Kenya. In a letter to one of them Joy touched on the panacea for loneliness she still longed to find.

SEPTEMBER 21, 1974

I try to make myself independent of spiritual and physical help as it is always painful when I get let down. I know that I have to pay a high price for not being a cabbage but sometimes I love to cuddle up on a comforting shoulder and share my ideas with a man. Well, that may remain an unfulfilled dream! I have several very good friends here, and all over the world, but no shoulder!

5

In 1975 it looked as though Joy might have discovered a man after her own heart. This letter arrived, out of the blue, from California.

MARCH 25, 1975

Dear Mrs. Adamson,

The papers tell me that you are now living on Lake Naivasha. I have read your books and followed your career with especial interest.

I am writing to ask you a favour. Year after year acquaintances visiting Kenya have promised to obtain photographs of the Moorish house I built at the end of the lake and nobody has kept their promises.

Would you be kind enough to have some colour photos made for me?

Wishing you much happiness and long life on beautiful Lake Naivasha.

Believe me, Yours sincerely,

C. S. Ramsay-Hill.

Oserian, which has been featured in many books and films about Kenya, is an exotic monument to balmier days, while Cyril Ramsay-Hill emerges from the correspondence that follows as perhaps the most polished member of the *White Mischief* set and its last articulate survivor. He creates an aura of wistful romance that opens and flowers with the forlorn courage and charm of a rose in December.

Joy's answer first put him in touch with the Zwagers at Oserian—which she referred to inadvertently as the "Gin" Palace—and then went on to give him a vivid picture of her life at Elsamere and her feelings for Naivasha. He quickly responded.

APRIL 20, 1975

Your warm and delightful letter brought tears to my eyes and I confess without shame.

I cannot imagine why the poor house is stuck with a label which sounds like a pub in the East End! The address was simply "Oserian," Naivasha. Oserian meant a place of peace and as that was the name of the local feature, it seemed appropriate; but there was never any peace in it.

My maternal grandmother was Spanish and descended from Pope Alexander VI, "Borja" in Spanish and "Borgia" in Italian. Her ancestor was the Pope's second bastard. Spending many holidays in the old house in Seville, dating from the sixteenth century, and being familiar with similar places in Morocco and Tunisia, I was always attracted to that type of house with its graceful arches and a fountain murmuring in a tiled courtyard; so when I came out to Kenya for a safari in 1923 and saw Lake Naivasha, I determined to build my dream house there in a perfect setting. I bought the 5,000 acres with about three miles of lake front for approximately half a crown an acre!

Oserian was no Moorish palace; it was an unpretentious five bedroom house, certainly very exotic and unique for the Kenya of the twenties. The master bedroom had French furniture. The bath room was certainly rather astonishing—it was my wife's taste. Does it still exist with its sunken bath and black and gold mosaic?

The library at the end of this side was pure Spanish with its high coloured ceilings and heavy beams. It was filled with 15th and 16th century Spanish originals, Spanish chairs with black leather seats, a painted Cordoban screen, a long refectory table with a centre cloth of faded red velvet from the altar of the cathedral at Seville.

Next to the library was a very small room with a heavy door always kept locked. It contained my secret library of rare Spanish books of romance and chivalry in splendid bindings and a very special collection of 18th century French originals, illustrated, of the choicest pornography of the Louis XV and Louis XVI period! Highly erotic pictures by Boucher, Lancret, Fragonard, and Watteau from the collection of the Duc de Richelieu. All to be found to-day in the Pierpont Morgan Library in New York!

I shall write to you again in a few days to appease your curiosity about "Oserian" in the twenties.

You are utterly "sympathique," I wish we had a word in English to express it!

Joy replied at length to this tantalizing letter, mentioning a picture of his wife, Mary. Since Mary had stayed on in the house with her next husband, the notorious Lord Erroll, Joy referred to his murder—and to her own friendship with June Carberry, who had dined with Erroll on the night he was shot.

> The life-size portrait of your wife is still hanging in what was your library.
>
> I knew June Carberry quite well and never forgot June's reply when I asked her how she got away in court without giving important evidence? She said "Well, one is not obliged to answer all the questions and the less one says in court, the less they have to convict you."

Joy did not have to wait long for the next installment of the Oserian saga.

JUNE 16, 1975

You amaze me that there is a picture of my wife Mary hanging in the Spanish library. I don't remember her sitting for anyone but Augustus John, who made a preliminary sketch of her Titian hair and green eyes—she was one of the most beautiful women I have ever seen—but the portrait was never finished. She had a falling-out with him over the price, or he pinched her bottom, I forget which.

Again, I was astonished to learn that June Carberry was mixed up in the murder of Erroll. Beryl Markham, whom I knew intimately and came here from New York in 1938 (I got her a job at Paramount Studios as technical adviser on an African picture starring another old friend Madeleine Carroll), told me that the Greswolde-Williams girl had driven off from the house at Ngong with Erroll, shot him with Jock Broughton's revolver and nipped back into the house and replaced the gun. Reason—Erroll, after getting his hands on all the money she had, had jilted her for Diana, the young heiress Jock Broughton brought out to Kenya, and would eventually have run off with her had he lived.

She added that Mary, before she died, was unrecognisable, bloated and alcoholic on the booze and drugs that Erroll forced on her. Erroll was a professional pimp—penniless, he lived on his wife's money (née Lady Idina Sackville) and then Mary's, and then on whatever woman was keeping him. I did not shoot him, although sorely tempted, as it was pointed out to me that I should certainly hang—it was better to lose a wife than one's life.

Yesterday there was a big "do" in Studio City for the Elsa Animal Appeal. I made my humble contribution by buying a picture of a Rendille woman which you painted at Laisamis.

My dear lady, I am as anxious to know you as you are to know me, so we must find a way. After all, you are a worldwide celebrity and I am the living relic of a vanished way of life and a decaying caste; albeit a highly civilised animal, many faceted like a man of the Renaissance, and with, thank God, a great if caustic sense of humour. I think you would find me entertaining and I feel already the strong pull of your personality across half the world.

Those who knew the three Greswolde-Williams sisters cannot believe the allegation in this letter. In her reply Joy reverted to the murder and sent him a pressing invitation to stay at Elsamere while she hunted for somewhere to release the leopard cub she hoped to adopt.

Ramsay-Hill was quick to answer.

JUNE 28, 1975

Your description of Elsamere and walking up into the hills and meeting eland give me desperate nostalgia and longing.

It is darling of you to ask me to house sit while you go off into the bush for years to make your leopard study but I want to be with you, and besides I would have no control over your servants. Remember I am an old-time Kenya hand.

I gave orders, and very strict ones, to Billea Issa, my head servant who was with Denys Finch Hatton for years, or to Sallatt (the poor fellow was burnt up in the crash of Denys's plane).*

These two very aristocratic Somali gentlemen (each had his own boy to look after him) ran the household silently and efficiently. I took them to Europe twice. They ordered Savile Row suits and each of them sported a gold-headed Malacca cane. Their conduct was always irreproachable even when tempted by amorous French maids! I loved them dearly.

---

* According to Finch Hatton's biographer, Errol Trzebinski, it was a Kikuyu named Kamau who was killed with him in the crash.

In July Joy arranged for Arnold Schapiro, an American photographer who was staying with her, to take the remaining color slides of Oserian for which Ramsay-Hill had asked. Schapiro promised to deliver them to California himself.

Ramsay-Hill replied with, among other things, a long story about Frédéric de Janzé, whose wife, Alice, had wounded one of her Happy Valley lovers with a pistol at the Gare du Nord in Paris and later committed suicide in Kenya. His letter ended like this.

AUGUST 6, 1975

I lunched with Shapiro. Some of his films are exactly what I want, so thank you for your kind thought.

We were discussing all the wild stories as to how Erroll met his death and I told him that he was shot by the Greswolde-Williams girl. He said, confirming my story, that when in hospital at the age of 65 and about to die, she had confided to her nurse that it was she who had fired the fatal shot, which was exactly what Beryl Markham told me.

Years ago, one of my Dorobo scouts whom I employed the year round to spot a large bull for me, sent word that there was an elephant with big ivory in the area. We were just settled in when another safari arrived—Judd, a professional hunter whom I knew. We decided to spin a coin to decide on our territory. Judd won and chose to go along the river eastwards, so I went in the opposite direction.

The country is quite blind, dense thorn bush with open patches where the elephants fed on sansevera. Judd said "Tomorrow is my birthday and if I kill a bull it will be my 365th elephant." The bull charged from a dense patch of bush within ten yards of where Judd was standing and smashed him to pieces.

I am so anxious to meet you. Hope that fate may be kind and allow our paths to cross somewhere, sometime and soon—I am so old.

As if the whole correspondence were devised and scripted by Ramsay-Hill from the outset there was now a long silence. Then this card arrived.

Dear Mrs. Adamson,

I am so very sorry to have to tell you that our dear Ramsay passed away on February 3, 1976.

He became ill in the later part of November, and one thing after another seemed to go wrong.

I miss him so terribly.

Yours sincerely,

Polly Ramsay-Hill.

6

In her draft memoir, written at Naivasha, Joy said this about men.

I feel incomplete without a man to complement my feminine nature and to share my interests and philosophy. Even though I have realised that there never can be a perfect prince, and I am no perfect princess, I have not yet found a partner who is stronger than I and still complementary.

A little later she told Marjorie Villiers that she had never had an ideal partner "since Peter Bally, and later Billy Collins, about whom you know all the difficulties."

Despite these sentiments she still sometimes cast George in the role of her missing prince or knight. She had a knack of foreseeing the dangers that threatened his work long before he did.

I am glad that the Somali invasion has stopped for a time, but fear that there will be similar trouble when the next drought comes. Then not only your lions but you yourself may be in danger when the Somalis know that you are the cause of their being cleared out of Kora.

Her letters to him alternate between concern and recrimination.

OCTOBER 10, 1974

I am more than just hurt by your attitude and will alter my will as far as you are concerned. You now only want to escape into Kora from any responsibility you have; still less do you "respect our marriage" as you signed in the contract when we discussed divorce three years ago. You obviously rely on my loyalty not to let anybody know that you left me as a husband from 1959 to 1964, and treat me like a stranger when I visit you.

I am leaving for London on November 1 and have no address other than Collins. Billy is also fed up with your never writing a book, which would be a more dignified way of earning money than telling your guests how hard up you are and making it plain you want financial help from them.

Despite letters like this Joy was still moved by compassion for him whenever one of his lions was lost, wounded or killed. She was also deeply upset when he himself had an accident.

In April 1975, after she had returned to Kenya from London, where she had the sixth operation on her hand, George came to convalesce for two weeks at Elsamere. He had unwisely started a game of hide-and-seek with Arusha, a young lioness he had accepted from Rotterdam. She had ambushed him and broken his pelvis. Joy wrote to Marjorie Villiers afterward.

JUNE 10, 1975

We were on very friendly terms all the time he was here—nearer than for years, but not as intimate as a married couple could be.

Her affectionate letter to him after his visit expresses the compound of concern and nostalgia that went on pulling her to him.

Do you still have flu or the pain in your hip? Please never leave camp alone!!!!!!!
Did you take your face flannel or has Kaka pinched it? I miss you very much and you would have been perfect moral support after my accident. I often think how ironical life can be and wonder why we have to end it like this after all we have gone through together.

Joy's feelings about Billy Collins were just as ambivalent. In a letter to Helen Wolff she refers sarcastically to the knighthood he received for his achievements as a publisher and in another she said she was considering employing an agent as she no longer wanted Billy to have her "at his mercy." In 1975, after her operation in England, she told Helen that she and Billy had fallen out again—it was "the old story magnified."

Yet the battles were something of a game between them. "Billy is trying to get into my good books again," she wrote two months later. "I must confess I feel defeated and fall for his charm."

In January 1976, when she needed encouragement with her memoirs and was desperate for a leopard cub, Joy noted: "Billy— heart trouble." In fact the problem was not only his heart but also inoperable cancer.

He knew that he was taking a risk—on account of the altitude at Naivasha—when he planned to visit Joy in October and fly on to see the gorillas at Kahusi Biega in Zaire. Joy was thrilled by a letter from him, in which he counted the hours until he reached Kenya.

In preparation for his visit, she went to look for bongo in the mountain forest on the northern side of the lake so that she could show them to Billy. With a young friend, Ros Hillyar, she pushed her way up the steep, narrow, muddy tracks forced through the bamboo by buffalo. She lost all sense of time and, hurrying to get down before dark, slipped and broke her ankle.

For two hours, with the help of her friend, Joy dragged herself down on her backside, cut by the bamboo, scratched by thorns, stung by nettles and viciously bitten by siafu ants. At last they found Ros's husband, Bill, who had been anxiously waiting for them in the dark, blowing the horn of his car to guide them. Despite a recent heart operation he carried Joy across a swamp and they got her to the hospital in Nairobi by midnight.

Joy came around from an operation at 2 o'clock in the morning. From one nightmare she woke to another. She was told that Billy had died of a heart attack in England.

The first letter I received in response to my cable to her was scrawled in tortured capitals, wandering and written under sedation. The second was fluent, forthright and lucid.

You know what Billy meant to me. Life has become meaningless.
    Poor Pierre. I never wanted to take Billy away from her, only to give him what she could not and what he loved. He was always so young here and like a mischievous schoolboy. We had so much fun and were on the same wavelength.
    He knew that I loved him without ulterior motive. I only clashed

with him sometimes as being my publisher, which often complicated our personal relations. But he was always boss—the only boss I ever had. I do not want to write more books. Billy was the inspiration.

Once more Joy had adjusted her version of events to her emotional needs. In truth her personal feelings had interfered with her business arrangements and not vice versa, while Billy's skills as a publisher were the vehicle for her books and not their inspiration.

From then on she kept his photograph close to her and in November she wrote this to Helen Wolff.

It is still so hard to believe that Billy is dead. I always have a fresh carnation near my bed, and the fragrance reminds me of him. He loved carnations and I always had one ready for his buttonhole.

At least I believe he is near me when I smell the carnation, but oh I feel so dreadfully sad.

Her unhappiness was so intense that she declined into her most serious depression in many years. Mercifully reprieve was not long in coming.

It is impossible to throw more light on the relationship between Billy and Joy. Her diary for 1976 is empty from February onward, while in London, New York and the archive at Elsamere there are gaps in the files for the months that followed his death where letters have been discreetly removed.

Billy kept many of her personal letters to him, but they were immediately destroyed when he died. She put his to her in an attaché case with postcards, receipts, ribbon, a rose, opera programs and other keepsakes. The case turned up at Kora years later and its contents were burned.

The course of their relationship may not have run true; but Billy helped bring Joy the success for which she had always yearned, while she gave him not only the glorious adventure of Africa, to which he returned year after year, but an entirely new direction to his publishing. The African list that he founded, embracing many aspects of the continent's natural history, the origins of man and outstanding photography, is still significant twenty years later.

TWENTY-FOUR

Freedom at Kora

1971–1977

1

In his early years at Kora George enjoyed a freedom he had not known since he joined the Game Department in 1938. He had neither an office in Nairobi nor Joy to snort down his neck.

In the first two years his only regular companions, apart from his lions, had been Terence and Hamisi, Terence's Sudanese cook, although they were frequently camped some way up or down the river, extending the network of roads. Ken Smith would drop in for the night or a sundowner, and he was not the only one.

> Because of the complete failure of the rains, animals and birds are having a hard time. Twice a day I feed 24 guinea fowl, besides 5 white-headed buffalo weavers, a dozen starlings, hundreds of quelia and recently a covey of six francolin. Then, of course, there are the three ravens Croaky, Crikey and Creaky. Young Creaky has become an accomplished thief and has a mania for hiding things. A couple of days ago I watched him hiding rather smelly pieces of meat inside Terence's jersey, which was lying over the back of a chair. Terence was not pleased!
>
> I have ordered a bale of lucerne, with which I want to try feeding the dik-dik and hyrax. The dik-dik are becoming quite fearless and come close to the wire, but there is little room for them to eat. If I could afford it I would get a ton of lucerne and feed the hippo and waterbuck as well.
>
> Ken was here last week. He is the last white game warden!

This was the nucleus of George's entourage for the last twenty years of his life.

In the worst droughts he could not save hippos dying of starvation by the Tana. The ravens produced offspring so egregious that the next generation were called Mad, Bad and Worse and one grandchild, even more frightful, earned the name Arsehole. The birds were courageous parents, dive bombing and even hitting baboons if they came too close to their nests on the cliffs.

In the years to come George was feeding more than 100 guinea fowl—they were excellent watchdogs at night, roosting in the bushes around his camp. They gave his toes a painful peck if not fed on demand. The three types of hornbill—red-billed, yellow-billed and von der Deckens—were better mannered, waiting patiently for peanuts in the mess at mealtimes.

This roll call omits monitor lizards and snakes hunting for birds or mice in the roof, sunbirds nesting in the shower next to the hornets for protection, scorpions sheltering in shoes and blankets during the rains, naked mole rats, agama lizards which turned red when courting and vervet monkeys flaunting their bright blue balls from the tree near the mess hut.

Although Terence was entirely at one with George in protecting as much of wild Africa as possible, he deplored his taste in animal company. He dispersed the birds and squirrels at meals by waving a cane at them—he was an elephant man himself.

Once he and his road gang came across an elephant that had fallen into a disused well. The men begged him to shoot it for meat but he refused, sending them for barrow loads of rocks which he dropped into the well one by one, so that they did not hit the elephant. At last it was able to heave itself out and wander off unharmed.

His tenderest feelings were reserved for the trees, shrubs and plants, of which he had a comprehensive knowledge—mastering the English, Swahili and scientific names of every species found in the Kora triangle.

After Boy's death George struggled alone to help Christian and four other young lions hold their own against the local pride. Christian would always return from battle with frontal wounds, which George took as evidence of his courage. Finally relief came when Joy passed him a letter from a young man in his twenties, Tony Fitzjohn.

A foster child, he had been both a rebel and performer at school in England, and had thrown over a job as a management trainee to become a nightclub bouncer, an Outward Bound instructor and a long-distance truck driver in South Africa. The only books he had loved as a boy were the Tarzan stories, and it might have been Tarzan himself who turned up at George's camp. He seemed ideally suited for the unique opening at Kora.

George was delighted with his new lieutenant; predictably Joy was not. This was not because Tony rebuffed an alleged advance from her: she never made one. It was because he frankly reproached her when she swept into Kora and constantly either needled George or wheedled him to abandon the lions and join her at Naivasha. Joy was so incensed that on her return to Naivasha she picked up the radio and blasted George for this impertinence. Tony and the listening subscribers were astounded: George was outraged.

Thereafter Tony was banished to a tent on the river when she came, twice a year, to Kora. In an attempt to make amends he wrote her an exemplary letter of apology to which she replied.

> As you mention, what we cannot forget we may forgive. I will forgive you but as this will not change your character I think it is better if we do not meet again.

Joy also made it plain she preferred Terence to keep out of her way too. She had long ago nicknamed him "The Virgin"—there were good grounds for supposing he was not—and variously charged that he was stupid, senile or deliberately offensive; yet throughout her life she went for long walks with him.

These black clouds were dispersed when George's cousin Pam Carson paid the first of her cheerful visits to the camp and when, in 1972, to George's delight, Tony Ofenheim dropped in at Kora on her way to South Africa. In 1935 George had found her the largest lion in the Serengeti to shoot; this time he showed her Christian who was growing into the biggest in Kenya. Tall and handsome she smiles at the camera from a rock, with Christian, now wild, at her side. Tony Fitzjohn was touched and amused to see that after a few days she and George grew quite sentimental about each other.

George wrote to thank her for a donation that would keep the lions in camel meat for the rest of the year. He went on:

> I know I have something which is to be found nowhere else in the world and which with a little imagination could become a valuable asset to the country.

2

This is how one of George's days started at an age when most men are retired. Christian was still feeling the loss of Boy.

Waking to his lonely roars, I went to offer him companionship — and before long spotted him crouching, ready to ambush me. It was one of his favorite games; he would jump up and greet me without any rough-housing. But today he rushed me, and pinned me to the ground; I was totally helpless. With his great weight on my back, I could do nothing when he gripped me with his paws and took the back of my head and my neck in his jaws. One of his claws went into my arm.

Suddenly he let go. I was so bloody angry that I picked up a stick and went for him. He was off in a flash, realising full well that he had broken the rules. But he broke them again almost immediately, this time with Tony.

Christian beat him up with his paws, knocked him down several times and then dragged him along by his head. Tony saw red, bunched up his fists and punched Christian on the nose with all his considerable strength. Again Christian made no attempt to retaliate.

We realised that Christian had simply been working off his loneliness and frustration.

If Christian became wayward as he grew older, so did Tony, and George was once tempted to draw a parallel between them.

In appearance and temperament Tony was Christian's counterpart. He had a fine physique and good looks; he was fearless in dealing with lions; neither his energy nor his capacity for mischief were often restrained. Like Christian he had an unnerving habit of disappearing from camp without warning, for weeks on end, and of materialising again just as unexpectedly. There the parallel ended, for his dexterity with girl friends was in a different league from Christian's, and I never once found Christian with a bottle at his elbow.

Tony asked for, and received, no wages from George other than a home, the use of his transport and a liberal supply of beer or whatever other sundowners were available in camp. As a teetotaler, Terence regarded Tony's habits with disdain; George knew it and once told a friend that his brother would "jump in the Tana" rather than seek Tony's help. Others felt offended only when the volume and idiom of Tony's speech were affected. Perhaps it was unfair: no one objected when Christian gave vent to a full-throated roar.

In these early years of their partnership there was complete sympathy between George and Tony. George did not tell him things, he showed them to him. When Sue Harthoorn had asked George to teach her bush lore at Meru he had simply said: "Stop talking so much; listen, use your eyes, watch the wind and sniff it from time to time."

Jim Corbett, the naturalist and hunter whose adventures in India with tigers were as famous as George's in Africa with lions, wrote this:

> Jungle lore is not a science that can be learnt from text books; it can, however, be absorbed a little at a time, and the absorption can go on indefinitely, for the book of nature has no beginning, as it has no end.

It is clear that both George and Tony only became fully alive in a natural setting, just as they both loved danger. "Never try to shoot a charging animal until it is within ten feet of you," was one of George's rarely spoken tips.

Early in 1973, Christian felt sufficiently confident to strike out on his own. He crossed the Tana and was not seen again.

His successful release, and George's continued presence, persuaded the government, with the full support of the Tana River Council, to gazette the Kora Triangle as a national reserve at the end of the year. In future the grazing of stock there would be, technically, forbidden.

Between 1970 and 1977, George released seventeen lions at Kora. Only two of them, Christian and Arusha, were born in captivity; even Boy had been found in the NFD before he had joined the Scots Guards. The others, with the blessing of the Game Department, were sent to him as cubs or young lions from all over Kenya.

It was impossible to judge precisely how many lions Kora could stand at any one time because the dynamics of the population were so unpredictable. For instance, when Christian went off George was left with only one of his first eight protégés; but in 1976, after accepting five more, and following the birth of half a dozen cubs, he wrote:

> I had made up my mind not to take on any more lions, because of the expense of feeding them and, more important, because there are already as many lions in this area as it can comfortably support. About a month ago I was asked to take over two cubs, which had absolutely no future apart from lifelong captivity in some zoo. I just could not refuse them the chance of freedom.
>
> Of course, the cubs share our camp. Pillows, blankets, towels, shoes—everything is there for them to play with, at least that is what they think! Our nightly slumbers have become woken rudely by a wrestling match on top of us or blankets being dragged off as "kills."
>
> In about 6 or 8 months it should be possible to let them join [the others] who are becoming increasingly independent. They go off on long expeditions for four or five days at a time, five or six miles from camp.

Some of the orphans reached him in a state of distress, having been caged, put on display and jeered at. All of them had to be habituated first to him, as their pride leader, then to his other lions, as their pride, and finally to life in the bush.

Terence only ever really liked one of George's pride, a plucky little lion known as Supercub. Within a few months he was found dead, bitten through the back of his neck by a wild male. He was buried in the same *lugga* as Boy.

Usually the lions were more than two years old before they learned to kill a Lesser kudu or waterbuck; later they managed an elephant calf, a giraffe, and even tackled a hippo. A young lioness, Gigi, was alleged to have attacked a party of game rangers in a truck. They put a bullet through her leg, and since it was her hind leg George told their superiors that it must be the only recorded case of a lion charging backwards!

At about two years old the males began to wander farther and farther afield as Christian had. George agonized over their disappearance, noting the days, weeks or months that went by. Joy tried to console him.

Do not despair; have faith they are happy. We love our animals as our children but we have to try not to be possessive, and regard their lives as more important than our own need for them.

It would have been impossible to locate all the lions by the time-honored method of tracking on foot, and in 1974 a young American, Esmond Bradley Martin—who later became one of the world's experts in tracing the illegal traffic in ivory and rhino horn—gave George his first radio collars. George and Tony took the tracking antenna out in the Land-Rover and then climbed with it to the highest points in Kora, transforming their work. The results were even more rewarding with the help of a plane.

They found some of the lions on the northern bank of the Tana, heading for the happy hunting grounds of Meru, where Girl and the Bisleti lionesses were still at large. Joy had found the Mugwongo pride in the company of a strange male. Jonny Baxendale also encountered Girl, approaching her on foot to be sure of her identity, and wondering at the last moment what the outcome would be if he were mistaken!

The first two lionesses to produce cubs at Kora were served by a wild lion. As often happens in a pride, they mated and gave birth together—one of nature's economies. They could not both safely hunt simultaneously and when one of the mothers was killed, the other, Juma, adopted her cubs. Juma's party trick was to wriggle under the wire, causing George's guests to choke on their sundowners.

He noticed that the real troublemakers, the only lions except Boy with a tendency to make unprovoked attacks on people, were the adolescent males. Although this applied to just a few, he and Tony reflected their instinctive suspicions when naming them. One of Juma's sons, a little on the wild side, was named Shyman; a young male, Suleiman, had arrived as Solomon, but Tony thought the name of a shifty acquaintance was more appropriate; and one of Juma's grandsons was christened Shade. There was seldom any warning of violence.

I was having my tea in the main hut. Suddenly Haragumsa came rushing in to say that Tony was being attacked by the lions. Thinking that the cubs had knocked him over and were giving him a rough time, I seized a stick and dashed out. Tony was on the ground in the grip of a big lion. As I ran at them, yelling and brandishing the stick, the lion dropped Tony and slunk off a few yards, looking as if he might have another go. A further demonstration caused him to disappear.

Tony was covered in blood, with nasty gashes on his neck, head and arms. While Terence and Haragumsa cleaned up the damage, George radioed the Flying Doctor, who flew Tony to hospital in Nairobi the next morning. He had been exceedingly lucky; a deep wound on the side of his neck had exposed the carotid—another fraction of an inch and he would have been dead.

The culprit had disappeared before George could identify him, but the next day he noticed that Shyman had blood on his chest, was unusually aggressive and given a wide berth by the other lions. He shot him through the brain.

Writing to Tony in hospital George said:

There is nothing to blame yourself for. It could just as easily have happened to me. For the sake of the lions one can be thankful that it was not an African!

What does a bloody *mzungu* matter!

It is clear from their letters that neither George nor Joy ever entirely lost the prejudices about Africans that had been prevalent among whites when they each arrived in Kenya. Joy once repeated a remark made to her by Ewart Grogan, a robust leader of the pioneers in Kenya: "There is no colour bar, only a culture bar." Since their attitude in this was more historical than personal I feel it should be stated but not stressed.

Two years later Suleiman nearly put an end to activities in Kora altogether. Looking for a litter of cubs in a cave on some rocks, George was playfully shadowed by the young lion.

Suleiman jumped on my back, grabbing me by the neck and bringing me down on the steep hillside. I tried to beat him off, whacking him over my shoulder with a stick. This made him angry and he started to growl, sinking his teeth in the back of my neck. It was no longer play.

Luckily I was wearing my revolver because my search might well have brought me face to face with a cobra or leopard in the rocks. I drew the gun now with the notion of firing a shot over Suleiman's head to scare him off. When I pulled the trigger there was just a dull click. It happened a second time and with a fearful chill I realised I had probably forgotten to load it.

My hand was no longer steady as I broke the gun open to work out my chances. At least there was a round in each of the chambers and as Suleiman still had his teeth in my neck—I could feel the blood trickling down my shoulders and the sweat coming out on my forehead—I decided to try again. This time I managed to get two shots off into the air.

Suleiman bit harder. In sheer desperation I pointed the revolver backwards over my shoulder, and fired straight at him. Immediately he let go and, looking startled, went and sat twenty feet off. I could see blood on his muzzle and more on his neck.

George was flown to Nairobi; both he and Suleiman survived the ordeal, though Suleiman not for long.

Cast out of the pride by the other lions, he and his sister lived alone on the banks of the Tana. One morning his sister led George to Suleiman's body. From the churned up mud George could read the story of his death. The two lions had taken on a hippo, and Suleiman had been killed by a single snap of its vast jaws. Crocodiles had repeatedly tried to get at his corpse, but his sister had held them at bay. George buried him, and for days she kept vigil over his grave.

Of the seventeen lions George released he had been obliged to shoot Boy; four had been killed by lions or other animals; and he reckoned that four must have succumbed to snares, poachers or the herdsmen who still infiltrated the reserve, especially in a drought. Whenever they did so he dreaded the possibility that the lions might be killed as a reprisal for stock raids or, worse still, might attack a child or a herdsman.

The other eight lions survived to make their own lives in the bush. Against the normal survival rate of one in four, he achieved a success rate of nearly 50 percent. Beyond that he was in touch with about a dozen of their cubs, all of them born in the wild.

3

Which brings us to the heart of the matter: What did George really achieve through his work with the lions?

Some of his least inhibited critics were among the Kenyan cognoscenti—ranchers, safari guides, lodge and camp managers, sometime hunters and DCs. They are remarkable for their hospitality, warmth, enterprise and courage. A slightly questionable omniscience on all matters concerning game and an infectious, cynical, even malicious sense of humor are common to some of them; for years Joy had been a butt of their laughter. After the success of *Born Free,* George too became a target.

They variously credited Elsa with killing a man and several serious maulings; they multiplied the number of animals George shot for his lions to a massacre; and they were apt to confide that George was a bit of a poseur, loved backing into the limelight and had grown financially rapacious. It was simply drivel.

George's most intimate critic, Joy, maintained that he encouraged a dangerous familiarity between his lions and people. In the case of some lions she was right. She was also technically right that, by feeding his pride and exposing it to the publicity of articles and films, he impaired its rehabilitation. Yet she did the same with her own animals, claiming that it added to our knowledge and helped influence public opinion.

George's fiercest critic, Wilfred Thesiger, the distinguished explorer and writer who had settled in Kenya, was a friend of Peter Jenkins. His experience of lions, forcibly deployed in the newspapers to attack George, was extensive but dangerously incomplete and distorted by tunnel vision—a tunnel with the bore of his rifle, George observed. While a DC in the Sudan, Thesiger had shot more than seventy stock-raiding lions and two cubs of his own that he had raised for nine months.

He seemed to believe that wild lions never suffered accidents when hunting, while rehabilitated ones could not kill efficiently; that wild lions would never allow rehabilitated ones to integrate with them; and that wild lions offer no threat to man unless provoked and never take to man eating unless handicapped. On all these points the facts prove him wrong.

He did, however, voice the essential question to which people wanted an answer: Was George producing man-eaters?

His most informed critics, the professional game managers—like Mervyn Cowie and Peter Jenkins in Kenya, and John Owen and Myles Turner in Tanzania—were fully justified in pointing out the danger of continuing to feed and consort with rehabilitated lions in a national park, and in complaining about the disruption this created to its natural order. The ability, achievements and integrity of these and other professionals who opposed George were outstanding, but there seemed to be a tinge of prejudice and even jealousy among those who argued that his work was of little value to conservation because lions as a species were not endangered, and because Kora was not worth protecting; or when they denied he was making any scientific contribution because he kept no systematic records.

Both these contentions are questioned or confounded by authorities commanding a wider perspective and better qualified to pronounce on the issues.

The value of George's work for conservation was recognized by Prince Bernhard of the Netherlands, who made a financial donation to Kora when he was President of the World Wildlife Fund; by Dr. Bernhard Grzimek, President of the Frankfurt Zoological Society, who gave George valuable transport for Kora; and by Sir David Attenborough, who shared Desmond Morris's view that George and Joy had significantly shifted public opinion.

As for Kora, such was the need to preserve every unspoiled area offering a home to the country's persecuted game that the government had designated it a reserve in 1973 on the strength of George's presence. Ten years later, Richard Leakey, as Director of the National Museums of Kenya, and the Royal Geographical Society in London, sent a joint expedition—based in a camp on the Tana—to record the status of all the lesser-known flora and fauna in this rare, if not unique, wilderness. Furthermore, throughout George's time at Kora, Chief Shabu of Asako and the Tana River Council, the DC and the local MP, the Chief Game Warden, the Permanent Secretary and the Minister of Tourism and Wildlife, were in no doubt about the importance of conserving Kora's integrity for the people of Kenya.

As to the scientific value of George's work, an opinion must depend on how you define "Science"; however, Sir Julian Huxley's recognition of its importance has been reinforced recently by two of the world's leading experts on animal behavior. George kept no methodical records, nor did he formulate and test new theories, but he added to the sum of human knowledge about lions, extended our understanding of them, and opened opportunities for further research.

Elsa had revealed that a lioness was capable of a far wider range of behavior than had previously been suspected—she was not simply programmed by a series of instincts and conditioned reflexes. Subsequently the film lions had demonstrated that Elsa was not an exception. Finally, in Meru and at Kora, George had worked out how captive lions, even after several generations in confinement, could be successfully released in the wild.

George Schaller, now the greatest authority on the behavior of carnivores, agrees with Huxley that the Adamsons' love of Elsa elicited responses from her that scientists could not have discovered through their more objective methods. In an introduction to a new edition of *Born Free* in 1987, and in a subsequent letter to me, he made these two observations.

The Adamsons gave us truths about the species that cannot be found in a biologist's notebook . . .

Their efforts at reintroduction and rehabilitation taught the scientific community invaluable lessons and the conservation community will for ever be indebted to them . . .

In 1992 Jane Goodall, whose lifelong study of chimpanzees in the wild has produced some of the most striking discoveries about animal behavior in our time, wrote this.

The careful documentation by the Adamsons of individual animals, their unique personalities, and the events of their rich and varied lives, represents a major accomplishment for science.

They have a special place in history because they had the courage of their convictions and their success is a beacon for the long term goal of breeding endangered species for ultimate return to the wild.

It may still be asked if this knowledge was gained at unjustifiable risk to human safety.

It was claimed, for instance, that George's lions were not to be trusted because he destroyed in them a supposed "natural" fear of man. It is, however, perfectly clear from his experience of lions that no such automatic and natural fear exists in wild lions; some tend to shy away from him and some do not. It depends on their character or mood.

Among George's lions, as in every pride in Africa, there were some with relaxed and amiable dispositions, and others who were constantly on the lookout for a chance to stalk, pounce and kill. George himself accepted the proposition—to put it in anthropomorphic terms—that there were "good" lions and "bad" lions, but no safe ones.

All lions are born to attack or kill and will be likely to do so if aroused by hunger, alarm or the urge to claim a mate. The same likelihood occurs if they are injured, provoked or tempted by a child. For a human figure to drop to the ground, bend down or to squat is also likely to trigger an attack, as George discovered when filming *Born Free*. Muga, Tony, Terence and conceivably Stanley, were all caught unawares in this way.

George spelled out these dangers, "occupational hazards" as he called them, to everyone who worked with him, and the risks were accepted. He likened them to the danger inherent in motor racing; miners and construction workers, too, accept a comparable measure of risk.

George did not predispose his lions to attack people; they were no more dangerous than wild ones—almost certainly they were less so because the human beings they encountered were friendly, not hostile or provocative. The real danger lay in growing too familiar with them. Tony, Peter Jenkins and George himself had all paid varying prices for this, but the blame was theirs, not the lions'.

After George's death I asked all his staff, the game warden in Kora and the head of the Garissa antipoaching unit, if they knew of any attack by his lions on the local population. None of them did; any hint of one would have certainly produced either a claim or complaint.

4

It was the growth of George's reputation at Kora that seemed to irk Joy so much while she was at Naivasha. She refused to contribute a penny to his work despite pressure from virtually all her trustees— maintaining that he had withdrawn to his "little kingdom" because he felt "overshadowed" by her; that his treatment of the lions was a failure, betrayed Elsa and discredited her; and that he was leading a life of idleness he expected others to fund.

I have seldom seen a man of his age more active, content or concerned for the work he was doing. He was up at dawn, busy all day except for a siesta when it was more than 100°F in the shade and the last to put out the oil lamps at night.

On my first morning at Kora he took me in the Land-Rover to

search for the lions, stopping at times to call them or study the dust for spoor. I did a double take when what seemed, for a second, to be a pack of huge golden labradors—at least one of them collared—burst out of the bushes near my window. Immediately they leapt up to see if George was in the car.

The sight of him and Tony wandering with complete unconcern among the lions, all of them beautiful, many fully grown and a few of them especially dangerous, made such an exciting impact that the news of it spread rapidly. An ever-growing flow of visitors made their way to this remote corner of Africa: the King of Toro; Prince Bernhard, who insisted on being photographed beside George on his two-seater lavatory made from elephants' jawbones; the Austrian Ambassador to Kenya; and a succession of scientists.

Professor R. L. Brahmachary came from Calcutta to find out how lions would respond to sprays of diluted tigers' urine, and to collect balls of elephant dung for analysis. Dr. Adriaan Kortlandt brought a tiny car full of thorns from the Mara to test his theory that early man found them effective weapons against predators. He tied his thorns to an electric propeller and was delighted when George's lions refrained from taking the meat he put underneath it. The moment his propeller was still the lions dashed in and stole the meat.

In 1976 the Tana River Expedition from a London polytechnic—led by Nigel Winser, now Expeditions Director of the Royal Geographical Society—made Kora a base on its way down to the sea. Aart Visee, the vet from Rotterdam Zoo, brought Arusha to Kora and came back each year to watch her progress. He also brought the news when Elsa's sister, Lustica, died at the age of nineteen: no lioness lives so long in the wild.

Reporters turned up from all over the world; Bill Travers made another film, *Christian the Lion*. As with *The Lion from World's End*, George was delighted by it, it was seen by an enormous audience in America and it earned him a handsome income. More filmmakers arrived from America, Japan, Australia and elsewhere; the stars Candice Bergen and Ali McGraw were filmed with him on the Tana and in a balloon over the Mara. Candice Bergen gave him money to help with some leopards he hoped to release. Ali McGraw promised to bake him a chocolate cake but had no time to. She made up for it by recording a video in support of a trust named after him.

Without Tony Fitzjohn, George could never have managed the logistics of keeping Kampi ya Simba in wood, water and food. The mail had to be collected from ninety miles away and an ox or camel fetched for the lions once a week from Mbalambala. One carcass, decomposing in the sun, became grossly inflated. When Christian bit into it the discharge of gas knocked him out for at least half an hour.

A tireless and inventive mechanic, Tony kept the trucks on the roads that Terence was still extending with his gangs, using pangas and traditional tools for the exhausting work of clearing the bush. Terence would give George meticulous instructions for whatever he needed: "*mature* sisal poles" and "ten *Chinese* pangas, Kenyan ones are not good." He was precise about everything, including his imitations of an irritated rhino: "Chough, chough, chough. Never two or four snorts, always three."

George's most thankless task was his business with the Tana River Council. After 1974 the British provided the council with periodic grants-in-aid, each of about £1,500, so that they could repay George for the road work that he financed himself. Extracting and accounting for the money was a nightmare. Later he had to collect landing fees from every visitor who flew into Kora.

As he had done at Meru he wrote regular reports on the lions for the ministry. Soon these were broadened into newsletters for his friends and supporters overseas. Often the contents were somber.

The 1970s were a decade of slaughter for Kenya's game. The price of ivory and rhino horn rose; the National Parks were absorbed by the Game Department and their fees went to the treasury instead of to protect the parks; and a ban on all hunting removed the vigilant eyes of the professional hunters from the surveillance of the ranges most prolific in game.

When George arrived at Kora he estimated there were sometimes as many as 400 elephants in the triangle. During droughts some, with long memories, made their way over two hundred miles from Tsavo to the permanent waters of the Tana. Each year he found an increasing number of rotting elephant and rhino carcasses with their tusks and horns hacked out. Through the bush telegraph he usually discovered if the culprits were Wakamba or Somali, but sometimes game rangers were involved. Once a poacher was caught with a bag of lion claws he was selling for trinkets.

Even more of a threat to Kora and his lions were the invasions of livestock. He pointed out to Prince Bernhard thousands of Somali cattle and camels illegally grazing inside the reserve, while their owners slashed down the greenery for foodstuff; hundreds of acres of palm grove were set on fire to discourage predators and tsetse flies. Although some of the camels came to the defense of their young with bared yellow teeth, George's lions killed a number of cows, and if given a chance, the Somali herdsmen did not hesitate to shoot, spear, snare or poison them with bait soaked in a lethal brand of cattle dip.

It was always George who had to alert the authorities to this gradual degradation of Kora. They would respond to his summons, but during every one of my visits the police, the antipoaching unit or the game wardens called in at Kampi ya Simba to beg petrol, tires, batteries, spare parts, food, water, short-term loans or the use of George's radio, since theirs were out of order.

There was never a week in George's life that was dull; there was never a day that was idle. Even so, he was always willing to offer a welcome to anyone—man, woman, lion, goat or an egret with a broken leg.

In 1972, when Joy had suggested they raise together her ill-fated leopard cub, he had replied:

I would very much like to cooperate. It would be the answer to our life together. Kora is the only place in Kenya where this could be done independently of the National Parks.

In 1977 he urged her to bring another young leopard to Kora. It was their last chance of coming together again.

TWENTY-FIVE

Queen of Shaba

1976–1980

1

By the time George had released the last lion at Kora Joy had embarked on her own last great enterprise. In November 1976 the jinx that had always thwarted her ambition to raise a leopard was finally lifted.

After Billy Collins's death, Juliette Huxley, Julian's widow, had come to stay at Elsamere and succeeded in easing Joy's depression by wise advice and the sheer sparkle and warmth of her personality. Afterward Joy wrote:

> You have helped me so much just by being as you are. I shall never forget our talk at Lake Nakuru. The doctor could not give me the tablets you mentioned, but the ones he got help a lot.
>
> I could even play *Rosenkavalier* two nights ago to test my strength, as this was a special secret between Billy and me. He signed his last letter to me "Your Rosenkavalier."

At Nakuru Joy had experienced the luckiest mishap of her life. She and Juliette were both spellbound when the setting sun turned the sky, the hills and the water the same soft pink as the million flamingos on the lake. They never noticed that their car was sinking through the crust of soda on which it was parked.

Before Joy could set off in search of a ranger, one hurried out to give her a tow and told her that a leopard cub had recently been handed in to the Provincial Warden, Joseph Mburugu, who had been a ranger at Meru when she had arrived there with Pippa. Now, she asked him if she might adopt, and later release, the little leopard. He agreed.

Joy wrote to Marjorie Villiers.

The cub is heaven! I have only had her a few days and already she tries to be playful without drawing blood.

She was eight weeks old when I got her and I at once tried her on a freshly killed rabbit. She knew exactly how to tear the intestines first, then the cartilage, and ate a whole one in a day. She is now thriving on them.

I am already fond of her although I am punctured on my arms and legs. Now I have to find a location. Meanwhile Penny gets imprinted on me: that is vital.

Although Joy uses the term "imprint," it is not correct. The phenomenon, observed and so named by Konrad Lorenz, really applies to a newly hatched or newborn creature if it belongs to a species that automatically attaches itself to the first large moving entity on which its eyes properly focus.

Elsa may well have imprinted on Joy in this sense, Pippa certainly did not, nor did Penny. It is therefore all the more interesting that Joy induced the cheetah and the leopard to make a form of transference on to her so that she became their surrogate mother.

Within a few weeks Penny began to reveal her true nature.

My baby leopard is three months old. I can see in her eyes the deep, unfathomable conflict between love and the ability to murder.

There is already a bond between us, however frail, and I hope to learn from her about birth control, thought communication and leopard values.

With the help of her pills, and above all with the prospect of exploring the world of a leopard, Joy's morale and vitality began to pick up. Penny lived in a spacious enclosure just outside her room, and although the colobus monkeys dropped down on the wire to tease her they were always quick enough to dodge her claws. Like the eagle owls, Penny was fed chickens—she ate the bodies, they had the heads. She liked mole rats too, but spat out the teeth.

By the time she was six months old Joy had to wear a thick canvas apron, back and front, with canvas leg guards and gauntlets up to her elbows. She exercised Penny in the hills around Hell's Gate, like a dog on a very long lead, but needed a man to go with her. Although Joy sometimes provoked Penny to play, fussed her and even tried to drag her against her will—as she had occasionally done with Elsa

375

and Pippa—anyone bringing up a young leopard is likely to get bitten or scratched.

Penny was nearly a year old before the Wildlife Department found somewhere to release her that was suitable for a leopard, free of herdsmen, and acceptable to Joy. Despite several pressing invitations from George, she had turned down Kora as too hot and too remote from a reliable mail service. She chose Shaba instead.

Much has been made of the way Joy ill-used her African staff, but old Toitonguro had come out of retirement to provide goats for Pippa and the cubs. Now Makedde, the Turkana who had been with George when he found Elsa, and Kifosha, the Kikuyu who had cooked for her on Mount Kenya and through the five long years of her tribal safaris, both agreed to join her.

Whatever the hardships of her earlier endeavors, this was the toughest, given the character of a leopard, the country and her age. She needed the best support she could find, and she chose an impressive team to launch Penny in the wild.

Patrick Hamilton was the acknowledged expert on leopards in East Africa, and was completing a three-year study in Tsavo, where he had released a dozen that had been trapped for stock raiding. The females are so canny that he had caught only one.

However fast leopards in Asia were losing their habitat—and their numbers were rapidly falling—there were thought to be at least 100,000 in Africa. It was impossible to tell because they are so secretive that under pressure they become nocturnal and can live close to a village or farm with little chance of detection, as long as they resist their favorite prey—dogs.

Hamilton doubted if Joy would learn much about Penny once she took her to Shaba. Even with the help of radio tracking all his leopards had quickly disappeared. Fundamentally solitary, except when mating or raising their young, they quickly move off ranges already occupied and, like domestic cats, immediately try to find their way home when displaced.

But two factors were different. Penny was female and she was dependent on Joy. For both these reasons she might choose to settle where she found herself if there were no competition. Nevertheless, Joy, hoping she would thoroughly explore the country around Shaba, acquired the radio-tracking equipment that Hamilton prescribed.

Paul Sayer, the vet who had helped the Harthoorns with Boy at Naivasha, sedated Penny while they put on her thick transmitting collar, and again when they took her to Shaba. Joy's new assistant, Martin Clarke, showed his mettle when Penny, still under sedation, struggled out of the collar. He managed to replace it, holding a torch in his mouth while adding new holes to bolt it on tighter as she began to wake up.

If Hamilton had the most extensive knowledge of leopards, no one's was more dramatic than Rodney Elliott's, who selected Joy's campsite in Shaba. An old friend and colleague of George, he had once been disturbed by a violent commotion when an impala crashed into his tent post, followed by a leopard that dispatched it and it proceeded to eat it on the fly.

Later he had to release a trapped leopard. He withdrew to a tree with one of his scouts, focused his movie-camera and shouted to his driver to open the cage. Even when the leopard came straight for him he kept on filming, confident the scout would shoot if it did not change course. The leopard never swerved, the game scout never fired and Elliott never stopped filming till the camera was knocked from his hands. Badly mauled, he managed to draw his revolver in time to save his life.

Joy wrote to me happily at the end of August 1977.

We are off. Shaba is 100 square miles and 30 miles from Isiolo, so it is like coming home again after 17 years. I have had a meeting with the Isiolo Councillors who welcomed me knowing I am the Golden Goose who will finance the development of their reserve.

We have a special ten man camel unit to keep poachers and Somali guerillas away. Keep your fingers crossed, they are sitting thirty miles from Shaba, heavily armed with Russian rifles.

2

For connoisseurs of Kenya Shaba is the remote jewel among its northern reserves. Jonny Baxendale took me back to discover what traces of Joy we could find ten years after her death. I had visited her there only once, in the rains; now I saw the other side of the coin.

The jagged, pale blue mountains surrounding it, the harsh limestone plain strewn with rock and brutal lava, the ocher earth and dusty tracks, provide the frame and the canvas. The real colors, softness and life flow into the picture from the rippling red Ewaso Ngiro river along its northern boundary, and from the springs on the plain.

Doum palms, poplars, fig trees and thornbushes, great sweeps of golden grass swaying in the hot wind like ripe corn, and the bright green spears of rushes and reeds thrusting up to a cloudless sky offer grazing and browse for elephants, giraffes, zebras and antelope. A hunting ground for lions, they also give shelter and food to baboons, monkeys, porcupines and hyraxes, and to flights of waterfowl, songsters and large birds of prey.

Rodney Elliott had set Joy's last camp on a lovely site commanding this view. It stood on a rise in a grove of fever trees, looking across the plain to Mount Bodech, five miles away, just beyond the river. Even at noon on the hottest day a faint breeze stirred through the trees; Egyptian geese sunned in the marsh below, and a pair of immaculate crowned cranes rose slowly into the air, let out a cry and gently settled again. Suddenly the largest herd of oryx Jonny had ever seen trotted through the grass and halted in unison, tossing their long black horns, flicking their tails and twitching their ears.

Joy joked about her camp to George. It was "too elaborate and built for eternity! Cemented loo seats, a kitchen table good enough for the Ritz. We have eight tents, two showers, one rabbit boma, and a large boma for Penny."

> On our second walk we put up a herd of buffalo in thick acacia forest. She watched Grant's gazelle, a jackal, waterbuck and a hare hopping off in front of her.
>
> She keeps close to us, is frightened of the open plains without cover, and reluctantly goes round the swamp, but copes with thorns and lava grass remarkably well. She only moves between 6.00–8.00 am and 6.00–7.00 pm, pants during the day, and sleeps at night.

Joy was exhilarated by the chance of unlocking the secrets of a creature as tough, intelligent and quick to strike as she herself; she seemed to revel in the physical as well as the mental demands.

> I am now 68 and wish I could have fifty years ahead to do all I would like to do. Apart from a steel hip, a broken hand, elbow,

knee and ankle—all on the right side, but mended during the last two years so that I would never know that I have had the breaks—I am very fit (touch wood). I can stumble for hours across wobbling lava in the heat and drench myself, fully dressed, several times a day under the shower to keep mentally active.

George, with whom she could stay in touch by radio, sixty miles away as the crow flew, came over at Christmas and joined the fishing expeditions that were a feature of Sundays in camp. They all went—Makedde, Kifosha, Martin Clarke and Jock Rutherfurd, a retired farmer, engaged to take care of her security.

Fishing along the river was idyllic. It is true that we had to keep a look-out for crocodiles, and in the thick bush for buffaloes, but listening to the water bubbling over the shoals, the wind rustling through the palms and the rhythm of their swinging fronds, I felt that we had gone back to the days when George and I spent months on safari in the Northern Frontier District. Today George's hair is white but as I watched him patiently throwing his line again and again until he got a bite, it was as though time had been telescoped.

Joy's walks round Shaba steadily widened and Penny grew more independent, but Joy was worried that they never saw a sign of a male leopard within her range. Ken Smith, as ever, was able to help and arranged for a recently trapped male to be brought in which involved none of the risks of importing a lion.

Early in 1978 Penny began to disappear for weeks on end and Joy had to track her from the air—signals from her collar could be picked up only four miles away on the ground but up to forty in a plane. She was found six miles outside the reserve—Joy supposed on a honeymoon. Nothing came of this initial romance but awareness of Penny's presence must have spread by bush telegraph, for there were signs—scrapes and quiet rasping coughs like the sound of a saw—that leopards were in the vicinity.

When she came into estrus she would disappear and return to camp with scratches or love bites on the back of her neck—leopards seemed to mate in the manner of lions and cheetahs. At other times she would lie on the ground and roll on her back, purring in front of Joy's current assistant or Makedde—but never to Joy. How did she know their gender? George had frequently found that lionesses behaved in the same way with him.

On their walks Penny sensed that Joy was the frailest of her three companions and would try to knock her down. Half a dozen times she gave her painful bites that needed stitching. Nevertheless, Joy remained her mother: a source of food and security. The assistant, with the tracking device, became something of a playmate and was often allowed to stroke her. Makedde she respected as the *mzee* with a gun, and she tried no tricks on him. Nevertheless he never dropped his guard; he knew one Turkana whose throat and eyes had been slashed by a leopard, and another who had been scalped by one.

Toward the end of the year it was clear that after several disappointments Penny was pregnant. However, a month or two later she either miscarried, or her cubs were killed by lions. Joy had come across two prides inside and on the fringes of Shaba.

As so often happened after a crisis with one of her animals, Joy fell, and fractured her kneecap. She was in a cast from heel to groin. She had driven herself to the limit, both day and night.

She was busy revising *The Searching Spirit* and she was well ahead with a book about Penny. She was in constant correspondence with her committee in Nairobi about funding Shaba, to which she had already given transport, a camel unit, an airstrip and gate huts; she was now asked for fencing and water pipes. She was also trying to find partners to fund the release in the reserve of threatened species like rhinos and cheetahs.

Just as Shaba demonstrated Joy's finest qualities, it also brought out some of her worst. As Frank Minot had predicted some years before, her tendency to interfere had become even more pronounced. Her dispute with the Elsa Appeal in America, about their directorate, their methods of raising money and how they used it, was reaching its climax.

Her behavior closer to home seemed even more disturbed. In all she had a series of six assistants to help her with Penny; she had vetted them carefully beforehand and after a few weeks wrote to George and her friends expressing glowing opinions of each. These are extracts from her remarks on the six men a few weeks or months after their various departures.

He behaved very badly. I do not want his name in my book . . .
We are imprisoned 24 hours together and the tension has

become intolerable. I never get a response and they chat together, having more in common with each other through their low education and intelligence than with me . . .

How can I live with people who are not intellectually and socially my equal? . . .

He turned into a fanatical religious maniac and found an outlet in caressing Penny rather sensually . . .

I am told that he was in prison for cheating income tax and has a black mark with the firearms bureau . . .

I found him lying again. I cannot trust him any longer . . .

I met four of these men, though not the man with a record. Three were young, willing, devoted to Penny and pleasant but out of their depth when faced with a personality like Joy's. Jock Rutherfurd, the retired farmer, drank too much but was charming and invaluable in the bush, and one night, when his car broke down, walked all the way across the park unarmed in order not to leave Joy alone in camp. He once called the outraged Kifosha a "bugger" when he got out of hand, and put up with no nonsense from Joy either.

Somehow the rock in her life, Peter Johnson, managed through his sanity to keep the logistics of Shaba from foundering. He had firmly refused a salary—"I do not want to be your secretary or dogsbody"—and he did not mince his words about her problems with her staff.

The reason he did not discuss his departure with you is the whip wielding effect you have on the people you employ. I get the same complaint from all the people I have sent to you, whether black or white. You are terribly autocratic and demanding and in this day and age you cannot act as you did thirty years ago.

It was wise and forthright advice which she entirely—and fatally—ignored. Happily she listened to him when he urged her not to cut out George entirely from her latest will as she had done in 1970 when she was contemplating divorce.

Never willing or able to face up to her own shortcomings—her betrayals, rejections and unceasing aggression—Joy reproached George in almost every letter she wrote him, for their separate existence, and invited him to abandon Kora to live with her again.

I know the lions are everything you believe you have left in your life and without them you will feel desolate and lonely. But my dear George you are not alone and I really do often need you, not only for your practical help but mainly for being the nearest person I have—even if I have had to resign myself in all these last years to the fact that you did not seem to care whether I was dead or alive. If you could decide to close Kora now and move to Shaba, we could grow old together in the bush, in a place that we both know and love, where we are popular and where we can do useful work.

In one letter she tried to dissuade him from taking on Jock Rutherfurd at Kora when he left her at Shaba: there is an irony in the terms she chose for her warning.

You always trust people's face value and you are the easiest person to exploit. I told you that at Ijara in the first week we met.

How different his life would have been, for richer for poorer, had he looked beneath the surface when he accepted her first invitation to tea in 1943.

3

By January 1979 Penny was more than two years old and fully mature. A leopard has shorter legs than a cheetah and, however sinuous, is stockier. Penny was six feet from nose to tail, about two feet tall at the shoulder and weighed nearly eighty pounds. She was powerful enough to kill antelope two or three times her own weight, and to drag an animal at least as heavy as herself straight up a tree to store it in the fork of a branch.

She was exquisite to look at and frequently almost invisible. A leopard relies on concealment and a short rush to bring down its prey. The pattern on her coat was perfectly adapted to the needs of her hunting.

Any animal standing in the sunlight will appear lighter above and shadowed beneath. But if, like the leopard, its coat is darker along the spine, fading to white under the belly, it will cease to be obviously three-dimensional.

Finally, give such an animal a disruptive pattern of spots—black dots or rough rosettes of three, four or five petals on chestnut backgrounds—and it will virtually vanish among the broken shapes and shadows of the grass and bushes, or the branches of a tree. It was certainly impossible to pick out Penny in the thorny thickets to which she withdrew in the heat of the day.

Joy never saw Penny make a kill, although she was able to keep herself fed for several weeks on end. One of her principal lairs was on a bastion of rock inhabited by a colony of hyraxes, which slept on the ledges at night. Since Penny was primarily nocturnal, Joy assumed they provided her diet.

The only large prey Penny got her teeth into was a Grant's gazelle that Joy stole from a pride of lions. The leopard had no idea how to tackle it at first and twice Joy had to show her by cutting open the skin. Apart from hyraxes, Penny also fed herself on hares, birds and frogs. She probably also killed vervet monkeys and baboons, although once or twice the latter got the better of her, leaving her with nasty bites on her flanks and chest.

At last in February Joy recognized blood on Penny's neck as a love bite and expected her to bear cubs in about three months' time.

MAY 26, 1979

My dearest Marjorie,

Big news. Penny gave birth last night!

Yesterday she behaved very strangely, as if wanting to show us something, making a strange sound like chirping and leading us high up into a rocky outcrop. Whenever we tried to leave her she followed us again, leading us up the rocks, always waiting for us to follow.

Newly born cubs are most vulnerable, and the mother sits on them like an incubator for 3–5 days to keep the temperature even. She licks the anus of the cubs to stimulate digestion and never leaves them during this time.

I was amazed that Penny wanted us to be with her during the last three days and now deserted her cubs to meet us and drink. But I intended not to follow her to the cubs.

Joy wrote again three days later.

We believed the cubs should be left alone for a few days until they got stronger. She made her nursery high up on a large rocky outcrop, of forbidding cliffs, precipices, boulders and loose stones.

The third day after their birth she guided us to two tiny cubs, very dark grey but perfectly marked already and in remarkably normal proportion. Even their tails are longer than they are in lion and cheetah babies. I have never seen such young cubs, naturally still blind, but these little ones are already full of vigour, spank each other over the best teats, push each other aside, and struggle up Penny's big body, to fall off on the other side. One is definitely a male.

She looked at them so tenderly; it was unbelievable how she had changed already into the role of a mother. She often looked at us and while the little ones snuggled between her front feet she licked our hands and allowed us to stroke her, all so peaceful and happy—except when a hawk flew over us and Penny's eyes narrowed and followed it with a murderous expression.

Joy also wrote to tell Elspeth Huxley her news.

The general belief is that leopards are the most dangerous of all African animals, and leopardesses with young especially fierce. Either I am exceptionally lucky in having such a good-natured, highly intelligent and affectionate leopard to work with, or Penny proves that most of the accepted beliefs are a fallacy.

After her first impulse to show Joy her cubs Penny grew extremely secretive, and she withdrew to increasingly inaccessible lairs where Joy could not follow. Pieter and Makedde therefore took up supplies of water and rabbits. All the time Penny's mate seemed to be shadowing his family while she nursed the cubs.

It is a perfect nursery-mountain for Penny with many caves, clefts, shady trees and all high up from where she can see any baboon or lion approach. The only snag is that she has to walk at least one hour for water at a spring, allocated as a camping site for tourists. Thus we have to provide a water basin, freshly filled, and hope this will stop her deserting the cubs.

If Penny was in excellent condition, Joy was not. She continued to suffer from malaria; she spent some days at the Italian mission hospital in Wamba, where they treated her swollen liver and a mild form of typhoid; she was suffering from low blood pressure; and she wrote to Dr. Nevill, who had seen her through so many of her troubles in Nairobi, asking him to prescribe pills for dizziness.

She was also burdened with two more waifs—a young lion cub and a year-old leopard. After a month the lion was successfully reunited with its pride in the park at Samburu, and the leopard was released in Shaba. There was no way of knowing what became of it, but George assured her that it would survive on rats, mice, lizards and birds.

There was little local company for Joy and her latest assistant, Pieter Mawson—the twenty-two-year-old son of a Rhodesian game warden—who achieved an instant rapport with Penny. Joy wrote intensely appreciative letters about him to his parents. For a time there was no warden in Shaba, and the game scouts on the gate had no transport. The nearest neighbor, Roy Wallace, ran a tented camp for tourists about a dozen miles away on the river. Pieter went there for a drink and to relax in the evenings.

In September there was a major disaster in camp: for the second time one of the fridges blew up.

> Our first explosion almost killed my assistant when the kerosene spluttered all over him.
>
> Then I was alone in camp when I suddenly saw the same fridge ablaze. The fire caught the canvas roof of the mess tent and licked thirty feet up into the trees above. Our dining hut next to the tent was instantly blazing too, and within five minutes a very strong wind carried the terrifying column of fire toward the swamp in front of the camp.

For an hour Joy attempted to beat out the flames until she could no longer move. She was so desperate to prevent them from setting the whole bush alight that she left her radio transmitter, Penny's tracking device, 3,000 photographs, 1,500 slides, 4,000 feet of film, and most of her sketches of Penny to burn. Above all she reproached herself for allowing 30 rabbits to die in the ashes of their *boma*. The Ritz had not lasted forever after all.

For three hours she was alone in the holocaust until the rangers at the gate, who had seen the smoke, could reach her on foot.

As always in the bush, everyone came to the rescue. The Isiolo councilors sent out teams of carpenters and laborers to rebuild the camp—some of its posts still stand and stones mark the edges of its deserted paths. Pieter Mawson and Makedde struggled to keep Penny supplied with water and meat, and when Joy cracked her knee again Pieter supported her for miles across the treacherous lava until they reached the car.

Roy Wallace, of whom she had always been wary because she disliked the idea of tourists staying inside the reserve and because Pieter went there to drink, was quick to write. He offered her the free use of his camp and his radio and sent her two bottles of her favorite Cinzano.

Even so there were stresses at the end of the long, hot, days. To ease them Joy hobbled off alone on one of the walks that gave George such qualms, and would get back only just before dark, in time for the seven o'clock news on her radio. Pieter Mawson disappeared more often, and for longer, to unwind over sundowners with Roy Wallace. Phobic as always of other people's drinking, Joy launched into noisy recriminations and arguments whenever he came back. His general behavior began to change so much that Wallace, too, found him irksome.

There were other problems, with casual labor, in the camp. On December 10, Joy discovered that a metal trunk had been forced with a crowbar and that a camera, two large torches and some money were missing. She identified a young Turkana, Paul Ekai, as the thief, paid him off and sacked him.

On the brighter side, both Penny's cubs were thriving, and despite her attempts to introduce them to Joy, they refused to obey her. Joy was not in the least dismayed. Their birth and survival had given her new book the climax she had been waiting for, and leopards seldom, if ever, raise more than two cubs at a time in the wild. Virtually the entire script had gone off to Marjorie Villiers just before the fire, together with sufficient photographs and slides to produce a handsome and worthy companion to her earlier books.

Patrick Hamilton confessed that her method of imprinting or transference seemed by far the best way of entering the secret world of a leopard. Joy told Helen Wolff:

I believe that we have a really important book. I am corresponding with three leopard researchers in Cape Town, the USA and Israel. They all assure me that I am the only one to have the opportunity of learning about the mother-young relationship. Nothing is known about this because normally cubs are not seen for six months and then only very rarely.

Well, from their questionnaire I can answer 34 out of 38 questions already, even if Pasha—the male cub—keeps so aloof.

In fact he proves why leopards are so difficult to study as their innate instincts are far stronger than in other cats. All Pippa's and Elsa's cubs were very obedient to their mothers and tolerated us at close range; but Pasha—he is wild as he can be, and why should he co-operate? His father is wild, and Penny lives utterly wild with him except for the two hours in the mornings when she is with us. So he learns from his parents all he needs to survive.

So thrilled was she with these triumphs that in the middle of December she accepted, at only half an hour's notice, an invitation to fly to Paris to appear on television. A channel devoted an evening to showing *Born Free* and then discussing Joy's work in the context of modern conservation. She was one of a panel that included Brigitte Bardot, a trapper turned conservationist, a circus director and a man who claimed "the poor eskimos would starve if they were not allowed to kill baby seals."

Elated by the tribute, she went on to London and changed planes at Heathrow, where Marjorie Villiers and I went to see her. She approved the final details of her book, including the title, *Queen of Shaba;* she had just discovered that "queen" was the correct title for a female leopard. She told us about Paris and the presents she had bought for Pieter Mawson, for George—whom she was expecting for Christmas—and even for Terence and Tony Fitzjohn. Not since the day Billy Collins had promised to publish *Born Free* had we seen her so happy.

Three weeks later she was dead.

4

George never made it to Shaba for Christmas; the pilot who had offered to take him worked for an Austrian aid scheme and was called elsewhere. Pieter Mawson celebrated it with friends in Isiolo.

Having no radio in camp, Joy waited all day for George's plane to appear and as the light faded gradually gave up hope. She had bought a new taperecorder in Paris and at her request Ros Hillyar had sent her tapes of Schubert, Chopin, Brahms and her other favorite composers. That evening she listened to Mozart and Strauss. It had rained while she was away and all around her Shaba had broken into leaf: the forsaken landscape of dust clouds, ash and blackened silhouettes was suddenly, everywhere, green.

On January 3, 1980, she went for her usual walk at about half past six in the evening. Makedde was in Isiolo—he had just been married for the third time—and only Pieter Mawson and Kifosha were in camp. Kifosha lit the lamps and by 7:15, when it was quite dark, he and Pieter were worried that Joy was not back.

Pieter therefore drove out in the Toyota pickup to look for her along the track she always took. Two hundred yards from the camp he saw her body in the lights, lying on the road in a pool of blood. Trying to reverse he got stuck in the mud at the side of the track. So he ran to the camp, called Kifosha and drove back in Joy's station wagon. They looked at her body to make certain she was dead, and seeing a large wound on her left arm thought it must have been caused by a lion. She had heard one grunting in the swamp a few days before.

Leaving Kifosha with the body, Pieter drove back to camp to fetch a sheet and a blanket, a rifle and ammunition. He noticed the lights had gone out. With Kifosha's help he wrapped up Joy's body, laid it on the backseat of the station wagon and set off for Isiolo. He gave Kifosha the rifle and ammunition and told him to guard the camp.

Kifosha then discovered that not only were all the lights out but the two gates to the animal enclosure at the back—the outer one gave on to the bush—were open. Joy had bolted them both before she had gone out. Kifosha now secured the inner one, but was afraid to go farther. Next he saw that Joy's tent had been opened. A trunk had been forced and papers were scattered all around it. Not surprisingly the stalwart Kikuyu who had shown no fear of the Mau Mau was extremely alarmed.

Pieter stopped briefly at Roy Wallace's camp to borrow some petrol. He told him that Joy had been killed by a lion and pointed to her body at the back. He then picked up Dr. Wedel in Isiolo at about 9:00 P.M. and went on to the police station, where the doctor examined the body. He simply confirmed Joy's death after observing two wounds on her arm and one on the left side of her chest.

Half an hour later a chief inspector arrived and it was decided to take Joy's body to the hospital mortuary in Meru, where there was refrigeration.

The next morning the chief inspector, who was not entirely convinced that Joy had been killed by a lion, went back to Shaba with Pieter, where they were joined by a senior superintendent and other policemen. They examined the blood patch where Joy had died. Today it is marked by a cairn with a metal plaque to her.

The police found her walking stick, and had to tow the pickup to camp because the battery was missing.

There was a crowbar lying in Joy's tent, and a metal box, like the trunk, had been prized open. The crowbar, taken from the camp toolshed, was the one that had been used to force a lock on December 10. When they went to the animal enclosure they found prints of shoes leading into the bush. This convinced the police that murder had been committed and suspicions fastened on all Joy's employees, particularly on those who had quarreled with her, including Pieter Mawson and Paul Ekai, the young Turkana she had sacked.

This account of the investigation is based on a transcript of the legal proceedings that followed it.

On January 5, a postmortem was carried out by three doctors in Nairobi. They agreed that Joy had been killed by a sharp weapon, such as a *simi;* there were two cuts on her arms and a third that had penetrated eight inches into her rib cage, severing the abdominal aorta. Later, Peter Jenkins confirmed in evidence that the wounds could not possibly have been made by a lion.

For several days the suspects underwent intensive interrogation. Pieter's was especially severe and intimidating for his recent disagreements with Joy in camp had been noisy and impossible to conceal. On January 6 two more senior police officers arrived from Nairobi and very soon all the suspects were cleared except Paul Ekai, who could not be found.

Then, on the night of February 2 at Baragoi, nearly two hundred miles away, toward Turkana country, three men complained to the police that they had been roughed up by thugs. When one of them handed over his card with the name Paul Ekai, the sergeant recognized him as being on the "wanted" list, and he was detained.

On February 4 Ekai made a full confession to the murder. He said he had been incensed that when Joy sacked him he had not been paid the full wages he thought due to him. He had therefore returned and loitered near her camp in order to protest to her on her evening walk. She immediately grew very angry and he stabbed her in fury. George mentions in a letter that the sum of money in dispute was only about fifty shillings, but that Ekai was particularly aggrieved by his sacking as he had been beaten by the police at the time.

Throwing his *simi* into the swamp Ekai crept up to the camp, intending to rob her tin trunk for money and valuables. Before he had a chance to finish the job Pieter Mawson returned for the blanket and rifle. He therefore hid in the bush until Kifosha came back alone, when he took the battery from the pickup and made his way by a game path to his manyatta.

Ekai led the police to the battery and then took them on to a manyatta, where he pointed to a knife, scabbard and belt. The next day he led the police to a second manyatta and produced a haversack containing some of Pieter's clothes that had been stolen on December 10. From the roof of another house he extracted a torch that had been stolen from Joy on the same night.

Later, government scientists established that the bloodstains on the haversack belonged to Joy's blood group and not Ekai's. He must have handled it shortly after the murder.

It took a very long time for the case to reach a hearing. It lasted three months and although Ekai reneged on his confessions, he was convicted of murder on October 28, 1981.

There was some doubt about Ekai's age—somewhere between seventeen and twenty—and he was therefore sentenced to be detained during the President's pleasure. Had he been older the death sentence would have been obligatory. His lawyers appealed on his behalf, largely on the grounds that his confessions were neither voluntary nor true, but the three appeal judges found nothing to convince them that the confessions had been extorted from him and felt that the second robbery was irresistible proof that Paul Ekai had been at the camp on the night of the murder. On December 14, 1981, they upheld his conviction.

Since then an attempt has been made to revive suspicions that Mawson was in some way responsible for Joy's murder. Not long afterward he was killed in a car accident. He cannot defend his name and no evidence of his complicity has ever been produced.

5

Joy's death was headline news all over the world. George never believed she had been killed by a lion, but he was stranded at Kora for twenty-four hours and was unable to stifle the rumor at birth.

Her body was taken to a private mortuary, where Peter Bally came to pay his last respects. In her will Joy asked that her ashes be buried in Elsa's and Pippa's graves. Her funeral therefore took place in the Nairobi crematorium, which stands on the road to the game park.

George wrote:

> Her funeral was simple and quiet. None of Joy's oldest and closest friends was there that day for they were either dead or in Europe. But old friends of mine, friends of Joy's later years—Austrian, English and Kenyan—and friends of the wild animals and their country to whom she had given so much, were present.

Later he went, very quietly, with Peter Johnson, Peter Jenkins and Jack Barrah—another old friend in the Game Department—to place Joy's ashes in the two graves at Meru. At Elsa's he planted them under a stone that some Tharaka had dislodged to get at the honey in a bee's nest beneath it.

It was widely known that George and Joy had been living in separate camps for the last fifteen years, and some papers wrongly reported that they were legally separated or even divorced. The success of *Born Free* so eclipsed all her other achievements that only one obituary explored them or attempted to assess their variety or the full complexity of her character.

A tourist who had lost her way in Shaba with a friend and found herself expiring of thirst at the gate of Joy's camp, afterward wrote this to her.

> That was the best cup of tea I have ever tasted. We never dreamed anything as exciting would happen to us. Friends have asked "What's she like?" "Electric," we tell them.

It would be difficult to say more in a single word.

I believe Joy's unique success in retaining the trust of a leopard while she raised her cubs in the wild, against all odds, and in country as rugged as Shaba, was one of her two most valiant achievements.

The other was the series of marathon safaris she made to paint the peoples of Kenya.

Only a few degrees less exacting, and each of them extraordinary in themselves, were her successes in painting the Kenyan flora and in unraveling the riddles of her sphinx, the cheetah, whose ancestry may be the longest of the three great cats, but whose descent we have placed in jeopardy.

With the exception of her botanical apprenticeship to Peter Bally she accomplished all these feats through her own vision, energy, tenacity, courage and skill as an artist and photographer.

Her greatest achievement, living, writing and illustrating *Born Free*, could never have been fulfilled without these qualities too—but the whole phenomenon was dependent on George from beginning to end.

Of course its legacy is much greater than the continuing worldwide pleasure derived from the book and the film. It also goes far beyond the beautiful and living memorials endowed by Joy from her royalties—the parks of Samburu, Meru, Shaba and Hell's Gate—and the benefits to the countless Kenyans whose wildlife clubs she helped found and finance.

Most significantly *Born Free* was one of the torches that in 1960 were lit and held up in the darkness of our ignorance by a handful of visionaries.

With the zoologist Bernhard Grzimek, the artist Peter Scott, the underwater explorer Jacques Cousteau and the marine biologist Rachel Carson, George and Joy—a game warden and an artist— suddenly cast enough light for the world to perceive the terrible destruction of its natural treasure that was going on all over it.

This perception gave rise to the popular movements that became broadly known as "green"—concerned with the environment, conservation and the recognition of animals' rights. It also coincided with the first widely known studies of our fellow mammals in the wild. Young men and women woke up to the fact that if the proper study of mankind is man then they had better examine man's origins, his relatives and his habitat very fast indeed or it might be too late.

Ted Hughes, now the Poet Laureate of Great Britain, wrote this in a review of *Living Free*.

That a lioness, one of the great moody aggressors, should be brought to display such qualities as Elsa's, is a step not so much in the education of lions as in the civilisation of men. And insofar as it is more important to throw one's energy into forming traditions of kindness and summoning a spirit of sympathetic understanding, even in the smallest things, rather than exercising any further the overdeveloped weapons of the hands and the head, this book is a small gospel.

Starting out with no more than courage, curiosity and a love of independence, and receiving not a penny of help from anyone else, George and Joy were welcomed to the ranks of the outstanding men and women of our century who have devoted their lives to opening our eyes to the mysteries of the animal world. At different times and in their different ways Konrad Lorenz, Julian Huxley, Bernhard Grzimek, Armand Denis, Peter Scott, Gerald Durrell, David Attenborough, George Schaller and Jane Goodall have all paid tribute to Joy's achievements with George.

George Schaller's meticulous studies of lions and gorillas were followed by others, of snow leopards in the Himalayas and pandas in the bamboo forests of China. His eye for detail was never blind to the full wonder of the natural world. In his 1987 introduction to *Born Free* he wrote:

> When humans observe an animal they mainly see the fiction they have invented for it. The Adamsons gave us another and a new image of the lion . . .
> At her death in 1980 Joy left an unequalled devotion to the big cats. Books and a movie made Elsa a force for conservation in that she helped create a new consciousness on behalf of Africa's wild life.

Born Free inspired Iain Douglas Hamilton, who has done more than any single man to protect the elephant in Africa from terminal destruction, to become a zoologist. Desmond Morris found himself in possession of evidence that the book affected the attitude of a whole generation to animals, and to lions in particular. As with any shift of public opinion "the wind bloweth where it listeth."

One night, in 1976, Joy could not sleep and an epitaph floated into her mind in German. She sent it to Helen Wolff for translation, telling her about her wish for her ashes, and that she wanted no gravestone.

She was writing her autobiography at the time, *The Searching Spirit*, but she did not include these lines.

> The wind, the wind, the heavenly child,
> Is fanning the solitary stone.
> It strokes and caresses
> In the moonlit night,
> And watches over the mysterious deep.
> Wind, wind, thou heavenly child,
> Secret are thy ways.

When Helen Wolff wrote back to Joy she ended her letter:

I dash this off with my love, and in the hope that it will be daylight, not moonlight, when this reaches you; you are a sun person, all warmth and fire.

TWENTY-SIX

Last Battles

1980–1989

1

George was appalled by the manner of Joy's death. "Far better it had been a lion," he told several close friends. Among the hundreds of letters he received was one from Kifosha who said:

> Thanks a lot for your reward of 500 sh. I was with your assistant some time back and sent him to say *pole* to what happened. Please let God be your shepherd for this is not our home, we are all passing through.

Pole, the Swahili for "slowly," has also become a greeting that may be modified by expression, intonation and gesture into moving condolence.

Many Africans had cause to be grateful to George. Retired game scouts materializing from the bush and his own staff would approach him for small gifts, loans or advances on their wages.

One day Muga wrote to him.

> Much greeting from your one workmen Muga Bocho. In 1971 I was eaten by one of your lions called "Boy" in name and you send me to Garissa Hospital.
>
> My child is learning at Daku Sec. School. The first term I tried up my lovely best and paid his school fees, but this second term I don't think he will go to school due to school fee. So I hope I will be much helped by you Mr. George, Sir.

George frequently did contribute to the children's school fees and he always acceded to requests from Chief Shabu in Asako for help with the hospital or repairing the school. He sent help to Hamisi's assistant, Osman Bitacha, when his house fell down; and he was regarded by most of his men with the affection and respect due to a father, although some—like many children—could be moody and rebellious.

He had expected little from Joy and she left virtually everything to her Elsa Appeal, including the serial rights to *Queen of Shaba* for which the *Daily Mail* paid £125,000, swelling its assets to nearly half a million pounds—excluding the value of Elsamere.

She left George about £8,000 a year by way of a life interest in her Channel Islands trust, which approximately doubled his pension that had recently been improved and guaranteed by the British government. Recurring reports that Joy had left him nothing and that he was on the breadline were therefore nonsense. Life in the bush, apart from the cost of his transport and meat for the lions, was not expensive.

Even so, whatever he received was quickly swallowed by his work, for the grants-in-aid had dried up and unless he kept the roads open there was no chance of maintaining effective antipoaching patrols— nor could he and Tony have found his lions.

Their numbers had grown considerably. After a wild lion had joined them, and a dozen or more cubs had been born, there were twenty. As a result the last of his rehabilitated lions dispersed, never to be seen again. One of their offspring, a young lioness named Growe, settled near the Tana among the Kiume hills; another, Koretta, became matriarch of a pride around Kampi ya Simba.

Previously George's prides had always been dominated by males like Boy or Christian. Their descendants, born free, were led by females who occasionally, but briefly, accepted the authority of some wild male.

Apart from Joy's death and the altered behavior of his lions, 1980 was a far more fundamental watershed for George. Kora, this remote triangle of thornbush, began to be encircled, then infiltrated, by the economic, social and political columns of the twentieth century that had already trampled so much of Africa's landscape, put its game to the sword and undermined the whole structure of tribal tradition.

George treated the inevitable conflicts like every other crisis in his life. As if they were charging animals he waited until they were almost on him; then he coolly took his decisions and acted.

There was one further change. From now on the significance of his life lay not in what he did, but in what he had become: people came from all over the world simply to be with him and to listen to him.

2

One of the lions that crossed the Tana paid a friendly but uninvited call on George's nearest neighbor, Chris Matchett, who had set up a tented camp for safaris along the river. George rowed over in an inflatable dinghy, identified the lion and planned to bring it back on a raft. Instead it moved on.

Matchett's wife, Marie France, who looked after their young daughter and the clients in camp, was an inspired cook. On special occasions, like birthdays and Christmas, George was invited for the finest food in the African bush. In return Matchett brought safaris to Kampi ya Simba for the authentic flavor of Kenya, over supper with George and Terence.

No two men could tell them more about the country's tribes, landscape and wildlife, or the legacy of the British. After their long colonial service they had both, to their considerable surprise, found congenial niches under Jomo Kenyatta and his successor Daniel arap Moi. Nevertheless, both knew that Kora's immemorial defenses— the thorn bush ramparts and the moat of the Tana—were under threat.

The tribes had always fathered large numbers of children because so few survived but they continued to do so despite the impact of medicine on infant mortality. Kenya had the fastest growing population in the world: from five million in 1950 it was now more than twenty million. In the same way, improved veterinary knowledge had led to an explosion of livestock, and since the animals were the basic measure of man's wealth, no attempt was made to control their numbers. The trouble was that although they helped feed the extra mouths, they also devastated the ranges that had always supported them.

As a result the Somalis, who for centuries had been pushing farther into Kenya to secure additional wells and grazing, were more persistent than ever. A series of droughts now made their pressure more severe still, and the government seemed to have lost the will to hold them on the line of the Tana. George told them he had no wish to

397

deny them their use of the water holes, only to protect the destruction of the trees and the game.

While the Somalis crossed into the reserve from the north, the Orma moved in from the east. Flying each year from Nairobi, I saw how the Wakamba settlements advanced from the southwest until at last they appeared inside the boundary.

Perhaps the threat that most endangered Kora was oil. When its price soared at the end of the 1970s, and gold slumped, there were strange repercussions. For instance, the value of ivory and rhino horns rocketed as an investment. Hong Kong and Japan wanted tusks for carvings and seals; the Chinese powdered rhino horn for aphrodisiacs and oil-rich Yemenis rhino horn for dagger handles. They were readily supplied because after the civil wars all over Africa, rifles were easily come by. The last of the 150 rhino in Kora were wiped out and the elephants reduced from 400 to 40.

When the poachers had picked off the largest and most accessible animals, they turned to other forms of banditry. Somali shifta ambushed a bus on the edge of the Kora reserve, killing its driver and twelve passengers. They looted the bodies and made off with half a million shillings.

Oil also made itself felt in other ways. Airliners carried annual migrations of tourists to Nairobi and Mombasa, from which smaller planes and minibuses bore them away on safari to Kora and elsewhere. Chris Matchett started to plan jet boat trips down the Tana.

Very soon these tourists became the targets of shifta: visitors were threatened, robbed, shot and murdered in Tsavo, the Mara and Meru. Chris was returning to camp one night with his wife and daughter but was delayed on the way. His German manager and African assistant went ahead. When they approached Matchett's camp at dusk an ambush was waiting. Both men were killed by Somalis and the camp set on fire.

The Somalis also threatened the life of Bitacha, the most reliable of George's men, for telling him about their presence in the reserve, with the result that the police had beaten some of them. They put a price on George's head too. One evening his driver, Moti, went to Asako for supplies and failed to return. Next day a friend of George's took a plane to discover what had happened. He found Moti in the village, who said he had been warned that a posse of Somali shifta were planning to hijack his car on the road, drive it to Kora and kill George in his camp as a reprisal for keeping them out of the reserve.

Moti's final return was uneventful. As on a previous occasion the Somali chief vetoed the contract on George: on no account was the golden goose, who spent so much money on camel meat, to be assassinated! Unconvinced by reports of this reprieve, the Director of Wildlife, Daniel Sindiyo, grandson of the Maasai *laibon* painted by Joy in 1951, sent Ted Goss to order George out of the reserve for his safety.

George replied he would leave Kora only in handcuffs. As a consequence a number of precautions had to be taken. He had slit trenches—he called them funk holes—dug beside each of the huts: in fact they would have been little use in an emergency but represented formidable obstacles after a convivial evening in the mess. At sunset each night he issued to his staff his motley collection of firearms: four rifles, a 12-bore shotgun and the .38 revolver that had nearly let him down when he was savaged by Suleiman. There was also an ancient .303 rifle that was clipped into the Land-Rover next to the driving seat whenever he went to look for his pride.

George's staff wanted a holy man to exorcise the Somalis' spell on their camp; the Game Department sometimes posted armed rangers to a specially constructed enclosure a few hundred yards up the road. George raised an eyebrow when he heard that one of their commanders came from a banana and fish-eating tribe.

3

George's allies in the coming battles were frequently absent. Tony Fitzjohn's movements, like those of the lions, remained unpredictable, and even Hamisi and Terence were apt to come and go. Hamisi would take time off in Asako to look after his wife, children and goats or on sick leave. Terence occasionally disappeared to the coast— George hinting darkly that it was a case of *cherchez la femme.*

Hamisi might never have returned from one of his visits to the village. He was watering his goats in the river when his ankle was seized by a crocodile which pulled him out into the stream. He yelled for help and with great presence of mind began to gouge at the reptile's eyes with his thumbs. It dropped him. But while he was limping back through the shallows the croc grabbed him again. This time children who had rushed toward the commotion screamed at the tops of their voices and pelted the crocodile with stones. Hamisi managed to tear himself away but he still has an ivory scar on his ebony shin.

Originally Terence's cook, Hamisi gradually shifted his allegiance to George, although he shared Terence's deprecation of the lions. Like Terence's his face was nearly always inscrutable, but it was not difficult to deduce that both men resented noisy intrusions into their tranquil routine. For Hamisi they often meant very hard work.

It was astonishing, especially in later years, with the growing but wildly irregular numbers around the mess table, how well Hamisi fed everyone. On his traditional fireplace of three stones and smoldering brushwood he produced satisfying meals from almost anything or virtually nothing.

Terence's principal preoccupation away from Kora was his house at Malindi—its completion and decoration, later its letting, and finally its sale. At Kora he found a new interest in life after a visit from one of George's assistants at Meru, Hans Oppersdorff.

Oppersdorff showed Terence that, his days as a hydraulic engineer ironically over, he had a gift for water divining. He could locate lions too, by dowsing. Oppersdorff had used the technique in 1976 to help the Tana River Expedition find some rare Pels fishing owls just below Kora. Tracking George's lions now became miraculously easy.

Holding the photograph of a missing lion in one hand, from the other Terence dangled a plastic pendulum over a map of the reserve. According to the way it then swung, or if it hung still, he would mutter a verdict on the lion's location, disappearance or death. George said this arcane divination was accurate 50 percent of the time; his tracker, Abdi, gave much the same figure. It saved a great deal of effort and petrol.

After the lioness Growe had vanished for six months, Terence's pendulum located her among the Kiume hills twenty-five miles upstream. George went to investigate with one of the girls who had become a mainstay in camp. They arrived at sunset and within a few minutes the girl felt a tingle down her spine; turning, she saw a lioness about to spring. Luckily it was Growe who responded to George's quiet call and the camel meat he quickly tossed her.

Jan Gillett, the botanist from Kew who had worked so often with Joy, accompanied Terence on a hunt for some poachers using one of their snares in place of a photograph. It led them to a hide in the bush that was empty. However the bows and arrows they found gave

Terence a pointer to one of the villages. There the culprits were discovered.

I discussed the technique with a professional geologist, unaware that he knew Terence. He said he was quite unable to believe in dowsing but had been obliged to accept that it worked. He had once taken Terence up in a plane. Over country not yet prospected he plotted on a map a fault line that the geologists discovered only later with their instruments.

If he was not dowsing or busy on the roads Terence caught up with repairs to the camp. One morning he bent down to set fire to a pile of rotten palm thatch without first taking a quick look around. His face was immediately seized by the sinister young lion named Shade, who had been stalking George a few days before.

The labor gang and George quickly drove off the lion. Alan and Joan Root, who were filming in camp, disinfected Terence's wounds—his cheek was punctured and his eyelid torn—and flew him to Nairobi. He later confessed that he had never believed Livingstone's assertion that he felt no pain when he was mauled by a lion; now he knew it was true. Eventually the doctors patched up both his cheek and his eyelid, but his enchanting smiles were rarer than ever.

Within a few weeks of Terence's accident, Ken Smith, as Provincial Game Warden, told George quietly that the Director of Wildlife had decided no more lions were to be released in Kora, but was perfectly happy for him to try his hand with leopards. There was only one condition: the leopards must not be imported.

News of this long-awaited approval for a leopard project at Kora spread rapidly to friends in Australia, India, the Gulf, North America and Europe. In Paris it was picked up by Michel Jeanniot, a pilot with Air France, who had always been very generous on his visits to Kampi ya Simba.

Most of George's and Tony's visitors—many self-invited—arrived with a welcome offering of fresh food. If some neglected this courtesy, few failed to bring him a bottle of whisky. In July 1981 Jeanniot left the cockpit of the jetliner that he had just flown into Nairobi with a very large basket on his arm. It appeared to be full of French bread, cheeses and some bottles of wine: he was quickly nodded through customs.

By the time the basket reached Kora the two baby leopard cubs, hidden under the food, were growing restless. Their mother was owned by a nightclub proprietor in Paris. Jeanniot, who had fallen under the spell of Kora and could not bear to see her offspring grow up in a cage, knew that George had been given permission to raise leopards but was unaware of the embargo on immigrants.

As so often happens in Kenya, time tempered the law. Tony had already prepared a new camp about six miles away, on the far side of a tiny new airstrip that Terence and his gang had scraped in the bush. It included an enclosure for the leopards complete with a tree, platform and carefully built cavern of rocks. He and the leopards immediately settled in there, and the authorities let bygones be bygones.

In the last year or two Tony was occasionally apt to drink more than was congenial to others. He had also taken to leaving George for weeks, perhaps months, without warning or saying good-bye; he even threatened to leave for good. In fact, though, he did not want to quit either George or Kora. One of his friends, Anthony Marrian, wrote to George:

> He looks on you really as a father, and most of his drive is directed toward realising the things you have taught him.

Marrian understood and told George that Tony—like any maturing young man—must be allowed to grow up independently, be shown his work was appreciated and be given the satisfaction of earning a wage, however meager. With this support Tony demonstrated where his heart lay. He set off for Europe and North America and, by his enthusiasm and the force of his argument, persuaded small groups of generous friends to set up trusts in England, the United States and Canada to support the conservation of Kora. It was an excellent foundation for the new enterprise.

The first leopards were about two months old when they arrived. The female was given the name of the nearest water hole, Komunyu. After careful handling, feeding and medication, both were released fifteen months later when they were fully acclimatized to Africa.

Between 1983 and 1985 Tony was sent eight more leopards for release—all of them consigned to Kora after they or their mothers had been caught stock raiding. Despite the use of radio collars, and the help of Patrick Hamilton on whose advice Joy had relied so much for Penny, nine of the leopards wandered off and then disappeared. For a while they could be traced, from a plane, up to twenty miles away, but it was impossible to track their quicksilver movements for long.

Only Komunyu did not break the bonds that held her to Kampi ya Chui; it became the center of her range and she was always about. She seemed to resent women in camp and at least twice threw herself at them with her claws out, though never doing serious damage.

The existence of a separate camp was essential, for the leopards, like the cheetahs at Meru, had to be kept apart from the lions; it also gave Tony a raison d'être and space of his own. At the same time it doubled the logistical problems. By then there were ten trucks, tractors and trailers; there were more visitors, more pretty girls—George noticed Tony's bed in smithereens outside his hut after a night with one Amazon—many more sundowners and tales that cannabis was being brought up from Nairobi; competition and resentments were increasingly in the air. Inevitably there was more traffic on the radio between the two camps and the outside world.

Frustrated for years by the inadequacy of the radio in George's camp, Tony made sure his own equipment was sophisticated and powerful. Rumors about its purpose and loose talk on it, combined with Tony's increased flying activity, convinced the authorities that the camp was "a security risk": one official even alleged he was "a British spy." A spy to what end?

The probable explanation of this accusation is that an influential faction of Kenyan Somalis, in sympathy with the needs and aspirations of the herdsmen from the north, were anxious to see the last of George's energetic assistant. Although he had no direct connection with these people, the most powerful Somali in the country, General Mohamed, commander of the armed forces, kept an alert and protective eye on his tribe. Once or twice he urged the Wildlife Department: "Be gentle with my people," when it became necessary to turn them out of the reserve.

At his best Tony was diplomatic—friendly, funny and co-operative—in his dealings with the army, the police and the game wardens. But occasionally they saw him at his worst, which led them to refuse him a gun license—a situation dangerous for a man in a remote area dealing every day with lions, leopards and shifta.

Anthony Marrian had laid it on the line to him.

The party is over, Fitz. Your own future at Kora depends entirely on you. Have you got it in you? When they say they do not envisage you changing your spots any more than the beautiful leopards in your programme, are they right?

In the opinion of his friends three factors enabled Tony to demonstrate—if too late for Kora—that the answer to the first question was "yes" and to the second "no." His establishment of the Kora Wildlife Preservation Trusts; his determination to learn to fly in order to further his work; and his love for an unusually able and attractive girl who wrote to George, as many did, offering her help at Kora.

You cannot learn to fly and at the same time drink. In 1984, Tony went to America, gave up drink whenever it was likely to affect his flying and obtained his license. He was rewarded by friends of the Canadian trust with a plane.

His return to Kora was followed shortly by the arrival of a girl, Kimberley Ellis, who was dark and slim, and of whom an old cliché, she moved with the grace of a panther, was inescapably apt. Very soon she settled into Kampi ya Chui.

Before long Kim had the measure of this idiosyncratic community, which included Tony; his cheerful jacks-of-all-trades, Mohamed Maru and Oil Can; Komunyu, who, despite her suspicion of other women, accepted Kim; Lucifer, an orphan found dying as a baby by a pool on the big rock, who was now growing into a handsome young lion.

4

Like other men of his age George missed the company of his contemporaries. Few, apart from Tony Ofenheim in England, survived—and even she felt unable to make the journey to Kora again.

I am afraid that I will never return. First I am too old and secondly I would never wish to alter my memories of our long drives through the bush fetching up with the lions, bathing in the river, and the evenings sitting with you and Terence and Tony watching the sun go down.

I even enjoy in retrospect being bitten by a scorpion and how unsympathetic you were! Going for walks with Christian and he chasing a rhino when still quite young. Fishing with Tony, while keeping a wary eye on three hippos in the river.

There was, however, one old acquaintance, first met in 1941 during the Somalia campaign, whose company always enlivened the camp. Major Douglas Tatham Collins answered an SOS for help when George was suddenly deprived of both Terence and Tony. Like so many others who began to arrive at Kora, he treasured George's friendship and stayed on for six months.

Collins had a colorful past. Given to hunting with his brother—as George had been with Terence—he had suffered the tragic experience of killing him during a buffalo hunt near Mbalambala. Charged by the buffalo, at very short range, he hit it twice with his .470 before it bowled him over and knocked him out. His brother then put a bullet into the buffalo from the far side, but did not drop it. When Collins came to, his third shot shredded the buffalo's heart, but went straight through to hit his brother in the chest.

Despite this, his spirit remained unbroken and his company was always a tonic. A gifted talker, drinker and writer, he was also a renowned lover and eccentric. When he was a young subaltern his beautiful Somali mistress, sailing in a dhow to join him, was shipwrecked in a storm and drowned. Some time later he had pulled himself through severe cerebral malaria by donning his cricket pads and miming some sensational strokes with his bat. He turned himself to whatever was needed at Kampi ya Simba, especially looking after its guests.

George's best antidote to loneliness—apart from his lions—were the relays of visitors, men and women, young and old, who pitched up at Kora, longing to play some part in its life. Each year a section of the British Army contingent sent to train in Kenya during the winter came to give him a hand.

When the new airstrip between the two camps came into operation this sign was nailed to a tree at the edge of it.

LIONS ON ROAD—BUZZ CAMP AND WAIT AT PLANE TO BE COLLECTED

Buzz camp they did, usually during George's siesta.

Many were flown in by a handful of familiar pilots, including two Austrians. Fritz Strahammer, who flew for the Austrian aid organization Wings for Progress, gave his own time freely and soon chalked up a hundred flights to Kora. Andrew Meyerhold, a doctor whose hobby was flying, had lost his father in the Holocaust during the war.

Quiet and courteous, he devoted himself to Terence and George. He frequently flew up for the weekend, filling his plane with provisions or passengers eager to see George.

David Allen was, by contrast, Pan-like and extroverted, matching Tony Fitzjohn with joke for joke, girl for girl, and exploit for exploit. He made George laugh. One morning two of the girls whipped off their shirts and waved to him topless as his plane left the airstrip. Describing the scene, George said, with a throaty chuckle, "David had to circle several times to pick up his eyeballs."

He even managed to overcome, by his sheer exuberance, George's detestation of flying. He took him to Lake Rudolf in a vain search for the rock engravings Joy had found forty years before, and to the Mara for an uproarious reunion with the last of the wardens and white hunters George had known at Isiolo. "We swapped lies for hours!" George said later.

Up to 500 visitors a year converged on Kora. Apart from the planes, they dropped in by helicopter, camper van or Land Cruiser, in cars without four-wheel drive, or on motorbikes. Two girls rode out from England on bicycles to raise money for the protection of rhinos; a Scotsman, a Greek and a Japanese judo instructor were only just prevented from swimming across to Kora, through the crocodiles, when their canoe was stranded on the far bank of the Tana.

Most wrote to George because their love for animals—their cats, their dogs or their horses—provided a link, and confidence that he, with his lions, would have the largeness of heart to offer them the hand they could not find elsewhere. Whether they sought urgent escape from a man, a woman, depression or some other illness—or simply needed a change—George gave them sanctuary.

The young women, mostly in their twenties, were astonishingly varied and versatile. One owned five cats and wrote him cheerful letters composed of few words but covered with kisses in lipstick; one eloped with a member of his staff; one looked after sharks, pythons and tarantulas in a Viennese zoo; two gave him expert pedicures, cutting his notorious toenails; one had sailed the Atlantic in a small boat at the age of seventeen and worked as a cannonball in a circus; and one braved the dangers of kidnap, rape and murder to nurse Ugandans through the worst horrors of their civil war.

George came to regard them—like his lion and leopard cubs—as pupils in his "Rehabilitation School for Errant Young Ladies." Apart from target practice with a revolver or rifle down by the river there was very little formal tuition, but they began to keep an illustrated magazine in the mess hut. They repaid George with their companionship and the support he needed himself to cope with his housekeeping, accounts and tyrannous correspondence.

Only a picaresque novel could do justice to the characters of all ages and races, from all walks of life and its sidelines, who turned up out of curiosity, on impulse or assignment, for adventure, sensation or refuge. Somewhere in his diary George mentions that one day Tony arrived "together with Father Nicky, one Irish nurse, one black nurse and a man with a squeaky voice, followed by Chief Shabu and his retinue." There was also "a buck-toothed wench" in the party.

It did not matter who you were, what you had done or how you looked. No one was judged and everyone was treated precisely the same: the prince and the poor man, the rich and the handicapped, the sick and the celebrated, Dimitri Gorunov the ambassador from Moscow or Sister Mary of Lourdes from the mission near Kimangao. On the unique occasion when a journalist repaid this hospitality by attempting to ridicule George's life and companions at Kora she laced her article with untruths.

For nearly all who visited him, sundowners under the stars in George's company was the quintessence of Kora. Just three or four people on old canvas chairs in the warm night air. No need to speak. The distant bark of a jackal. Silence again. The soft clatter as Hamisi cooked supper on his stones. The croak of a frog in the water trough. A longer silence and the scent of drifting woodsmoke. A shooting star streaking across the sky. Ash grey silhouettes of the lions, just visible against the bushes.

Whatever George's visitors were seeking, most found respite from the demons of civilization, as Jung had when he came to Kenya in 1926. Kora also lifted the spirit. The only other place where I have experienced a similar sensation was at a Franciscan friary: it offered a similar freedom from the distinctions and demands of life in a city, the same openness to the restoring rhythms of the natural world. For many Kora was an ashram in Eden.

The force that brought the whole experience together was George himself; its proclamation was the roar of a lion on the rocks above camp as the moon rose in the sky. He loved above all things, at the end of his life, to spend a night in the bush on the roof of his Land-Rover, sharing his mattress and a bottle of whiskey with a friend. On this occasion he was alone.

Night out at upper Komunyu. About 10 pm heard an elephant at the water hole, drinking and then approaching. Switched on the Aldis lamp and found it was less than twenty feet away. It turned at the flash and quite slowly, without panic, wandered off. A big bull with tusks of about 60 or 70 pounds. A fine night. Wonderful to lie naked in the starlight with the cool breeze playing over one's body, listening to the sounds of the night.

Once I followed a pair of francolins, with half a dozen chicks, making for George's hut. The croon of a laughing dove rippled down from the roof, a ground squirrel sat on his lap eating peanuts, the francolins headed for the grain scattered around his chair.

Years later, while finishing this book, I came across this impression of Buddha in the wilderness, quoted in a memoir of Kenya, *Speak to the Earth.*

Oft times while he mused—as motionless
As the fixed rock his seat—the squirrels leaped
Upon his knee, the timid quail led forth
Her brood between his feet, the blue doves pecked
The rice-grains from the bowl beside his hand.

5

Peaceful moments like these epitomized the atmosphere at Kora, and George remained constantly relaxed except when he was sometimes oppressed by a surfeit of strangers. Nevertheless, hostile forces and time itself were gathering for their final attack.

Neither George nor Tony Fitzjohn would have had any use for the Litany that prays for deliverance "from the world, the flesh and the devil; from pestilence and plague; from battle, murder and sudden death." Nevertheless, both of them, their staff, their visitors, their lions and their leopards too, could have done with its protection. Though the threat of typhoid and cholera, reported in Mbalambala, quickly receded, other problems did not.

George was not getting any younger. His hand was shakier than ever, he could not take a photograph, and writing was extremely difficult, although he could quell the shakes with a couple of strong gins. His eyesight could not be dealt with so easily.

In 1984 he bowed to pressure from Tony Ofenheim and one of his visitors, Dr. Wolfgang Koos—a distinguished Viennese surgeon who had once owned a lion—to have his eyes treated. He accepted the generous offer of the Austrian Society of the Friends of Kenya to pay for his plane tickets and an operation in Vienna.

The examination, removal of a cataract and implant of a lens entailed two trips to Europe, since the correct lens was not immediately available. It was on the first of these that Bill Travers kidnapped him and brought him to England for a month to record the interviews that were the starting point for the script of *My Pride and Joy*.

It was on the second, in March 1985, that the surgeon inserted a Multiflex plastic lens, with ultraviolet protection, in his right eye. Ernestine Nowak, who had worked so closely with Joy on the illustration of her books, and who had now retired to Vienna, went to see him in hospital, where she encountered one of his "young ladies."

> We were talking about all sorts of things when suddenly a girl burst into the room. She took no notice of me, settled herself on George's bed and got hold of his feet. While she concentrated on his toe nails George had such an expression of utter bliss on his face that I felt like an intruder, so I made my excuses and left!

The eye operation restored George's vision perfectly. He found he could both read and drive at night without glasses.

Terence had always been less robust than George, and his frail body had begun to falter under a series of assaults—an accident in Malindi, when his car was hit broadside; a stroke that paralyzed his leg; and breathing and gallbladder problems needing intensive care in Nairobi. He was seen through these troubles by two men. His doctor, Andrew Meyerhold, who flew himself to Kora whenever he was needed, and Ongesa, one of the older men on George's staff, who had a healing touch as a masseur.

There was a limit to what they could do, however, and nothing could prevail against a thrombosis in 1986.

April 4   Terence in a bad way all last night, groaning and gasping. Got up several times to look at him. 6.30 am tried to get through to Andrew Meyerhold, finally managed. Said he would try to get an aircraft and come in this afternoon. Late in the morning Terence was sleeping, although his breathing was labored and fast. About 12.30 pm. Ongesa came to me and said Terence had stopped breathing. He was dead!

Writing from England, Tony Ofenheim balanced her sympathy with a philosophical attitude that George shared.

I was so sorry to hear about Terence and you must miss him very much, but I am sure he was glad to go as his health was so bad. Quick and painless—and that is something we all wish for ourselves.

Terence was buried in the same *lugga* as Boy, next to the one young lion that he had liked, Supercub. A sprinkling of the flowers he had loved always pushed up nearby in the rains, and in the evenings George went down to water the desert roses planted around his headstone.

Walking back to camp, George was quite likely to bump into Koretta and her pride, all of them wild, which were being filmed by a Japanese company. It was Koretta's brother Shade who had bitten Terence in the face, and unwisely George had spared his life. Two and a half years later he had crossed the river and was shot by a game warden, after killing a Somali girl who tried to drive him away from her goats.

There must have been a rogue gene in the family, for in 1986 one of Koretta's daughters, aptly named Boldie, attempted to carry off Tomoko, the star of the Japanese film, by her scalp. She had been interviewing George and at the end of the day she and the crew were watching Koretta's pride on a camel carcass. While Tomoko was enjoying a gin and tonic to one side of the car, and George was on the other using the radio, Boldie crept up on her. Perhaps the petite Japanese girl presented the same temptation as a child; in any case, just as Boy had let go of Mark Jenkins, Boldie now left Tomoko as soon as George rushed at her.

Tomoko was flown to hospital in Nairobi and a week later was able to return to Kora—to face an equally terrifying experience. The entire Japanese crew were sitting down to supper at Kampi ya Chui, when Komunyu made her way over the wire and appeared in the mess hut.

Despite Tony's efforts to make a serious introduction between the leopard and his guests—as one might with a guard dog—Komunyu chose her target and sank her teeth in the back of Tomoko's neck. She seemed to resent her as previously she had other women. Again Tomoko was flown to Nairobi and again, with outstanding courage, she insisted on coming back to finish the film.

Both Boldie and Komunyu managed to avoid death sentences, but Koretta's pride was doomed. Before long they were poisoned by Somalis after attacking their cattle.

If the death of Terence and disappearance of Koretta cut George off from the past, he now suffered a third blow that struck at the future. He had always hoped that Tony would succeed him at Kora; but the sensitivity of the security forces to Tony's presence in a trouble spot went against him. Suddenly the Director of Wildlife— still Daniel Sindiyo—closed down the leopard project. Following a visitation by the Provincial and District Commissioners, the chairman of the local council and the chief of police, together with a large retinue, it was also made clear that despite Tony's initiation of the Kora Preservation Trust he was no longer persona grata inside the reserve.

In the face of this intense disappointment Tony showed his mettle. He took Kim to Tanzania to look for a reserve in need of protection— where he could put into practice all he had learned in the last sixteen years. He found one at Mkomazi, on the other side of the frontier from Tsavo, and at the invitation of the Tanzanian government, he set about planning to move there.

With George's blessing the name of the Kora Trust was changed to the George Adamson Wildlife Preservation Trust so that funds raised in its name could be applied to the Mkomazi project as well. Kampi ya Chui was closed and dismantled, and although George took on the staff to help with his own work, two other inhabitants paid a heavy price.

Tony had always kept young Lucifer at his camp rather than George's; now that the lion was homeless he tried to join Growe. But she was preoccupied with her own offspring and her consort, a wild male, would not accept him. He therefore struck off forlornly to look for a mate.

Then Komunyu disappeared. Signals seemed to show she was near George's camp, up on Christian's Rock. At first no one could find her there, but on a second search Tony, Oil Can and George peered over a sheer drop and saw her body decomposing on a ledge below. She had been driven to her death by baboons.

It is hardly surprising that under these pressures George's health began to deteriorate seriously in 1987 and 1988. He was flown to hospital four times with breathing problems, blood poisoning and a mysterious allergy.

Andrew Meyerhold maintained that the basic decline was due not to age, but depression after Terence's death. The two brothers had never been demonstrative toward each other, but separation—after nearly eighty years' companionship, under the blue skies of India, the long gray spell of their school days in England and their eventful, crisscrossing lives in the African bush—took its toll.

Nevertheless, George possessed a formidable will to live, which as always was reinforced by his team of "errant young ladies." Further incentive was provided when the lioness Growe, who had been living with her pride in the Kiume hills, and had not been seen for six months, suddenly appeared, killed a large bull giraffe and claimed Koretta's empty territory. She knew she could count on the occasional meal there and that it would be safer than the hills near the Tana frequented by herdsmen.

Among the young women who helped keep George going through the last decade of his life there were up to half a dozen who roused in him, when he was on either side of eighty, emotions and flickers of the old Adam, which took him back many years. Some were extremely attractive and inspired feelings more powerful than paternal—or grand-paternal—affection. When this happened he grew suspicious, and then angry, if they spent too long with one of the younger men in camp.

My secretary has gone back to the jungles of America. The last straw was when she kept Terence and myself waiting for supper while being laid by a visitor.

Despite these rare lapses each was invaluable and brought a different combination of gifts and skills to looking after his health, letter writing, bookkeeping and the exhausting entertainment of his innumerable visitors. They threw parties for him, slept out on the roof of the Land-Rover with him and went swimming in the river. Once or twice, when drinking, music and laughter began soon after sundown and continued—with the encouragement of a convivial Irish father from the local mission—until long after moon-up, they even risked dancing with him. It was all good, clean, fun and gave a kiss of life to George's morale.

The last of the girls to bring him such joy was English—Georgina Edmonds, known as Doddie to everyone. Intelligent and attractive, she animated his days with her dog, her goat and her humor, and found fulfillment herself in the sanctuary of Kora.

Not all the spirits around Kora were benign. A few took advantage of George's laissez-faire attitude. There was something about him of the holy innocent or fool, who found it hard to reprove, to say "no," or to withhold his signature from a paper put in front of him.

He also appeared oblivious to the emotions and situations he unwittingly generated among the young men and women in camp. Jealousies and disagreements, bad blood and occasionally worse behavior, intensified in the isolation of the bush. Rumors of them spread and were exaggerated in Nairobi, and in 1988 questions were even raised in Parliament about "the white hippie community" at Kora.

Some of George's most stalwart supporters, Ted Goss, Monty Ruben and Andrew Meyerhold immediately urged him to be more careful in controlling how many people, and who, he allowed to come and stay in his camp. The allegations in Nairobi were quickly refuted and soon overtaken by reports of a different kind of trouble at Kora.

Fighting had broken out between the Wakamba and Somalis: one Somali was killed and several wounded. But however many problems the Somalis had caused him, George did not hesitate to help get their wounded to the hospital as fast as he could.

More ominously still, a gang of shifta ambushed a Game Department patrol on the edge of the reserve: a warden was wounded and three rangers killed.

6

In 1988 an English company, Yorkshire Television, decided to make a film about the last phase of George's long life in Africa before it was too late. To do so it had to obtain the permission of the new Director of Wildlife, once again Dr. Perez Olindo.

Olindo was fighting a desperate rearguard action to protect the last strongholds of game in Kenya. He had inherited an almost impossible assignment. Starved of funds by the government, the Wildlife Department was inadequately staffed and armed, its morale was at a nadir and it was riddled with corruption. Some rangers had even joined in the slaughter that, during twenty years, had reduced Kenya's elephant population from 100,000 to 15,000 and virtually exterminated its rhinos.

Since the protracted disputes over the lions in Meru, Olindo's views on George's activities had changed. George personified the preservation of Kora for wildlife, and Olindo now saw films about George in the same light as his minister had viewed them twenty years before. Anything that drew the world's attention to the current crisis commanded his support. Furthermore he agreed that to give the film a sharper point George should be shown releasing another batch of lions.

In July George therefore received three cubs, two weeks old, whose mother had been shot killing cattle on a ranch at Lewa Downs, near Mount Kenya. By then he had the temporary assistance of Gareth Patterson, a young man who had acquired bushcraft and a devotion to lions while working as a ranger in South Africa and Botswana. He helped to keep an eye on Growe and her pride, was making a systematic search for Lucifer and looked forward to understudying George in the release of the three new cubs, Batian, Rafiki and Furaha.

The film was shot in September. It is a vivid and moving portrayal of George's last stand against the advance of time and the growing pressure on the crumbling defenses of Kora. Perez Olindo flew up to appear in it. Perhaps the most striking moment in the film is when he and George gaze down at the decomposing corpses of an elephant mother and her calf, still buzzing with flies, and George made this emphatic assertion.

"It should be a capital offence to kill one. I think the life of an elephant is worth at least a hundred humans." He was not asked how he had arrived at this opinion, but one explanation might run something like this. Thirty years before he and Joy had recognized, through their relationship with Elsa that lions and some other animals were far closer to us than people were prepared to admit. Apart from Eugene Marais's study of baboons in South Africa, no zoologist had then completed a systematic study of large mammals in the wild, but as time went on a few scientists and naturalists reached similar conclusions.

The fact that only about 1.5 percent of our DNA differs from a chimpanzee's means they are closer to us than they are to gorillas or orangutans. We therefore need to look at them differently if we are to understand both them and ourselves. In her book *Through a Window*, Jane Goodall offers parallel after parallel between chimpanzees' behavior and our own—from deceit, hunting and warfare to family life, friendship and a semblance of altruism. In one case an old chimpanzee defended his keeper from a murderous attack by two females who wrongly thought the man was threatening their young.

Advances in our knowledge of elephants also reveal parallels between them and ourselves. Daphne Sheldrick discovered that if their orphans are to survive the trauma of a family massacre they need at least as much company, care and play as a human child does to recover. When they are regularly harassed by poachers, or their ranges are restricted and overcrowded, they are prone to the same conditions of the blood and heart as men under stress. Elephants trained to work in the forests of Burma can work out solutions to new problems on their own. On at least two occasions elephants have been known to protect the life of a wounded man.

Most of us look at an animal, prejudiced by our ignorance of it and convinced that because it lacks a language like ours, and therefore a culture, it is our inferior. Most of us are only concerned for its survival if its whole species is endangered.

George, on the other hand, with the clearer eyes of experience, recognized an animal's capacities for what they actually were, and regarded it as an equal. He wanted to save each one, as an individual, from unnecessary captivity, suffering or death.

This was the foundation of his moral concern for the animals. He knew that they constituted no threat to the human race. On the other hand, he regarded man as what he called "the most destructive creature on earth," while his rate of breeding was out of control. Given the reckless genocide of the elephants that had taken place over the previous twenty years, and that they could well be driven to extinction in the wild, his computation that one elephant was worth a hundred human lives was a reasonable, if deliberately provocative, verdict.

Toward the end of the Yorkshire Television film Perez Olindo said, on camera, that in his opinion George had made a greater contribution to conservation than anyone else in the country. Before he left he told George privately that the government was about to raise Kora to the status of a National Park.

Nevertheless, on the very next day, there was a security alert in the province that temporarily delayed further filming in Kora. Alarm bells started ringing in Nairobi and London, with two direct consequences.

Earlier in the year George had decided to leave his entire estate to the Elsa Appeal (renamed the Elsa Conservation Trust). Since it was perfectly apparent that he and anyone with him was now vulnerable to attack by shifta at any time the trustees immediately made a formal request to the Wildlife Department that George's assistant be allowed to carry firearms. They also asked George should be licensed to use hand-held radios linking him at all times with his staff and the local game rangers. With great generosity the television crew offered their own walkie-talkies.

Second, in November the government posted to Kora a force of eighty armed men of the paramilitary General Service Unit; when they had to be moved in February 1989, they were replaced by seventy Anti Stock Theft Police who carried out armed patrols of the park. George wrote to Tony Ofenheim.

> Government is taking strong action to push the Somalis and their herds across the river. Now, for the first time in all the years I have been here, the reserve is without a single Somali!

For the moment Kora was safe, both for Kampi ya Simba and for Growe and her pride. With six new cubs they numbered fourteen.

Each day George walked his own three young lions down to the river with his latest assistant, Neil Lindsay, and his tracker, Abdi. Eager though he was to release the three permanently, Growe made it perfectly clear, by snarling at them through the wire in the evenings, that she would not accept them into her pride. Not yet ready to kill, and competition for her own young, they would be more of a liability than an asset.

Even though Kora was peaceful, poachers continued to ravage the game and bandits to threaten the tourists in the rest of the country. Suddenly aware that this violence could spell disaster to the whole Kenyan economy, President Moi appointed a new Director of Wildlife, Richard Leakey. With his worldwide reputation as an expert on the origins of man, his outspoken views on Kenya's inability to manage its game and his proven willingness to grasp nettles, he seemed the only person capable of turning imminent defeat into a lasting victory.

Within a few days of his appointment Leakey announced his first measures. Poaching became a capital offense and a shoot-to-kill directive was sent to the rangers in the parks. Yet until he could build up their numbers, re-arm and entirely retrain them, every park in the country was still at risk, and in July two tourists were shot and killed in Meru. By way of response the security force in Kora was immediately transferred across the river.

A week later Neil Lindsay had to go to the nearest permanent police post, ninety miles away at Mwingi, to report that he had found Somali footprints in Kora again.

TWENTY-SEVEN

Death in the Afternoon

1989

1

Bad news travels extraordinarily fast in Kenya. On Sunday, August 20, 1989, a dozen or so subscribers to the Laikipia radio network, scattered all over the country, warmed up their sets ready for the evening transmission that usually runs for thirty or forty minutes. At 7:30 precisely a cool, clear woman's voice broke the silence.*

"Good evening all stations. The time is 7.30 pm. This is Delta 26 acting as control on the evening schedule of the Laikipia Security Network. Any station with police or emergency traffic come in now."

Normally there is a pause for a few seconds and a faint crackling before Control goes on to ask each station in turn if it has any calls to make. That night there was no such silence.

A tense, high-pitched African voice immediately came up on the air. "Control this is Delta 40, it is an emergency, an emergency, over."

"All other stations please stand by," Jane McKeand, the Control, said calmly. "Delta 40 please go ahead with your message, over."

"Control from Delta 40, I am in the camp at Kora," the African said. "There has been an accident. Shifta bandits have attacked and shot Mr. Adamson. I repeat, they have shot Mr. Adamson."

For some moments Control did not react, but then she began to speak slowly, almost incredulously. "Delta 40 can you please identify yourself and repeat your message, over."

The African replied in clear, staccato sentences although his tenseness came through the fuzz of the static.

"My name is Samuel Mwaura. I am Game Warden of the Kora

---

* I am indebted to Mrs. Kuki Gallman for the transcript of the transmission which follows.

National Reserve. Shifta have shot George Adamson dead. I have taken over Kampi ya Simba. Please call the Director of Wildlife. His telephone number is —— Over."

Control acknowledged the message and went on. "Is there any station who can make a phone call, over?" There was a shadow in the tone of her question. It echoed the shock of everyone who was listening.

"Delta 30 calling Control," a military voice intervened. "Thank you for your report, Mwaura. I shall call the Director now. Please stand by, over."

One of the listeners was Kuki Gallmann, who combines a 90,000-acre ranch with a remarkable private game sanctuary. She knew Richard Leakey, the new Director of Wildlife, and had been making notes of these exchanges.

"Delta 16 to Control," she broke in. "I'm sorry to interrupt, but the Director's correct telephone number is ——" She dictated it twice.

The new number was acknowledged by Delta 30.

"Thank you 16," said Control. "All stations please stand by, over." For agonizing minutes the operators stayed tuned to the frequency, hearing only the static.

At last the clipped matter-of-fact English voice broke the strained silence. "Delta 30 calling. Do you read me, Mwaura?" Mwaura responded tautly and Delta 30 went on.

"The Director will fly up to Kora at first light. You are to wait there with all concerned. Please will you have the body waiting at the airstrip, over."

Samuel Mwaura acknowledged the instruction. "I will have Mr. Adamson's body at the airstrip tomorrow morning before daylight. Thank you, over and out."

Jane McKeand's voice came up again, kind and composed but distressed, as every one listening now was. Her husband Julian had made the trek with George, Joy and Elsa along the shores of Lake Rudolf.

"Delta 30 thanks you very much for your assistance. I am sure all stations will join me in the grief at this terrible accident. Is there any other station with urgent traffic?"

Nothing more was heard.

2

At about six o'clock on the previous evening George had sat down at his typewriter. For sixty years his diary had reflected every facet of his life, but his hand was so shaky that in the last year only three words appear in his own writing. Many of the entries were written for him by his companions and assistants; his own were irregular, typed and then stuck in.

He finished as it was getting dark and added the heading for August 20. Then, taking care not to trip into one of his funkholes, he went over to his mess hut to prime and light the Tilley lamps. Unusually, for a weekend, he was alone in camp with just one guest, Inge Ledertheil.

Four visitors had left him and flown back to Nairobi that afternoon.

Inge Ledertheil, in her early forties, was German. She had written to George five years before, without introduction, to ask if she might visit him. He had agreed, as he usually did to requests of that kind. She spoke virtually no English, was enchanted by Kampi ya Simba, had asked if she might come again and had left on his table a pink elephant stuffed with hard-earned banknotes. Since then she had been back a number of times.

There were nine of George's staff in camp that night. Hamisi, of course, and Osman Bitacha, Hamisi's assistant, a slight, wiry man, with a little mustache and a placid expression. His eyes sometimes flashed, with anger if he was describing a theft of tools from George's store, or with amusement when he recalled that Terence had the appetite of a starling.

Then there were Mohamed Maru, now George's headman; Moti, the driver; and Kiya and Ongesa, who were older than the rest. Ongesa was the kindly man with a limp who had nursed Terence so devotedly through his last illness. The others were Hassan, Deru, and Ali, the mechanic, also known as Oil Can. Abdi, George's tracker, was on leave in Asako.

Toward sundown many of the occupants of Kampi ya Simba went to roost—the ravens, sunbirds, weavers and marabou storks. As soon as darkness fell frogs would croak, bubble or belch, and the guinea fowl would let out an occasional screech. The three young lions in their enclosure next to George's hut were alert, with their ears pricked, and grew restless. Perhaps they caught a scent or a sound from Growe's pride outside.

It was impossible to predict when she and her companions would turn up, for they were apt to disappear for weeks, but George had long believed in the lions' awareness of the arrival and departure of the people who matter to them. Abdi told me: "It was as if George and the lions could speak to each other through radios in their hearts."

On that Saturday evening Growe suddenly arrived at the Camp of the Lions. Her pride was now fourteen strong. George went out to throw them some goat meat, and they lay outside the wire for most of the night.

3

Sunday morning passed quietly and toward lunchtime, after an eleven o'clock gin—the ritual of George's morning restorative having survived for fifty years—he began typing a letter to a nurse in England; now that he could see properly again he had no difficulty in tapping it out slowly with a forefinger. He told her in the letter how far behind he was with his correspondence and accounts.

Not long after 12:30 P.M. he was interrupted by the drone of a plane, and a small single-engine six-seater dipped low over the camp. Moti, his driver, was having a siesta in his *kikoi*. George told him to put on his trousers and go to the airstrip.

Before he could do so, Inge volunteered to take the Land-Rover parked near the camp gate. Bitacha, who was on general duty, went with her.

It usually took about a quarter of an hour to get to the airstrip along the rough but well-worn track between the gray thornbushes, where doves, and occasionally tiny dik-dik, darted off at the approach of a car, and hornbills glided away with a croak. After nearly ten minutes on the road Inge and Bitacha suddenly heard shots and saw three figures running through the bush. It is impossible to know exactly what happened next because their impressions vary, though not in essentials. I base this account on all the evidence I have received and, where it is contradictory, on probability.

More shots followed and Inge slowed down: bullets slammed into the front tires and the differential. Then she stopped and three Somalis approached. One was wearing a camouflage uniform like a game ranger's and at least two carried automatic rifles.

They immediately demanded money and then watches, cameras and binoculars. Inge could not understand them, but Bitacha got out with his hands in the air and protested they had nothing of value. As he stood in front of the Land-Rover, one of the Somalis seized Inge's watch, pulled her out and hustled her beside Bitacha. When they began to slap her and prod her with their guns she turned out her pockets. She also rolled up her T-shirt, and after that her shorts, to show them she had no money. One of the men then angrily pulled her toward the bushes with obvious intentions.

Although she cannot remember doing so, Bitacha says she screamed and tried to cling to him for protection but according to her he ran into the bush. It is difficult to see how he could have done this because when Inge caught hold of him the shifta started to beat him with a crowbar that had been stolen from the airstrip a few days before. They ordered him to sit on the ground and deliberately smashed his thigh with it.

By now, it seems, Inge was making such a noise that the shifta became nervous. One suggested shooting Bitacha, but the others said no, they would finish with the woman first and then kill them both. According to Inge a second man now helped the first to push her away into the bush.

4

Back in camp, the headman, Mohamed Maru, was the first to react to the fusillade up the road. He ran to George's hut at the far end of the compound and George broke off his typing. Together they called Hassan, Kiya and Ongesa, and all of them clambered into George's battered Land-Rover embellished with a lively graffito of a guinea fowl calling "All aboard for the Nightingale."

George had buckled on his pistol, and his ancient .303, with four rounds in the magazine, stood upright in its rest between him and Mohamed, who was in the passenger seat. Hassan, Kiya and Ongesa sat behind.

A few minutes later George came around a corner and was confronted, about fifty yards ahead, by the scene of the ambush. He took in the implications instantly and knew he must do something drastic if any of them were to survive. Throughout his life he had faced dangers of all kinds without flinching—in the path of charging buffalo, elephants or lions he had been obliged to make split-second decisions.

The radio transmitter on his dashboard was useless to him. Tony Fitzjohn's camp had been dismantled; no one left in his own camp could handle the radio there; and the Game Warden at Asako was off the air. Very briefly he slowed down or stopped the car.

The sound of his approach had alerted the Somalis to potential trouble; one of Inge's attackers had already gone back to the Land-Rover and now the second one, who had been pulling at her clothes, left her too.

It is quite clear that George took in the situation, and calculated, exactly, the odds and the stakes. He drew his pistol, engaged in low gear and accelerated toward the gunmen. Beside him Mohamed had also been calculating the odds. There could only be one result if George drove at the Somalis. "Stop. Don't do it. Go back," he said.

When George ignored him and put down his foot, Mohamed seized the rifle beside him, shut his eyes and rolled out into the bush at the edge of the track. As he did, he shouted to Hassan to join him. Hassan leaped through the window.

With hope born of desperation, Inge forced herself back to the track and was close enough to exchange looks with George.

Bitacha said he saw what happened next. The shifta nearest to him aimed at the Nightingale and put at least one bullet through the windshield. George drove at him and fired his pistol in return.

Someone shouted a command to kill him, while two men ran alongside the Land-Rover and pumped bullets into it. George made it past the stationary Land-Rover but a bullet hit him in the leg and broke it. The car slewed off the track to the right and came to rest against a tree, crumpling the metal and shattering glass.

By then the Nightingale was perforated by shots and George had received a bullet in the back that emerged from a massive hole in his chest, just below his left shoulder. Ongesa and Kiya were also shot in the back. Somehow Ongesa managed to stagger out of the car and take a few unsteady paces before he collapsed. All three men were dead, and the floor of the Nightingale was soon running with blood.

During the mayhem Inge ran off and hid behind a termite mound and Bitacha dragged himself into the bush.

4

Meanwhile the party on the airstrip grew increasingly puzzled.

The plane was being flown by Wernher Schillinger, a chief engineer with Lufthansa, stationed in Nairobi. He had not been to Kora before but his copilot, Naveed Rasul, an Asian employed by a Kenyan air charter firm, was familiar with the Kora procedures, as was a Mrs. Hoffmann who was bringing her husband to meet George for the first time. Together with the two other passengers they had brought supplies for the camp and intended to return to Nairobi after lunch.

They had all seen the two Land-Rovers parked at George's camp when they buzzed it, and after waiting forty-five minutes at the strip Schillinger decided to fly back and have another look at the camp with his copilot. They left their four passengers on the ground.

Finding no Land-Rovers in Kampi ya Simba they flew back along the track toward the airstrip at about 150 feet. Three quarters of the way along it, about half a mile from the airstrip, they saw the two cars, one on the road and the other about twenty-five yards ahead of it, askew in the bush. A figure, motionless and possibly dead, lay on the road. There was nothing else to be seen.

Schillinger circled above the road, looking vainly for clues to the mystery, and returned to the airstrip. He supposed there had been some kind of accident and wanted to walk back to investigate, but the others would not let him in case there had been violence and he fell into a trap himself.

Instead the entire party circled the scene again for five minutes, flew once more over the camp and headed for Mulika Lodge in Meru, about twenty minutes to the north, on the other side of the Tana.

The second appearance of the plane above their heads broke the shifta's nerve, and they vanished into the bush.

5

Back in camp, downwind of the shooting, the rest of George's staff had heard the second volley and grown extremely alarmed.

Moti, the driver, who had narrowly escaped death from the shifta in 1964, and had been warned of the plan to ambush him on his way back to George's camp in 1980, set off in George's white Suzuki pickup to raise the alarm with the Game Warden at Asako, in the opposite direction from the ambush. He took Deru with him and left behind Hamisi and Oil Can.

In the meantime Mohamed and Hassan were hurrying back to camp. Realizing the danger of keeping to the track and being followed by the shifta, they made a detour and approached from the direction of the river, threading their way between Kora Rock and Kora Tit.

They rapidly described the ambushes to Hamisi and Oil Can, although they were still ignorant of the final horror. The four men then set off on foot for Asako, locking the gates behind them. They heard the plane heading their way and watched it pass over them. Mohamed thought he could make out an Asian and a pilot and one, if not two, passengers. The plane headed northward toward Meru; by then it was about 2:15 P.M.

There was a security post next to the lodge and at approximately 2:30 Schillinger reported exactly what he had seen to the policeman there. He offered to fly five armed men back to Kora immediately but was told that this was not possible without higher authority. After lunching in the lodge he returned to the post at 3:00 P.M. to be informed that Kora had been closed as a security precaution and that an army plane had been sent in to find out what had happened.

Schillinger's party spent the afternoon at Meru and returned to Nairobi at about 6:00 P.M. He reported exactly what he had seen, his subsequent actions and his conversations with the security post. He was so deeply disturbed by the events of the day that he sat up drinking late into the night. At 1:30 A.M. his most pessimistic fears were confirmed by a message from Mr. Hoffmann, who had been drinking in the bar of another hotel. There he had picked up, in a chance conversation with some journalists, news of the disaster at Kora that was already beginning to spread through Nairobi. It was the first they had heard of any shooting because the wind had carried the sound of the gunshots in the opposite direction.

6

By 2:30 P.M. Moti and Deru had reached Asako in the Suzuki pickup and told what little they knew to the Game Warden, Samuel Mwaura. Mwaura was then faced with an exceedingly difficult problem. He had no working transport of his own, his radio batteries were exhausted and he did not know the strength of the shifta, only that they possessed automatic weapons, and his own men merely carried single-shot .303s.

However, within half an hour he had mustered about a dozen armed men, drawn from his own game rangers and members of the local antipoaching unit. At about three o'clock they set off for Kora in a county council Land-Rover and the Suzuki. On the way they met Mohamed, Hassan, Hamisi and Oil Can walking toward them. By 4:00 P.M. they all arrived at Kampi ya Simba, where most of George's staff were dropped off.

The Land-Rover, with Moti following in the Suzuki, then carried the patrol on toward the ambush. No one knew what carnage might await them, or indeed whether they might not run into a burst of fire themselves.

Mwaura stopped the cars well short of where Mohamed and Hassan had baled out of the Nightingale. Keeping to the track himself, he deployed his patrol on either side in the bush and slowly advanced toward the killing ground.

In time they came across Inge still lying on the mound. When she caught a glimpse of Mwaura's rangers in a camouflage jacket, exactly like one of the shifta's, she was convinced the Somali's had returned and was only calmed when Moti appeared.

Mwaura's patrol then found Bitacha lying in the bush where he had hidden himself. As they approached he too was alarmed that the Somalis had come back, until he recognized one of the rangers.

He said that after the shifta had fled Inge had first checked that George and the others were dead and then sought him out in the bush. He tried to persuade her to go back to the camp for help, but she refused, and returned to the termite mound. She denies this ever happened but there is no doubt that she was, understandably, in a state of traumatic shock.

Mwaura immediately arranged for the Suzuki to take Inge and Bitacha back to camp and, after briefly investigating the surrounding bush, followed with the bodies in the Land-Rover. When the tragic cortege reached Kampi ya Simba George's body was laid on his bed. It was four and a half hours since the initial attack and no search, of any kind, had been organized. Despite what the police post in Meru had told Wernher Schillinger, neither the police nor the army had sent anyone to investigate the mysterious accident he had reported.

Mwaura went straight to George's radio set but did not know how to make an emergency call and Inge knew so little English that she had never been asked to handle it. The staff had not been trained in its use either, because there had always been George, Terence, Tony, Doddie or some regular visitor to put through special calls.

For the next two hours Mwaura struggled ineffectually to make contact with Control in Nairobi, and in the meantime Inge found painkillers for Bitacha and made a simple splint for his leg. At seven o'clock it grew dark. Pursuit of the murderers could not begin for another twelve hours.

At 7:30 P.M. the receiver in George's mess hut suddenly came to life with the help of a car battery and the steady voice of the Laikipia control came up on the air.

7

Mwaura's first instinct had been to get Bitacha and Inge to the hospital by road as fast as possible, but Richard Leakey had told him to stay put, until his own arrival, for very good reasons.

He had taken over as Director of Wildlife only a few months previously, when the department had its back to the wall. The intensifying massacre of elephants and rhinos with automatic weapons, spearheaded by the Somali shifta, had led to even worse lawlessness. The death toll had included the ambushed busload of Wakamba, the three rangers and the game warden shot near Kora and the two tourists killed across the Tana near Meru. There had been other atrocities too. The circumstances of Julie Ward's murder in the Mara Reserve, during the previous year, were quite different but had created widespread alarm.

Leakey had to decide then, on the strength of this single radio call, whether George's murder was a deliberate assassination, part of a concerted effort to destabilize the government by the disruption of tourism, a reprisal against the tough measures he was already taking to crack down on poaching, or just an act of casual banditry. He spent most of the night in consultation with the President's office, which was responsible for the country's security.

It was finally decided that Richard Leakey and Philip Kilonzo, Kenya's Commissioner of Police, would fly in at dawn with a show of strength. They would evacuate any casualties with the three bodies and set in motion the machinery of search and retribution.

Soon after dawn on Monday, August 21, a large air force helicopter brought the Director and the Commissioner to the reserve. By then the police and an armed antipoaching unit had arrived in four more helicopters from Provincial Headquarters. For more than two hours they carried out a sweep around the airstrip, the site of the ambush and the camp.

When Bitacha was closely questioned about the shifta he said he was certain he would recognize them again, and was convinced that one lived across the river in Mbalambala.

Later in the morning Leakey left in the helicopter, taking with him Bitacha, George's body and Inge. Ongesa's and Kiya's bodies were flown to Nairobi for postmortem examination a few hours later; Mwaura followed by road and brought with him relatives of the two men to identify the bodies.

As soon as Richard Leakey's party reached Nairobi, Bitacha was taken to the best hospital, where surgeons treated his wounds and bruises and prepared to set his broken femur. George's old friend Monty Ruben, who had done so much for him during the last twenty years, went to the mortuary to identify his body.

At Richard Leakey's special request he had also come to Leakey's office in the museum, picked up Inge and taken her to German-speaking friends who found her a flight back to Germany.

With great consideration the authorities spared Inge all the forbidding procedures that normally attend assault, robbery, intended rape, and murder, but for some reason they decided not to ask her for any form of statement. She flew home to Germany that night.

TWENTY-EIGHT

The End of the Safari

1989–1993

1

George's funeral took place on Saturday, September 2, 1989.

After he had shot and buried Boy, the lion he had probably loved even more than Elsa, he had said he would like to be buried beside Boy "without any fuss." But when Terence had died in 1987 George changed his mind; he wanted to be buried farther down the same *lugga*, next to his brother. There they dug his grave.

More than a hundred and twenty people came to the service in one of the remotest corners of Kenya. Half were African, half European—friends, associates, admirers and reporters from the press, radio and television. They flew to Kenya from all over the world and many made the last stage of the journey to Kora by air, too. Most of the twenty-five little planes had to drop their passengers on the tiny airstrip and then wait twenty or even fifty miles away until the funeral was over.

An impressive array of guards was posted in the surrounding bush and escorted visitors along the road, through the place of the ambush, to the camp. By noon the mess hut began to fill up, but George's usual mealtime companions made off in astonishment. For once the vervet monkeys, ground squirrels, guinea fowl, hornbills, doves and Superb starlings deserted the table from which George always tossed them peanuts, millet and maize.

The British High Commissioner, Sir John Johnson, his wife, Jean, and many others too began to unpack their picnic lunches in the shade of the crowded mess hut. None of George's family—only Pam Carson and other distant cousins survived—could be there, but there was someone to pay tribute from every phase of his life in Kenya over the last sixty-five years.

Nevil Baxendale, George's oldest and closest friend, with whom he had sailed and fished in the 1920s, and shared his marathon marches in search of gold and adventure, now dead, was represented by his son, Jonny, George's godson. He brought a large wreath with a broad white ribbon.

The Game Department, which he had joined in 1938, was now one with the National Parks, and its head, Richard Leakey—the son of Joy's patron and mentor—was coming to give the address.

As soon as the news of George's death had broken, Douglas Collins had agreed to take over the camp. He was the one who presided at the wake dressed only in sandals, shorts, a scarlet cravat and a small white sun hat. George would have approved, he had particularly asked for no fuss.

Ken Smith, who had been with George on the day he had found Elsa, who had succeeded him in the NFD and become the éminence grise of his fortunes at Kora, came to see him laid to rest there—as did Julian and Jane McKeand.

Bill Travers, who had become as close a friend as any, and Virginia McKenna, whom George had loved from the days when they had played with the lions on the foothills of Mount Kenya, flew out from England. Ted Goss and Peter Jenkins, so different in their attitude to the film lions in Meru, were united in mourning. Peter Jenkins who had seen Joy's ashes interred on one bank of the Tana, now watched George's body returning to the dust on the other.

In the last twenty years a whole generation of young had found at Kora a home, a vocation or respite from the bedlam of the twentieth century. Tony Fitzjohn, George's mainstay for sixteen of them, drove up from Tanzania. No one knew better than he how much George had given to this proud stretch of Africa and its wildlife, or had longer experience of the friendship, laughter and wonder that pervaded Kampi ya Simba.

The "Rehabilitation School for Errant Young Ladies" was represented by George's best-loved graduate, Doddie Edmonds, who had hurried back from England. "Oh for Doddie!" he wrote in the letter he left unfinished to drive to his death. He had missed her terribly whenever she was away.

Just before 2:00 P.M. the assembled crowd began to leave camp and walk slowly under the blazing sun to the waiting grave. The three young lions, no longer cubs, stretched their muscles and looked disdainfully down from the roof of their palm-thatched shelter.

Punctually at two o'clock, a huge air force helicopter brought

George back to Kora for the last time. It lowered itself next to the camp and the coffin, covered with flowers, was lifted into a Land-Rover. With Richard Leakey and others in the helicopter was his deputy, Joseph Mburugu. As assistant warden in Meru, Mburugu had welcomed Joy and Pippa there, and eleven years later he had given her Penny.

George would have given a wry smile at the gathering around the grave. The press photographers and television cameras were jostling together on the mound of stones and sand dug from the bed of the *lugga*. The mourners grouped themselves in a semicircle, making the most of a patch of scant shade cast by the gray, skeletal branches of an almost leafless thorn tree. A uniformed guard from the Wildlife Department lined the approach.

Just to one side, at the head of Terence's grave, the desert rose that George had watered in the evenings was in flower. All around a heat haze shimmered off the rocks and sand.

The pallbearers who lifted the coffin from the Land-Rover were also game rangers and were followed to the grave by the Reverend Simon Maina. While he began to intone the burial service, Hamisi, who had remained so impassive throughout the twenty years of drudgery and drama, of laughter and tragedy at Kora, could control his grief no longer. His loud and heart-rending sobs were as moving a tribute to the trust and affection George inspired as the letter from Mohamed read out by George's faithful friend and executor, Peter Johnson.

Before the coffin was lowered the guard of honor fired a salute over the grave, the "Last Post" and "Reveille" rang from two bugles and Richard Leakey proclaimed his government's absolute resolve to meet violence with implacable force and to stamp out forever the threat of the gun to the wildlife and people of Kenya.

One by one George's friends and colleagues dropped a handful of sand onto the coffin. Then the pallbearers began to shovel back the soil and the dust rose in a golden cloud over the flowers and wreaths which lay already wilting in the heat.

In the late afternoon the High Commissioner, who had first served in Kenya many years before, returned to the grave when the dust had settled. Sitting under the tree, listening to the croak of the hornbills, his eye wandering over the surrounding hills in the slanting sunlight, John Johnson was convinced there was no more perfect place in which to be buried.

2

George managed to find a silver lining to almost any cloud, and tragic as his death was, we should do the same.

His memorial service in London, some months after the funeral, ended with a Celtic blessing that included the prayers:

> May your days be long on this rich earth . . .
> May the sun shine warm upon your face.

Those prayers were certainly granted.

He suffered neither the lingering death of an invalid nor a fatal attack by one of his lions, as some friends feared might happen as he grew older, less steady and more prone to forget his gun when he went out to meet the pride.

Although he would have derided the idea, his death was a martyr's. Had he not arrived in the nick of time Inge's molestation might have been even worse than it was; and had he turned back, instead of charging the shifta, the visiting plane would not have spotted trouble on the road and circled it to scare off the gunmen. Inge and Bitacha would have been shot.

Taking the broadest view, the spontaneous anger and dismay that George's death caused all over the world had an immediate impact on Kenyan opinion. It may have been too late and too little but the government rapidly passed an act requiring all Somalis to identify and register themselves.

More impressively, Richard Leakey started to raise, and put into intensive SAS-style training, a cadre of paramilitary rangers willing and able to fight gangs of poachers in the field and defeat them. He recruited the most warlike peoples from the northern frontiers of Kenya to man this new force.

At George's request all the loans he had made to his staff were forgiven at his death. Generous compensation for loss of service was paid to those who survived. None had been with him for fewer than seven years; Hamisi had been at Kora for fifteen, and before that as long again with Terence.

There were substantial payments—from the state and insurance— for the families of the two men who died. Kiya's eldest son, who grew bananas and herded thirty goats, had eight children to support. Ongesa's son by his first wife was in the army, but his eldest son by his second wife had not yet left school and his youngest was only six. Most Africans are good neighbors, and the villagers, under their chief, who came to the burials at Asako would see to it that the two families did not starve.

George's main concern in his last ten years was that his work would be carried on and that Kora, in which a lodge near the river had been recently planned, should not be abandoned to grazing and poaching after his death. He had asked on the last page of *My Pride and Joy:* "Who will raise their voices, when mine is carried away, to plead Kora's case?" He hoped very much that young Africans would take up the cudgels: some of them have, and the wildlife of Kenya will soon be entirely in their hands.

The Elsa Conservation Trust renewed a pledge they had given the Wildlife Department a year earlier that they would grant £100,000 to help develop Kora, so long as the park was fully protected by the Kenyan government. Any penny that George left would therefore continue the fight to protect what he cared for most.

In Europe Bill Travers and Virginia McKenna have intensified their efforts to protect animals in captivity and to revolutionize our attitudes to zoos; the movement is now spreading to America. The threatened closure of Regent's Park Zoo in London, whose treatment of the Kenyan elephant Pole Pole sparked off the creation of Zoo Check, is a measure of the public's growing condemnation of traditional zoo management.

Many zoos and medical research centers, if not most, are still prepared to lock up, in jail cell or concentration camp conditions, animals as intelligent and sensitive as elephants, chimpanzees, gorillas and orangutans, lions, leopards and cheetahs, tigers and bears—to name only a few of the species in which scientists have diagnosed acute distress revealed by their repetitive behavior, which is "stereotypic" or mad. It is time we dismantled this Gulag Archipelago we have imposed on these animals.

Five years after he prospected the Mkomazi reserve in Tanzania, Tony Fitzjohn has brought new life to an area three times the size of Kora. The game is returning to it. There were eleven elephants when he arrived, now there are sometimes six hundred. With the government's backing, his plans for introducing and breeding new stocks of black rhinos and wild dogs, two of the most seriously threatened species in Africa, are about to be put into action.

In the meantime several young men, to whom George's work at

433

Kora was a revelation, have also responded to his challenge. Neil Lindsay has trained for three years to become a game warden. When Richard Matthews, whose father was a friend of George's, found he was unable to join the Kenya Wildlife Service he produced two fine films on leopards and lions instead.

The decision about the future of George's last three lions rested with Richard Leakey, since every wild animal born in Kenya belongs to the state. Bearing in mind that several of their predecessors had attacked George or one of his colleagues at Kora, Leakey accepted an offer from Gareth Patterson to release Batian, Rafiki and Furaha in a private reserve at Tuli in Botswana.

He did so only to encounter setbacks as bitter as George's. Batian, the adventurous male, followed cattle that had strayed into the reserve back across its border and was illegally shot by a farmer.

His affectionate sister Furaha met a far more bizarre end. The body of a tracker was discovered mauled, near where she was nursing three cubs sired by a wild male. On the order of Botswana's Department of Wildlife and National Parks she and her cubs were shot before a postmortem was carried out on the tracker. Two months later the doctor reported that the man had been killed by a bullet, and his body partly eaten not by a lion, but a hyena. Patterson is now fighting for the future of Rafiki.

An even stranger story attaches to the fate of Growe, the matriarch of George's last wild pride. On Douglas Collins's first night in camp Growe arrived with a gaping red wound ringing one of her legs; she could hardly walk. She and her pride were all very hungry but there was no meat in the camp and she reluctantly led them away.

The state of Growe's leg greatly disturbed the staff, especially Abdi, who believed her foot had been grabbed by a crocodile; Collins suspected a snare. He had no truck available to fetch an ox or a camel, but he bought some goats so that he could feed Growe until she could hunt again. However, neither she nor her pride came to Kampi ya Simba.

While I was writing this chapter I remembered a letter from abroad which mentioned that on the day after his murder George appeared to a Mrs. Whitfield during a seance in England for healing animals *in absentia*. Connie Whitfield, who had known George slightly in Kenya, was unaware that he was already dead when this apparition occurred. In answer to my enquiry she wrote:

He came to me for help for a lioness that was in distress miles from water, with a broken leg and in dry, arid country. This beast must have been relying on George for sustenance, and in his thoughts preceding his death; but he was very, very upset when he came.

3

The wheels of justice sometimes grind slowly in Kenya, while the shifta slip through the bush as swiftly as caracals. It was nearly three years before the only suspect accused of the murders was brought to trial. For some reason the prosecution did not call Inge Ledertheil as a witness nor, as the judge pointed out, did they even present a statement from her. He therefore felt it unsafe to convict on Bitacha's evidence alone: there were, after all, three men involved in the incident. The accused man was acquitted.

The real motives behind the ambush have never been discovered but it looks increasingly likely that there may have been a small group of local Somalis determined to remove George, the one fragile barrier between them and the water, grazing and browse inside the reserve, before it was too late. If implemented, the plans for Kora's status as a national park and the creation of a lodge on the Tana, would entail rigid enforcement of the embargo on entry.

An antipoaching unit in Meru also picked up intelligence that an influential Somali, owning large herds, grew angry when two of his men were shot by police evicting them from Kora. He blamed George for their deaths and once more put a price on his head. Either story or both may be true and would account for the crude and haphazard way in which the ambush and murders were carried out.

So far the assassins have successfully bought time for themselves. More than three years after George's death his camp has been burned and is derelict, his grave has been vandalized, the park is unprotected; Somali herdsmen and poachers range through it at will.

Richard Leakey, who has successfully stamped out poaching in all other parks, has prepared a plan to integrate Kora with Meru, Bisanadi and Rahole, on the north bank of the Tana, more easily managed and defended than Kora in isolation. However he has not yet been able to mobilize the necessary legislation and security to achieve this.

The world is now waiting to see if the Kenyan government will back the promises which he, as the Director of their country's Wildlife Service, made in their name at George's funeral—that thuggery and poaching would be eliminated from Kenya's reserves so that Kora, among them, will once more be safe. If they do not, at a time when refugees are flooding across the border from Somalia, the line of the Tana may be irreparably breached, causing everlasting damage to wildlife, to tourism and to the management of the country itself.

4

One of the most articulate epicureans of his generation, Cyril Connolly, famous for his love of fine silver, rare books and good wine— also hot baths—wrote this in *The Unquiet Grave*, long before he fell in love with East Africa toward the end of his life.

> The spiritual life of man is the flowering of his bodily existence: there is a physical life which remains the perfect way of living for natural man, a life in close contact with nature, with the sun and the passage of the seasons, and one rich in opportunities for equinoctial migrations and home-comings. This life has now become artificial, out of reach of all but the rich or the obstinately free, yet until we can return to it we are unable to appreciate the potentialities of living.

There can hardly be a more apt description of the way George lived and perhaps it explains why so many men and women, including "the seekers and the lost," as Virginia McKenna called them when she spoke at his memorial service, were drawn to him at Kora. They felt they might learn something about the secret of life from him.

His obstinate pursuit of freedom, for himself, for others and above all for animals, kept George on safari until his last breath left him. It was as if he shared Robert Louis Stevenson's belief that "to travel hopefully is a better thing than to arrive, and the success is to labour."

He recognized that man's unique development of language, and our preoccupation with our cultures that stem from it, have blinded nearly all of us to the foundation of our existence, our root stock as animals. We have chosen to ignore these origins largely because of our inherited prejudice that animals are absolutely inferior to us rather than relatively different.

If we open our eyes we shall see, for the first time, that we are sharing our world not with a dwindling menagerie of animals over whom we have dominion, but a galaxy of living creatures endowed with many of the same faculties as we are, and with others that we have lost or never possessed—all of which entitle them to freedoms and rights no different from our own.

For nearly two months Douglas Collins and Richard Matthews stayed on to take care of Kora, but when a large band of Somalis and shifta, some of them armed, were seen on the Tana they had to pull out.

They turned the key in the padlock of Kampi ya Simba and headed for Nairobi, while Hamisi, Mohamed, Abdi and the others went home to Asako, looking forward to the day when they could come back and work for a secure and transfigured national park.

Until he left Kora, Douglas Collins made daily entries in George's diary, and went regularly to check on his grave. Anxious that his old friend should not lack for refreshment on the last leg of his journey he had buried a bottle of gin beneath the coffin; determined that George should never be forgotten at Kora he started building a stone cairn above it.

One of Collins's diary entries refers to the passage from *Out of Africa* in which Karen Blixen writes about the grave of her lover, Denys Finch Hatton. She reports that the Maasai had often seen a lion and lioness lying there at sunrise and sunset. Collins continues that on the evening of September 16th he went down to complete the cairn.

I noticed a curious thing. The wreaths and bunches of withered flowers had been blown away by a strong wind. A particularly heavy wreath [had been dragged back and] was only just out of position; on it was a broad white ribbon with the obvious teeth marks of a lion. I found the spoor and it was that of a large male. Scouting round I found further pug marks and evidently the grave had been visited by a pride. All I could do then was wonder.

Perhaps, through their hearts, George's pride were keeping in touch with him on the last stage of his safari.

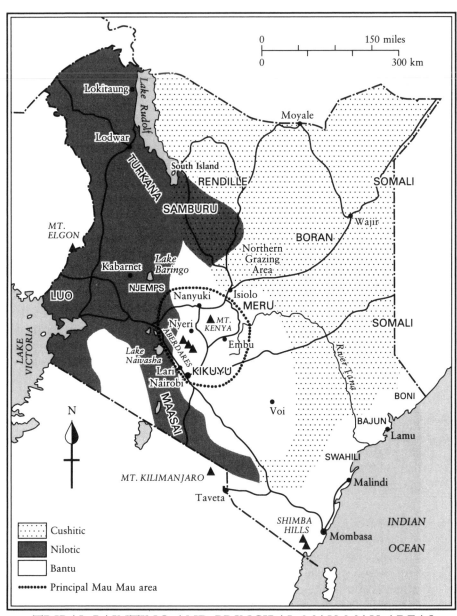

TRIBAL PAINTING AND PRINCIPAL MAU MAU AREAS

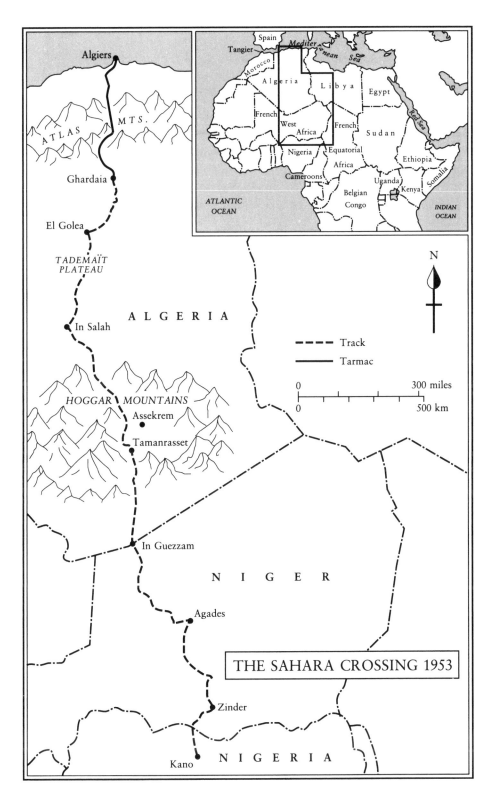

THE SAHARA CROSSING 1953

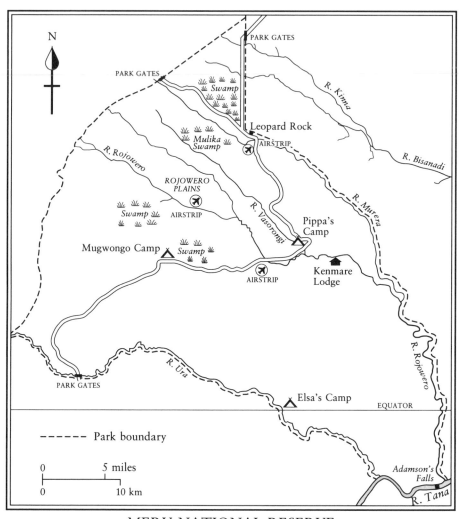

N

PARK GATES

PARK GATES

Swamp

Leopard Rock

Mulika Swamp

AIRSTRIP

R. Rojowero

ROJOWERO PLAINS

AIRSTRIP

Swamp

R. Vasorongi

Pippa's Camp

Mugwongo Camp

Swamp

AIRSTRIP

Kenmare Lodge

R. Kinna

R. Bisanadi

R. Murera

R. Rojowero

PARK GATES

R. Ura

Elsa's Camp

EQUATOR

- - - - - Park boundary

0   5 miles

0   10 km

Adamson's Falls

R. Tana

MERU NATIONAL RESERVE

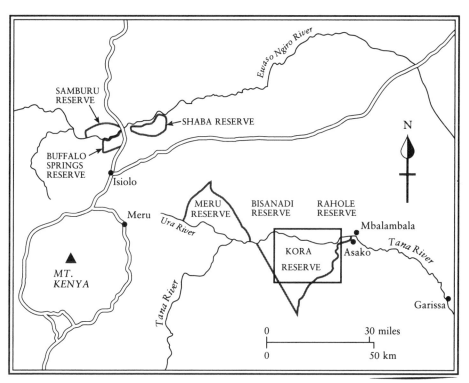

SAMBURU
RESERVE

SHABA RESERVE

Ewaso Ngiro River

BUFFALO
SPRINGS
RESERVE

Isiolo

N

Meru

MERU
RESERVE

BISANADI
RESERVE

RAHOLE
RESERVE

Mbalambala

Ura River

Tana River

Asako

KORA
RESERVE

MT.
KENYA

Tana River

Garissa

0		30 miles
0		50 km

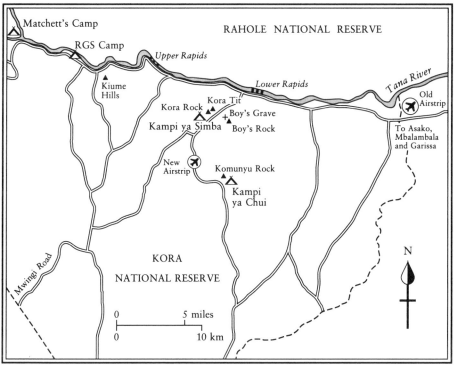

Matchett's Camp

RAHOLE NATIONAL RESERVE

RGS Camp

Upper Rapids

Lower Rapids

Tana River

Kiume
Hills

Old
Airstrip

Kora Tit

Kora Rock

Boy's Grave

Kampi ya Simba

Boy's Rock

To Asako,
Mbalambala
and Garissa

New
Airstrip

Komunyu Rock

Kampi
ya Chui

Mwingi Road

KORA

NATIONAL RESERVE

0		5 miles
0		10 km

N

KORA NATIONAL RESERVE
AND DETAIL
441

NOTES

The indented quotations in the text are identified below by the page numbers on which they appear and the first two or three words of the quotations. Published sources are listed in the Bibliography. Most of the unpublished sources are held in the Adamson archive owned by the Elsa Conservation Trust.

Abbreviations

GA   George Adamson
JA   Joy Adamson
BC   Sir William (Billy) Collins
AH   Adrian House
VM   Virginia McKenna

TO   Dr. Angela (Tony) Ofenheim
BT   Bill Travers
MV   Marjorie Villiers
HW   Helen Wolff

CHAPTER 1   1942–1943
8 *What men call* Lord Byron, *Don Juan,* Stanza 63.
14 *While we were* GA, diary, 1943.
14 *In the evening* Ibid.
14 *Joy asked me* Ibid.
15 *The Ballys and* Ibid.

CHAPTER 2   1906–1924
17 *I saw Halley's* GA, draft memoir.
19 *Dear Mummie* GA, letters, 1914–1923.
20 *Dear Mummie* Terence Adamson, letters, 1914–1923.
21 *At Bombay we* GA, draft memoir.
22 *I saw Aunt* GA, letters, 1914–1923.
23 *I remember George* F. W. Robins, letter to AH, 1991.

CHAPTER 3   1924–1934
25 *We arrived late* GA, *Bwana Game,* p. 36.
27 *We would never* GA, *My Pride and Joy,* p. 31.
33 *The design of* Ibid., p. 36.
33 *At 3.00 pm, three* Ibid., p. 37.

CHAPTER 4   1935–1942
37 *T. is really* GA, diary, 1935.
37 *Tony has gone* Ibid.

38 *One evening we* GA, *Bwana Game,* p. 73.
40 *On my safaris* GA, *My Pride and Joy,* p. 60.
40 *In the morning* GA, diary, 1937.
43 *I went up* Elspeth Huxley, letter, February 9, 1938 (Public Records Office. CO533/498/14).
45 *Juliette has made* GA, diary, 1938.
45 *Spent a wonderful* Ibid.
45 *Devil of a* Ibid.
45 *Sent a note* Ibid.
46 *Mathews Range* Ibid.
47 *I saw a* GA, *Bwana Game,* p. 102.
47 *As I waited* GA, *My Pride and Joy,* p. 59.
48 *Simultaneously her chain* Ibid., p. 59.
49 *This is a* GA, diary, March 14, 1939.

CHAPTER 5   1943–1944
51 *She wants to* GA, diary, 1943.
51 *Peter hinted to* JA, draft memoir.
53 *I do love* GA, diary, 1943.
53 *I realised today* Ibid.
53 *In the course* Ibid.
54 *This short time* JA, draft memoir.
54 *One day she* GA, legal statement, 1947.
58 *The weather was* Alan Davidson, letter to his family, January 14, 1943.
59 *When night falls* Ibid.

60 *In the late* "Leslie," letters, January and February, 1963.
61 *Got up to* GA, diary, 1943.
61 *During these months* JA, draft memoir.
61 *Left Joy, omens* GA, diary, 1943.
62 *This morning after* Ibid., 1944.

CHAPTER 6   1906–1944
64 *Like Dian's kiss. Endymion.*
66 *As you were* Traute Hofmann (JA's mother) to JA, c. 1969.
66 *You had a* Ibid.
66 *In school you* Ibid.
71 *Thus I was* JA, *The Searching Spirit*, p. 35.
72 *It proved a* Ibid., p. 31.
74 *How fatal such* JA, draft memoir.
76 *I scribbled down* JA, *The Searching Spirit*, p. 39.
77 *I noticed especially* JA, draft memoir.
78 *I battled during* Ibid.
82 *My poor darling* Peter Bally, letter to JA.
83 *This morning my* JA, essay, April 9, 1940.
84 *I was in* JA, draft memoir.

CHAPTER 7   1944–1946
89 *The pride had* JA, draft memoir.
90 *She got in* GA, diary, 1944.
90 *This has been* Ibid.
95 *My feelings now* Ibid.
96 *Joy accused B.* Ibid., 1945.
96 *She read through* GA, legal statement. 1947.
97 *She has applied* GA, diary, 1945.
100 *Some of the* JA, *Born Free*, p. 44.
101 *About 1.00 am* GA, diary, 1946.
102 *He that but* Coventry Patmore. *The Victories of Love*, Bk. 1, 2.
103 *Feel very sad* GA, diary, 1946.

CHAPTER 8   1946–1947
104 *Rather outspoken* JA, diary, 1946.
109 *I have in* JA, letter to Louis Leakey.

CHAPTER 9   1938–1947
117 *At Banya a* GA, letter to JA, June 20, 1948.
117 *He was as* Harry Benson, letter to AH, April 5, 1991.
118 *Next thing I* GA, letter to JA, December 17, 1948.
119 *The old woman* GA, Kenya Game Department, Annual Report, 1952.

121 *The ingredients vary* Peter Bally, Ibid.
122 *There were over* GA, Ibid.
123 *I met again* GA, letter to JA, April 8, 1950.
123 *Eric Rundgren turned* GA, letter to JA, March 16, 1950.
125 *Put my plan* GA, diary, 1949.
127 *Up at Lalalei* GA, *My Pride and Joy*, p. 55.
127 *Just as we* Ibid.
132 *I had the* C. G. Jung. *Memories, Dreams, Reflections* p. 293
132 *When I look* GA, letter to JA, October 18, 1948.

CHAPTER 10   1947–1953
134 *Waited for nearly* GA, diary, 1947.
135 *The old associations* GA, legal statement, 1947.
135 *Bally came over* Ibid.
135 *Joy ignored my* Ibid.
137 *May I seek* Viktor von Klarwill, letter, March 19, 1980.
138 *Your dear friend* GA, letter to JA, August 24, 1948.
138 *I remember hearing* David Shirreff, letter to AH, February 19, 1991.
139 *We had a blow* JA, draft memoir.
139 *After being away* GA, letter to Captain A. Ritchie and JA, June 20, 1948.
140 *Dear Joy* GA, letter to JA, October 18, 1948.
141 *Some took advantage* JA, draft memoir.
141 *Got back today* GA, letter to JA, November 29, 1948.
142 *Got your very* Ibid., February 4, 1949.
143 *Joy had come* GA, diary, 1949.
144 *Off to Neumann's* JA, diary, 1949.
144 *Mail from Joy* GA, February 22, 1949.
144 *Posted registered letter* diary, Ibid., 1949.
145 *The Government decided* David Shirreff, letter to AH. February 19, 1991.
145 *His wife has* GA, letter to JA, January 28, 1950.
146 *Went to see* GA, diary, 1950.
147 *I hope and* GA, letter to JA, June 1950.
147 *Pity you are* GA, letter to JA, June 20, 1950.
147 *Spent the morning* GA, diary, 1950.
148 *Letter from Peter* Ibid., August 24, 1950.

227 *Took Elsa to* JA, diary, 1958.

229 *My excitement is* MV, letter to BC and Mrs. William Collins, 1959.

230 *I am keeping* MV, letter to BC 1959.

230 *There are 21* JA, letter to MV, 1959.

231 *First I have* MV, letter to BC, 1959.

232 *Had I been* Lord William Percy, letter to MV, September 5, 1959.

232 *From your letter* GA, letter to JA, 1959.

233 *On Thursday morning* Ibid.

233 *On a recent* René Babault, letter to GA, April 1, 1959.

234 *No one who* Lord William Percy, letter to MV, June 20, 1959.

235 *We got a* JA, letter to MV, 1959.

235 *George found the* Ibid.

235 *I had nothing* Ibid.

237 *Elsa is now* GA, letter to Harry Watt, December 2, 1959.

237 *Elsa's story is* Elspeth Huxley, letter to MV, January 20, 1959.

238 *This book is* Peter Scott, letter to BC or MV, 1960.

CHAPTER 16   1960–1962

239 *I am really* JA, letter to BC, July 4, 1960.

240 *About the leaflet* JA, letter to MV, September 14, 1960.

241 *You are certainly* GA, letter to TO, March 18, 1960.

242 *She also dealt* JA, *Living Free*, p. 48.

243 *Their visit was* JA, letter to MV, 21 Sept. 1960.

244 *It is important* Julian Huxley, Introduction to *Living Free*, p.x.

244 *About 3.30 I* BC, broadcast, 1960.

245 *So another beautiful* Ibid.

245 *The interesting thing* Ibid.

247 *George tells me* JA, diary, September 17, 1959.

247 *After about 10 minutes* GA, diary, November 5, 1959.

247 *It is funny* GA, letter to TO, 1960.

248 *I slept with* GA, letter to TO, February 19, 1961.

249 *During the night* Ibid.

249 *My Elsa gone* GA, diary, January 24, 1961.

250 *The cubs have* GA, letter to Ken Smith, April 13, 1961.

251 *Oh, Marjorie I* JA, letter to MV, April 10, 1961.

252 *The Tanganyika* GA, letter to Ken Smith, June 25, 1961.

254 *Terrible drive back* JA, diary, 1961.

254 *I am retired* GA, letter to TO, December, 1961.

CHAPTER 17   1962–1964

256 *She has had* MV, letter to Lady Reece, August 14, 1962.

256 *One day Joy* David Bateman. letter to AH, February 18, 1991.

257 *Leicester. I cried* JA, diary, 1962.

257 *My contact with* C. T. Astley Maberley, letter to JA, August 22, 1960.

257 *My husband's cousin* Una Lady Troubridge, letter to JA, March, 1960.

259 *Sleepless. Morning final* JA, diary, ' 1962.

259 *I feel like* JA, letter to HW, February 11, 1963.

260 *When I got* GA, letter to TO, November 30, 1962.

260 *I saw her* Ibid.

261 *For the next* Ibid.

261 *The political situation* Ibid.

261 *I, who made* Ibid.

261 *I am very* GA, letter to JA, January 1963, 13.

266 *Elsa had also* Desmond Morris, *Animal Days*, p. 218.

267 *You well know* GA, letter to JA, September, 1963.

268 *I will pay* JA, letter to GA, August 24, 1963.

268 *Came on a* GA, letter to Ken Smith, September 15, 1963.

269 *At one time* GA, letter to Major E. W. Temple Boreham, 15 Jan. 1959.

269 *Our Prime Minister* GA, letter to JA, December 10, 1963.

269 *Grimwood needs urgent* JA, letter to AH, May 2, 1964.

270 *Since you left* GA, letter to JA, January 20, 1964.

CHAPTER 18   1964–1965

272 *I am very* GA, letter to JA, June 13, 1961.

276 *After you left* JA, letter to VM and BT, April 5, 1965.

277 *When she first* GA, letter to TO, December 17, 1964.

278 *At this moment* Ronald Ryves, letter to GA.

278 *I find it* GA, letter to Carl Foreman, April 22, 1965.

278 *As you well* Carl Foreman, letter to GA, May 26, 1965.

279 *And George, let* Ibid.

279 *I know that* JA, letter to VM and BT, April 28, 1965.

279 *The greatest problem* Frank Minot, letter to GA, April 15, 1965.

280 *Ugas in particular* GA, letter to Stephen Ellis, April 24, 1965.

281 *I cannot find* Ronald Ryves, letter to GA, May 30, 1965.

282 *A kindly American* GA, letter to VM and BT, March 24, 1966.

282 *This wonderful success* JA, letter to VM and BT, October 21, 1965.

CHAPTER 19   1965–1968

284 *Experts told me* JA, letter to HW, July 3, 1965.

285 *Yesterday when out* JA, letter to VM and BT, January 6, 1966.

285 *On August 24* JA, letter to VM and BT, August 31, 1966.

285 *Two days ago* JA, letter to HW, September 5, 1966.

286 *The cubs are* JA, letter to HW, December 1, 1966.

287 *I have been* JA, letter to HW, April 30, 1965.

287 *All of us* Jomo Kenyatta, speech; see Elspeth Huxley's *Out in the Midday Sun*, p. 202.

288 *I was charged* JA, letter to VM and BT, October 21, 1965.

290 *It is truly* JA, letter to HW, February 28, 1968.

290 *We have your* Peter Johnson, letter to JA, December 19, 1968.

291 *I do not* JA, letter to Traute Erdmann (sister) October 7, 1968.

292 *I feel worried* JA, letter to HW, August 14, 1967.

293 *When you first* JA, letter to HW, January 24, 1968.

293 *I certainly did* HW, letter to JA, February 5, 1968.

294 *It was torture* JA, letter to HW, March 2, 1967.

CHAPTER 20   1965–1968

298 *Age has not* GA, letter to TO, July 26, 1965.

298 *They have hunted* Ibid.

298 *I went to* VM, letter to GA, October 5, 1965.

298 *The people in* GA, letter to TO, October 23, 1965.

300 *Toni and his* GA, letter to VM and BT, May 5, 1966

300 *It suddenly charged* GA, diary, October 19, 1966.

301 *He and Boy* GA, letter to TO, December 9, 1966.

301 *Luckily I had* Ibid.

301 *About 3.00 am* GA, letter to VM and BT, December 31, 1966.

302 *I got in* GA, *My Pride and Joy*, p. 149.

303 *You can always* JA, letter to VM, May 18, 1965.

304 *They were quite* GA, letter to TO, December 9, 1966.

305 *He now betrays* JA, letter to Ken Smith, September 22, 1968.

306 *Another aspect deserves* GA, letter to David Brown, December 31, 1966.

309 *Got back to* GA, diary, 1968.

309 *WHO IS LORD* GA, *Bwana Game*, 1968, p. 309.

CHAPTER 21   1969

310 *The rain is* JA, letter to HW, November 29, 1968.

311 *Sooner or later* JA, letter to HW, 8 December, 1968.

312 *I have no* JA, letter to HW, February 6, 1969.

312 *I am getting* JA, letter to HW, March 9, 1969.

313 *I WAS DEAD* JA, letter to MV, September 14, 1969.

314 *Peter Jenkins drove* GA, *My Pride and Joy*, p. 162.

315 *The next morning* Ibid., p. 163.

316 *Peter much exercised* GA, diary, 1969.

318 *There is a* JA, letter to MV, October 10, 1969.

318 *I do not* JA, letter to Sue Harthoorn, October 9, 1969.

318 *This morning your* JA, letter to BC, November 6, 1969.

319 *On October 17* GA, letter to Alan Davidson, December 6, 1969.

320 *On October 29* Ibid.

321 *Once again Boy* Ibid.

322 *I do not* JA, letter to MV, October 23, 1969.

CHAPTER 22 1969–1971

325 *Billy Collins was* JA, letter to HW, March 21, 1970.

326 *They gave me* GA, letter to TO, March 14, 1970.

329 *Kora is about* GA, letter to TO, December 11, 1970.

333 *I have no* BT, letter to GA, January 6, 1970.

334 *Boy is just* GA, letter to JA, January 27, 1971.

334 *On most nights* GA, *My Pride and Joy*, p. 202.

335 *All that happened* GA, letter to JA, June 10, 1971.

336 *Just as Kimani* Ibid.

336 *Lions very quiet* GA, diary, June 6, 1971.

338 *The saddest part* BT, letter to GA, July 5, 1971.

338 *When I read* JA, letter to GA, June 16, 1971.

338 *My current occupation* GA, diary notes, 1971.

CHAPTER 23 1971–1976

341 *Since I wrote* JA, letter to GA, September 24, 1972.

342 *I tried to* JA, letter to HW, November 25, 1977.

342 *Some terrible foreboding* JA, diary extracts, 1971–1973.

347 *Finally I got* JA, letter to HW, December 7, 1975.

347 *One of the* JA, letter to MV, February 14, 1972.

348 *I am sorry* Traute Hofmann (JA's mother), letter to JA, December 20, 1973.

348 *I try to* JA, letter to Mrs. C. E. (Peach) Taylor, September 21, 1974

349–53 *Dear Mrs. Adamson* C. S.

Ramsay-Hill (copyright his heirs and successors), letters exchanged with JA, March 25 to August 6, 1975.

354 *Dear Mrs. Adamson* Polly Ramsay-Hill, card to JA, March 1976.

354 *I feel incomplete* JA, draft memoir.

354 *I am glad* JA, letter to GA, October 22, 1972.

354 *I am more* JA, letter to GA.

355 *We were on* JA, letter to MV,

355 *Do you still* JA, letter to GA, May 10, 1972.

356 *You know what* JA, letter to AH, October 20, 1976.

357 *It is still* JA, letter to HW, November 18, 1976.

CHAPTER 24 1971–1977

358 *Because of the* GA, letter to JA, July 13, 1973.

360 *As you mention* JA, letter to Tony Fitzjohn, February 10, 1973.

360 *I know I* GA, letter to TO.

361 *Waking to his* GA, *My Pride and Joy*, p. 223.

361 *In appearance and* Ibid., p. 222.

362 *Jungle lore is* Jim Corbett, *Jim Corbett's India*, p. 249.

363 *I had made* GA, letter to TO, March 6, 1976.

364 *Do not despair* JA, letter to GA, August 5, 1972.

364 *I was having* GA, letter to TO, July 14, 1975.

365 *There is nothing* GA, letter to Tony Fitzjohn, June 25, 1975.

365 *Suleiman jumped on* GA, *My Pride and Joy*, p. 17.

369 *The Adamsons gave* George Schaller, foreword to *Born Free*, Pantheon edition, 1987.

369 *Their efforts at* George Schaller, letter to AH, April 10, 1991.

369 *The careful documentation* Jane Goodall, letter to AH, August 28, 1992.

369 *I would very* GA, letter to JA, October 10, 1972.

CHAPTER 25 1976–1980

374 *You have helped* JA, letter to Juliette Huxley, December 1, 1976.

375 *The cub is* JA, letter to MV, December 1, 1976.

375 *My baby leopard* JA, letter to HW, December 20, 1976.

377 *We are off* JA, letter to AH, August 23, 1977.

378 *On our second* JA, letter to Paul Sayer, September 4, 1977.

378 *I am now 68* JA, letter to Elspeth Huxley, December 30, 1970.

379 *Fishing along the* JA, *Queen of Shaba*, p. 68.

380 *He behaved very* JA, letters, 1978–1979.

381 *The reason he* Peter Johnson, letter to JA, January 30, 1978.

382 *I know the* JA, letter to GA, May 29, 1978.

382 *You always trust* JA, letter to GA, April 20, 1978.

383 *My dearest Marjorie* JA, letter to MV, May 26, 1979.

383 *We believed the* JA, letter to MV, May 29, 1979.

384 *The general belief* JA, letter to Elspeth Huxley, May 28, 1979.

384 *It is a perfect* JA, letter to MV, May 29, 1979.

385 *Our first explosion* JA, letter to HW, September 19, 1979.

386 *I believe that* JA, letter to HW, November 2, 1979.

391 *Her funeral was* GA, *My Pride and Joy*, p. 271.

391 *That was the* Ethelyn Stringfellow, letter to JA, September 13, 1979.

392 *That a lioness* Ted Hughes, review in the *New Statesman*, London, November 10, 1961.

393 *When humans observe* George Schaller, foreword to *Born Free*, Pantheon edition, 1987.

394 *The wind, the wind* JA, letter to HW, August 13, 1976.

394 *I dash this* Helen Wolff, letter to JA, August 23, 1976.

CHAPTER 26   1980–1989

395 *Thanks a lot* Kifosha, letter to GA, July 27, 1980.

395 *Much greeting from* Muga Bocho, letter to GA, April 24, 1989.

402 *He looks on* Anthony Marrian. letter to GA, October 8, 1979.

403 *The party is* Anthony Marrian, letter to Tony Fitzjohn, February 5, 1982.

404 *I am afraid* TO, letter to GA, February 12, 1987.

408 *Night out at* GA diary, April 23, 1984.

408 *Oft times while* Vivienne de Watteville, *Speak to the Earth*, p. 205.

409 *We were talking* Ernestine Nowak, letter to AH, November 23, 1992.

409 *Terence in a* GA, diary, April 4, 1986.

410 *I was so sorry* TO, letter to GA.

412 *My secretary has* GA, letter to TO.

416 *Government is taking* Ibid., January 3, 1989.

CHAPTER 28   1989–1993

436 *The spiritual life* Cyril Connolly, *The Unquiet Grave*, p. 34

437 *I noticed a* Douglas Collins, GA's diary, 1989.

BIBLIOGRAPHY

Books by George Adamson (published by Collins Harvill, London)

AUTOBIOGRAPHY
Bwana Game, 1968
My Pride and Joy, 1986

Books by Joy Adamson (published by Collins Harvill, London)

ELSA THE LIONESS AND HER CUBS
Born Free, 1960
Living Free, 1961
Forever Free, 1962

PIPPA THE CHEETAH AND HER CUBS
The Spotted Sphinx, 1969
Pippa's Challenge, 1972

PENNY THE LEOPARD AND HER CUBS
Queen of Shaba, 1980

PAINTING EXPEDITIONS
The Peoples of Kenya, 1967
Joy Adamson's Africa, 1972

AUTOBIOGRAPHY
The Searching Spirit, 1978
Friends from the Forest, 1981

FOR CHILDREN
Elsa, 1961
Elsa and Her Cubs, 1965

FOR CHILDREN
Pippa the Cheetah and Her Cubs, 1970

Books Illustrated by Joy Adamson

Jex-Blake, A. *Gardening in East Africa.* 2nd, 3rd and 4th eds., London: Longman Green, 1939, 1949, 1957.
Jex-Blake, Lady Muriel. *Some Wild Flowers of Kenya.* London: Longman Green, 1948.
Eggeling, W. J. *The Indigenous Trees of Uganda Protectorate.* Glasgow: Uganda Protectorate, 1951.
Greenway, P. G. and Dale, I. R. *Kenya Trees and Shrubs.* London: Buchanan Estates and Hatchards, 1961.

General

Allen, Charles. *Tales from the Dark Continent.* London: André Deutsch, 1979.
Amin, Mohamed and Moll, Peter. *Portraits of Africa.* London: Harvill Press, 1983.
Attenborough, David. *Life on Earth.* London: Collins & BBC, 1979.

——*The Living Planet*. London: Collins & BBC, 1984.
——*The Trials of Life*. London: Collins & BBC, 1991.
Bache, Eva. *The Youngest Lion*. London: Hutchinson, 1934.
Barker, E. *Austria 1918–72*. London: Macmillan, 1973.
Bartlett, Jen and Des. *Nature's Paradise*. London: Collins, 1967.
Blixen, Karen (Isak Dinesen). *Out of Africa*. London: Putnam, 1937.
Blundell, Michael. *Collins Guide to the Wild Flowers of East Africa*. London: Collins, 1987.
Blunt, Wilfred. *The Art of Botanical Illustration*. London: Collins, 1953.
Bourke, Anthony and Rendall, John. *A Lion Called Christian*. London: Collins, 1971.
Carcasson, R. H. *A Field Guide to the Coral Reef Fishes of the Indian and West Pacific Oceans*. London: Collins, 1977.
Carnegie, V. M. *A Kenyan Farm Diary*. Edinburgh: William Blackwood & Sons, 1930.
Carr, Norman. *Return to the Wild*. London: Collins, 1962.
Cass, Caroline. *Joy Adamson*. London: Weidenfeld and Nicolson, 1992.
Chenevix Trench, Charles. *The Desert's Dusty Face*. Edinburgh: William Blackwood & Sons, 1964.
Coe, Malcolm. *Islands in the Bush*. London: George Philip, 1985.
Cole, Sonia. *Leakey's Luck*. London: Collins, 1975.
Connolly, Cyril. *The Unquiet Grave*. London: Hamish Hamilton, 1951.
——*The Sunday Times Magazine*. London: December 21, 1969.
Corbett, Jim. *Jim Corbett's India*. Selected by R. E. Hawkins. Oxford: Oxford University Press, 1978.
Corfield, F. D. *Historical Survey of the Origins and Growth of Mau Mau*. London: HMSO, 1960.
Cott, Hugh. *Looking at Animals*. London: Collins, 1975.
Crewe, Quentin. *In Search of the Sahara*. London: Michael Joseph, 1983.
De Watteville, Vivienne. *Speak to the Earth*. London: Methuen, 1935.
Diamond, Jared. *The Third Chimpanzee*. London: Radius, 1991.
Douglas Hamilton, Iain and Oria. *Among the Elephants*. London: Collins Harvill, 1975.
——*Battle for the Elephants*. London: Doubleday, 1992.
Douglas Home, Charles. *Evelyn Baring: The Last Proconsul*. London: Collins, 1978.
Drake-Brockman, P. L. *Etawah District: Gazeteers of the United Provinces*. Vol 11, 1911.
Dyer, Anthony. *Classic African Animals: The Big Five*. New York: Winchester Press, 1973.
Fedders, Andrew and Salvadori, Cynthia. *Peoples and Cultures of Kenya*. Nairobi and London: Transafrica & KDTC, 1980.
Fitze, K. S. *Twilight of the Maharajas*. London: John Murray, 1956.
Fox, James. *White Mischief*. London: Jonathan Cape, 1982.
Gall, Sandy. *Lord of the Lions*, London: Grafton Books, 1991.
Gallman, Kuki. *I Dreamed of Africa*. London: Viking, 1991.
Gelder, Michael, Gath, Dennis, and Mayon, Richard. *Oxford Text Book of Psychiatry*. 2nd ed. Oxford: Oxford University Press, 1989.
Goodall, Jane. *In the Shadow of Man*. London: Collins, 1971.
——*Through a Window*. London: Weidenfeld and Nicolson, 1990.
Grzimek, Bernhard and Michael. *Serengeti Shall Not Die*. London: Hamish Hamilton, 1960.
Guggisberg, Charles. *Simba*. Cape Town: Howard Timmins, 1961.
Haltenorth, T. and Diller, H. *A Field Guide to the Mammals of Africa*. London: Collins, 1980.
Hamilton, Patrick. *The Leopard and the Cheetah*. Nairobi: Report for the Kenya Government, privately printed, 1981.
Hart, Susanne. *Life with Daktari*. London: Geoffrey Bles, 1969.

Hook, Hilary. *Home from the Hill.* London: The Sportsman's Press, 1987.

Huxley, Elspeth, ed. *Nine Faces of Kenya.* London: Collins Harvill, 1990.

——*Out in the Midday Sun.* London: Chatto and Windus, 1985.

——*White Man's Country* 2 vols. London: Chatto and Windus, 1935.

Ingrams, Harold. *Seven across the Sahara.* London: John Murray, 1949.

Jung, C. G. *Memories, Dr.eams, Reflections.* London: Collins, 1963.

Kenyatta, Jomo. *Facing Mount Kenya.* London: Secker and Warburg 1937.

Kingdon, Jonathan. *East African Mammals: Carnivores.* London: Academic Press, 1977.

Kitson, Frank. *Gangs and Counter-gangs.* London: Barrie & Rockcliff, 1960.

Leakey, Mary. *Olduvai Gorge: My Search for Early Man.* London: Collins, 1979.

Leakey, Richard and Lewin, Roger. *The People of the Lake.* London: Collins, 1979.

Lovell, Mary. *Straight on till Morning.* London: Hutchinson, 1987.

Lovelock, James. *Gaia: A New Look at Life on Earth.* Oxford: Oxford University Press, 1982.

Luard, Nicholas. *The Wildlife Parks of Africa.* London: Michael Joseph, 1985.

MacArthur, Wilson. *The Desert Watches.* London: Rupert Hart-Davis, 1954.

MacDonald, David. *Velvet Claws.* London: BBC, 1992.

McKenna, Virginia and Travers, Bill. *On Playing with Lions.* London: Collins, 1966.

McNeile, Rev. R. F. *A History of Dean Close School.* Cheltenham: Dean Close School, 1966.

Majdalany, Fred. *State of Emergency.* London: Longman Green, 1962.

Matthiessen, Peter and Porter, Eliot. *The Tree Where Man Was Born.* London: Collins, 1972.

Moorehead, Alan. *No Room in the Ark.* London: Hamish Hamilton, 1959.

Morris, Desmond. *Animal Days.* London: Jonathan Cape, 1979.

Moss, Cynthia. *Portraits in the Wild.* London: Hamish Hamilton, 1978.

Patterson, Gareth. *Lion's Legacy.* London: Robson Books, 1991.

Pickering, George. *Creative Malady.* London: George Allen & Unwin, 1974.

Pfeifer, Netta. *A Soul's Safari.* Punjab: Radha Soami Satsang Beas, 1978.

Reader, John. *Missing Links.* London: Collins, 1981.

Reader, John, and Croze, Harvey. *Pyramids of Life.* London: Collins, 1977.

Reece, Alys. *To My Wife 50 Camels.* London: Collins Harvill, 1963.

Ricciardi, Mirella. *Vanishing Africa.* London: Collins, 1971.

Schaller, George. *The Serengeti Lion.* London: University of Chicago Press, 1972.

——*The Year of the Gorilla.* London: Collins, 1964.

Scott, Peter. *Travel Diaries of a Naturalist.* Vol. 1. London: Collins, 1983.

Sheldrick, Daphne. *Orphans of Tsavo.* London: Collins, 1966.

Smith, Anthony. *The Great Rift.* London: BBC, 1988.

Telavich, B. *Modern Austria: Empire and Republic, 1815–1986.* Cambridge: Cambridge University Press, 1987.

Tichy, Herbert. *Kenya.* Innsbruck: Pinguin-Verlag, 1980.

Trzebinski, Erroll. *Silence Will Speak.* London: Heinemann, 1977.

——*The Lives of Beryl Markham.* London: Heinemann, 1993.

Turnbull, Richard. *The Darod Invasion.* Dar-es-Salaam: privately printed, 1961.

Van Lawick-Goodall, Hugo and Jane. *Innocent Killers.* London: Collins, 1970.

Waugh, Evelyn. *Remote People.* London: Duckworth, 1931.

Williams, John. *A Field Guide to the Birds of East Africa.* Expanded edition, London: Collins, 1980.

——*A Field Guide to the National Parks of East Africa.* London: Collins, 1967.

Wood, Michael. *Go an Extra Mile.* London: Collins, 1978.

Ylla. *Animals in Africa.* London: Harvill Press, 1954.

INDEX

For books by George and Joy Adamson see their separate entries under "Writings"

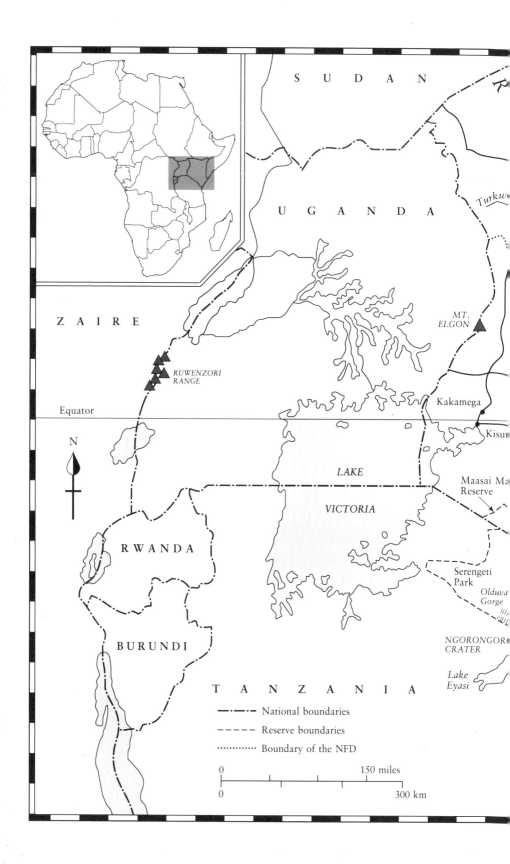

SUDAN

UGANDA

Turkw

ZAIRE

MT.
ELGON ▲

▲▲
▲
▲
*RUWENZORI
RANGE*

Kakamega

Equator

Kisu

N

LAKE

Maasai Ma
Reserve

VICTORIA

RWANDA

Serengeti
Park

Olduva
Gorge

BURUNDI

*NGORONGOR
CRATER*

*Lake
Eyasi*

T A N Z A N I A

—·—·— National boundaries

— — — Reserve boundaries

············ Boundary of the NFD

| 0 | | | 150 miles |
| 0 | | | 300 km |